S0-AZQ-850

Authors & Artists for Young Adults

ISSN 1040-5682

Authors & Artists for Young Adults

VOLUME 73

THOMSON
GALE

Detroit • New York • San Francisco • New Haven, Conn. • Waterville, Maine • London

Authors and Artists for Young Adults, Volume 73

Project Editors
Michael LaBlanc and Jennifer Greve

Editorial
Katy Balcer, Dwayne D. Hayes

Permissions
Kelly A. Quin, Lisa Kincade, Tim Sisler, Emma Hull, Andy Specht

Imaging and Multimedia
Lezlie Light

Composition and Electronic Capture
Tracey L. Matthews

Manufacturing
Cynthia Bishop

LIBRARY OF CONGRESS CATALOG CARD NUMBER 89-641100

ISBN-13: 978-0-7876-7792-3
ISBN-10: 0-7876-7792-2
ISSN 1040-5682

Printed in the United States of America
10 9 8 7 6 5 4 3 2 1

Contents

Introduction

Authors and Artists for Young Adults is a reference series designed to serve the needs of middle school, junior high, and high school students interested in creative artists. Originally inspired by the need to bridge the gap between Gale's *Something about the Author,* created for children, and *Contemporary Authors,* intended for older students and adults, *Authors and Artists for Young Adults* has been expanded to cover not only an international scope of authors, but also a wide variety of other artists.

Although the emphasis of the series remains on the writer for young adults, we recognize that these readers have diverse interests covering a wide range of reading levels. The series therefore contains not only those creative artists who are of high interest to young adults, including cartoonists, photographers, music composers, bestselling authors of adult novels, media directors, producers, and performers, but also literary and artistic figures studied in academic curricula, such as influential novelists, playwrights, poets, and painters. The goal of *Authors and Artists for Young Adults* is to present this great diversity of creative artists in a format that is entertaining, informative, and understandable to the young adult reader.

Entry Format

Each volume of *Authors and Artists for Young Adults* will furnish in-depth coverage of approximately twenty-five authors and artists. The typical entry consists of:

—A detailed biographical section that includes date of birth, marriage, children, education, and addresses.

—A comprehensive bibliography or filmography including publishers, producers, and years.

—Adaptations into other media forms.

—Works in progress.

—A distinctive essay featuring comments on an artist's life, career, artistic intentions, world views, and controversies.

—References for further reading.

—Extensive illustrations, photographs, movie stills, cartoons, book covers, and other relevant visual material.

A cumulative index to featured authors and artists appears in each volume.

Compilation Methods

The editors of *Authors and Artists for Young Adults* make every effort to secure information directly from the authors and artists through personal correspondence and interviews. Sketches on living authors and artists are sent to the biographee for review prior to publication. Any sketches not personally reviewed by biographees or their representatives are marked with an asterisk (*).

Highlights of Forthcoming Volumes

Among the authors and artists planned for future volumes are:

Gillian Armstrong	Charlotte Perkins Gilman	Jerome Robbins
William Bell	Malcolm Gladwell	O.E. Rolvaag
Gianlorenzo Bernini	H. Rider Haggard	Richard Sala
Matthew Brady	Nancy Holder	Clark Ashton Smith
Kate Brian	Dorothy Hoobler	Will Smith
Deb Caletti	Katherine Kirkpatrick	Elizabeth George Spear
Mark Delaney	Johanna Lindsey	Wislawa Szymborska
Paul Dini	Robert Longo	Jean Toomer
Paul Laurence Dunbar	Sujata Massey	Lily Tuck
Lee Falk	Katsuhiro Otomo	Rick Veitch
John Ford	Nam June Paik	Sarah Weeks
Bob Fosse	Hal Roach	Jack Williamson

Contact the Editor

We encourage our readers to examine the entire *AAYA* series. Please write and tell us if we can make *AAYA* even more helpful to you. Give your comments and suggestions to the editor:

BY MAIL: The Editor, *Authors and Artists for Young Adults,* 27500 Drake Rd., Farmington Hills, MI 48331-3535.

BY TELEPHONE: (800) 347-GALE

Authors and Artists for Young Adults
Product Advisory Board

The editors of *Authors and Artists for Young Adults* are dedicated to maintaining a high standard of excellence by publishing comprehensive, accurate, and highly readable entries on writers, artists, and filmmakers of interest to middle and high school students. In addition to the quality of the entries, the editors take pride in the graphic design of the series, which is intended to be orderly yet appealing, allowing readers to utilize the pages of *AAYA* easily, enjoyably, and with efficiency. Despite the success of the *AAYA* print series, we are mindful that the vitality of a literary reference product is dependent on its ability to serve its readers over time. As critical attitudes about literature, art, and media constantly evolve, so do the reference needs of students and teachers. To be certain that we continue to keep pace with the expectations of our readers, the editors of *AAYA* listen carefully to their comments regarding the value, utility, and quality of the series. Librarians, who have firsthand knowledge of the needs of library users, are a valuable resource for us. The *Authors and Artists for Young Adults* Product Advisory Board, made up of school, public, and academic librarians, is a forum to promote focused feedback about *AAYA* on a regular basis, as well as to help steer our coverage of new authors and artists. The advisory board includes the following individuals, whom the editors wish to thank for sharing their expertise:

- **Eva M. Davis,** Youth Department Manager, Ann Arbor District Library, Ann Arbor, Michigan

- **Joan B. Eisenberg,** Lower School Librarian, Milton Academy, Milton, Massachusetts

- **Susan Dove Lempke,** Children's Services Supervisor, Niles Public Library District, Niles, Illinois

- **Robyn Lupa,** Head of Children's Services, Jefferson County Public Library, Lakewood, Colorado

- **Caryn Sipos,** Community Librarian, Three Creeks Community Library, Vancouver, Washington

- **Stephen Weiner,** Director, Maynard Public Library, Maynard, Massachusetts

Acknowledgments

Grateful acknowledgment is made to the following publishers, authors, and artists for their kind permission to reproduce copyrighted material.

DONNA ANDREWS. Andrews, Donna, photograph by Mary A. Dusing. Courtesy of Donna Andrews.

TEX AVERY. Bugs Bunny stamp, photograph. United States Postal Service/AP Images. / Droopy Dog and Red Hot Riding Hood, photograph. Everett Collection. / American bomber attacks German Blitz Wolf, 1942, cartoon by Tex Avery, photograph. Everett Collection.

JAY BENNETT. Bennett, Jay, photograph by Mary Bennett. Courtesy of Jay Bennett. / From a cover of *Coverup,* by Jay Bennett. Fawcett Juniper Books, 1991. Copyright © 1991. Used by permission of Ballantine Books, a division of Random House, Inc. / Bennett, Jay. From a cover of *The Skeleton Man,* by Jay Bennett. Ballantine Books, 1988. Copyright © 1988. Used by permissions of Ballantine Books, a division of Random House, Inc. / Bennett, Jay, photograph by Mary Bennett. Courtesy of Jay Bennett.

DAVID BREASHEARS. Still from the movie, "Everest," photograph. Kobal Collection. Reproduced by permission. / Still from the movie "Everest," climber on ladder being filmed by cameraman, photograph. MacGillivray Freeman Film/The Kobal Collection. Reproduced by permission. / Still from the movie "Everest," David Breashears with camera, photograph. © IMAX Pictures/Everett Collection.

AUGUSTEN BURROUGHS. Burroughs, Augusten, photograph. Photo by Jeremy Montemagni/Everett Collection. / Cross, Joseph, with Augusten Burroughs, photograph. © Sony Pictures/Everett Collection.

JOHN CARPENTER. Carpenter, John, Deauville Festival, 1996, photograph. Eric Robert/Corbis/Sygma. / Still from the movie "Assault on Precinct 13," photograph. The Kobal Collection. Reproduced by permission. / Still from the movie "Escape from New York," photograph. Avco Embassy/The Kobal Collection. Reproduced by permission. / Still from the movie "Halloween," photograph. Falcon International/The Kobal Collection. Reproduced by permission. / Still from the movie "The Thing," photograph. Universal/The Kobal Collection. Reproduced by permission. / Woods, James, in a scene from the film, "John Carpenter's Vampires," 1998, photograph by Neil Jacobs. The Kobal Collection. Reproduced by permission. / Carpenter, John, directing the film, "In the Mouth of Madness," 1995, photograph. The Kobal Collection. Reproduced by permission.

GENNIFER CHOLDENKO. Choldenko, Gennifer. From a cover of *Al Capone Does My Shirts,* by Gennifer Choldenko. Puffin Books, 2004. Used by permission of Puffin Books, a division of Penguin Putnam Books for Young Readers. / Ulriksen, Mark, illustrator. From a cover of *Notes from a Liar and Her Dog,* by Gennifer Choldenko. Puffin Books, 2001. Reproduced by permission of Puffin Books, a division of Penguin Putnam Books for Young Readers. / Choldenko, Gennifer, photograph by Pat Stroud. Courtesy of Gennifer Choldenko.

GREG HILDEBRANDT. Hildebrandt, Greg, and Tim. From a cover of *Star Wars: The Art of the Brothers Hildebrandt,* by Bob Woods. Del Rey Book, 1997. Copyright © 1997. Used by permission of Del Rey Books, a division of Random House, Inc.

JAMES WELDON JOHNSON. Johnson, James Weldon, photograph. / "Alexander's Ragtime Band," with Jack Haley as drummer Davey Lane, Douglas Fowler as Snapper, Alice Faye as singer Stella Kirby, Don Ameche as pianist Charlie Dwyer, Tyrone Power as violinist Roger Grant, and Wally Vernon on trumpet, photograph. © John Springer Collection/Corbis. / Douglas, Aaron, illustrator. From a cover of *God's Trombones,* by James Weldon Johnson. Viking Penguin, 1955. Copyright 1927 The Viking Press, Inc., renewed © 1955 by Grace Nail Johnson. Used by permission of Viking Penguin, a division of Penguin Group (USA) Inc. / Johnson, James Weldon, photograph. Time Life Pictures/Getty Images.

WILLIAM KENNEDY. Kennedy, William, photograph. © Jerry Bauer. Reproduced by permission. / Kennedy, William, photograph. © Bettmann/Corbis. / Nicholson, Jack, still from the movie "Ironweed," photograph. Tri-Star/The Kobal Collection. Reproduced by permission. / Hines, Gregory, still from the movie "The Cotton Club," photograph. Zoetrope/Orion/The Kobal Collection. Reproduced by permission.

IMRE KERTESZ. Kertesz, Imre. From a cover of *Kaddish for an Unborn Child,* by Imre Kertesz, translated by Tim Wilkinson. Vintage International, 2004. Copyright © 2004 by Random House, Inc. Used by permission of Vintage Books, a division of Random House, Inc. / Kertesz, Imre. From a cover of *Fatelessness: A Novel,* by Imre Kertesz, translated by Tim Wilkinson. Vintage International, 2004. Copyright © by Random House, Inc. Used by permission of Vintage Books, a division of Random House, Inc. / Kertesz, Imre, 2005, photograph. Getty Images. / Kertesz, Imre, with Nobel Prize, photograph. AFP/Getty Images. / "Fateless" movie set, photograph. Buda Gulyas/Reuters/Corbis.

JEPH LOEB, III. Still from the television series "Smallville," photograph. Warner Bros TV/The Kobal Collection. Reproduced by permission. / Sale, Tim, illustrator. From a cover of *Spiderman Blue,* by Jeph Loeb. Marvel Characters, Inc., 2004. © 2004 Marvel Characters, Inc. Reproduced by permission. / Loeb, Jeph, photograph. Albert L. Ortega/WireImage.com. / Loeb, Jeph, at 2005 Wizzard of Oz, photograph. Albert L. Ortega/WireImage.com.

JOE MANTELLO. Mantello, Joe, 2004, photograph. © Zack Seckler/Corbis. / Mantello, Joe, photograph. AP Images. / Still from the movie "Love, Valour, Compassion," photograph. Fine Line Features/Lider/The Kobal Collection/Attila Dory. Reproduced by permission. / Billboard for "Glengarry Glen Ross," 2005, photograph. Getty Images. / Menzel, Idina, as Elphaba in "Wicked," photograph. AP Images

ELIZABETH MOON. Ruddell, Gary, illustrator. From a cover of *Once a Hero,* by Elizabeth Moon. Baen Books, 1997. Reproduced by permission. / Parkinson, Keith, illustrator. From a cover of *The Deed of Paksenarrion,* by Elizabeth Moon. Baen Books, 1992. Reproduced by permission. / Moon, Elizabeth, photograph by Nancy Whitworth. Courtesy of Elizabeth Moon.

HENRY MOORE. "Reclining Figure No. 5," sculpture by Henry Moore, London, England, 1966, photograph. Archive Photos, Inc. /Getty Images. / Moore, Henry, with his "Seated Nude" sculpture, photograph. AP Images. / Moore, Henry, photograph. John Swope Collection/Corbis. / "Three Figures," sculpture by Henry Moore. Photo by Joe Schilling/Time Life Pictures/Getty Images. © The Henry Moore Foundation. This image is not to be reproduced or altered without permission of the Henry Moore Foundation. / "Draped Reclining Figure," sculpture by Henry Moore, photograph by Joe Schilling/Time Life Pictures/Getty Images. © The Henry Moore Foundation. This image is not to be reproduced or altered without permission of the Henry Moore Foundation. / Moore, Henry, photograph by Kurt Hutton/Picture Post/Getty Images © The Henry Moore Foundation. This image is not to be reproduced or altered without permission of the Henry Moore Foundation.

TERRY MOORE. Moore, Terry, illustrator. From a cover of *Strangers in Paradise High School!* by Terry Moore. Abstract Studio, 2002. Reproduced by permission. / Moore, Terry, photograph. Courtesy of Terry Moore.

LOUISE PLUMMER. Plummer, Louise. From a cover of *The Unlikely Romance of Kate Bjorkman,* by Louise Plummer. Laurel-Leaf Books, 1995. Used by permission of Random House Children's Books, a division of Random House, Inc. / Plummer, Louise. From a cover of *My Name is Susan Smith, The 5 is Silent,* by Louise Plummer. Dell Publishing, 1991. Used by permission of Dell Publishing, a division of Random House, Inc. / Plummer, Louise. From a cover of *The Romantic Obsessions & Humiliations of Annie Schlmeier,* by Louise Plummer. Dell, 1987. Used by permission of Random House Children's Books, a division of Random House, Inc. / Plummer, Louise, photograph by Tom Plummer. Courtesy of Louise Plummer.

ROBERT J. SAWYER. Sawyer, Robert J., photograph by Carolyn Clink. © 2003 Robert J. Sawyer. Reproduced by permission of Robert J. Sawyer. / Sawyer, Robert J., standing next to a display of his paperback novels at the World's Biggest Bookstore, photograph. © 2003 Robert J. Sawyer. Reproduced by permission. / Donato, illustrator. From a cover of *Hominids,* by Robert J. Sawyer. Tom Doherty, 2002. Reproduced by permission of the illustrator. / From a cover of *Calculating God,* by Robert J. Sawyer. Tor Books, 2000. Reproduced by permission. / Martiniere, Stephan, illustrator. From a cover of *Mindscan,* by Robert J. Sawyer. Tor Books, 2005. Reproduced by permission.

GARY D. SCHMIDT. Cameron, Scott, illustrator. From a cover of *Lizzie Bright and the Buckminster Boy*, by Gary D. Schmidt. A Yearling Book, 2005. Cover art © 2005 by Scott Cameron. Used by permission of Random House Children's Books, a division of Random House, Inc. / Martinez, Ed, illustrator. From a cover of *Anson's Way*, by Gary D. Schmidt. Puffin Books, 1999. Cover illustration copyright © Ed Martinez, 1999. Reproduced by permission of Puffin Books, a division of Penguin Putnam Books for Young Readers. / Schmidt, Gary, onstage with Katherine Paterson at Calvin College's Faith and Writing Festival, photograph by John Corriveau. Courtesy of Gary Schmidt. / Schmidt, Gary D., photograph by Myrna Anderson. Courtesy of Gary Schmidt. / Farnsworth, Bill, illustrator. From a cover of *The Sin Eater,* by Gary D. Schmidt. Lodestar/Dutton Books, 1996. Jacket illustration © Bill Farnsworth, 1996. Used by permission of Lodestar Books, a division of Penguin Group (USA) Inc.

JAMES R. SHEPARD. McVay, Ryan/Photodisc, photographer. From a cover of *Project X*, by Jim Shepard. Vintage Books, 2004. Copyright © 2004 by Jim Shepard. Used by permission of Alfred A. Knopf, a division of Random House, Inc. / Shepard, Jim, photograph by Barry Goldstein. Courtesy of Jim Shepard.

MARY STEWART. Stewart, Mary, photograph. © Jerry Bauer. Reproduced by permission.

ALLAN STRATTON. Stratton, Allan, photograph by Pierre Gautreau. Courtesy of Allan Stratton. / Stratton, Allan, photograph. Courtesy of Allan Stratton. / Stratton, Allan, and friends at a lunch booth, photograph. Courtesy of Allan Stratton.

WENDY WASSERSTEIN. Weintraub, Abby, illustrator. From a cover of *Shiksa Goddess*, by Wendy Wasserstein. Vintage Books, 2002. Copyright © 2001 by Wendy Wasserstein. Used by permission of Alfred A. Knopf, a division of Random House, Inc. / Wasserstein, Wendy, photograph. Pace Gregory/Corbis Sygma. / The Heidi Chronicles, photograph. Time Life Pictures/Getty Images/ Pataki, George, Wendy Wasserstein, John Hayes, 2004, Tribeca, photograph. Getty Images. / Rudd, Paul, and Jennifer Aniston, photograph. 20th Century Fox/Laurence Mark/The Kobal Collection/Barry Wetcher. Reproduced by permission. / Jackness, Andrew, illustrator. From an illustration in *Pamela's First Musical*, by Wendy Wasserstein. Hyperion, 1996. Copyright © 1996. All rights reserved. Reprinted by permission of Hyperion Books for Children.

WALLACE WOOD. Wood, Wallace, illustrator. From an illustration in *Atom Bomb*, by Wallace Wood for "Two-Fisted Tales." Entertaining Comics, 1953. Courtesy of Glenn Wood. / Wood, Wallace, illustrator. From an illustration in *Bucky's Christmas Caper*, by Wallace Wood. Courtesy of Glenn Wood. / Christmas card hand-drawn by Wallace Wood. Courtesy of Glenn Wood. / Wood, Wallace, photograph. Courtesy of Glenn Wood. / Wood, Wallace, photograph. Courtesy of Glenn Wood.

Donna Andrews

■ Personal

Born in Yorktown, VA. *Education:* University of Virginia, B.A.

■ Addresses

Office—11654 Plaza America Dr., #313, Reston, VA 20190. *E-mail*—donna@donnaandrews.com.

■ Career

Author. Former member of communications staff of a financial organization in Washington, DC.

■ Member

Mystery Writers of America, Sisters in Crime, Private Investigators and Security Association.

■ Awards, Honors

Malice Domestic/St. Martin's Press Best First Traditional Mystery Award, 1997, Agatha Award, Anthony Award, *Romantic Times* Award, and Barry Award, all for best first novel of 1999, and Lefty Award, for funniest mystery book of 1999, all for *Murder with Peacocks*; Agatha Award, best novel of 2002, for *You've Got Murder*; Toby Bromberg Award for Excellence, *Romantic Times*, for the most humorous mystery of 2003, for *Crouching Buzzard, Leaping Loon*.

■ Writings

"MEG LANGSLOW" SERIES

Murder with Peacocks, Thomas Dunne Books (New York, NY), 1999.

Murder with Puffins, Thomas Dunne Books (New York, NY), 2000.

Revenge of the Wrought-Iron Flamingos, Thomas Dunne Books (New York, NY), 2001.

Crouching Buzzard, Leaping Loon, Thomas Dunne Books (New York, NY), 2003.

We'll Always Have Parrots, Thomas Dunne Books (New York, NY), 2004.

Owl's Well That Ends Well, Thomas Dunne Books (New York, NY), 2005.

No Nest for the Wicket, Thomas Dunne Books (New York, NY), 2006.

"TURING HOPPER" SERIES

You've Got Murder, Berkley Prime Crime (New York, NY), 2002.
Click Here for Murder, Berkley Prime Crime (New York, NY), 2003.
Access Denied, Berkley Prime Crime (New York, NY), 2004.
Delete All Suspects, Berkley Prime Crime (New York, NY), 2005.

OTHER

Contributor to anthologies, including *The Mysterious North*, edited by Dana Stabenow.

■ Sidelights

Donna Andrews is the author of two popular mystery series: the "Meg Langslow" series, featuring the sleuthing lady blacksmith Meg Langslow, and the "Turing Hopper" series, in which an Artificial Intelligence Personality solves crimes. While the Langslow novels provide as many laughs as they do clues, the Turing Hopper books explore the developing world of computer technology through straightforward mystery puzzles. A *Kirkus Reviews* critic dubbed Turing Hopper "one of the most cleverly conceived detectives of the decade."

Andrews was born in Yorktown, Virginia. She enjoyed reading as a child, but only developed a love for mysteries while attending the University of Virginia. After graduating with a major in English and Drama, Andrews found a job on the communications staff of a financial organization in the Washington, DC, area. Over some twenty years at the company, Andrews claims in a statement posted on her Web site to have "developed a profound understanding of the criminal mind" by observing the office politics around her. In 1997 Andrews entered her first complete mystery novel manuscript, *Murder with Peacocks*, in the Malice Domestic/ St. Martin's Press Best First Traditional Mystery contest and won.

The first book in the "Meg Langslow" series, *Murder with Peacocks*, finds Meg committed to being a bridesmaid at three different summer weddings in her hometown. She cannot back out of the awkward arrangement: the weddings involve her best friend, her brother's fiancée, and her own mother. Worse, she has to participate in the preparations for the weddings as well. One bride wants live peacocks on the lawn, another has her heart set on a Native American herbal purification ceremony, and Meg's mother thinks her living room should be completely redecorated for the home nuptials. Amid the confusion, Meg finds herself falling for the attractive Michael Waterston, son of the town dressmaker and a drama professor at the local college—that is, until her mother confides that Michael may be gay. Her summer really falls apart when one of the wedding guests is found murdered. When she and her father begin an informal investigation, they find themselves the targets of suspicious accidents that may be the work of a killer. According to Monica Pope in a review of the novel for the *Mystery Reader*, Andrews "has concocted a comical and entertaining set of events, an utterly odious victim and villain, and a cast of truly delectable characters." The *Publishers Weekly* critic found that "Andrews's debut provides plenty of laughs for readers who like their mysteries on the cozy side." *Murder with Peacocks* went on to win a host of awards in the mystery field, including the Agatha Award from the Mystery Writers of America and the Anthony Award.

In Meg's second outing, *Murder with Puffins*, she is involved with Michael Waterston—who is not gay—and the two of them travel to her Aunt Phoebe's cottage on Monhegan Island, a tiny island off the coast of Maine. When they arrive, they find that not only Phoebe but Meg's father, mother, and brother have already taken the place over. Ferry service is suspended due to a threatening hurricane, leaving the couple stranded with a host of annoying birdwatchers who have come to the island to see the puffins. When the island's most famous citizen, an artist and former beau of Meg's mother, is found murdered, Meg's father is the prime suspect. Meg is called upon to solve the case herself. Jenny McLarin in *Booklist* praised Andrews's "dry humor and offbeat characters." Pam Johnson in the *School Library Journal* concluded that *Murder with Puffins* "wends its way to a satisfying ending, treating readers to an entertaining cast of characters in an interesting locale."

Meg has a booth at the Yorktown Colonial Crafts Fair being held in conjunction with a reenactment of the British surrender at Yorktown in the series's third installment, *Revenge of the Wrought-Iron Flamingos*. The relationship with Michael is going well; the couple is now engaged to be married. Meg's future mother-in-law, Mrs. Waterston, is running the historical reenactment. Meg has also been charged with heading up the anachronism police, who are supposed to watch for any lapses from colonial attire, such as wristwatches or zippers. She hopes Mrs. Waterston will not discover the wrought-iron flamingos she has stashed away to deliver to the client who commissioned them, but her secret is out when one of the flamingos is used as a murder weapon. Jenny McLarin in *Booklist* judged the novel to be "a better-than-average entry in a consistently entertaining, if slightly lightweight, series." Rex E. Klett, in his review for the *Library Journal*, believed that "a fearless protagonist, remarkable supporting characters, lively action, and a keen wit put this at the top of the list."

Meg is helping out her brother Rob in *Crouching Buzzard, Leaping Loon*. Rob's computer games company, Mutant Wizards, needs an office manager to sort out conflicts among the technologically talented but socially inept staff members. Meg does her best, but when the staff practical joker is found dead, she must step in and solve the murder. The list of suspects grows long when she discovers that the joker was also a blackmailer. A *Kirkus Reviews* critic called *Crouching Buzzard, Leaping Loon* a "frantically inventive farce." "There's a smile on nearly every page and at least one chuckle per chapter," a critic for *Publishers Weekly* claimed. Writing in the *Romantic Times,* Tara Gelsomino concluded: "This may be the funniest installment of Andrews's wonderfully wacky series yet. It takes a deft hand to make slapstick or physical comedy appealing, yet Andrews masterfully manages it (the climax will have you in stitches)."

Andrews's *We'll Always Have Parrots* finds Meg's fiancée, Michael—who usually works as a theatre professor—a member of the cast for the cult television program "Porfiria, Queen of the Jungle." The couple attend a convention of the show's fans at a local hotel and find the place decorated with jungle vines, palm trees, and live monkeys and parrots. The hotel management has given up trying to impose any order on the proceedings, and even Meg, who must constantly fight against her tendencies to take charge of every situation, knows when she is defeated. But when the show's hated woman star turns up dead, Meg, convinced that the police are just not doing the job, wades in to solve the crime herself. About the only people Meg does not suspect are the nerdy, extravagantly costumed fans, who blithely go their own way, partying until the wee hours and having so much fun they are almost oblivious to the murder in their midst. McLarin found that "Meg remains an imminently likable heroine, and the wacky supporting characters make *Parrots* a hoot." In a review for *BooksnBytes*, Harriet Klausner concluded that "Andrews furnishes a fabulously loony entry in her delightful offbeat series."

In *Owl's Well That Ends Well*, Meg and Michael buy an old house "as is." The disclaimer means that the building is filled with old junk, some valuable, some not. The couple decide to hold a big yard sale to clear out the house. Soon, Meg's large extended family is bringing over their own belongings to sell. The sale is a huge success, with buyers coming in from all over. But the proceedings are rudely interrupted when a body is discovered in a trunk that is for sale. The body turns out to be Gordon McCoy, a slick antiques dealer who had a score of enemies. When one of Michael's fellow professors, who is on the committee considering him for tenure, becomes the principal suspect, Meg sets out to find the real killer. While a critic for *Kirkus Reviews* called the novel "a creaking mystery surrounded by rampant goofiness," Harriet Klausner, in her review for *BooksnBytes*, claimed that the book will appeal to "fans of amusing mysteries that play for laughs as opposed to serious drama." "Andrews playfully creates laughable, wacky scenes that are the backdrop for her criminally devious plot," wrote Jo Peters in the *Romantic Times*. "Settle back, dear reader and enjoy another visit to Meg's anything-but-ordinary world."

In *No Nest for the Wicket*, Meg finds a dead body while playing a game of "eXtreme croquet" on her own property. It was to be a friendly game involving friends and family. Meg and Michael needed a break from the endless restoration work on their old house. But, while searching for a missing croquet ball, Meg stumbles upon Lindsay Tyler, a former history professor, who has been bashed in the head with a croquet mallet. Did her death have anything to do with an ongoing protest against a local development company? Meg's resulting investigation is, according to a reviewer for *Mystery News*, "288 pages of laugh-out-loud, barely controlled chaos." The *Kirkus Reviews* critic noted that "Andrews is a reliable source for those who like their murder with plenty of mayhem." A reviewer for *Publishers Weekly* admired "the author's sense of fun and a lively, charming cast."

A Detecting Artificial Intelligence

Andrews took an unexpected change of direction with the launch of her "Turing Hopper" series, featuring an Artificial Intelligence Personality. Living only in the virtual universe of computers, the "female" Turing Hopper interacts with others in an almost human manner. She is, in fact, the end result of a corporate research program to develop life-like artifical intelligence. Because of the qualities programmed into her, Turing has begun to believe herself a sentient being capable of independent thoughts and actions. In the series debut, *You've Got Murder,* Zachary Malone, Turing's friend and programmer, turns up missing. Able to access databases, security cameras, and other computer resources, and with the legwork of Tim Pincoski and Maude Graham, employees at the corporation where she is installed, Turing conducts a virtual search to locate the missing man. Turing, according to a critic for *Kirkus Reviews,* "fills the bill with more energy and charm than most fictional detectives." The reviewer for *Publishers Weekly* called *You've Got Murder* "a unique effort executed with great skill." Toby Bromberg, writing in the *Romantic Times,* believed that Andrews "may have come up with a new subgenre! All characters, human and non, are a delight and definitely hold appeal for techies and non-techies alike."

Andrews continued the series with *Click Here for Murder,* in which computer programmer Ray Santiago is brutally murdered, and Turing Hopper must find the culprit before others are killed. Turing soon learns, with the help of Maude Graham, another computer-whiz, that Ray was deeply involved in a high-tech role playing game in which he was living out an alternate personality. The players of this game are being hounded by the killer, and the search for him takes Turing and her colleagues on a dangerous chase through the cyber and real worlds. Although Turing cannot actually pursue the killer herself, it falls to her to put the pieces together. The critic for *Publishers Weekly* noted that "those who are computer literate will most appreciate the author's talent for blending information-age details with an enjoyable crime puzzle." Dawn Dowdle, in a review for *BooksnBytes,* found that, despite the odd nature of the protagonist, "Andrews has written it so well that you truly believe a computer could do this."

Access Denied finds Turing on the hunt for her clone, an artifical intelligence personality named T2. The clone has been kidnapped by Nestor Garcia. Turing learns that Garcia's credit cards have been used to order merchandise for delivery at a nearby address. She dispatches Tim Pincoski to check the site. But when a dead body is found at the empty house, Tim becomes the prime suspect in a murder. "As Turing works on the puzzle, racing against time," noted the critic for *Publishers Weekly,* "she observes everything with the wry, witty musings on human-computer relations that make this 'techno-cozy' series a true standout." Jenny McLarin in *Booklist* concluded that "readers will appreciate the entertaining Turing, who struggles to make sense of humans while becoming humanlike herself."

If you enjoy the works of Donna Andrews, you may also want to check out the following books:

Diane Mott Davidson, *Dying for Chocolate,* 1992.
Valerie Wolzien, *Weddings Are Murder,* 1999.
Edie Clare, *Never Tease a Siamese,* 2002.

Delete All Suspects finds Turing investigating the victim of a hit-and-run, 22-year-old Eddie Stallman, the head of a computer company. But Eddie's grandmother does not want to know anything about the suspicious accident that has left her grandson hospitalized, she wants to know whether his company was involved in any illegal activity. It soon becomes obvious that there may be more going on than Turing was told. Is the woman who hired Turing really Eddie's grandmother at all? The *Publishers Weekly* critic found that the story is "full of surprising twists and turns." "Andrews concocts a farfetched plot," McLarin admitted, "but readers (justifiably) enamored with Turing won't care."

■ Biographical and Critical Sources

PERIODICALS

Booklist, May 1, 2000, Jenny McLarin, review of *Murder with Puffins,* p. 1610; August, 2001, Jenny McLarin, review of *Revenge of the Wrought-Iron Flamingos,* p. 2094; February 1, 2004, Jenny McLarin, review of *We'll Always Have Parrots,* p. 952; December 15, 2004, Jenny McLarin, review of *Access Denied,* p. 710; November 1, 2005, Jenny McLarin, review of *Delete All Suspects,* p. 26.
Denver Post (Denver, CO), January 1, 2006, Tom and Enid Schantz, review of *Delete All Suspects,* p. F10.
Kirkus Reviews, November 15, 1998, review of *Murder with Peacocks,* p. 1631; August 1, 2001, review of *Revenge of the Wrought-Iron Flamingos,* p. 1067; February 15, 2002, review of *You've Got Murder,* p. 221; November 1, 2002, review of *Crouching Buzzard, Leaping Loon,* p. 1568; April 1, 2003, review of *Click Here for Murder,* p. 506; October 15, 2004, review of *Access Denied,* p. 985; February 15, 2005, review of *Owl's Well That Ends Well,* p. 198; June 1, 2006, review of *No Nest for the Wicket,* p. 546.

Kliatt, September, 2004, Bette Ammon, review of *We'll Always Have Parrots* audiobook, p. 66.

Library Journal, January, 1999, Rex E. Klett, review of *Murder with Peacocks,* p. 163; September 1, 2001, Rex E. Klett, review of *Revenge of the Wrought-Iron Flamingos,* p. 238; May 1, 2003, Rex E. Klett, review of *Click Here for Murder,* p. 158; July 1, 2005, Ann Kim, review of *Delete All Suspects,* p. 58.

Mystery News, April-May, 2003, review of *Crouching Buzzard, Leaping Loon;* June/July, 2003, review of *Click Here for Murder;* April-May, 2004, review of *We'll Always Have Parrots;* February-March, 2005, review of *Access Denied;* December, 2005-January, 2006, review of *Delete All Suspects;* August-September, 2006, review of *No Nest for the Wicket.*

Publishers Weekly, November 23, 1998, review of *Murder with Peacocks,* p. 62; April 17, 2000, review of *Murder with Puffins,* p. 54; September, 2001, review of *Revenge of the Wrought-Iron Flamingos,* p. 58; March 18, 2002, review of *You've Got Murder,* p. 80; January 20, 2003, review of *Crouching Buzzard, Leaping Loon,* p. 60; April 21, 2003, review of *Click Here for Murder,* p. 42; January 26, 2004, review of *We'll Always Have Parrots,* p. 235; November 29, 2004, review of *Access Denied,* p. 26; September 26, 2005, review of *Delete All Suspects,* p. 66; June 19, 2006, review of *No Nest for the Wicket,* p. 44.

School Library Journal, October, 2000, Pam Johnson, review of *Murder with Puffins,* p. 194.

ONLINE

Best Reviews, http://pnr.thebestreviews.com/ (July 7, 2006), Harriet Klausner, reviews of *Delete All Suspects, Revenge of the Wrought-Iron Flamingos, You've Got Murder,* and *Click Here for Murder.*

BooksnBytes, http://www.booksnbytes.com/ (September 11, 2004), Tuggy Curan, review of *Murder with Peacocks,* and Harriet Klausner, reviews of *Murder with Puffins, Revenge of the Wrought-Iron Flamingos, You've Got Murder,* and *Crouching Buzzard, Leaping Loon.*

Donna Andrews Home Page, http://www.donnaandrews.com (December 28, 2006).

Lady M's Mystery International, http://www.mysteryinternational.com/ (September 11, 2004), Diane Klechefski, review of *The Revenge of the Wrought-Iron Flamingos.*

Murder Express, http://www.murderexpress.net/ (November, 2002), Lelia Taylor, review of *Crouching Buzzard, Leaping Loon.*

Myshelf.com, http://www.myshelf.com/ (September 11, 2004), Susan McBride, review of *Revenge of the Wrought-Iron Flamingos.*

Mystery Reader, http://www.themysteryreader.com/ (September 11, 2004), Monica Pope, reviews of *Murder with Peacocks* and *Murder with Puffins.*

Reviewers Choice, http://www.reviewers-choice.com/ (October, 2006), Sunnie Gill, review of *No Nest for the Wicket.*

Romantic Times Book Club, http://www.romantictimes.com/ (July 7, 2006), Toby Bromberg, reviews of *Murder with Peacocks, Murder with Puffins, Revenge of the Wrought-Iron Flamingos,* and *You've Got Murder,* Tara Gelsomino, review of *Crouching Buzzard, Leaping Loon,* and Jo Peters, reviews of *Click Here for Murder, We'll Always Have Parrots,* and *Owl's Well That Ends Well.**

Tex Avery

■ Personal

Birth name, Frederick Bean Avery; born February 26, 1908, in Taylor, TX; died of lung cancer August 26, 1980, in Burbank, CA; son of George Walton and Mary Augusta (maiden name, Bean) Avery. *Education:* North Dallas High School, graduated 1927; attended Chicago Art Institute.

■ Career

Animator, cartoonist, director. Universal-Walter Lantz Cartoons, animator, 1930-35; Warner Bros., animator and director, 1936-41; Paramount, animator, 1942; MGM, animator and director, 1942-55; Cascade Productions, animator and producer of commercials, 1956-78; Hanna-Barbera Cartoons, animator and director, 1978-80. Animated films as director: *Golddiggers of '49*, 1936, *The Blow-out*, 1936, *Plane Dippy*, 1936, *I'd Love to Take Orders from You*, 1936, *Miss Glory*, 1936, *I Love to Singa*, 1936, *Porky the Rain Maker*, 1936, *The Village Smithy*, 1936, *Milk and Money*, 1936, *Don't Look Now*, 1936, *Porky the Wrestler*, 1937, *Picador Porky*, 1937, *I Only Have Eyes for You*, 1937, *Porky's Duck Hunt*, 1937, *Uncle Tom's Bungalow*, 1937, *Ain't We Got Fun*, 1937, *Daffy Duck and Egghead*,1937, *Egghead Rides Again*, 1937, *A Sunbonnet Blue*, 1937, *Porky's Garden*, 1937, *I Wanna Be a Sailor*, 1937, *The Sneezing Weasel*, 1937, *Little Red Walking Hood*, 1938, *The Penguin Parade*, 1938, *The Isle of Pingo Pongo*, 1938, *A Feud There Was*, 1938, *Johnny Smith and Poker-Huntas*, 1938, *Daffy Duck in Hollywood*, 1938, *Cinderella Meets Fella*, 1938, *Hamateur Night*, 1938, *The Mice Will Play*, 1938, *Daffy's Romance*, 1939, *A Day at the Zoo*, 1939, *Thugs with Dirty Mugs*, 1939, *Believe It or Else*, 1939, *Dangerous Dan McFoo*, 1939, *Detouring America*, 1939, *Land of the Midnight Fun*, 1939, *Fresh Fish*, 1939, *Screwball Football*, 1939, *The Early Worm Gets the Bird*, 1940, *Cross Country Detours*, 1940, *The Bear's Tale*, 1940, *A Gander at Mother Goose*, 1940, *Circus Today*, 1940, *A Wild Hare*, 1940, *Ceiling Hero*, 1940, *Wacky Wild Life*, 1940, *Of Fox and Hounds*, (plus voice of Willoughby the dog) 1940, *Holiday Highlights*, 1941, *The Crackpot Quail*, 1941, *Haunted Mouse*, 1941, *Tortoise Beats Hare*, 1941, *Hollywood Steps Out*, 1941, *Porky's Preview*, 1941, *The Heckling Hare*, (plus voice of Willoughby the dog) 1941, *Aviation Vacation*, 1941, *All This and Rabbit Stew*, 1941, *The Bug Parade*, 1941, *Aloha Hooey*, 1941, *The Cagey Canary*, (completed by Bob Clampett) 1941, *Crazy Cruise*, 1942, *Speaking of Animals down on the Farm*, 1942, *Speaking of Animals in a Pet Shop*, 1942, *Speaking of Animals in the Zoo*, 1942, *The Blitz Wolf*, 1942, *The Early Bird Dood It*, 1942, *Dumb-Hounded*, 1943, *Red Hot Riding Hood*, 1943, *Who Killed Who?*, 1943, *One Ham's Family*, 1943, *What's Buzzin', Buzzard?*, 1944, *Screwy Squirrel*, 1944, *Batty Baseball*, 1944, *Happy-Go-Nutty*, 1944, *Big Heel-watha*, 1945, *The Screwy Truant*, 1945, *The Shooting of Dan McGoo*, 1945, *Jerky Turkey*, 1945, *Swing Shift Cinderella*, 1945, *Wild and Woolfy*, 1946, *Lonesome Lenny*, 1946, *The Hick Chick*, 1946, *Northwest Hounded Police*, 1946, *Henpecked Hoboes* (plus voice of Junior) 1947, *Hound Hunters*, (plus voice of Junior) 1947, *Red Hot Rangers*, (plus voice of Junior) 1947, *Uncle Tom's Cabana*, 1947, *Slap Happy Lion*, 1947, *King Size Canary*, 1947, *Little Tinker*, 1948, *What Price Fleadom*, 1948, *Half-Pint*

Pygmy, (plus voice of Junior) 1948, *Lucky Ducky,* 1948, *The Cat That Hated People,* 1949, *Bad Luck Blackie,* 1949, *Senor Droopy,* 1949, *The House of Tomorrow,* 1949, *Doggone Tired,* 1949, *Wags to Riches,* 1949, *Little Rural Riding Hood,* 1949, *Outfoxed,* 1949, *Counterfeit Cat,* 1950, *Ventriloquist Cat,* 1950, *The Cuckoo Clock,* 1950, *Garden Gopher,* 1950, *The Chump Champ,* 1950, *The Peachy Cobbler,* 1951, *Cock-a-Doodle Dog,* 1951, *Dare-Devil Droopy,* 1951, *Droopy's Good Deed,* 1951, *Symphony in Slang,* 1951, *The Car of Tomorrow,* 1951, *Droopy's Double Trouble,* 1951, *The Magical Maestro,* 1952, *One Cab's Family,* 1952, *Rock-a-Bye Bear,* 1953, *Little Johnny Jet; TV of Tomorrow,* 1953, *The Three Little Pups,* 1953, *Drag-a-long Droopy,* 1954, *Billy Boy,* 1954, *Homesteader Droopy,* 1954, *Farm of Tomorrow,* 1954, *The Flea Circus,* 1954, *Dixieland Droopy,* 1954, *Crazy Mixed-Up Pup,* 1955, *Field and Scream,* 1955, *The First Bad Man,* 1955, *Deputy Droopy,* (codirector) 1955, *Cellbound,* (codirector) 1955, *I'm Cold (Some Like It Not),* 1955, *Chilly Willy in the Legend of Rockabye Point (The Rockabye Legend),* 1955, *SH-H-H-H-H;* remakes of *Wags to Riches* and *Ventriloquist Cat,* 1956, *Millionaire Droopy,* 1956, *Cat's Meow,* 1958, *Polar Pests,* 1958. Also creator of commercials for Kool-Aid, Pepsodent, Raid, and Frito-Lay, 1956-78.

■ Awards, Honors

First Prize, Venice Publicity Festival, for *Calo-Tiger,* 1958; Television Commercials Council Award, 1960; Annie Award, ASIFA, 1974.

■ Writings

Much of Avery's work has been collected on *The Golden Age of Looney Tunes: 1933-48,* MGM/UA, 1992, and *The Compleat Tex Avery, 1942-1957,* MGM/UA, 1993.

■ Adaptations

Avery's work was the inspiration for the television show, *The Wacky World of Tex Avery,* DIC Entertainment, 1997. *The Tex Avery Show,* 1999-2002 (television show replaying cartoons from Warner Bros. and MGM).

■ Sidelights

"The cartoons of Tex Avery represent a style of animation that is the absolute antithesis to the [Walt] Disney school of filmmaking," according to a critic for *International Dictionary of Films and Filmmakers.* "Whereas Disney strove for realism (with such technical devices as sound, Technicolor, and the multiplane camera), Avery strove for the absurd and the surreal." And according to most writers on animation, Avery was more than successful in this effort. Animator, director, and producer of animated shorts at Warner Bros. and MGM from the 1930s to the 1950s, Avery is credited with developing some of the most screwball cartoon characters in the genre, including Bugs Bunny, Daffy Duck, Porky Pig, Droopy Dog, Chilly Willy, Screwy Squirrel, and Red Hot Riding Hood. To Avery also goes the credit for Bugs Bunny's famous line, "What's up, doc?" Writing in *Time* magazine, Richard Corliss noted that Avery's "best cartoons inhabit a dog-eat-cat, male-chase-female, everyone-humiliate-everyone-else world—a place of constant war over food crises and turf disputes. It is a world wholly aware of itself as an artistic fabrication." Corliss further observed: "By keying the insane pace, wild exaggeration, mock-cheerful tone and inside references that today define so much of movie and TV entertainment, Avery practically invented pop culture's Postmodernism." For *World and I* contributor Robert L. Tefertillar: "It takes a great director like Avery to blend humor, music, character, and animation into a masterpiece." Avery created almost 150 cartoon shorts over a career lasting half a century. After leaving cartooning for a time in the 1960s, he turned his hand to television advertising, where he created further memorable characters, including the bugs for the Raid commercials, and the Frito-Lay mascot, Frito Bandito. Avery's legacy indeed lives on, as Corliss noted. Gordon Flagg, writing in *Booklist,* commented that "today's cartoons owe far more to Avery's over-the-top style than to Disney's staidness." Gary Morris, writing for *Bright Lights Film Journal,* observed: "In a field teeming with talent, Avery stood out."

Texas Beginnings

Born Frederick Bean Avery in Taylor, Texas, in 1908, the future animator was said to be related to Judge Roy Bean (the man who told defendants that they would of course get a fair trial before hanging), and to the frontiersman Daniel Boone. He grew up listening to the tall tales of Texas and also enjoying illustration. Graduating from high school in 1926, he attended the Chicago Art Institute. After trying unsuccessfully to start a syndicated comic strip, he moved to California, where he worked for a time on the Los Angeles docks and slept on the beach to save money. Finally he was able to find a job at the Walter Lantz unit at Universal, where he spent five years as an assistant animator, "in-betweening," as it is called in the trade; that is, doing the sequential poses for a character in motion. It was at the Lantz unit that Avery learned the animation craft. Quickly it became apparent that Avery was moving beyond the limitations of animation; that he was determined to make characters move in a fluid and antic manner that had never been seen before in cartoons.

Avery was, early in his career, known for his storytelling, athleticism, and sense of fun. However, an accident during a bit of playful rough-housing at Lantz ended in Avery being blinded in his left eye. "This grim event was a turning-point," according to Morris. "By all accounts, along with his eye he lost much of his fun-loving spirit, put on weight, and turned for solace to a driving perfectionism that provided both inspiration and frustration." Some critics theorize that Avery's subsequent lack of depth perception accounts, in part, for his zany style as a director.

In 1935, Avery left Universal for Warner Bros., where he became a full-time cartoon director, joining other talented members of the animation unit such as Chuck Jones and Bob Clampett. The fast-talking Avery managed to convince the head of the studio to let him lead an animation team headquartered in an old bungalow on a back lot of Warner Bros., at Sunset Boulevard. This bungalow, home to a significant termite population, was soon dubbed "Termite Terrace," and Avery's team was put in charge of the black-and-white cartoons in the *Looney Tunes* line. At Warner Bros., he was still known as Fred Avery. By 1941 he had become Tex Avery.

Days at the Termite Terrace

A critic for *St. James Encyclopedia of Popular Culture* noted that Avery and his fellow artists at Termite Terrace "set about creating a new cartoon sensibility which was more adult, absurd, and filled with slapstick." They pushed the limits of cartooning beyond the staid humor of the Disney studios, having their characters speak directly to the audience, using split screen effects, and especially employing rapid changes in pacing. The tone of the cartoons was also heavily satiric. An early example of Avery's satire on popular culture is the 1936 *I Love to Singa*, parodying the movie *The Jazz Singer* and its star, Al Jolson. Avery's cartoon featured a protagonist called "Owl Jolson."

Avery excelled at characterization and gags. Instead of the cute and cuddly characters of the Disney studio, Avery, along with Jones and Clampett, gave the world "unflappable wits like Bugs Bunny, endearing buffoons like Porky Pig, or dazzling crazies like Daffy Duck," according to Morris. Porky Pig became one of the first creations of Avery and his team, reviving a standard *Looney Tunes* character with a new dash of vitality. With *Porky's Duck Hunt* from 1937, Avery introduced the irascible Daffy Duck, a zany bird that became so popular that he ultimately had his own cartoon series. Most significant were Avery's contributions to the development of Bugs Bunny, transformed from a rabbit character in several cartoons from 1938. However it is the 1940 cartoon *A Wild Hare* in which the fully developed Bugs is introduced, along with his trademark "What's up, doc?" This was a popular phrase at Avery's high school, and became Bugs Bunny's incisive line, helping to portray the rabbit as a streetwise character rather than a charming Disney-like creation. Avery was also instrumental in the development of the befuddled Elmer Fudd, introduced in *A Wild Hare*, and adapted from the earlier character, Egghead. As the contributor for *St. James Encyclopedia of Popular Culture* commented, "Avery's style became so important to the studio and imitated by his colleagues that he became known as the 'Father of Warner Bros. Cartoons.'" Writing in *Entertainment Weekly*, Steve Daly described this style as "the weawwy scwewy stuff—the raw, early, hyperkinetic work of fledgling directors elated at smashing the cuddly Disney mold."

Avery also transformed the fairy tale—a staple of the Disney studio—into an updated and rather sexy version. As Gary Morris wrote for *Images Journal:* "It was in the Hollywood cartoon short, and especially the work of Tex Avery at Warner Bros. and MGM, that a truly modern version of the fairy tale emerged." In particular, Avery contributed risqué take offs on the Little Red Riding Hood of Charles Perrault fame. Beginning with his 1937 *Little Red Walking Hood*, Avery stood the fairy tale premise on its head. Both at Warner Bros. and later at MGM he created several spin offs of popular fairy tales. According to Morris in *Images Journal:* "These cartoons represent an assault on the [Bruno] Bettelheim school that sees fairy tales as the source of moral instruction for youth, and, closer to home, on the Disney aesthetic." Morris continued: "Avery's versions of these archetypal stories, made to satisfy both children and adults, attempt to reverse Bettelheim by 'bringing chaos out of order.' . . . Avery's fairy tales jettison the whole idea of morality, along with other troublesome concepts like logic, sense, and sexual repression."

Development of Bugs Bunny may be one of Avery's claims to fame; the rabbit was also part of the reason

Avery's first release for MGM, the 1942 cartoon *The Blitz Wolf*, parodied Adolf Hitler and the Nazi war machine.

he left Warner Bros. studios. The rabbit's fourth outing under the directorship of Avery, the 1941 *The Heckling Hare*, brought his association with Warner Bros. to a close. A gag ending with a sexual innuendo was cut without Avery's consent, and he left, joining MGM, where he would stay for the next dozen years, and perhaps his most creative ones.

MGM and Beyond

At MGM Avery was given larger budgets for his cartoons and more freedom in his subject matter. His first release, the 1942 *Blitz Wolf*, a satiric parody of Adolf Hitler, was nominated for an Academy Award for Best Short. Perhaps his best known and

best loved character from the MGM years is Droopy Dog, introduced in the 1943 *Dumbhounded*. He also created Screwy Squirrel during these years, and continued to push the limits of fairy tales with his sexy Red Hot Riding Hood, introduced in the 1943 cartoon of the same title. The wolf, in Avery's version of the story, is unable to control his lust for Red: his eyeballs pop out, his tongue lolls on the ground. To get by the censors, Avery eventually added segments that he knew would be beyond bounds. These were cut, leaving the central story—and its racy bits—untouched.

Avery also enjoyed satirizing some of what society thought was wonderful. He took on the idea of technological progress in *The House of Tomorrow, The Car of Tomorrow,* and *The TV of Tomorrow,* and parodied John Steinbeck's literary classic *Of Mice and Men* with his *Lonesome Lenny.* He even poked fun at the singer Frank Sinatra with his *Li'l Tinker.* His style at MGM, having started as lushly realistic, slowly developed into faster paced and less realistic, as if he were trying to erase all connection with live action in his cartoons—to create a separate cartoon reality of nonstop action and gags.

By 1954, however, Avery had decided to move once more, this time returning to Universal to work again with Walter Lantz. This association lasted for only cartoons, however, one of them in which he introduced the penguin character Chilly Willy. A contract dispute led to his leaving Universal and cartoons for many years. During the 1960s, Avery turned to television commercials, with major accounts including Raid and Frito-Lay. His Frito Bandito, with all the stereotypes inherent in the name, became so controversial that ultimately Frito-Lay had to stop the mascot's use.

If you enjoy the works of Tex Avery, you may also want to check out the following animators:

The works of Bob Clampett and Chuck Jones, best known for their work on the "Looney Tunes" series of cartoons; John Kricfalusi, creator of *Ren and Stimpy*; and Matt Groening, creator of *The Simpsons.*

Toward the end of his life, Avery returned to theatrical cartooning, working for Hanna-Barbera Cartoons, once his competitors. Here he drew for the Saturday morning cartoon show *Kwicky Koala.* He died at his desk at Hanna-Barbera on August 26, 1980. Since his death, Avery has been canonized as one of the most influential animators and directors in cartooning history. "Bending the physics of movie reality was Avery's obsession," wrote Daly in *Entertainment Weekly.* He is remembered for the assortment of cartoon characters he created or helped to develop, as well as for his breakneck speed of animation and action. "His work," according to the critic for *International Dictionary of Films and Filmmakers,* "has certainly influenced a number of younger animators, although no one has yet been able to completely match Avery's achievement: the totally crazy cartoon." Similarly, Morris, writing in *Bright Lights Film Journal,* concluded, "Like the characters, the work always outlives the author, and a bit of Avery continues to live whenever someone says, 'What's up, doc?'"

The sultry, sexy vixen in Avery's 1943 work *Red Hot Riding Hood* was modeled after pin-up girl Betty Grable.

■ Biographical and Critical Sources

BOOKS

Adamson, Joe, *Tex Avery: King of Cartoons,* Da Capo Press (New York, NY), 1975.
Benayoun, Robert, *Le mystère Tex Avery,* Editions du Seuil (Paris, France), 1988.

Canemaker, John, *Tex Avery: The MGM Years, 1942-1955*, Turner Press (Atlanta, GA), 1996.

International Dictionary of Films and Filmmakers, Volume 4: *Writers and Production Artists*, 4th edition, St. James Press (Detroit, MI), 2000.

St. James Encyclopedia of Popular Culture, St. James Press (Detroit, MI), 2000.

Schneider, Steve, *That's All Folks!: The Art of Warner Bros. Animation*, Henry Holt (New York, NY), 1988.

PERIODICALS

Booklist, November 15, 1996, Gordon Flagg, review of *Tex Avery: The MGM Years, 1942-1955*, p. 562.

Entertainment Weekly, January 10, 1992, Steve Daly, review of *The Golden Age of Looney Tunes: 1933-48*, p. 74; March 19, 1993, Steve Daly, review of *The Compleat Tex Avery, 1942-1957*, p. 66.

Horn Book Magazine, January-February, 1993, Lane Smith, "The Artist at Work,"

People, April 3, 1989, Ralph Novak, review of "Bugs Bunny Classics," p. 20; November 12, 1990, David Hiltbrand, review of "What's Up Doc?," p. 13.

Time, August 8, 1994, Richard Corliss, "Like 'The Mask'? Try Tex Avery's Cartoons," p. 58.

World and I, May, 2000, Robert L. Tefertillar, "Controversial Cartoons."

ONLINE

Bright Lights Film Journal Online, http://www.brightlightsfilm.com/ (May 29, 2006), Gary Morris, "A Quickie Look at the Life & Career of Tex Avery."

Dan Markstein's Toonopedia, http://www.toonopedia.com/ (May 29, 2006), "Tex Avery."

Images Journal, http://www.imagesjournal.com/ (May 29, 2006), Gary Morris, "The Fairy Tales of Tex Avery."

Internet Movie Database, http://www.imdb.com/ (May 29, 2006), "Tex Avery."

Tex Avery Tribute, http://www.texavery.com (May 29, 2006).*

Jay Bennett

■ Personal

Born December 24, 1912, in New York, NY; son of Pincus (a businessman) and Estelle (Bennett) Shapiro; married Sally Stern, February 2, 1937; children: Steven Cullen, Randy Elliott. *Education:* Attended New York University. *Religion:* Jewish. *Hobbies and other interests:* Music, art, ballet, travel, sports.

■ Addresses

Home—64 Greensward Lane, Cherry Hill, NJ 08002.

■ Career

Writer, 1930—. Worked as a farmhand, factory worker, lifeguard, mailman, salesman, and at other occupations. Scriptwriter for radio and television dramas during 1940s and 1950s; Grolier Education Corp., New York, NY, senior editor of encyclopedias, c. 1960. Guest lecturer at universities. *Military service:* U.S. Office of War Information, English features writer and editor in Overseas Division, 1942-45.

■ Member

Mystery Writers of America (member of board of directors), Authors Guild, Authors League of America, Writers Guild, Dramatists Guild (life member).

■ Awards, Honors

Edgar Allan Poe Award for best juvenile mystery novel, Mystery Writers of America, 1974, for *The Long Black Coat,* and 1975, for *The Dangling Witness; Variety* Award for television script for *Monodrama Theatre;* Shakespeare Society award for television adaptation of *Hamlet.*

■ Writings

YOUNG ADULT MYSTERIES

Deathman, Do Not Follow Me, Meredith Press (New York, NY), 1968.

The Deadly Gift, Meredith Press (New York, NY), 1969.

Masks: A Love Story, F. Watts (New York, NY), 1971.

The Killing Tree, F. Watts (New York, NY), 1972.

The Long Black Coat, Delacorte (New York, NY), 1973.

The Dangling Witness, Delacorte (New York, NY), 1974.

Say Hello to the Hit Man, Delacorte (New York, NY), 1976.

The Birthday Murderer, Delacorte (New York, NY), 1977.

The Pigeon, Methuen (New York, NY), 1980.

The Executioner, Avon (New York, NY), 1982.

Slowly, Slowly I Raise the Gun, Avon (New York, NY), 1983.

I Never Said I Loved You, Avon (New York, NY), 1984.

The Death Ticket, Avon (New York, NY), 1985.

To Be a Killer, Scholastic, Inc. (New York, NY), 1985.

The Skeleton Man, F. Watts (New York, NY), 1986.

The Haunted One, F. Watts (New York, NY), 1987.

The Dark Corridor, F. Watts (New York, NY), 1988.

Sing Me a Death Song, F. Watts (New York, NY), 1990.

Coverup, F. Watts (New York, NY), 1991.

Skinhead, F. Watts (New York, NY), 1991.

The Hooded Man, Fawcett-Juniper (New York, NY), 1993.

Death Grip, Fawcett-Juniper (New York, NY), 1993.

ADULT NOVELS

Catacombs, Abelard-Schuman (New York, NY), 1959.

Murder Money, Fawcett (New York, NY), 1963.

Death Is a Silent Room, Abelard-Schuman (New York, NY), 1965.

Shadows Offstage, Nelson (New York, NY), 1974.

PLAYS

No Hiding Place (three-act), produced in New York, NY, 1949.

Lions after Slumber (three-act), produced in London, England, 1951.

OTHER

The Guiccoli Miniature (stories), Scholastic, Inc., 1991.

Author of numerous radio scripts, including *Miracle before Christmas* and *The Wind and Stars Are Witness*; author of television scripts for *Alfred Hitchcock Presents*, *Harlem Detective*, *Crime Syndicated*, *Wide, Wide World*, *Cameo Theater*, and *Monodrama Theater*.

■ Adaptations

One of Bennett's novels for adults was adapted as a film produced by Warner Bros.

■ Sidelights

Called a "recognized master of mystery and suspense novels for young adult readers" by a contributor for *St. James Guide to Young Adult Writers*, Jay Bennett is the author of over a score of such works, from his 1968 *Deathman, Do Not Follow Me*, to his 1993 title, *Death Grip*. Though suspenseful thrillers, Bennett's novels also deal with serious themes. Moral dilemmas are presented in novels such as *The Dangling Witness* and *The Deadly Gift*, while teenage drinking is at the core of *Coverup*, teen suicide is investigated in *The Dark Corridor*, and white supremacy groups inform the 1991 *Skinhead*. Bennett has also written two young adult romance novels, *Masks: A Love Story*, and *I Never Said I Loved You*, books which also tackle social problems important to teens, such as interracial romance.

Bennett frequently features protagonists who are outsiders, who go it alone against heavy odds. As a critic for *St. James Guide to Young Adult Writers* noted, such outsider and "loner" characters often "find through the course of the novels that it is difficult to survive alone, and its is this discovery that becomes the thematic framework for [Bennet's] stories." Writing in *Something about the Author Autobiography Series* (*SAAS*), Bennett noted: "I speak to the loner in our society. There are so many loners, especially among the young and I say to them in my novels, You cannot make it alone, you have to reach out and embrace another human being and human values. There is no other way, or you are lost." Referring to Bennett's writing style, the contributor for *St. James Guide to Young Adult Writers* noted that his "writing is clear and simple, again appealing to many young readers; but his concise prose is rich in meaning and fully expressive." Bennett's novels have earned two prestigious Edgar Allan Poe Awards, have sold over four million copies, and have been translated into sixteen languages. As Teri S. Lesesne and Kylene G. Beers observed in *Journal of Adolescent and Adult Literacy*, "With male protagonists and good page-turning mysteries, Jay Bennett's novels have appealed to many readers over the years."

Theme of the Loner

Born in New York, NY in 1912, Bennett has been a professional writer since the 1930s. He began his writing career as a playwright and scriptwriter for radio and television. He also worked as an encyclopedia editor for a time. His earliest books were writ-

Bennett working at his typewriter.

ten for adults, but by 1968 he had turned to juvenile fiction, publishing his first young adult title, *Deathman, Do Not Follow Me*. That book established many of the themes Bennett would work on throughout his long career as a fiction writer. When a priceless Van Gogh painting disappears from the Brooklyn Museum, teenager Danny Morgan finds himself in mortal danger. Morgan, a loner, learns that this outsider status a liability in dealing with the eerie "Deathman," who threatens him. Another loner is the protagonist of Bennett's second young adult novel, *The Deadly Gift*. One night teenager John-Tom Dawes picks up a briefcase left behind by a man waiting for a bus. Inside is 10,000 dollars, enough to fund his college education. Faced with the moral dilemma of finding the rightful owner and keeping the money for his education, John-Tom is soon drawn into a web of violence by a crime syndicate that claims the money.

The Long Black Coat, from 1973, was Bennett's first Edgar Allan Poe Award winner. This thriller features Phil Brant, whose life has become overshadowed by the death of his older brother, Vinnie, in Vietnam. However, soon Phil is menaced by two men who helped commit a bank robbery with Vinnie before he shipped out for Vietnam. They believe Phil knows where the proceeds from that robbery are hidden, but he is ignorant of such things. His searches ultimately lead him to his older brother who did not die in Vietnam after all. *The Dangling Witness*, Bennett's second Edgar Allan Poe Award-winning title, features another male teenager who becomes unwittingly involved in crime. Matthew Garth is an usher at a movie theater and the only witness to a murder. Matt is fearful of going to the police, as the murderer knows Matt saw him. He is eventually helped in the moral quandary by a police detective and the victim's sister. Ultimately Matt must face and deal with the violence that he so much despises.

Psychological Insights

Bennett's works also demonstrate psychological insights into his characters who as often fall victim to their own neuroses as they do to the stalkers and hoodlums who threaten them. In *The Birthday Murderer*, Shan Rourke is certain that he was responsible for a fatal accident when he was only a five-year-old. Though he has no memory of the incident, the adults present have told him about it. Now, when he is threatened as a result of this long-distant accident, Shan must come to terms with his memories. A love-hate relationship between brothers is the emotional backdrop for *The Death Ticket*, in which teenage Gil is half-owner of a winning lottery ticket which a group of criminals wants to secure.

Bennett explored international terrorism with *The Pigeon*, in which Brian Cawley is set up to be the "pigeon" in the death of his girlfriend. With the help of a former teacher, Brian tries to track down the real killers, a search that leads him to a Neo-Nazi group with plans to bomb the Staten Island ferry. Another dead girlfriend is the plot engine for *The Dark Corridor*. Kerry Lanson assumes that the death of his girlfriend Alicia is suicide, until it is discovered that she had drugs in her body at the time of death. Alicia's father—owner of a multi-million dollar business empire which Alicia was being prepared to take over—blames Kerry for introducing her to drugs. However, Kerry is sure that Alicia did not use drugs; he soon becomes suspicious enough to mount his own investigation, which brings him face to face with the murderer. Reviewing *The Dark Corridor* in *School Library Journal*, Merilyn S. Burrington praised Bennett's "well-constructed plot," and his "masterful employment of light and dark to paint a hellish atmosphere."

Bennett's *The Skeleton Man* is a "taut, suspenseful crime novel," according to *School Library Journal* contributor Phyllis Graves. Once again, sudden money brings danger to a teen protagonist. Ray's Uncle Ed leaves him a bequest of 30,000 dollars, but Ed was a gambler with debts owed to criminals. When Ray ignores demands for the return of the money, a killer threatens Ray's girlfriend, and he decides to give up the money. However, the long

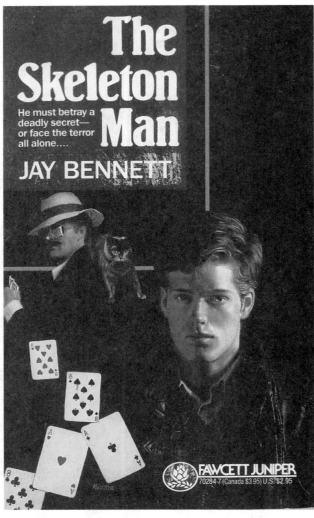

A young man is threatened by criminals after his uncle, a problem gambler, bequests him a large sum of money in this 1986 novel.

nett's [spare] style is sure to appeal to reluctant readers." Kowen also thought the author "maintains the suspense and intrigue at an intense level throughout the book."

Tackles Social Issues

Bennett's work in the 1990s deals with various social issues. As the contributor for *St. James Guide to Young Adult Writers* noted of his *Coverup:* "the issues of teenage drinking and the homeless combine to provide the chilling effect, when the hero Brad cannot remember what happened the night before when he had been drinking with his friend Alden, the judge's son . . . [and Brad] . . . learns the terrible truth about the ability of those in power to cover up scandal, even death by auto." Reviewing the novel in *School Library Journal,* Judie Porter commented, "Bennett, the master of short sentences, has suspensefully plotted another mystery that is sure to appeal to reluctant readers."

If you enjoy the works of Jay Bennett, you may also want to check out the following books:

Lois Duncan, *I Know What You Did Last Summer,* 1973.
Patricia Windsor, *The Sandman's Eyes,* 1985.
Caroline B. Cooney, *The Face on the Milk Carton,* 1990.

---

arm of the law interferes just in time. This novel, like all of Bennett's, is noted for dialogue of short sentences which moves the plot quickly, well-drawn characters, and a minimum of detail to speed the reading.

With *Sing Me a Death Song,* Bennett looks at the efficacy of capital punishment. Jason Feldon knows he has to go it alone in uncovering the truth about a murder that his mother is scheduled to be executed for—in less than a week. A compelling argument against the use of the death sentence, Bennett's story was praised by Randy Brough in *Voice of Youth Advocates* as a "taut, spare, poignant" mystery sure to appeal to young adult readers. Kenneth E. Kowen, writing in *School Library Journal,* felt that "Ben-

Another topical concern is the subject of *Skinhead.* Jonathan Atwood, the grandson of a powerful millionaire, is summoned to Seattle by a stranger, the dying Alfred Kaplan, author of a work in progress about the white supremacy movement. While there, Jonathan receives a death threat from an unidentified source. He remains in Seattle, although he is aware that he is under surveillance by local white supremacists, or "skinheads," who apparently have connected him to Kaplan and the unpublished book manuscript. This connection puts Jonathan's life in danger. Not only must he now confront these skinheads, but he must also deal with his own family background and his sense of right and wrong. Bruce Anne Shook, reviewing the title in *School Library*

Journal, recommended the book for reluctant readers for its "generous doses of adventure mingled with unpredictable violence and a little romance."

Writing in *SAAS,* Bennett summarized his goals and motivations for writing young adult fiction: "All through my years I have been intensely interested in the young and their problems and hopes. Their dreams and despairs. . . . My wife still calls me a child who will never grow up and in one sense she's absolutely right. And that's why it's so easy for me to write my books for that readership. But there's more to it than that. I feel very strongly that it's up to the young to help turn things around. We can't go on much longer the way we are."

Brad wakes up with a terrible hangover and the feeling that something has gone terribly wrong....

Coverup

JAY BENNETT
Author of *Skinhead*

"Bennett has suspensefully plotted another mystery.... [A] page turner"

■ Biographical and Critical Sources

BOOKS

Contemporary Literary Criticism, Volume 35, Gale (Detroit, MI), 1985, pp. 52-53.

Donelson, Kenneth L., and Aleen Pace Nilsen, *Literature for Today's Young Adults,* Scott, Foresman (Glenview, IL), 1980, pp. 228-257.

Something about the Author Autobiography Series, Volume 4, Gale (Detroit, MI), 1987, pp. 75-91.

St. James Guide to Young Adult Writers, 2nd ed., St. James Press (Detroit, MI), 1999.

PERIODICALS

Best Sellers, January, 1981, review of *The Pigeon,* p. 349.

Booklist, June 1, 1971, review of *Masks: A Love Story,* p. 829; November 1, 1972, review of *The Killing Tree,* p. 238; April 1, 1976, review of *Say Hello to the Hit Man,* p. 1100; October 15, 1977, review of *The Birthday Murderer,* p. 366; May 15, 1980, review of *The Pigeon,* p. 1356; April 1, 1982, review of *The Executioner;* June 1, 1985, review of *To Be a Killer,* p. 1389; November 15, 1985, review of *The Death Ticket,* p. 481; November 1, 1986, review of *The Skeleton Man,* p. 402; March 15, 1991, review of *Sing Me a Death Song,* p. 1480; May 1, 1991, review of *Skinhead,* p. 1705; November 1, 1991, review of *Coverup,* p. 505; March 15, 1992, review of *Coverup,* p. 1366.

English Journal, February, 1969, review of *Deathman, Do Not Follow Me,* pp. 295-296; April, 1970, review of *The Deadly Gift,* p. 591; January, 1979, review of *The Birthday Murderer,* p. 57.

Journal of Adolescent and Adult Literacy, December, 1996-January, 1997, Teri S. Lesesne and Kylene G. Beers, review of *Coverup,* p. 316.

Kirkus Reviews, December 1, 1969, review of *The Deadly Gift,* p. 1265; April 1, 1971, review of *Masks,* p. 379; April 1, 1973, review of *The Long Black Coat,* p. 395; January 1, 1974, review of *Shadows Offstage,* p. 9; April 15, 1976, review of *Say Hello to the Hit Man,* p. 481; November 15, 1977, review of *The Birthday Murderer,* p. 12105; October 1, 1986, review of *The Skeleton Man,* p. 1513; September 15, 1987, review of *The Haunted One,* p. 1388; November 15, 1988, review of *The Dark Corridor,* p. 1670; February 1, 1990, review of *Sing Me a Death Song,* p. 176; April 1, 1991, review of *Skinhead,* p. 467; September 15, 1991, review of *Coverup.*

Kliatt, April, 1991, review of *Sing Me a Death Song,* p. 4; January, 1993, review of *Coverup,* p. 4; March, 1994, review of *Death Grip,* p. 4.

New York Times Book Review, August 22, 1965, review of *Death Is a Silent Room,* p. 26; July 7, 1968, review of *Deathman, Do Not Follow Me,* p. 16; November 10, 1974, review of *The Dangling Witness,* pp. 8, 10; May 2, 1976, review of *Say Hello to the Hit Man,* p. 38.

Publishers Weekly, August 14, 1972, review of *The Killing Tree,* p. 46; May 7, 1973, review of *The Long Black Coat,* p. 65; June 3, 1974, review of *Shadows Offstage,* p. 157; August 12, 1974, review of *The Dangling Man,* p. 58; March 8, 1976, review of *Say Hello to the Hit Man,* p. 67; August 22, 1977, review of *The Birthday Murderer,* p. 66; July 18, 1980, review of *The Pigeon,* p. 62; January 29, 1982, review of *The Executioner,* July 1, 1983, review of *Slowly, Slowly I Raise the Gun,* p. 103; September 27, 1985, Jean F. Mercier, review of *The Death Ticket,* p. 97; October 28, 1988, Kimberly Olson Fakih and Diane Roback, review of *The Dark Corridor,* p. 83; February 1, 1991, Diane Roback and Richard Donahue, review of *Skinhead,* p. 81.

School Library Journal, May, 1970, review of *The Deadly Gift,* p. 92; May, 1974, review of *Shadows Offstage,* p. 69; May, 1976, review of *Say Hello to the Hit Man,* p. 77; December, 1977, review of *The Birthday Murderer,* p. 62; February, 1978, review of *Deathman, Do Not Follow Me,* p. 35; May, 1980, review of *The Pigeon,* p. 86; November, 1980, Robert E. Unsworth, review of *The Pigeon,* p. 46; May, 1982, review of *The Executioner,* p. 84; December, 1983, review of *Slowly, Slowly I Raise the Gun,* p. 84; August, 1984, review of *I Never Said I Loved You,* p. 80; October, 1986, Phyllis Graves, review of *The Skeleton Man,* pp. 185-186; November, 1987, Robert E. Unsworth, review of *The Haunted One,* p. 112; November, 1988, Merilyn S. Burrington, review of *The Dark Corridor,* p. 124; April, 1990, Kenneth E. Kowen, review of *Sing Me a Death Song,* pp. 139-140; May, 1991, Bruce Anne Shook, review of *Skinhead,* p. 108; August, 1991, Judie Porter, review of *Coverup,* p. 195.

Times Educational Supplement, July 29, 1988, review of *The Skeleton Man,* p. 21.

Times Literary Supplement, August 19, 1988, review of *The Skeleton Man,* p. 917.

Voice of Youth Advocates, August, 1982, review of *The Executioner,* p. 28; February, 1984, review of *Slowly, Slowly I Raise the Gun,* p. 337; August, 1984, review of *I Never Said I Loved You,* p. 143; August 1990, Randy Brough, review of *Sing Me a Death Song,* p. 158; June, 1994, review of *Death Grip,* p. 80.

Washington Post Book World, October 7, 1979, review of *The Birthday Murderer,* p. 15.

Wilson Library Bulletin, April, 1992, Cathi Dunn MacRae, review of *Skinhead,* p. 99.*

David Breashears

■ Personal

Born December 20, 1955, in Fort Benning, GA; son of a U.S. Army officer.

■ Addresses

Home—Boston, MA. *Agent*—c/o Author Mail, Simon & Schuster, 1230 Avenue of the Americas, New York, NY 10020.

■ Career

Documentary filmmaker and writer. Worked in construction in early career; University of Colorado, Denver, CO, climbing instructor; Public Broadcasting Service (PBS), climbing rope rigger on *Free Climb*; American Broadcasting Company Sports (ABC Sports), guide and apprentice sound man, 1980; ABC American Sportsman, sound technician and cameraman on ascent of Mt. Everest, 1981; ABC American Sportsman, cameraman on second ascent of Mt. Everest, 1982; ABC and Mutual of Omaha, team leader on ascent of Everest, 1986; *Cliffhanger*, cameraman and climbing advisor, 1993; *Ice Princess*, director of photography and field producer, 1995; *Seven Years in Tibet*, director of photography, 1996; *Front-line* (WGBH-TV) documentary *Red Flag over Tibet*, director of photography and producer, 1996; Everest IMAX filming expedition, *Everest*, co-director, co-producer, and photographer, 1996; PBS, *Nova* program, "Everest: The Death Zone," co-producer and photographer, 1997; *Kilimanjaro: To the Roof of Africa*, director, producer, cinematographer, 2002. Member of advisory board, Rowell Fund for Tibet.

■ Awards, Honors

Emmy Award, 1983, for outstanding technical achievement; three other Emmy Awards for cinematography; Telluride Mountain Film Festival Grand Prize, 1994, for documentary *Red Flag over Tibet*; Best Climbing Film, Telluride Mountain Film Festival, 1997, for *Everest: The Death Zone*.

■ Writings

High Exposure: An Enduring Passion for Everest and Other Unforgiving Places (memoir), Simon & Schuster (New York, NY), 1999.

(With Audrey Salkeld) *Last Climb: The Legendary Everest Expeditions of George Mallory*, National Geographic Society (Washington, DC), 1999.

Also author of afterword and contributor of photographs to *Everest: Mountain without Mercy*, by Broughton Coburn, National Geographic Books

(Washington, DC), 1997; author of introduction to *Kilimanjaro: To the Roof of Africa*, by Audrey Salkeld, National Geographic Books (Washington, DC), 2002.

■ Work in Progress

Everest, Working Title Films/Universal, co-producer, second unit director.

■ Sidelights

David Breashears is a filmmaker and mountaineer whose 1998 IMAX film, *Everest*, became an unexpected box office and critical success. The first IMAX-format movie shot on Everest, Breashears's film grossed over forty million dollars and helped popularize not only mountaineering, but also the IMAX format. Breashears had abundant preparation for this film: in 1983 he transmitted the first live pictures from the summit, and in 1985 he became the first American to twice reach the summit of Everest. A veteran climber and mountaineer, he became a pioneer in the use of the 70mm IMAX format, as well. An Emmy Award-winning director and cinematographer, he has worked on feature films such as the 1993 *Cliffhanger,* and the 1996 *Seven Years in Tibet.* In 2002 he turned his attention to the heights of the African continent with his *Kilimanjaro: To the Roof of Africa.* Breashears has also proved himself adept as an author, penning his memoir, *High Exposure: An Enduring Passion for Everest and Other Unforgiving Places,* and coauthoring *Last Climb: The Legendary Everest Expeditions of George Mallory.*

Wandering Youth

Breashears was born in Fort Benning, Georgia, in 1956, the son of a U.S. Army officer. Born into a military family, Breashears became accustomed at an early age to moving about the world. As Breashears disclosed in *High Exposure,* his father was abusive, and he spent much of his youth in Greece, where his father was stationed. Living in Athens, he would spend large amounts of time wandering the ruins of the Acropolis. As a teenager, he and his family returned to the United States, settling in Colorado. There Breashears began enjoying mountain climbing. Tall and slim, he was built for rock climbing. As a fifteen-year-old, Breashears attended

the National Outdoor Leadership School (NOLS) in Wyoming, where he learned the basics of mountaineering and rock climbing. Breashears later noted of that experiences, as quoted on the NOLS Web site, "My instructors taught me not only how to be safe, but also about being respectful and patient." This patience would later pay large dividends in his many ascents of Everest, when he was willing to wait for bad weather to pass before making a climb.

Breashears attended college for a short time after high school graduation, but the academic life was not for him. Instead, he taught rock climbing at the University of Colorado. He largely stumbled into film, securing a job as a rope rigger for a PBS documentary about the peak Half Dome in Yosemite National Park. Though this expedition did not reach the summit, it did give Breashears an indication of how he could make a living as a climber. He began a long association with ABC sports, working in various capacities on short films about climbing. Working as a soundman on a documentary about climbing Everest, Breashears had to take over the camera work as well when the cameramen were unable to climb an icy rock face. He showed that he was not only a seasoned climber, but also talented with a camera. Thus, in the late 1970s, Breashears began his filmmaking career, and he has subsequently worked on over forty documentaries as climbing advisor, cameraman, and/or director.

Mountaineering and Filming

In 1983 Breashears earned his first Emmy for cinematography for his live broadcast of climbers reaching the summit of Everest on ABC's *Ascent of Mount Everest.* His fascination with Everest continued, not only as a mountaineer, but also as a filmmaker. He returned in 1986 as director of photography for the ABC-TV production *American Women on Everest,* in 1987, as director of photography and producer for *Everest: The Mystery of Mallory and Irvine,* in 1990, as cinematographer for the BBC-TV production, *Galahad of Everest,* and in 1991, as writer and director of photography for the PBS production *Taller than Everest.* In the 1990s, he also worked on feature films, as well as producing the award-winning 1994 documentary, *Red Flag over Tibet.*

Red Flag over Tibet is an examination of life in Tibet after fifty years of Chinese communist rule. Narrated by author Orville Schell, the film documents the many abuses the Tibetan people have suffered.

David Breashears, a mountaineer and documentary filmmaker, has earned four Emmy Awards for his technical achievements in cinematography.

Over a million people have been killed by the government since China invaded and conquered Tibet in 1949. Torture is routinely used against political dissenters. A strongly Buddhist nation, Tibet has seen some seven thousand temples and religious monasteries deliberately destroyed by the Chinese. Walter Goodman in the *New York Times* called the film "an indictment both of the Chinese for their military conquest and of the United States for taking no effective action against Beijing."

Breashears faced his biggest challenge concerning Everest with his decision to film an ascent of the 29,000-foot peak with the 70mm IMAX camera, to provide a huge image of the mountain. However, to make his film, Breashears needed to reduce the weight of the eighty-five pound camera. Carrying the camera at high altitude required a weight reduction of about fifty percent. Also, the camera, battery, and film would have to withstand temperatures of around minus forty degrees. Solutions to these problems included a Mylar-based film rather than the usual acetate-based one, thus making it more resistant to tearing and less likely to crack in the cold. Using plastic parts, the camera weight, with lens, battery, and film, was also reduced to forty-eight pounds, though the camera tripod still weighed seventy-five pounds. However, no amount of planning could alter the fact that the film would have to be changed frequently: the IMAX camera shoots five hundred feet of film in just ninety seconds. Breashears could not use gloves when changing the film, and knew he would have to withstand severe cold as a result.

Next, Breashears needed to get his climbing team organized, and this included the well-known American climber Ed Viesturs, as well as the sherpa Jamling Norgay, son of Tenzing Norgay, who, along with Sir Edmund Hillary, was one of the first climbers to reach Everest's summit, in 1953. His team set out in May 1996, and while waiting for the weather to clear so that they could make a safe ascent, Breashears and his production company and climbers became involved in an event that focused world attention on Everest. A fierce storm struck and stranded a group of climbers on the mountain. Instead of continuing filming, Breashears and his crew put away their cameras and helped as best they could in rescue efforts. Eight climbers ultimately lost their lives, and Breashears and his crew were praised for their heroic efforts trying to save the men. He made the conscious decision not to film the rescue efforts, but rather to put all available manpower into the rescue effort.

Speaking with Peter Potterfield of the *Mountain Zone,* Breashears expounded on the difficulties of filming *Everest:* "There were so many challenges with this film. . . . It's a documentary, so the story took care of itself, but in a very sad and unantici-

Breashears pioneered the use of the 70mm IMAX camera for his 1998 film *Everest,* which chronicled an ascent of the world's highest peak.

pated way. In the end, making that movie came down to so much more than technical problems, which were in themselves trying. There was even some question, after the tragic deaths near the summit, of whether we would continue." But Breashears and his team decided to go ahead with the project, documenting the ascent of Everest by Viesturs without oxygen. This in itself was an amazing feat. Writing in *Current Health 2,* Nancy Dreher quoted Breashears on the difficulty of high-altitude climbing: "Climbing about 26,000 feet, even with bottled oxygen, is like running on a treadmill and breathing through a straw."

Before release of their movie in 1998, the author and mountaineer Jon Krakauer brought home the tragic events of the deaths on Everest with his bestselling *Into Thin Air.* Thus, with the release of *Everest,* audiences were primed for a new experience. Not only climbers and fans of large-format films flocked to IMAX theaters around the country, but its audience also included regular moviegoers in search of a new and exciting experience. In the event, the movie was a huge success, climbing into the top twenty of box office charts and grossing more money than many Hollywood extravaganzas. This success brought IMAX out of the museum circuit and into the multiplexes. The film also scored high critical marks. Writing in the *Christian Science Monitor,* Jennifer Wolcott noted, "There's nothing like the IMAX experience to land you on that 29,028-foot mountain." Wolcott went on to observe that the "huge screen, cliffhanger seats, and crystal-clear images create a virtual climbing experience not to be missed." For *Variety* contributor Godfrey Cheshire, *Everest* "combines real-life tragedy and derring-do with eye-popping scenery for an effect that's as dramatic as it is fascinating and spectacular." Writing in the *Los Angeles Times,* Pamm Higgins commented that the film "also packs in a geology lesson on the formation of the Himalayas." Also reviewing the film for the *Los Angeles Times,* Kenneth Turan felt that it "not only shows us the beauty of the mountain, it also details how painfully arduous getting up and down on it is." Similar praise came from *New York Times* critic Lawrence Van Gelder, who found *Everest* "an absorbing film and a story of hope and hubris." Speaking with Potterfield, Breashears commented, "We didn't set out to make such a powerful movie. . . . What makes all of us associated with the project so pleased is that it is *not* a climber's movie—people from all walks of life, of all ages, find much to enjoy in that film."

Frigid temperatures, dangerous ice walls, and a fierce blizzard were just some of the challenges Breashears faced during the filming of *Everest*.

An Author and Director

Breashears followed up the shooting of *Everest* with a PBS special, *Everest: The Death Zone,* in which he investigates the difficulty of climbing at heights where only thin amounts of oxygen is available. This marked his fourth ascent of Everest. Thereafter, he turned to books for a time, penning his own memoir, *High Exposure,* as well as a study of the Everest mountaineer George Mallory in *Last Climb.* Breashears's *High Exposure* in part provides a written account of the events on Everest in 1996 which *Library Journal* critic Joseph L. Carlson found as "equally breathtaking" as his film. *Booklist* contributor Gilbert Taylor thought the same book was a "riveting combination of true adventure and biography." Writing in the *New York Times Book Review,* Bruce Barcott observed that with *High Exposure,* "Breashears reveals how a shy, scrawny kid can grow up to become the world's premier high-altitude filmmaker." Reviewing Breashears's col-laborative effort with Audrey Salkeld on *Last Climb, Sports Illustrated* reviewer Ron Fimrite called it the "definitive account" of three British attempts at climbing Everest in the 1920s.

If you enjoy the works of David Breashears, you may also want to check out the following books:

Peter Matthiessen, *The Snow Leopard,* 1978.
Jon Krakauer, *Into Thin Air: A Personal Account of the Mount Everest Disaster,* 1997.
Steven Callahan, *Adrift: Seventy-six Days Lost at Sea,* 2002.

For a time, Breashears did not think he would work with the bulky IMAX camera again, but with *Kilimanjaro: To the Roof of Africa,* a thirty-eight minute film, he returned to the large format to present a five-day ascent to the top of the 19,340-foot Tanzanian peak by a group of hikers who range in age from twelve to sixty-four. Speaking with Tamara Wieder of the *Boston Phoenix Online*, Breashears explained his inspiration for the second IMAX film: "As a climber, I find [Kilimanjaro] a much more interesting mountain than Everest, and I also find it much more interesting as a filmmaker. As a storyteller, I thought that hearing the stories of ordinary people experiencing the biggest climb of their lives, which doesn't *have* to be Everest, that that has a very broad appeal." For David Barton, reviewing *Kilimanjaro* in the *Sacramento Bee*, "the real drama is in the spectacular vistas caught by Breashears." Similarly, Arthur Salm, writing in the *San Diego Union-Tribune*, thought the "spectacular landscape is infinitely more varied than Everest's great sheets of ice and rock." Salm also noted that the viewers "root for very nice, very determined people to reach their reasonable goal."

Though Breashears has filmed in exotic locations around the world, he is still primarily associated with Everest. He made a fifth ascent of the mountain in 2004, as part of a film crew for a feature film about the 1996 tragedy. "Everest is this great magnet," Breashears told Tony Kahn of *NOVA Online*. "It's a symbol of achievement and accomplishment. . . . People will continue to come here with great hopes and dreams and some of them will make it and some of them will die. And that's the nature of climbing on the highest mountain in the world."

■ Biographical and Critical Sources

BOOKS

Breashears, David, *High Exposure: An Enduring Passion for Everest and Other Unforgiving Places*, Simon & Schuster (New York, NY), 1999.

PERIODICALS

Booklist, April 15, 1999, Gilbert Taylor, review of *High Exposure: An Enduring Passion for Everest and Other Unforgiving Places*, p. 1450; April 1, 2000, Stephanie Zvirin, review of *High Exposure*, p. 1448.

Christian Science Monitor, May 15, 1998, Jennifer Wolcott, review of *Everest*, p. B1.

Current Health 2, January, 1998, Nancy Dreher, "Keeping Your Heart and Lungs in Peak Condition," p. 6.

Library Journal, June 1, 1999, Joseph L. Carlson, review of *High Exposure*, p. 146.

Los Angeles Times, March 6, 1998, "A Focus on Preparation Paid Off for 'Everest,'" p. F1, Pamm Higgins, "'Everest' Takes Your Breath Away," p. F38; October 16, 1998, Kenneth Turan, review of *Everest*, p. F1.

New York Times, February 22, 1994, Walter Goodman, review of *Red Flag over Tibet*; March 26, 1999, Lawrence Van Gelder, review of *Everest*, p. E1.

New York Times Book Review, May 9, 1999, Bruce Barcott, "Social Climbers," review of *High Exposure*, p. 46; December 5, 1999, Susan Reed, "Rocky Horror," review of *Last Climb: The Legendary Everest Expeditions of George Mallory*, p. 32.

Publishers Weekly, April 26, 1999, review of *High Exposure*.

Sacramento Bee (Sacramento, CA), August 1, 2003, David Barton, review of *Kilimanjaro: To the Roof of Africa*.

San Diego Union-Telegram (San Diego, CA), May 15, 2003, Arthur Salm, review of *Kilimanjaro*.

Science Activities, winter, 2002, review of *Kilimanjaro*, p. 8.

Sports Illustrated, November 29, 1999, Ron Fimrite, review of *Last Climb*, p. R22.

Variety, March 16, 1998, Godfrey Cheshire, review of *Everest*, p. 64.

ONLINE

Boston Phoenix Online, http://www.bostonphoenix.com/ (March 14, 2002), Tamara Wieder, "Mountain Man."

CIRES, http://www.cires.colorado.edu/ (June 1, 2006), "Making Films on Mountains: Professional Biography—David Breashears."

EverestNews.com, http://www.everestnews2004.com/ (June 1, 2006), "David Breashears and Ed Viesturs Summit Everest Again!"

Internet Movie Database, http://www.imdb.com/ (June 1, 2006), "David Breashears."

Literati.net, http://www.literati.net/ (June 1, 2006), "About David Breashears."

Mountain Zone, http://www.mountainzone.com/ (June 1, 2006), Peter Potterfield, "IMAX *Everest* Film Shatters All Records."

NOLS Web site, http://www.nols.edu/ (June 1, 2006), "Our Grads: David Breashears."

NOVA Online, http://www.pbs.org/ (May 13, 1997), "Interview with David Breashears and Tony Kahn."*

Augusten Burroughs

■ Personal

Original name, Christopher Robison; name legally changed, c. 1983; born 1965, in Pittsburgh, PA; son of John (a professor) and Margaret Robison; partner of Dennis Pilsits (a graphic designer).

■ Addresses

Agent—Christopher Schelling, Ralph M. Vicinanza Ltd., 303 W. 18th St., New York, NY 10011; fax: 212-691-9644.

■ Career

Writer. Radio commentator, National Public Radio, 2003—. Previously worked as a copywriter, dog trainer, store clerk, waiter, and store detective.

■ Awards, Honors

Nominated for a Quill Award for *Magical Thinking*, 2005.

■ Writings

Sellevision, St. Martin's Griffin (New York, NY), 2000.
Running with Scissors: A Memoir, St. Martin's Press (New York, NY), 2002.
Dry: A Memoir, St. Martin's Press (New York, NY), 2003.
Magical Thinking: True Stories, St. Martin's Press (New York, NY), 2004.
Possible Side Effects, St. Martin's Press (New York, NY), 2006.

Contributor to periodicals, including *Details.*

■ Adaptations

Running with Scissors was adapted for audio, read by the author, Audio Renaissance, 2003; *Sellevision* and *Running with Scissors* are being adapted for film.

■ Work in Progress

Better Not Cry, a collection of holiday stories; a television series for Showtime; another memoir.

■ Sidelights

Augusten Burroughs has written several over-the-top memoirs that raise questions about their truthfulness. But the wild plots—involving child abuse, drug addiction, and mental illness—and the often laugh-out-loud approach he takes to such grim subjects have earned Burroughs a loyal audience. According to Cathie Beck in the *Rocky Mountain News:* "Burroughs has made a name for himself by writing brilliant, self-deprecating stories about everything from addiction to coy school teachers to pedophiliac psychiatrists." The approach has served him well. Burroughs's book *Running with Scissors: A Memoir* has sold over one million copies.

Burroughs was born Christopher Robison in 1965 in Pittsburgh, Pennsylvania, and raised in western Massachusetts. At the age of eighteen, he fashioned the name Augusten Burroughs for himself and has legally used that name ever since. Burroughs went through a series of jobs, culminating finally as an "alcoholic advertising executive," as Erika Gonzalez explained in the *Rocky Mountain News.* After suffering from alcohol poisoning, which brought on several days of horrifying hallucinations, Burroughs found the strength to walk to a nearby store and buy more alcohol. "I thought, well, if I keep drinking, I'm going to die. I'm going to have a heart attack and I was OK with that because I felt like I had lost everything," he told Gonzalez. But the thought that he had never tried serious writing, something he had always wanted to do, nagged at him. A few days after cleaning himself up, he sat down to write, producing a novel inside of a week.

Burroughs's first book is the campy novel *Sellevision,* set in the world of home-shopping networks. In the story, on-air personality Max exposes himself while promoting toys, is fired, and finds a new career in adult pornography. The prim and proper Peggy Jean Smythe, who pushes Princess Di memorabilia, takes fan criticism to heart and finds refuge in drugs and drinking, oblivious to the fact that her husband is seducing the girl next door. When Peggy goes into rehab, two replacements, one of whom is the executive producer's mistress, are stalked via e-mail. A *Publishers Weekly* reviewer wrote that "this kaleidoscope of gleefully salacious intrigue aims to titillate and amuse in a purposefully over-the-top way." *Booklist* reviewer James Klise concluded that "the material sparkles, just like the Diamonelle earrings on the shopping channels."

Based on his childhood diaries, Burroughs claims, *Running with Scissors: A Memoir* was twenty years in the writing and a lifetime in the making. Although Burroughs has changed the names of his characters, he avows that this is his life story, beginning when he was an adolescent in the 1970s. *Entertainment Weekly* contributor Karen Valby wrote that Burroughs "wins the year's Best Scene Opener award with this dandy: 'We were young. We were bored. And the old electroshock therapy machine was just under the stairs in a box next to the Hoover.'"

Burroughs describes his father as an emotionally distant and alcoholic professor and his mother as a manic depressive confessional poet. After they split, his mother went to therapy with Rodolph Harvey Turcotte (Dr. Finch in the book). Finch's household includes his hunchback wife, Agnes, their six children, and an assortment of live-in patients, all of whom share a filthy pink Victorian mansion in Northampton, Massachusetts. Finch's unorthodox practice includes reading the future in his patients' feces. Burroughs's mother never improves under Finch, and after coming out as a lesbian and moving in with her teenaged lover, she signs her son over to the psychiatrist, who accepts guardianship. Burroughs, like the Finch children, receives no adult guidance. He befriends Hope and Natalie Finch, with whom he shares substance abuse and delinquency. A *Kirkus Reviews* contributor noted that Burroughs "strongly delineates the tangled, perverse bonds among these high-watt eccentrics and his childhood self, aspiring to a grotesque comic merger of John Waters and David Sedaris."

With the help of Finch, Burroughs fakes a suicide attempt to get out of school. Neil Bookman, a man in his thirties and the "adopted son" of Finch, molests Burroughs with Finch's approval. Thomas Haley wrote in the *Minneapolis Star Tribune* that "this association overshadows most other events in Burroughs's book, not only because it is potentially the most harmful, but because it so clearly exemplifies Augusten's perpetual victimization by those older and supposedly more mature than him." Haley concluded by saying that Burroughs's memoir "is too brutal and disturbing, despite the frequent laughs, to be read as an inspirational or life-affirming memoir. But *Running with Scissors* is nonetheless a stirring and stunning testament to a boy's strength in an environment of unfathomable heartache and dysfunction."

Scott Tobias wrote for the *Onion A.V. Club* online that "the sole comfort of reading this profoundly disturbing memoir, outside of Burroughs's brave comic perspective, lies in knowing that he lived to write it." Burroughs did survive, however. He distanced himself from his mother, came out as being gay, left Finch at seventeen, earned his GED, and became a copywriter. His abuse of alcohol and drugs led him into rehab at age thirty. His only connection to his own family was his older brother, John, who had not been subject to the life Burroughs experienced in the Finch household.

Virginia Heffernan, who reviewed the memoir in the *New York Times Book Review,* wrote that it "promotes visceral responses (of laughter, wincing, retching) on nearly every page" and "contains the

Joseph Cross (left), who portrays Burroughs in the 2006 film adaptation of *Running with Scissors,* meets with the author on the movie set.

kind of scenes that are often called harrowing but which are also plainly funny and rich with child's-eye details of adults who have gone off the rails." Galina Espinoza noted in a *People* review that many of the characters in Burroughs's life acknowledge the truth of parts of the memoir but deny others. His father declined to comment. His parents were both in their late sixties when the book was published, and his mother was confined to a wheelchair after a stroke in 1989. Turcotte lost his medical license in 1986 and died in 2000.

Lambda Book Report contributor Seth J. Bookey wrote that *Running with Scissors* "does a beautiful job of reflecting on the bizarre without fetishizing or sentimentalizing it, or being victimized by it. Distance, via time, allows Burroughs to laugh at it all, but underneath all the kitsch (and filth), this memoir perfectly captures how an adult generation abdicated all authority. The only thing more fascinating than Augusten's neglect going unnoticed by anyone who could have helped is that he had the self-determination not to get stuck in the quicksand of his elders."

The sequel to *Running with Scissors, Dry: A Memoir,* was published in 2003. Also written in memoir format, *Dry* focuses on Burroughs's descent into and struggles with alcoholism. This section of the memoir begins with the protagonist as a nineteen-year-old with only an elementary school education and a long legacy of troubles stemming from his insane mother, his alcoholic father, and the psychiatrist who raised him. He finds his only escape in drink and fills twenty-seven garbage bags with empty liquor bottles. His employer, concerned for his health, has him sent away for a month of rehab; naturally, more wild adventures and fantasies ensue. "With irreverent and humorous touches, Burroughs manages to personalize the difficulties of recovery without ever lapsing into sentimentality," said Nancy R. Ives in the *Library Journal. Dry* is considered by many reviewers to be a deeper story than Burroughs's previous memoir, providing readers with more insight into his personality. The main character is "less the walking quirk this time and more just a brave, funny, unhappy human being," wrote Lev Grossman in *Time.* Other reviewers preferred Burrough's more bombastic prior work and see too many indications of authorial self-indulgence in *Dry*. Steve Wilson, reviewing the memoir in *Book*, noted that while the story analyzes Burroughs's recovery from alcohol addiction, "his new addiction is memoir writing, and that he may well have overdosed on it after only two books."

Following *Dry*, Burroughs released *Magical Thinking: True Stories*, a collection of colorful, sometimes shocking, stories full of delicious details and self-deprecating humor. The term "magical thinking" describes Burroughs' belief that people can influence the world around them simply with their thoughts. Among the many stories included in this collection are "My Last First Date," in which Burroughs discusses the first time he met his current boyfriend, and "Telemarketing Revenge," which Allison Block of *Booklist* described as "a raunchy solution for relentless nocturnal callers." Other stories describe Burroughs' anguish over killing a mouse in his bathtub, his legal run-in with a cleaning lady, his wish for his boss's horrific demise, and numerous other tales from his strange and interesting life.

Like his previous books, *Magical Thinking* "showcases Burroughs's sharp, funny and sometimes brilliant writing," wrote a critic for *Publishers Weekly*. The critic compared Burroughs to essayists David Sedaris and David Rakoff, but noted that he is very much an individual. "Burroughs ambles toward insight in a continual state of self-examination and just happens to have peculiar adventures along the way," the reviewer noted. In her review for *Booklist*, Block expressed the opinion that *Magical Thinking* "offers an irresistible display of sanity hanging by a thread." Likewise, a critic for *Kirkus Reviews* commented: "Dementedly original and unstoppable: Burroughs deserves a shelf all to himself, just as an unpredictable convict might require protective custody."

In the 2006 collection Possible Side Effects, R.J. Stevenson related in the *Winnipeg Free Press*, "Burroughs relates his travails and observations through different points in his life. By turns wry and neurotic, these collected essays aim to amuse and enlighten. Topics such as blind dates, lesbian personal ads, eBay etiquette, pet ownership, Nicorette addiction, voyeurism and dry skin compete for space with his requisite errant relatives." The *Publishers Weekly* reviewer found that "Burroughs has superb comic sensibility, throwing off sparkling riffs on everyday humiliations in a voice that's alternately caustic and warm, bitchy and self-deprecating." According to the *Kirkus Reviews* critic, Burroughs "again turns his whirligig neuroses into something resembling a book." Sue McClellan, writing in the *Library Journal*, found that "the ostensibly real-life stories suggest an eccentric childhood indeed and are sure to enthrall readers."

If you enjoy the works of Augusten Burroughs, you may also want to check out the following books:

Frank McCourt, *Angela's Ashes*, 1996.
David Sedaris, *Me Talk Pretty One Day*, 2000.
Jeanette Walls, *The Glass Castle*, 2005.

When asked by Heather V. Eng in the *Boston Herald* how people react when they find that he has made them characters in his books, Burroughs replied: "Dennis [his partner] laughs and rolls his eyes when I write about him. For my brother, I think it changed his life. He always felt defective because of our parents and our childhood. *Running with Scissors* liberated him. He related to the book and it was embraced by his friends. But the thing is, my focus is not to write about other people. I write about myself. When other people are in my work, they're seen through my eyes, in relation to me."

Burroughs lives in western Massachusetts with his partner, Dennis Pilsits. The couple recently built a house near where Burroughs's brother lives. "I battened down the hatches of my personal life very, very much," Burroughs admitted to Gonzalez. "I live a very small life next to my brother and I have exactly the same friends that I've had for many, many years—many of whom have never read any of my books."

■ Biographical and Critical Sources

BOOKS

Burroughs, Augusten, *Running with Scissors: A Memoir*, St. Martin's Press (New York, NY), 2002.
Burroughs, *Dry: A Memoir*, St. Martin's Press (New York, NY), 2003.

PERIODICALS

Advocate, September 14, 2004, "Through a Joke, Darkly," review of *Magical Thinking: True Stories*, p. 80.
Book, July-August, 2003, Steve Wilson, review of *Dry*, p. 77.

Booklist, August, 2000, James Klise, review of *Sellevision*, p. 2109; July, 2004, Allison Block, review of *Magical Thinking*, p. 1795; April 1, 2006, Brad Hooper, review of *Possible Side Effects*, p. 4.

Boston Herald, April 30, 2006, Heather V. Eng, review of *Possible Side Effects*, p. 30.

Entertainment Weekly, June 28, 2002, Karen Valby, review of *Running with Scissors: A Memoir*, p. 136; December 26, 2003, review of *Dry*, p. 83; May 12, 2006, Nicholas Fonseca, review of *Possible Side Effects*, p. 85.

Globe & Mail (Toronto, Canada), May 6, 2006, Marnie Woodow, review of *Possible Side Effects*, p. D13.

Kirkus Reviews, July 15, 2000, review of *Sellevision*, pp. 977-978; May 15, 2002, review of *Running with Scissors*, p. 714; April 15, 2003, review of *Dry*, p. 581; July 1, 2004, review of *Magical Thinking*, p. 612; March 1, 2006, review of *Possible Side Effects*, p. 217.

Lambda Book Report, September, 2002, Seth J. Bookey, review of *Running with Scissors*, p. 14; November-December, 2004, Owen Keehnen, "True Confessions," p. 43.

Library Journal, June 1, 2002, Nancy R. Ives, review of *Running with Scissors*, p. 162; July, 2003, Nancy R. Ives, review of *Dry*, p. 95; April 15, 2006, Sue McClellan, review of *Possible Side Effects*, p. 75.

Los Angeles Times Book Review, July 22, 2002, Merle Rubin, review of *Running with Scissors*, p. E3.

New York Times, June 20, 2002, Janet Maslin, review of *Running with Scissors*, p. B9.

New York Times Book Review, July 14, 2002, Virginia Heffernan, review of *Running with Scissors*, p. 7; October 10, 2004, John Leland, "Running to Home Depot," p. 12.

People, September 23, 2002, Galina Espinoza, review of *Running with Scissors*, p. 229.

Publishers Weekly, July 31, 2000, review of *Sellevision*, p. 69; June 3, 2002, review of *Running with Scissors*, p. 77; April 21, 2003, review of *Dry*, p. 48; July 12, 2004, review of *Magical Thinking*, p. 50; May 23, 2005, Jason Anthony, "Authors Craving Some of That Hollywood Movie Money before Actually Doing What They're Paid to Do—Write Books—Have Two Choices," p. 10; February 20, 2006, review of *Possible Side Effects*, p. 143.

Rocky Mountain News (Denver, CO), November 5, 2004, Erika Gonzalez, "Just like Magic: Burroughs Spins Best-selling Stories from Threads of His Strange, Tortured Life"; May 12, 2006, Cathie Beck, review of *Possible Side Effects*, p. 29D.

Seattle Post-Intelligencer (Seattle, WA), May 23, 2006, John Marshall, review of *Possible Side Effects*, p. E1.

Star Tribune (Minneapolis, MN), August 11, 2002, Thomas Haley, review of *Running with Scissors*.

Time, May 26, 2003, Lev Grossman, "Drinking out Loud," p. 77.

USA Today, May 11, 2006, David Daley, review of *Possible Side Effects*, p. 6D.

Winnipeg Free Press, June 4, 2006, R.J. Stevenson, review of *Possible Side Effects*, p. B8.

Writer, May, 2005, "Augusten Burroughs," p. 66.

ONLINE

Augusten Burroughs Home Page, http://www.augusten.com (July 10, 2006).

BookSense.com, http://www.booksense.com/ (December 3, 2002), interview with Burroughs.

Curled up with a Good Book, http://www.curledup.com/ (December 3, 2002), review of *Running with Scissors*.

Entertainment Weekly Online, http://www.ew.com/ (July 10, 2006), Karen Valby, "Burroughs Deep."

Onion A.V. Club, http://www.theonionavclub.com/ (August 21, 2002), Scott Tobias, review of *Running with Scissors*.*

John Carpenter

■ Personal

Born January 16, 1948, in Carthage, NY; son of Howard Ralph (a music professor) and Milton Jean (Carter) Carpenter; married Adrienne Barbeau (an actress), January 1, 1979 (divorced, 1988); married Sandy King (a producer), December 1, 1990; children: (first marriage) John Cody. *Education:* Western Kentucky University, B.A., 1968; attended University of Southern California Film School, 1968-72. *Hobbies and other interests:* Helicopter piloting, music, Elvis, old Cadillacs, National Basketball Association.

■ Addresses

Office—Big Deal Productions, Inc., 5632 Van Nuys Blvd., Van Nuys, CA 91411. *Agent*—William Morris Agency, One William Morris Pl., Beverly Hills, CA 90212.

■ Career

Writer, composer, director, actor, producer. Director of such motion pictures as *The Thing*, 1982; *Christine*, 1983; *Starman*, 1984; *Big Trouble in Little China*, 1986;

Memoirs of an Invisible Man, 1992; and *John Carpenter's Vampires*, 1998. Also director (as Johnny Carpenter) of short films *Revenge of the Colossal Beasts, Gorgo Versus Godzilla, Terror from Space, Sorcerer from Outer Space, The Warrior and the Demon,* and *Gorgon, the Space Monster.* Director of such television productions as *Elvis.* Producer of such films as *The Philadelphia Experiment, Dark Star,* and, with Debra Hill, *Halloween II* and *Halloween III: Season of the Witch.* Editor (under pseudonym John T. Chance) of the film *Assault on Precinct 13.* Composer of scores for such films as *Halloween, The Fog, Escape from New York, Christine, Big Trouble in Little China, Prince of Darkness* (under pseudonym Martin Quatermass), and *They Live.* Performer in rock group Coup de Ville.

Film appearances include *No Place to Land*, 1958; (uncredited) *The Thing* (also known as *John Carpenter's The Thing*), 1982; (uncredited; man in helicopter) *Starman* (also known as *John Carpenter's Starman*), 1984; (with the Coupe de Villes) *The Boy Who Could Fly*, 1986; (as Rip Haight; helicopter pilot) *Memoirs of an Invisible Man*, 1992; Trench Coat Man, *The Silence of the Hams* (also known as *Il Silenzio dei Prosciutti*), 1994; (uncredited; man in phone booth) *Village of the Damned*, 1995; and *Scoring Resident Evil*, 2002.

Television appearances include *Fear in the Dark,* 1991; *Masters of Illusion: The Wizards of Special Effect,* 1994; *Firstworks,* 1988; *The Reality Trip,* 1996; *Masters of Fantasy: John Carpenter,* Sci-Fi Channel, 1998; *The Directors,* 1999; *Guns for Hire: 'The Making of the Magnificent Seven,'* 2000; *The American Nightmare,*

2000; *Mario Bava: Maestro of the Macabre*, 2000; *Dario Argento: An Eye for Horror*, 2000; *AFI's 100 Years, 100 Thrills: America's Most Heart-Pounding Movies*, 2001; and *Hidden Values: The Movies of the Fifties*, 2001.

Video/DVD appearances include *100 Years of Horror: Witchcraft and Demons*, 1996; *100 Years of Horror: Sorcerers*, 1996; *100 Years of Horror: Maniacs*, 1996; *After Sunset: The Life and Times of the Drive-In*, AMC, 1998; *Unmasking the Horror*, 1998; *Halloween Unmasked*, 2000; *Scoring Ghosts of Mars*, 2001; *Red Desert Nights: Making 'Ghosts of Mars,'* 2001; *Tales from the Mist: Inside 'The Fog,'* 2002; and *Scoring Resident Evil*, 2002.

Credited as part of miscellaneous film crew in *The Quiet Room* (also known as *La Stanza di Cloe*), 1996, and *Scoring Resident Evil*, 2002.

Horror Hall of Fame, member of board of directors; Emerald Productions, founder; Hye Whitebread Productions, cofounder, 1979.

■ Member

Directors Guild, Writers Guild of America—West, American Society of Composers, Authors, and Publishers.

■ Awards, Honors

Academy Award, best short subject (live action), 1970, *The Resurrection of Bronco Billy*; Golden Scroll Award (with others), best special effects, 1976, for *Dark Star*; London Film Festival special award, 1977; Edgar Allan Poe Award, best made-for-television mystery movie, Mystery Writers of America, 1978, for *Someone's Watching Me!*; New Generation Award, Los Angeles Film Critics Association Awards, 1979; Critics' Prize, Avoriaz Film Festival, 1980, for *The Fog*; American Institute for Public Service Jefferson Award, outstanding public service benefiting local communities, 1980; Grand Prize Award nomination, Avoriaz Fantastic Film Festival, 1984, for *Christine*; International Fantasy Film Award nomination, best film, 1989, for *They Live*; CableACE Award (with Bill Phillips), writing a movie or miniseries, 1991, for *El Diablo*; International Fantasy Film Award nomination, best film, 1993, for *Memoirs of an Invisible Man*; International Fantasy Film Award nomination, best film, 1994, for *Body Bags*; Critics Award, Fantasporto, and International Fantasy Film Award nomination,

best film, 1995, both for *In the Mouth of Madness*; George Pal Memorial Award, Academy of Science Fiction, Fantasy and Horror Films, 1996; Saturn Award, best music, and Bram Stoker Award nomination, other media, 1999, both for *John Carpenter's Vampires*; Best Film Award nomination, Catalonian International Film Festival, 2001, for *Ghosts of Mars*.

■ Writings

SCREENPLAYS

(with Jim Rokos; and editor and composer) *The Resurrection of Bronco Billy*, 1970.

(With Dan O'Bannon; and director and composer) *Dark Star*, Jack H. Harris, 1974.

(And director, actor, and composer) *Assault on Precinct 13*, Irwin Yablans, 1976.

(With Debra Hill; and director, actor, and composer) *Halloween*, Compass, 1978.

(With David Zelag Goodman) *The Eyes of Laura Mars*, Columbia, 1978.

(With Debra Hill; actor, composer, and director) *The Fog*, Avco-Embassy, 1980.

(With Nick Castle; and director and composer) *Escape from New York*, Avco-Embassy, 1981.

(With Debra Hill; and composer) *Halloween II* (also known as *Halloween II: The Nightmare Isn't Over!*), Universal, 1981.

(With Desmond Nakano and William Gray) *Black Moon Rising* (also a story), New World, 1986.

(Under pseudonym Martin Quatermass; and director) *Prince of Darkness*, Universal, 1987.

(Under pseudonym Frank Armitage; and director) *They Live* (adapted from Ray Nelson's short story "Eight O'Clock in the Morning"), Universal, 1988.

(With Alan Howarth; and composer) *Halloween 5: The Revenge of Michael Myers*, Galaxy International, 1989.

(With Jim Lang; and director and composer) *In the Mouth of Madness*, New Line Cinema, 1995.

(With Dave Davies; also director, actor, and composer) *Village of the Damned*, Universal, 1995.

(With others; and composer) *Halloween: The Curse of Michael Myers* (also known as *Halloween 666: Curse of Michael Myers* and *Halloween: The Origin of Michael Myers*), Dimension Films, 1995.

(With Shirley Walker; and director and composer) *John Carpenter's Escape from L.A.*, Paramount, 1996.

(With others; and composer) *Halloween H20: 20 Years Later* (also known as *Halloween: H20* and *Halloween: H20 (20 Years Later)*), Dimension Films, 1998.

Meltdown, 1999.

(And director and composer) *Ghosts of Mars*, Screen Gems, 2001.

(With Debra Hill; and composer) *Halloween: Resurrection 2002*, Dimension Films, 2002.

TELEPLAYS

Zuma Beach, NBC-TV, 1978.

(And director) *Someone's Watching Me!* (also shown as *High Rise*), NBC-TV, 1978.

(With Greg Strangis) *Better Late Than Never*, NBC-TV, 1979.

El Diablo, 1990.

Blood River, 1991.

(With Jim Lang; also executive producer, segment director, and composer) *Body Bags*, Showtime, 1993.

Silent Predators, 1999.

Cigarette Burns (episode of *Masters of Horror*), Showtime, 2005.

■ **Adaptations**

The Fog and *Assault on Precinct 13* were both adapted for feature films, 2005, based on Carpenter's earlier screenplays and productions; various "Halloween" films have been based on Carpenter's characters.

■ **Work in Progress**

Psychopath, feature film, as writer and director; *Halloween: Retribution*, as composer.

■ **Sidelights**

John Carpenter is, according to Eric Beetner writing for *Latent Image*, "the modern master of terror and suspense." Others have dubbed the director, screenwriter, producer, composer, and sometimes actor the "master of the horror film," as Marco Lanzagorta noted on the *Senses of Cinema* Web site. The same critic went on to observe that "this is a reasonable title, bearing in mind that [Carpenter] has proved to be not only a director with a visually and thematically consistent body of work, but also a true visionary of the horror genre." The writer and director of the 1978 classic, *Halloween*, Carpenter

single-handedly gave rise to the slasher movies of the 1970s and 1980s, and also created one of the most profitable independent movies in film history. Carpenter has mined the horror genre in numerous other films, including *The Thing, The Fog, Christine, In the Mouth of Madness, John Carpenter's Vampires,* and *Village of the Damned,* but has also done action movies, including *Assault on Precinct 13* and *Escape from New York,* science fiction with *Dark Star, Starman,* and *Ghosts of Mars,* humor with *Memoirs of an Invisible Man,* and kung fu camp with *Big Trouble in Little China.* "Regardless of their subject matter," wrote Lanzagorta, "the films directed by John Carpenter are characterized by his mastery of the cinematographical craft, and by the showcasing of engaging narratives that convey a profound commentary on the many social, racial, gender and sexual anxieties of our modern world."

Not all critics find the Carpenter oeuvre to be consistent, however. For the contributor to *International Dictionary of Films and Filmmakers,* Carpenter "currently stands as an out-of-time B specialist . . . [whose] later directorial output has not exactly failed to live up to the promise of his earliest films, but nor has it been able to match their perfect achievements." For this reviewer, the films and television movies made after about 1980 are inferior to his earlier products, such as *Halloween*: "Although there are pleasures to be found in most of his subsequent works, Carpenter has never quite recaptured the confidence and streamlined form of the early pictures." Yet Carpenter has a large fan base, and several of his films have become cult classics, despite mainstream critical disapprobation.

The Making of a Filmmaker

Born in Carthage, New York, in 1948, Carpenter was raised in Bowling Green, Kentucky, where his father taught music history and theory at Western Kentucky University. An only child, Carpenter grew up in the seclusion of a log cabin situated on the immense grounds of the university museum. His father, a violinist, was a large influence on the future auteur director, for Carpenter learned to play violin, piano, and guitar as a youngster, and would later go on to compose original synthesized music for most of his films. "I heard classical music constantly," Carpenter recalled for James Stevenson in a *New Yorker* profile. "Wall-to-wall string quartets." Carpenter also grew up with books; there was no family television until he was twelve. Carpenter began composing and writing stories at an early age, but quickly he became a fan of movies. His first movie experience was *The African Queen.* Even more exciting for him was the 1953 film *It Came*

The occupants of a remote police station come under attack from a vicious street gang in Carpenter's action film *Assault on Precinct 13.*

from Outer Space, for which the audience wore special glasses to see in 3-D. Carpenter told Stevenson: "The first shot was of this meteor—it came right off the screen and exploded in my face. I couldn't believe it! It was everything I'd ever wanted! After that, I was addicted to films. I made movies in my head. The cabin and the museum grounds became my movie set, my back lot. I made up little stories."

At eight, Carpenter received an 8mm camera. Using the stop motion, he created special effects for a science fiction movie he and his school friends created. However, by high school Carpenter had discovered girls, as he told Stevenson, and left movies behind for a time. Yet the early influence of the filmmakers he enjoyed as a child—Howard Hawks and John Ford—has held throughout his professional career. After attending his undergraduate years at Western Kentucky University, Carpenter once again became interested in film, and went to the film school of the University of Southern California. There he first worked on the short live-action film *The Resurrection*

of *Bronco Billy,* which he cowrote, composed the music for, and edited. This first production won an Academy Award. Still a student filmmaker, Carpenter was on his way.

Early Successes

A further student film, *Dark Star,* was a black satire on spacemen and science fiction films. The primary plot involves the crew of an interstellar space ship on a mission to destroy stars about to become supernovas. The critic for *International Dictionary of Films and Filmmakers* called this work "one of the miracles of the 1970s, an intelligent and approachable science-fiction film . . . with a satiric bite carried over from the *written* sf of the 1950s." Carpenter served as writer, director, producer, and score composer on this film that, upon release, was not successful, but which later became a cult classic among Carpenter fans.

On the strength of these early films, Carpenter found funding for an action film he had written,

Assault on Precinct 13, "a lean, generic, action machine," according to the contributor for *International Dictionary of Films and Filmmakers,* about a street gang that besieges a remote police station. This film demonstrates not only Carpenter's debt to Hawks in its theme of heroes who must confront impossible odds, but it also "clearly showcases Carpenter's distinctive visual and thematic style," according to Lanzagorta. His use of the wide screen format of Panavision also began in this film.

Carpenter next turned to the horror genre for his 1978 film, *Halloween,* set in a small Illinois town on the night of Halloween. A small boy, Michael, inexplicably murders his sister and is sent to an institution for the mentally insane. Exactly fifteen years later he escapes and returns to his hometown, where he terrorizes three teenage girls played by Jamie Lee Curtis, P.J. Soles, and Nancy Loomis. Donald Pleasance plays the psychiatrist who has treated Michael for fifteen years without results. With total costs of approximately 300,000 dollars, *Halloween* grossed over 80 million dollars, making it proportionally the most profitable film ever. Lanza-

gorta called this the "most successful of [Carpenter's] career, and one of the most influential and enduring movies of the horror genre." This movie spawned a host of sequels, most of which Carpenter had no involvement with, other than the use of his characters and some of the theme music he composed for the original film. The critic for *International Dictionary of Films and Filmmakers* felt this "slender but masterly confection . . . should not be blamed for the floodgates it opened when it became an unexpected box office bonanza."

This success brought more production money to Carpenter, allowing him to produce with larger budgets. In 1980 he wrote and directed *The Fog,* a maritime ghost story, and the following year developed one of his dream projects, *Escape from New York.* The latter is a futuristic science fiction action film set in a Manhattan that has been turned into a immense penal colony. When a helicopter carrying the president of the United States goes down in this huge prison, a Vietnam veteran, Snake Plissken is tasked with the job of saving the American leader. Writing in the *New York Times,* Vincent Canby called *Escape from New York* "a toughly told, very tall tale," and Carpenter's "most ambitious, most riveting film to date."

In the futuristic thriller *Escape from New York,* a war hero turned criminal must rescue the president of the United States after Air Force One crashes in Manhattan, which serves as a maximum security prison.

From Independent Production to Hollywood

Carpenter's next four feature films were not written by him; they were the product of the Hollywood system. He adapted the Howard Hawks film *The Thing from another World* for his own 1982 movie, *The Thing,* also relying on the original 1951 short story by Christian Nyby for inspiration. Set in Antarctica, the film tells of a creature from outer space, frozen in the polar ice for millennia, that is unwittingly set free by scientists. The result was a "controversially downbeat but genuinely effective movie," according to the critic for *International Dictionary of Films and Filmmakers.* Other critics disagreed, however. Canby, writing in the *New York Times,* for example, found *The Thing* a "foolish, depressing, overproduced movie that mixes horror with science fiction to make something that is neither one thing or the other." Audiences agreed; *The Thing* was a box office failure for Carpenter.

The director found more success in two other studio films, *Christine,* adapted from a Stephen King novel, and *Starman,* about an alien who assumes a dead man's body and becomes involved with the widow of this dead man. An unlikely love story, it brought

An alien wreaks havoc on an Antarctic outpost in *The Thing,* Carpenter's remake of Howard Hawks's classic 1951 film *The Thing from Another World.*

Carpenter recognition (as had the 1979 television production *Elvis*) as a director adept in human drama. With *Big Trouble in Little China,* Carpenter filmed a tribute to Hong Kong kung fu movies, featuring Kurt Russell, who has starred in numerous Carpenter productions. The *International Dictionary of Films and Filmmakers* contributor called this a "wacky kung fu-monster-comedy-musical-action-adventure-horror-fantasy . . . [that] never quite catches the magic of the Hong Kong films upon which it is obviously based." Similarly, Michael Wilmington, writing in the *Los Angeles Times,* found the same film an attempt at "mock-Oriental movie magic that goes leaden about a third of the way through—and finally detonates into great, whomping firebombs of overcalculated, underinspired absurdity." Other critics, however, had a more positive assessment of *Big Trouble in Little China. New York Times* critic Walter Goodman called it an "upscale send-up," while Lanzagorta felt it was one of Carpenter's "finest films to date."

Returns to Lower-Budget Filmmaking

Growing dissatisfied with the interference in the creative process he experienced in Hollywood, Carpenter returned to low-budget production in the late 1980s. His 1987 film, *Prince of Darkness,* presents a battle between a Catholic priest, a nuclear physicist, and Satan. Canby, writing in the *New York Times,* found this a "surprisingly cheesy horror film." Wilmington, writing in the *Los Angeles Times,* was also unimpressed, complaining that "much of the movie remains an accretion of carnage and glop." However, Lanzagorta was more upbeat in his assessment: "Technically, this film is close to flawless, and the escalating intensity of the last 15 minutes is an example of superlative pace and rhythm."

Poverty and the costs of capitalism are examined in one of Carpenter's personal favorites, the 1988 *They Live,* something of an updated *Invasion of the Body Snatchers,* in which Earth is invaded by aliens who want to exploit the planet and its inhabitants economically. This film earned more positive critical remarks. Wilmington, writing in the *Los Angeles Times,* felt "you can forgive the movie everything because of the sheer nasty pizzazz of its central concept." Lanzagorta commended Carpenter's dissection of social problems in this movie, calling it "the most imaginative, provocative and incisive criticisms of these subjects found in cinema history."

Carpenter took a four-year break from feature film work, returning in 1992 to direct the comedic *Memoirs of an Invisible Man,* which he followed up with *In the Mouth of Madness,* an homage to the horror writer H.P. Lovecraft. The critic for *International Dictionary of Films and Filmmakers* noted that many of Carpenter's fans feel this latter movie is "the most terrifying film he'd made since the halcyon days of *Halloween* and *The Thing.*" Kevin Thomas, writing in the *Los Angeles Times,* felt Carpenter was in "top form" with this film. Similar praise came for his next production, the remake of *Village of the Damned,* which *New York Times* critic Janet Maslin thought was Carpenter's "best horror film in a long while" and "one scarifying trip down memory lane." Likewise, Thomas, writing in the *Los Angeles Times,* called it a "sleek and scary remake."

Mixed reviews met Carpenter's 1996 sequel to *Escape from New York.* Stephen Holden, writing in the *New York Times,* found *John Carpenter's Escape from L.A.* a "hopelessly choppy adventure spoof that doesn't even try to match the ghoulish surrealism of its forerunner." Holden felt that this sequel "wants mostly to play it for laughs while serving up a series of silly comic book stunts." Thomas, writing in the *Los Angeles Times,* however, thought Carpenter was "at the top of his game" with this film that "brilliantly imagines a Dante-esque vision of the City of Angels 17 years from now as a hell on Earth." Thomas also commended Carpenter's mix of "humor and high adventure."

Carpenter turned to the lore of vampires in his 1998 feature, *John Carpenter's Vampires,* using as a premise a Vatican Special Forces team led by actor James Woods that is attempting to track down and destroy the King of Vampires and his helpers. Most critics felt that Carpenter was off mark with this production. The contributor for *International Dictionary of Films and Filmmakers* complained that the film "surrendered itself completely to the gore and sleaze that had become endemic to the horror genre by this point." Writing in the *Washington Post,* Michael O'Sullivan noted: "Carpenter is at his best when his is trying to frighten the pants off you, but

John Carpenter on the set of *In the Mouth of Madness.*

the toothless narrative is so dead that there's no need to take a wooden stake to this sucker." Similarly, Lawrence van Gelder, writing in the *New York Times,* called the same film "simple-minded nonsense" and "ridiculous without being awful enough to be hilarious."

If you enjoy the works of John Carpenter, you may also want to check out the following films:

Dawn of the Dead, directed by George A. Romero, 1978.
Alien, directed by Ridley Scott, 1979.
Army of Darkness, directed by Sam Raimi, 1992.

With his 2001 science fiction and horror film, *Ghosts of Mars*, Carpenter blended many of the effects from his earlier films to create a futuristic fantasy with Western overtones. Greg Braxton, writing in the *Los Angeles Times*, felt the movie "could carry the subtitle: 'John Carpenter's Greatest Hits.'" For Rita Kempley, writing in the *Washington Post*, the film was "fun but idiotic." Other reviewers had a less positive assessment. Thomas, in the *Los Angeles Times*, thought *Ghosts of Mars* "is arguably the horror/sci-fi director's most routine movie." Reviewing the same film in the *New York Times*, Elvis Mitchell noted that Carpenter "has to be the last hippie still making movies." Mitchell went on to observe: "He has dug his heels and continues to pack his films with anticonformity messages; there can't be another director who has worked the theme of losing one's individuality more consistently. That theme is also the basis of 'John Carpenter's Ghosts of Mars.' Unfortunately, though its heart and mind are in the right place, it's like a zombie picture directed by one of the undead." For Gabe Klinger, writing in *Senses of Cinema*, the same film was an "interesting failure."

Though some claim that Carpenter's career is in its decline, the director, as well as other critics, would disagree. As Klinger noted: "To say John Carpenter is in his twilight years is somewhat cynical. One might say he is in the process of finding a new niche." Speaking with Richard Meyers of *Millimeter* magazine, Carpenter early on summed up his stance on filmmaking: "My whole philosophy of movies is that movies are not intellectual, they are not ideas, that is done in literature and all sorts of other forms. Movies are *emotional*, an audience should cry or laugh or get scared. I think the audience should project into the film, into a character, into a situation, and *react*. The great thing about some of the B

James Woods and his team about to enter a dark haven for vampires in *John Carpenter's Vampires*.

movies or the *film noir,* say, is that the audience did just that. . . . So in terms of extending the genres, . . . I'm not as interested in that as I am in getting the audience to react, really to project into the film, and come away having had an experience." And in an interview with Braxton, Carpenter concluded, "All I really want is to have a body of work. . . . And to survive."

■ Biographical and Critical Sources

BOOKS

Contemporary Theatre, Film and Television, Volume 53, Gale (Detroit, MI), 2004, pp. 72-75.

Cumbow, Robert C., *Order in the Universe: The Films of John Carpenter,* Scarecrow Press (Lanham, MD), 2000.

International Dictionary of Films and Filmmakers, Volume 2: *Directors,* 4th edition, St. James Press (Detroit, MI), 2000.

Maltin, Leonard, *Leonard Maltin's 1996 Movie & Video Guide,* Signet (New York, NY), 1995.

Muir, John Kenneth, *The Films of John Carpenter,* McFarland & Co. (Jefferson, NC), 2000.

PERIODICALS

Film Comment, January-February, 1999, Kent Jones, "American Movie Classic: John Carpenter."

Los Angeles Times, July 2, 1986, Michael Wilmington, review of *Big Trouble in Little China,* p. 10; October 23, 1987, Michael Wilmington, review of *Prince of Darkness,* p. 23; October 25, 1988, Michael Wilmington, review of *Halloween 4,* p. 4; November 4, 1988, Michael Wilmington, review of *They Live,* p. 6; February 28, 1992, Peter Rainer, review of *Memoirs of an Invisible Man,* p. F6; February 3, 1995, Kevin Thomas, review of *In the Mouth of Madness,* p. F6; April 28, 1995, Kevin Thomas review of *Village of the Damned,* p. F10; October 2, 1995, Jack Matthews, review of *Halloween: The Curse of Michael Myers,* p. F8; August 9, 1996, Kevin Thomas, review of *John Carpenter's Escape from L.A.,* p. F1; August 10, 1996, Steven Smith, "There's Simply No Escape from L.A.," p. F1; October 30, 1998, Kevin Thomas, review of *John Carpenter's Vampires,* p. F22; August 23, 2001, Greg Braxton, "Chill Seeker," p. F10; August 24, 2001, Kevin Thomas, review of *Ghosts of Mars,* p. F6.

Millimeter, April, 1980, Richard Meyers, "Interview: Budget-Conscious Director, John Carpenter."

New Yorker, January 28, 1980, James Stevenson, "Profiles: People Start Running."

New York Times, July 19, 1981, Vincent Canby, review of *Escape from New York,* p. C6; November 24, 1981, Aljean Harmetz, "Carpenter: A Maverick in Spendthrift Filmland," p. C7; June 25, 1982, Vincent Canby, review of *The Thing,* p. C14; July 2, 1986, Walter Goodman, review of *Big Trouble in Little China,* p. C29; October 23, 1987, Vincent Canby, review of *Prince of Darkness,* p. C26; February 28, 1992, Janet Maslin, review of *Memoirs of an Invisible Man,* p. C17; April 28, 1995, Janet Maslin, review of *Village of the Damned,* p. C8; August 9, 1996, Stephen Holden, review of *John Carpenter's Escape from L.A.,* p. C5; October 30, 1998, Lawrence van Gelder, review of *John Carpenter's Vampires,* p. E1; August 24, 2001, Elvis Mitchell, review of *Ghosts of Mars,* p. E1.

Wall Street Journal, October 22, 1999, "Talking Head: John Carpenter," p. W2.

Washington Post, October 28, 1987, Richard Harrington, review of *Prince of Darkness,* p. D15; October 30, 1998, Michael O'Sullivan, review of *John Carpenter's Vampires,* p. N65; August 24, 2001, Michael O'Sullivan, review of *Ghosts of Mars,* p. T37.

ONLINE

IGN, http://www.filmforce.ign.com/ (July 11, 2005), Jeff Otto, "Interview: John Carpenter."

Internet Movie Database, http://www.imdb.com/ (June 5, 2006), "John Carpenter."

Latent Image, http://pages.emerson.edu/ (June 6, 2006), Eric Beetner, "Director's Profile: John Carpenter."

Official John Carpenter Web site, http://www.johncarpenter.com (June 5, 2006).

Science Fiction Weekly, http://www.scifi.com/ (June 6, 2006), Michael McCarty and Mark McLaughlin, "John Carpenter Looks Back at *Halloween* on Its 25th Anniversary."

Senses of Cinema, http://www.sensesofcinema.com/ (June 5, 2006), Marco Lanzagorta, "John Carpenter," and Gabe Klinger, "Stalled Auteurism: John Carpenter's *Ghosts of Mars.*"

VideoVista, http://www.videovista.net/ (June 6, 2006), Octavio Ramos, Jr., "Surviving Shadow Logic: John Carpenter."*

Gennifer Choldenko

■ Personal

Born 1957, in Santa Monica, CA; married; children: Ian, Kai. *Education:* Brandeis University, B.A.; Rhode Island School of Design, B.F.A.

■ Addresses

Home—Tiburon, CA. *Agent*—c/o Author Mail, Penguin Putnam, 375 Hudson St., New York, NY 10014. *E-mail*—choldenko@earthlink.net.

■ Career

Writer. Worked in various jobs, including horse back riding instructor for seeing-and hearing-impaired children.

■ Awards, Honors

Junior Library Guild selection, New York Library Top 100 Book selection, and Cuyahoga County Library Best Book selection, all 1997, and National Parenting Center Seal of Approval, 2001, all for *Moonstruck: The True Story of the Cow Who Jumped over the Moon;* Best Book of the Year, *School Library Journal* and Center for Children's Books, California Book Award, Winner Children's Fiction Division, IRA-CBC Children's Choice Book, all 2001, all for *Notes from a Liar and Her Dog;* Top Shelf Fiction for Middle School Readers, *Voice of Youth Advocates,* and Top Ten Children's Books, *San Francisco Chronicle,* both 2004, Newbery Honor Book, Carnegie Medal nomination, ALA Notable Book, Best Book of the Year, from *School Library Journal, Publishers Weekly,* and *Kirkus Reviews,* Books for the Teen Age list, New York Library, CBC-NCSS Notable Social Studies Trade Books, Special Needs Award, U.K., Beatty Award, California Library Association, Judy Lopez Honor Award, Northern California Book Award, Parents' Choice Silver Medal, all 2005, all for *Al Capone Does My Shirts.*

■ Writings

Moonstruck: The True Story of the Cow Who Jumped over the Moon, illustrated by Paul Yalowitz, Hyperion (New York, NY), 1997.

Notes from a Liar and Her Dog, Putnam (New York, NY), 2001.

Al Capone Does My Shirts, Putnam (New York, NY), 2004.

How to Make Friends with a Giant, illustrated by Amy Walrod, Putnam (New York, NY), 2006.

If a Tree Falls at Lunch Period, Harcourt, 2007.

Choldenko's books have been translated into German, French, Spanish, Italian, Chinese, Japanese, Serbian, Catalan, and Korean.

■ Adaptations

Notes from a Liar and Her Dog was adapted for audiocassette, Listening Library, 2001; *Al Capone Does My Shirts* was adapted for audiocassette, Recorded Books, 2004.

■ Work in Progress

Louder, Lili, illustrated by Steve Schindler, for Putnam, 2007; *Putting the Monkeys to Bed,* illustrated by Tom Pohrt, Putnam, 2008.

■ Sidelights

Gennifer Choldenko is the author of several children's books, including picture books as well as novels for middle school children. Noted for her humor and offbeat perspective, Choldenko was a 2005 Newbery Honor Book-winner for her novel *Al Capone Does My Shirts.* In her novels, Choldenko deals with serious topics, from chronic lying and tense family relationships to autism, but with a light and witty touch and a fast pace. Choldenko's first work, *Moonstruck: The True Story of the Cow Who Jumped over the Moon,* was not published until the author was forty. On her author Web site she explained her late arrival as a writer: "My strongest influence to become a writer and my strongest influence not to become a writer were the same person, my dad." Choldenko's father wrote every day, but also had a regular job as a business executive. He never published any of his work; from his example she learned two things, as Choldenko went on to note: "One was that writing was a blast and two was it would break your heart. It took me a long time to come to terms with this for myself and to be willing to take the risks necessary to pursue a career as a writer."

Late Bloomer

Choldenko was one of a family of four children, born in 1957 in Santa Monica, California. Her family was a boisterous one, so loud, that, as she com-

mented on her Web site, "strangers sometimes asked us if our parents were deaf." Horses were Choldenko's first love as a child; she spent long hours on the back of her horse riding the hills of southern California. The youngest in the family, she was dubbed Snot Nose by her siblings. "I've always loved to write," Choldenko told *Authors and Artists for Young Adults (AAYA).* "I wrote and illustrated my first book at age 8 called 'The Adventures of Genny Rice.' It was the story of a grain of rice's adventures down the garbage disposal. As a kid, I loved to write stories and make up songs and tell stupid (but original) jokes which my family called 'Gennifer Jokes.' When I was in high school, I collected favorite words, made up my own language and wrote a lot of poetry. In college, I wrote fiction with a vengeance. Not surprisingly, my favorite subject in school was English. I remember staying up late at night in high school working on compositions. I was a perfectionist even then, so I would write and re-write my essays over and over again. I have two B.A. degrees. One is in English and American Literature from Brandeis University. I was actually a Creative Writing major, but they hadn't yet established CW as a separate major, so my degree says English and American Literature. I graduated Cum Laude with Honors. My second degree is a B.F.A. in illustration from Rhode Island School of Design."

As part of Choldenko's class work at the Rhode Island School of Design, under the tutelage of David Macaulay, she was assigned the project of writing and illustrating a picture. However, she had no luck with her project ideas; all of them were rejected by Macaulay. Finally, as the semester was nearing its end, Macaulay suggested that Choldenko simply illustrate a public domain fairy tale, along the lines of "Hansel and Gretel" or "Goldilocks and the Three Bears." In an interview for *Downhomebooks.com,* Choldenko said of this experience: "There went my dreams of being a children's book author. I should have gone to law school, I thought. But after feeling sufficiently sorry for myself for an hour or so, I began to wonder if there had been other authors who had had a tough go of it. That made me think of Mother Goose. My favorite Mother Goose rhyme is the cow jumped over the moon . . . and then out popped *Moonstruck.* I pretty much wrote it in one night."

This class project ultimately became Choldenko's first publication, a humorous take on the traditional nursery rhyme "Hey Diddle Diddle." Her *Moonstruck* brings new light to bear on the perplexing line "And the cow jumped over the moon," which has puzzled young and old listeners alike. According to the story's narrator—a horse—the black-and-white bovine in question accomplished the high-flying task after training with a group of agile horses that regularly made the leap into the night sky to skim the top of the moon and return to Earth. Calling the book "a giggle from beginning to end," a *Publishers Weekly* contributor noted that the author "clearly had fun setting tradition on its ear, and her glee is evident throughout." In *Booklist* Ilene Cooper dubbed *Moonstruck* "fractured and funny," and called it "a fun read-aloud—and a tribute to hard work."

Moonstruck was Choldenko's debut, and she has followed up its success with several more picture books for children, including the 2006 story *How to Make Friends with a Giant,* about the unlikely friendship between the shortest kid in the class, Jake, and the tallest, the new kid, Jacomo. Jake helps Jacomo literally fit in with his fellow classmates in this picture book illustrated by Amy Walrod. Though written in 2000, the book did not see publication until 2006, waiting in queue at the publishers for the illustrator Walrod.

Turns to Novels for Children

Choldenko turned her humorous talents to longer tales, beginning with *Notes from a Liar and Her Dog,* the author's 2001 book for middle-grade readers. This book features preteen Antonia "Ant" MacPherson, a middle sister who finds herself constantly on the outs with her two bookend ballerina sisters—the perfect "Your Highness Elizabeth" and the equally perfect "Katherine the Great"—as well as with her parents. In fact, Ant's mother finds her middle daughter a trial. As Choldenko noted for *Downhomebooks.com:* "My own feeling about Mrs. MacPherson is that she is able to be an adequate mom with Elizabeth and Kate, but that something about Ant just pushes her buttons like crazy. It is a 'perfect storm' situation. Ant brings out the worst in her." Ant's only confidants are a Chihuahua named Pistachio and best friend Harrison, an artist who is obsessed with poultry. As conditions at home and in school continue to deteriorate, Ant decides she must have been adopted. She resorts to fabricating elaborate falsehoods as a way to mask her unhappiness until a sixth-grade teacher sensitive to the girl's emotional problems steps in and helps Ant face responsibility for contributing to the problems within her family. Noting that Choldenko "vividly captures the feelings of a middle child torn between wanting to be noticed and wanting to be invisible," a *Publishers Weekly* contributor praised *Notes from a Liar and Her Dog* as a "funny and touching novel [that] portrays the tug-of-war within this strong heroine and taps into very real emotions." Connie Tyrrell Burns added in *School Library Journal*

A sixth-grader feels overshadowed by both her older and younger sisters in this 2001 novel for young adults.

that the author's "first-person narrative is humorous, tongue-in-cheek, and as irreverent as her independent heroine." Similar praise came from *Booklist* contributor Susan Dove Lempke, who concluded: "Funny, moving, and completely believable, this is a fine first novel." And for *Bookseller* critic Wendy Colling, *Notes from a Liar and Her Dog* "is impossible to put down—it's funny and moving and reflects real insecurities."

Choldenko explores the difficulties of moving to a new home in an unusual coming-of-age novel with the 2004 *Al Capone Does My Shirts.* Moose Flanagan is twelve and none too enthused about the fact that he and his family must move to the island prison of Alcatraz in 1935, where his father will work as a prison guard so that his young sister, Natalie, who is autistic, can attend the special Esther P. Marinoff School in San Francisco. Moose moves to Alcatraz when infamous inmates included Capone the mobster. He has to leave his winning baseball team behind, and once settled at Alcatraz he sees very little of his busy father, while his mother is so involved with Natalie's illness that she pays him little attention. However, Moose is helped in acclimatizing to life on Alcatraz by the warden's daughter, feisty Piper, who never ceases to get the pair of them into mischief.

Choldenko was inspired to write this book by a newspaper article she read about the early days of Alcatraz and the little-known fact that families of the guards and prison officials actually lived on the island. Following that, she served as a docent on the former prison island, researching the history of the institution and its inmates and support staff. Additionally, Choldenko took inspiration from her own sister, Gina, who suffered from autism. The prison setting of Alcatraz became a metaphor for Choldenko, for her sister had once drawn a picture

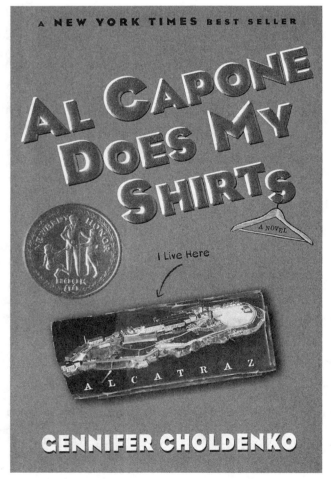

This Newbery Honor winner provides readers with a sense of what it was like for children growing up on Alcatraz Island while their parents worked at the prison.

of herself in prison and then said, "This is Gina," as the author recounted on *Downhomebooks.com.* "This was an important moment in the life of our family because it was the first time we understood that she understood the terrible limits of her illness," Choldenko further noted. The author took the title from a joke that she has the children make about the prisoners and their prison jobs. In fact, Al Capone did work in the prison laundry; military personnel stationed in San Francisco during World War II used to make a similar joke: "Al Capone does my shorts."

Critics reacted warmly to this novel. *Booklist* contributor Ed Sullivan commented, "With its unique setting and well-developed characters, this warm, engaging coming-of-age story has plenty of appeal." In a starred *Publishers Weekly* review, a contributor added similar praise, calling *Al Capone Does My Shirts* an "exceptionally atmospheric novel [that] has equally unusual characters and plot lines." The same reviewer declared it "fast-paced and memorable." *School Library Journal* reviewer Miranda Doyle thought the same novel was "told with humor and skill," while Paula Rohrlick, writing in *Kliatt,* felt the book was a "sensitive portrait of autism and how it affects a family." Rohrlick went on to conclude that it was "an affecting novel." Likewise, Jennifer Brown, reviewing the novel in *People,* commended the "funny situations and plot twists [that] abound." A critic for *Kirkus Reviews* found that the "pacing is exquisite" and that, overall, the book is a "great read." Awards committees agreed with the critics. In addition to being chosen as a Newbery Honor Book, *Al Capone Does My Shirts* was also a "best book of the year" for numerous review journals, and was short-listed for England's prestigious Carnegie Medal.

In an interview for *Quercus,* Choldenko remembered how she learned of having won the Newbery Honor: "When the phone rang at 4:15 a.m. in the morning, it was the biggest shock I've ever had in my life. Because a good friend of mine was the author of a Caldecott Honor Book, I knew awards phone calls came early, but when the phone rang, I literally could not believe it. I lay in bed giving myself a little talking to. 'Now you're imagining the phone ringing. You are really going around the bend, girl.' Eventually the phone stopped ringing. A minute later it began again. Whoever it was would not give up. It was my husband who finally answered the phone. 'It's Susan Faust,' he told me. 'Chairman of the Newbery Committee. She wants to talk to you.' I'd like to tell you that I was completely poised and had many erudite comments to make to the Chairman of the 2005 Newbery Committee at 4:19 that morning, but when she said *Al Capone Does My Shirts* won the Newbery Honor all I could say was 'Oh my God' over and over again. It was very embarrassing, but the truth is: in the end I am always ready for disappointment. Until that morning I had very little experience with having my dreams come true."

A typical working day for Choldenko, she told *AAYA*, begins with her children: "I have two amazing children: Ian age 12 and Kai age 7. I drop them off at school then head straight for my desk. I would like to tell you that my house is always in perfect order, the dishes are put away and the laundry is folded, before I begin writing, but alas that isn't true. While my kids are at school, my bottom is pasted to my chair and my hands are glued to the keyboard. I pick my kids up about four thirty and then presto chango I'm Mom again. Dinner gets made, the dishes get done, the laundry gets put away. I always hope that no one comes to visit during the witching hour: five to six P.M. when I'm scurrying around trying to clean everything up."

If you enjoy the works of Gennifer Choldenko, you may also want to check out the following books:

Audrey Couloumbis, *Getting Near to Baby*, 1999.
Cynthia Kadohata, *Kira-Kira*, 2004.
Gary D. Schmidt, *Lizzie Bright and the Buckminster Boy*, 2004.

Choldenko continues to write both novels for middle readers and picture books. However, as she noted on *Downhomebooks.com:* "Picture books are fun to work on but novels are my lifeblood." The author further commented: "I've got so many novels I want to write, I better live a very long time so I have time to write them all. It takes me two to three years to write a novel, because I do so many revisions. I enjoy revising though, so it's not like the process is torture. In fact, my favorite part of novel writing is the initial wild idea stages and revision."

Choldenko told *AAYA* about her future writing plans: "Last week I sent my next novel *If a Tree Falls at Lunch Period* to copyediting! I am very excited about this because I have been working on this novel for about four years. I think it is my funniest novel so far, and yet it is also addresses a topic about which I am deadly serious. It's a very fast

read, but I'm hoping that after you finish reading the last page, you will continue to think about the book for a very long time."

"What I love most about being a published author," Choldenko told *AAYA*, "is having the time to write. Writing for me isn't a means to getting published, it is the reward in and of itself. That doesn't mean I'm not interested in being published because of course I am. But there is simply nothing more fun than working on a story. Nothing."

■ **Biographical and Critical Sources**

PERIODICALS

Booklist, March 1, 1997, Ilene Cooper, review of *Moonstruck: The True Story of the Cow Who Jumped over the Moon*, p. 1169; April 15, 2001, Susan Dove Lempke, review of *Notes from a Liar and Her Dog*, p. 1550; October 15, 2001, Lolly Gepson, review of *Notes from a Liar and Her Dog* (audiobook), p. 428; February 1, 2004, Ed Sullivan, review of *Al Capone Does My Shirts*, p. 976.

Bookseller, January 18, 2002, Wendy Cooling, review of *Notes from a Liar and Her Dog*, p. 48.

Horn Book, March-April, 2005, "Newbery Medal," p. 235.

Kirkus Reviews, March 1, 2004, review of *Al Capone Does My Shirts*, p. 220.

Kliatt, March, 2004, Paula Rohrlick, review of *Al Capone Does My Shirts*, p. 8; November, 2004, Julie Scordato, review of *Al Capone Does My Shirts* (audiobook), p. 41.

People, May 3, 2004, Jennifer Brown, review of *Al Capone Does My Shirts*, p. 46.

Publishers Weekly, February 10, 1997, review of *Moonstruck*, p. 83; May 14, 2001, review of *Notes from a Liar and Her Dog*, p. 82; August 6, 2001, review of *Notes from a Liar and Her Dog* (audiobook), p. 26; July 7, 2003, review of *Notes from a Liar and Her Dog*, p. 74; February 2, 2004, review of *Al Capone Does My Shirts*, p. 78.

School Library Journal, April, 1997, Patricia Pearl Doyle, review of *Moonstruck*, p. 91; April, 2001, Connie Tyrrell Burns, review of *Notes from a Liar and Her Dog*, p. 139; October, 2001, Brian E. Wilson, review of *Notes from a Liar and Her Dog* (audiobook), p. 92; March, 2004, Miranda Doyle, review of *Al Capone Does My Shirts*, p. 203; September, 2004, B. Allison Gray, review of *Al Capone Does My Shirts* (audiobook), p. 76; October, 2004, review of *Al Capone Does My Shirts*, p. S53.

Washington Post Book World, "For Young Readers," February 6, 2005, p. 12.

ONLINE

Downhomebooks.com, http://www.downhomebooks. com/ (June 9, 2006), "Gennifer Choldenko Interview."

Gennifer Choldenko Home Page, http://www. choldenko.com (June 8, 2006).

Penguin Group (Canada) Web site, http://www. penguin.ca/ (June 9, 2006), "Gennifer Choldenko."

Quercus, http://www.windingoak.com/quercus/ (July, 2006), "Receiving the Call: An Interview with Author Gennifer Choldenko."

Greg and Tim Hildebrandt

■ Personal

Greg Hildebrandt: Born January 23, 1939, in Detroit, Mich.; son of George J. (an executive) and Germaine (Lajack) Hildebrandt; married Diana F. Stankowski, June 8, 1963; children: Mary, Laura, Gregory. *Education:* Attended Mienzinger's Art School, Detroit, MI.

Tim Hildebrandt: Born January 23, 1939, in Detroit, MI; died June 11, 2006 from complications related to diabetes; son of George J. (an executive) and Germaine (Lajack) Hildebrandt; married Rita Murray, July 10, 1965; children: Charles. *Education:* Attended Mienzinger's Art School, Detroit, MI.

■ Addresses

Home—12 Rock Spring Rd., West Orange, N.J. 07052. *Office*—90 Park Ave., Verona, N.J. 07044. *Agent*—Jean L. Gruder, 90 Park Ave., Verona, N.J. 07044. *E-mail*—brothershildebrandt@spiderwebart.com.

■ Career

Greg Hildebrandt: Freelance illustrator and writer, 1958—. With brother, Tim Hildebrandt, illustrated three calendars based on J.R.R. Tolkien's *Lord of the Rings,* 1976-78, and posters for the films *Star Wars,* 1977, *Barbarella,* 1979, and *Clash of the Titans,* 1981. Consultant to Columbia Pictures. "Terry and the Pirates" comic strip, illustrator, 1995. Illustrator for comics, magazines, calendars, pinups, collectible cards, games, and collectible coins. Owner of Spiderwebart Gallery, Hopatcong, NJ. *Exhibitions:* Work has been shown in individual and group shows in New York, NY, Philadelphia, PA, Birmingham, MI, and San Francisco, CA. *Military service:* U.S. Army, 1959-63.

Tim Hildebrandt: Worked for four years as artist in animation department and as film designer for Jam Handy Organization, Detroit, MI; worked for six years as head of film department and filmmaker for Society for the Propagation of the Faith, New York, NY; freelance illustrator; production designer for Swashbuckler Films. With brother, Greg Hildebrandt, illustrated three calendars based on J.R.R. Tolkien's *Lord of the Rings,* 1976-78, and posters for the films *Star Wars,* 1977, *Barbarella,* 1979, and *Clash of the Titans,* 1981. Sole illustrator of poster for the film *The Secret of NIMH,* 1984. "Terry and the Pirates" comic strip, illustrator, 1995. Illustrator of comics, magazines, and collectibles. *Exhibitions:* Work has been exhibited in major shows in New York, NY, Philadelphia, PA, Birmingham, MI, and San Francisco, CA. *Military service:* U.S. Army, 1957-60.

■ Awards, Honors

Greg Hildebrandt: Gold Medal, with brother Tim Hildebrandt, Society of Illustrators; Book of the Year list, with Tim Hildebrandt, Child Study Association of America, 1973, for *Giant Panda*.

Tim Hildebrandt: Gold medal, with brother Greg Hildebrandt, Society of Illustrators; Book of the Year list, with Greg Hildebrandt, Child Study Association of America, 1973, for *Giant Panda*; award of merit at Society of Illustrators Annual Show, 1987, for cover illustration of the book *The Children of Arabel*, published by New American Library; Golden Eagle award for the film *Project Hope*, produced by Jam Handy Organization; awards from Society of Illustration for illustrations in children's books.

WRITINGS BY GREG HILDE-BRANDT:

WRITTEN AND ILLUSTRATED

(With Tim Hildebrandt) *How Do They Build It?*, Platt (New York, NY), 1974.

(With Tim Hildebrandt and Jerry Nichols) *Urshurak* (fantasy novel), Bantam (New York, NY), 1979.

(With Tim Hildebrandt) *A Christmas Treasury*, Unicorn (Parsippany, NJ), 1984.

Greg Hildebrandt's Favorite Fairy Tales, Little Simon (New York, NY), 1984.

(With Tim Hildebrandt) *From Tolkien to Oz*, Unicorn (Parsippany, NJ), 1985.

(With Tim Hildebrandt) *Greg Hildebrandt's Book of Three-Dimensional Dragons*, Little, Brown (Boston, MA), 1994.

(With Tim Hildebrandt) *Greg and Tim Hildebrandt, the Tolkien Years*, Watson-Guptill Publications (New York, NY), 2001.

(With Justin Boring) *War on Flesh*, Volume one, Tokyopop (Los Angeles, CA), 2005.

Also the writer and illustrator, with brother Tim Hildebrandt, of "The Emerald 7" miniseries for *Frank Frazetta Fantasy Illustrated* magazine.

ILLUSTRATOR

Charles Dickens, *A Christmas Carol*, Little Simon (New York, NY), 1983.

Bram Stoker, *Dracula*, Unicorn (Parsippany, NJ), 1985.

Bonnie Worth, *Peter Cottontail's Surprise*, Unicorn (Parsippany, NJ), 1985.

Frank L. Baum, *The Wizard of Oz*, Unicorn (Parsippany, NJ), 1985.

Edgar Allen Poe, *Poe: Stories and Poems*, Unicorn (Parsippany, NJ), 1986.

Carlo Collodi, *The Adventures of Pinocchio*, Unicorn (Parsippany, NJ), 1986.

Charles E. Carryl, *Davy and the Goblin*, Unicorn (Parsippany, NJ), 1988.

J.M. Barrie, *Peter Pan*, Unicorn (Parsippany, NJ), 1988.

Gaston Leroux, *The Phantom of the Opera*, Unicorn (Parsippany, NJ), 1988.

J. Walker McSpadden, *Robin Hood*, Unicorn (Parsippany, NJ), 1989.

Simone Zapun, *Wonderful Wild Animals*, Grosset & Dunlap (New York, NY), 1989.

Lewis Carroll, *Alice in Wonderland*, Unicorn (Parsippany, NJ), 1990.

'Twas the Night Before Christmas and Other Holiday Favorites, Unicorn (Parsippany, NJ), 1990.

Tad Williams, *Child of an Ancient City*, Maxwell Macmillan (New York, NY), 1992.

L. Frank Baum, *The Wonderful Wizard of Oz*, Courage Publishing, 2003

Magical Storybook Treasury, Courage Publishing, 2006

ILLUSTRATOR WITH BROTHER, TIM HILDEBRANDT

Audrey Hirsch and Harvey Hirsch, *A Home for Tandy* (fiction), Platt & Munk (New York, NY), 1971.

Watty Piper, editor, *Mother Goose: A Treasury of Best-Loved Rhymes*, Platt & Munk (New York, NY), 1972.

Aileen Fisher, *Animal Disguises* (fiction), Bowmar (New York, NY), 1973.

Barbara Shook Hazen, *A Nose for Trouble* (fiction), Golden Press (New York, NY), 1973.

Anthony Hiss, *The Giant Panda Book* (nonfiction), Golden Press (New York, NY), 1973.

Gloria Skurzynski, *The Remarkable Journey of Gustavus Bell* (fiction), Abingdon (Nashville, TN), 1973.

Sarah Keyser, *The Pop-up Action Circus Book*, Platt & Munk (New York, NY), 1973.

Sarah Keyser, *The Pop-up Action Construction Book*, Platt & Munk (New York, NY), 1973.

Simone Zapun, *Games Animals Play* (nonfiction), Platt & Munk (New York, NY), 1974.

(Contributing illustrator) J.R.R. Tolkien, *Smith of Wooton Major and Farmer Giles and Ham* (fiction), Ballantine (New York, NY), 1975.

Bill Larson, *Let's Go to Animal Town: A Book About Things That Go!*, Golden Press (New York, NY), 1975.

Annie Ingle, *The Big City Book* (fiction), Platt & Munk (New York, NY), 1975.

Winifred Rosen Casey, *The Hippopotamus Book* (nonfiction), Golden Press (New York, NY), 1975.

Kathleen N. Daly, *The Wonder of Animals* (nonfiction), Golden Press (New York, NY), 1976.

Kathleen N. Daly, *Dinosaurs* (nonfiction), Golden Press (New York, NY), 1977.

Kathleen N. Daly, *Today's Biggest Animals* (nonfiction), Golden Press (New York, NY), 1977.

Kathleen N. Daly, *Hide and Defend* (nonfiction), Golden Press (New York, NY), 1977.

Kathleen N. Daly, *Unusual Animals* (nonfiction), Golden Press (New York, NY), 1977.

(Under joint pseudonym The Brothers Hildebrandt) Terry Brooks, *The Sword of Shannara* (adult fantasy novel), Random House (New York, NY), 1977.

Ruthanna Long, *The Great Monster Contest* (fiction), Golden Press (New York, NY), 1977.

(Under joint pseudonym The Hildebrandts) *Who Runs the City?*, Platt & Munk (New York, NY), 1978.

(Under joint pseudonym The Hildebrandts) *Animals!*, Platt & Munk (New York, NY), 1978.

(Under joint pseudonym The Hildebrandts) *Here Come the Builders!*, Platt & Munk (New York, NY), 1978.

Clement C. Moore, *The Night Before Christmas* (poem), Golden Press (New York, NY), 1981.

The Cricket Book of Mother Goose, Platt & Munk (New York, NY), 1987.

Star Wars Episode I Great Big Flap Book, Random House (New York, NY), 1999.

Walt Simonson, *Superman: The Last God of Krypton*, DC Comics (New York, NY), 1999.

Also illustrator of numerous book covers with Tim Hildebrandt.

WRITINGS BY TIM HILDEBRANDT:

WRITTEN AND/OR ILLUSTRATED

(With Greg Hildebrandt) *How Do They Build It?*, Platt (New York, NY), 1974.

(With Greg Hildebrandt and Jerry Nichols) *Urshurak* (fantasy novel), Bantam (New York, NY), 1979.

(With Greg Hildebrandt) *A Christmas Treasury*, Unicorn (Parsippany, NJ), 1984.

(With Greg Hildebrandt) *From Tolkien to Oz*, Unicorn (Parsippany, NJ), 1985.

The Shoemaker and the Christmas Elves, Derrydale Books (New York, NY), 1993.

(With Greg Hildebrandt) *Greg Hildebrandt's Book of Three-Dimensional Dragons*, Little, Brown (Boston, MA), 1994.

The Fantasy Art Techniques of Tim Hildebrandt, Sterling Publishing (New York, NY), 2000.

(with Greg Hildebrandt) *Greg and Tim Hildebrandt, the Tolkien Years*, Watson-Guptill Publications (New York, NY), 2001.

Also the writer and illustrator, with brother Greg Hildebrandt, of "The Emerald 7" miniseries for *Frank Frazetta Fantasy Illustrated* magazine.

ILLUSTRATOR:

Othello Bach, *Lilly, Willy, and the Mail-Order Witch* (juvenile fiction), Caedmon (New York, NY), 1983.

Rita Hildebrandt (wife), *The Fantasy Cookbook*, Bobbs-Merrill (Indianapolis, IN), 1983.

Othello Bach, *Hector McSnector and the Mail-Order Christmas Witch*, Caedmon (New York, NY), 1984.

Rita Hildebrandt, *Merlin and the Dragons of Atlantis* (novel), Bobbs-Merrill (Indianapolis, IN), 1984.

Michael Coney, *Fang, the Gnome*, New American Library (New York, NY), 1988.

Bruce Coville, *The Unicorn Treasury*, Doubleday (New York, NY), 1988.

■ Sidelights

Greg and Tim Hildebrandt have followed in an impressive tradition of brothers who have created fantasy for children, young and old. In the nineteenth century, there were the Brothers Grimm, who collected folk tales such as "Cinderella," "Snow White," and "Little Red Riding Hood." In the mid-twentieth century Walt Disney, aided financially by brother Roy, created Mickey Mouse and Donald Duck. The Hildebrandt twins have also helped to bring fantasy worlds alive for an entire generation. They worked together on and off as artists and illustrators for almost five decades, until the death of twin Tim in 2006. Together they painted hundreds of book covers, illustrated books, calendars, advertisements, movie posters, film production designs, and trading card games. Their joint name, the Brothers Hildebrandt, became synonymous with the fantasy world of J.R.R. Tolkien, when, in the 1970s, they illustrated several calendars of *The Lord of the Rings* books. The 1978 addition went on to become the best-selling calendars ever, and two decades after publication, one of the original illustrations fetched $150,000 in auction. The brothers also became well known for their movie poster for the original *Star Wars* film. Thereafter, they continued to do artwork for various aspects of the *Star Wars* franchise, from trading cards to games. Greg Hildebrandt has also made a name for himself independently of brother Tim as the illustrator of such children's book classics as *The Wizard of Oz, The Adventures of Pinocchio, Peter Pan, Alice in Wonderland,* and *The Phantom of the Opera*. According to a contributor for *RoGallery.com*, the Brothers Hildebrandt "are among the best known illustrators in the world." This same writer went on to praise their "virtuoso ability to capture light and form, their classic compositions, and their sensitive isolation of a moment of action or of serenity." For *SciFi.com* contributor A. Jaye Williams, the twins "have long been a mainstay in the fields of both fantasy and science-fiction art." Speaking with Williams, Tim Hildebrandt noted: "What we love about the whole SciFi/Fantasy genre is that it deals with pure imagination. Being able to fully utilize your creative thoughts is awesome. The whole medium of painting is self-satisfying for us. It's hands-on work. It's organic. You use tools that were invented by the cave men as an extension of your own hand to move colors around and form an image that's locked up inside your head."

Born Artists

Born in Detroit, Michigan, in 1939, the brothers were identical twins, with Greg five minutes older than Tim. At the age of two, the twins were already being taught to draw with crayons by their father. Quickly the boys appropriated the crayons from their father and began drawing within the lines of figures. Coming of age during a golden age of comics as well as of cartooning, the Hildebrandt boys were deeply influenced by comics such as *Green Lantern, Wonderwoman, Batman,* and *Superman,* and by comic strips such as "Steve Canyon," "Prince Valiant," and "Terry and the Pirates." Half a century later they would try to revive "Terry and the Pirates," illustrating the strip for a year in 1995. They also grew up on the cartooning magic of the Walt Disney Studio, enjoying such animated features as *Snow White and the Seven Dwarfs, Pinocchio,* and *Fantasia.* By the time they were eight, the twins were busy trying to copy the drawings they loved in comics and cartoons; in this effort they also had their first self-taught lessons in anatomy and perspective. Added to this was a love for science fiction novels and films, including *Frankenstein, When Worlds Collide,* and *The War of theWorlds.*

As they grew older, the Hildebrandts were also inspired by the works of contemporary illustrators, such as N.C. Wyeth, Maxfield Parrish, and Howard Pyle. Painterly influences include the works of Pieter Brueghel the Elder, Hieronymous Bosch, Claude Monet, and Rembrandt van Rijn. For a time the Brothers Hildebrandt wanted to become Disney animators. To further this ambition, they entered the Meinzinger Art School in Detroit. However, after six months they left that school, realizing that they already knew as much as their teachers. Instead, they went to work for the advertising firm, Jim Handy Company, where they learned some of the craft of animating and filmmaking. It was there they also made their first commercial sale, an abstract landscape purchased by the company vice president.

In 1963, they moved to New Jersey, where they worked for Bishop Fulton J. Sheen, making documentary films about hunger and poverty intended for a high school audience. Part of their efforts was *Project Hope,* a short documentary chronicling the efforts of a medical relief ship. They won a Golden Eagle award for this work, and continued to travel to Europe, Africa, and South America, making documentaries, until 1969, when they decided to focus on book illustration.

Worlds of Fantasy and Science Fiction

For the next six years, the brothers illustrated books for publishers such as Holt, Reinhart & Winston, Western Publishing, and other major New York houses, adding their artwork to scores of textbooks and children's books, as well as illustrating hundreds of book covers. They had made enough of a name for themselves, that by 1975 they were offered a commission to illustrate the next year's Tolkien calendar for Ballantine Books. Their 1976 effort proved so successful that they went on illustrate the next two years as well, with the 1978 calendar selling over a million copies. As Williams noted, the Hildebrandts have become "the painters most responsible for how we've pictured J.R.R.Tolkien's *Lord of the Rings* characters." This sudden fame for the Brothers Hildebrandt, as they had by then become known, secured them other high-profile work, including the 1977 poster for the film *Star Wars,* and book illustration for Terry Brooks's 1977 fantasy title, *The Sword of Shannara.* In 1979, the brothers, working with Jerry Nichols, produced their own fantasy novel, *Urshurak,* which won a degree of critical acclaim and reached the bestseller list of the *New York Times.*

A Decade of Separation and Beyond

By 1981, however, the brothers felt a need to take a break from each other. They wanted to pursue their own career paths and prove to themselves that they could each function without the other. In fact, for the next decade, they not only worked apart from one another, but also saw each other very infrequently. "The split was absolutely essential," Tim Hildebrandt told Mark Sanders in an interview for *TwinStuff.com.* "We were working together since we were born. . . . We kept up with what the other one was doing, but we didn't speak to each other for years." During this time, Greg Hildebrandt continued with book and magazine cover illustration, and began to supply work for collectibles: plates, figurines, dolls, and swords. He also was active in advertising, doing artwork for Dr. Pepper, among others. In addition he became involved in greeting cards, and illustrated a calendar for the "Merlin Trilogy" by Mary Stewart. During these years, he also began illustrating a series of some of the classic fairy tales for children, books which have since become accepted classics of their kind.

Meanwhile, brother Tim was also active in illustration, doing the artwork for numerous calendars, including the 1984 calendar for "The Dragonriders of Pern" series by Anne McCaffery. He also illustrated covers for science fiction and fantasy magazines and novels. He teamed up with his wife Rita Hildebrandt on *The Fantasy Cookbook*. And like his brother, he additionally became involved in advertising, supplying images for companies such as Levi's. For a larger project, he supplied illustrations for a proposed theme park in Kansas based on *The Wizard of Oz*.

The brothers were finally reunited in the early 1990s after more than a decade apart. Their first collaboration thereafter was *Greg Hildebrandt's Book of Three-Dimensional Dragons*, with dragons painted in pieces to provide "five striking pop-ups of fantastical creatures," according to a *Publishers Weekly* reviewer. Included among these are such pseudo- historical creatures as the Lindworm and the dragon that St. George killed. Writing in *School Library Journal*, John Sigwald found this book a "sure thing."

If you enjoy the works of the Brothers Hildebrandt, you may also want to check out the following:

The work of fantasy and science fiction artists such as Boris Vallejo, Julie Bell, Michael Whelan, Alan Lee, and John Howe.

The Brothers Hildebrandt continued to collaborate throughout the 1990s and into the new millennium, working on collectible cards, posters for Marvel Comics and DC Comics, and even a miniseries of their favorite superhero, Superman, providing the

art work for the 1999 *Superman: The Last Gold of Krypton*. Their illustrations for this work "don't disappoint," according to Tom Knapp, writing for the online *Rambles*. Knapp went on to note that the brothers "have always had a flair for dramatic, realistic-looking fantasy art," concluding the readers will "love the art" in this Superman edition. They also did a pirate story, "The Emerald 7," for the *Frazetta Fantasy Magazine*, and completed set designs for movies. In 1997, their collected art for the *Star Wars* movies, *Star Wars: The Art of Greg and Tim Hildebrandt*, was published. Four years later, on the eve of the release of the film of *Lord of the Rings*, their collected Tolkien art was presented in *Greg and Tim Hildebrandt, the Tolkien Years*, a "glorious feast,"as *Library Journal* contributor Michael Rogers noted. With the advent of the terrorist attacks on New York and Washington, DC, in 2001, they created commemorative paintings honoring the fallen victims and heroes, with proceeds going to help the families of survivors.

Each brother also continued to work on his own art, with Greg Hildebrandt focusing on genre illustrations, including a series of pin-ups, and Tim Hildebrandt more on fine art painting. Diabetes, however, slowed the work of Tim Hildebrandt, and he ultimately died of complications of that illness on June 11, 2006. Speaking with Sanders, Greg Hildebrandt summed up his own and his brother's life-long obsession with art: "What it takes to be an artist is that you have to live an isolated life. You have to have the isolation to stay in that room and complete your work. We were lucky because we were there for each other."

■ **Biographical and Critical Sources**

BOOKS

Beahm, George, *The Essential J.R.R. Tolkien Sourcebook: A Fan's Guide to Middle-Earth and Beyond*, New Page Books, 2003.

Summers, Ian, *The Art of the Brothers Hildebrandt*, Ballantine (New York, NY), 1979.

Woods, Bob, *Star Wars: The Art of the Brothers Hildebrandt*, Ballantine (New York, NY), 1997.

PERIODICALS

Editor & Publisher, September 23, 1995, "About Art in 'Terry,' p. 42."

Kliatt, November, 2005, George Galuschak, review of *War on Flesh*, Volume One, p. 24.

Library Journal, August, 2001, Michael Rogers, review of *Greg and Tim Hildebrandt, the Tolkien Years*, p. 99.

Publishers Weekly, December 12, 1994, review of *Greg Hildebrandt's Book of Three-Dimensional Dragons,* p. 63; October 10, 2005, review of *War on Flesh,* Volume One, p. 43.

School Library Journal, January, 1995, John Sigwald, review of *Greg Hildebrandt's Book of Three-Dimensional Dragons,* p. 130; April, 2002, Patricia White-Williams, review of *Greg and Tim Hildebrandt, the Tolkien Years,* p. 189.

ONLINE

Brothers Hildebrandt Official Web site, http://www.brothershildebrandt.com (June 9, 2006).

Dragon*Con, http://www.dragoncon.org/ (June 13, 2006), "Biography: Greg & Tim Hildebrandt."

Rambles, http://www.rambles.net/ ((June 14, 2006), Tom Knapp, review of *Superman: The Last God of Krypton.*

RoGallery.com, http://www.rogallery.com/ (June 9, 2006), "Gregory and Timothy Hildebrandt (1939—)."

SciFi.com, http://www.scifi.com/ (June 13, 2006), A. Jaye Williams, "Greg and Tim Hildebrandt Soar with *Star Wars* and Transform Tolkien."

TwinStuff.com, http://www.twinstuff.com/ (June 9, 2006), Mark Sanders, "The Brothers Hildebrandt."*

James Weldon Johnson

■ Personal

Born James William Johnson, June 17, 1871, in Jacksonville, FL; died following an automobile accident, June 26, 1938, in Wiscasset, ME; buried in Brooklyn, NY; son of James (a restaurant head-waiter) and Helen Louise (a musician and school-teacher; maiden name, Dillette) Johnson; married Grace Nail, February 3, 1910. *Ethnicity:* African American *Education:* Atlanta University, A.B., 1894, A.M., 1904; graduate study at Columbia University, c. 1902-05.

■ Career

Poet, novelist, songwriter, editor, historian, civil rights leader, diplomat, lawyer, and educator. Stanton Central Grammar School for Negroes, Jacksonville, FL, teacher, later principal, 1894-1901; *Daily American* (newspaper), Jacksonville, founder and co-editor, 1895-1896; admitted to the Bar of the State of Florida, 1898; private law practice, Jacksonville, 1898-1901; songwriter for the musical theater in partnership with brother, J. Rosamond Johnson, and Bob Cole, New York, NY, 1901-06; United States Consul to Puerto Cabello, Venezuela, 1906-09, and to Corinto, Nicaragua, 1909-13; *New York Age* (newspaper), New York, NY, editorial writer, 1914-24; National Association for the Advancement of Colored People (NAACP), New York, NY, field secretary, 1916-20, executive secretary, 1920-30; Fisk University, Nashville, TN, professor of creative literature and writing, 1931-38; elected treasurer of the Colored Republican Club, New York, NY, and participated in Theodore Roosevelt's presidential campaign, both in 1904; lectured on literature and black culture at numerous colleges and universities during the 1930s, including New York, Northwestern, and Yale Universities, Oberlin and Swarthmore Colleges, and the Universities of North Carolina and Chicago. Served as director of the American Fund for Public Service and as trustee of Atlanta University.

■ Member

National Association for the Advancement of Colored People (NAACP), American Society of Composers, Authors, and Publishers (charter member), Academy of Political Science, Ethical Society, Civic Club (New York City).

■ Awards, Honors

Spingarn Medal, National Association for the Advancement of Colored People (NAACP), 1925, for outstanding achievement by an American Negro;

Harmon Gold Award for *God's Trombones*; Julius Rosenwald Fund grant, 1929; W.E.B. Du Bois Prize for Negro Literature, 1933; named first incumbent of Spence Chair of Creative Literature at Fisk University; honorary doctorates from Talladega College and Howard University.

■ Writings

The Autobiography of an Ex-Colored Man (novel), Sherman, French (Boston, MA), 1912, republished as *The Autobiography of an Ex-Coloured Man*, Knopf (New York, NY), 1927, Arden Library, 1978.

(Translator) Fernando Periquet, *Goyescas; or, The Rival Lovers* (opera libretto), G. Schirmer (New York, NY), 1915.

Fifty Years and Other Poems, Cornhill (Boston, MA), 1917, AMS Press (New York, NY), 1975.

(Editor) *The Book of American Negro Poetry*, Harcourt (New York, NY), 1922.

(Editor) *The Book of American Negro Spirituals*, Viking (New York, NY), 1925.

(Editor) *The Second Book of Negro Spirituals*, Viking (New York, NY), 1926.

God's Trombones: Seven Negro Sermons in Verse (poetry), illustrations by Aaron Douglas, Viking (New York, NY), 1927, Penguin (New York, NY), 1976.

Saint Peter Relates an Incident of the Resurrection Day, privately printed, 1930.

Black Manhattan (nonfiction), Knopf (New York, NY), 1930, Arno, 1968.

Along This Way: The Autobiography of James Weldon Johnson, Viking (New York, NY), 1933, Da Capo (New York, NY), 1973, reprinted with a new introduction by Sondra K. Wilson, 2000.

Negro Americans, What Now? (nonfiction), Viking (New York, NY), 1934, Da Capo (New York, NY), 1973.

Saint Peter Relates an Incident: Selected Poems, Viking (New York, NY), 1935, AMS Press (New York, NY), 1974.

(Editor) *The Books of American Negro Spirituals* (contains *The Book of American Negro Spirituals* and *The Second Book of Negro Spirituals*), Viking (New York, NY), 1940, reprinted, 1964.

The Creation (poetry), illustrated by James Ransome, Holiday House (New York, NY), 1994.

The Selected Writings of James Weldon Johnson, Volume I: *The New York Age Editorials (1914-1923)*, edited and with an introduction by Sondra K. Wilson, Oxford University Press (New York, NY),

1995, Volume II: *Social, Political, and Literary Essays*, edited and with an introduction by Sondra K. Wilson, Oxford University Press (New York, NY), 1995.

Lift Ev'ry Voice and Sing: A Pictorial Tribute to the Negro National Anthem, illustrated by Jan Spivey Gilchrist, Scholastic (New York, NY), 1995.

Complete Poems, edited and with an introduction by Sondra K. Wilson, Penguin (New York, NY), 2000.

Lift Every Voice and Sing: Selected Poems, with a preface by Sondra K. Wilson, Penguin (New York, NY), 2000.

James Weldon Johnson: Writings, Library of America (New York, NY), 2004.

Contributor of articles and poems to numerous newspapers and magazines, including the *Chicago Defender*, *Times-Union* (Jacksonville, FL), *New York Age*, *New York Times*, *Pittsburgh Courier*, *Savannah Tribune*, *Century*, *Crisis*, *Nation*, *Independent*, *Harper's*, *Bookman*, *Forum*, and *Scholastic*. Poetry represented in many anthologies; songs published by Joseph W. Stern & Co., Edward B. Marks Music Corp., and others; author of numerous pamphlets on current events published by the NAACP, *Nation*, *Century*, and others.

Johnson's papers are included in the James Weldon Johnson Collection of Negro Arts and Letters deposited in the Beinecke Library of Yale University.

■ Sidelights

James Weldon Johnson's boundless energy and concern for the plight of African Americans combined to produce an extraordinary career. As a poet, journalist, social activist, and educator, Johnson sought new standards for the treatment of blacks in the early decades of the twentieth century. He was simultaneously a mainstream American writer, a leader of the National Association for the Advancement of Colored People (NAACP), and a collector of the most poignant songs and poems produced by black Americans prior to 1930. In *Black Poets of the United States: From Paul Laurence Dunbar to Langston Hughes*, Jean Wagner called Johnson "doubtless one of the most distinguished and influential personalities the black world has ever known."

Johnson distinguished himself equally as a man of letters and as a civil rights leader in the early decades of the twentieth century. A talented poet and novelist, Johnson is credited with bringing a new standard of artistry and realism to black literature in such works as *The Autobiography of an*

An accomplished poet, journalist, and songwriter, Johnson also served as the executive secretary of the National Association for the Advancement of Colored People during the 1920s.

Ex-Coloured Man and *God's Trombones: Seven Negro Sermons in Verse.* His pioneering studies of black poetry, music, and theater in the 1920s also helped introduce many white Americans to the genuine Afro-American creative spirit, hitherto known mainly through the distortions of the minstrel show and dialect poetry. Meanwhile, as head of the NAACP during the 1920s, Johnson led determined civil rights campaigns in an effort to remove the legal, political, and social obstacles hindering black achievement.

Johnson was a "Renaissance man" before the term was popular. In his own time, Johnson was admired for his intellectual breadth, self-confidence, and leadership qualities. More than half a century after his death, he is recognized for his original contributions to American letters, his preservation of essential African American songs and poems, and his temperate civil rights agitation. Eugene Levy noted in an essay for *Black Leaders of the Twentieth Century:*

"In both roles [as literary figure and activist] Johnson fought to move beyond the severe constraints set by racial prejudice and discrimination to shape the attitudes and actions of both black and white Americans."

A Cultured Upbringing

Johnson was born in Jacksonville, Florida, in 1871, and his upbringing in this relatively tolerant Southern town may help explain his later political moderation. Both his father, a resort hotel headwaiter, and his mother, a schoolteacher, had lived in the North and had never been enslaved, and James and his brother John Rosamond grew up in broadly cultured and economically secure surroundings that were unusual among Southern black families at the time. Johnson's mother stimulated his early interests in reading, drawing, and music. "A precocious child, James was quickly reading Charles Dickens, Sir Walter Scott, John Bunyan, and Jacob and Wilhelm Grimm," noted Keneth Kinnamon in the *Dictionary of Literary Biography.* Johnson attended the segregated Stanton School, where his mother taught, until the eighth grade.

Since high schools were closed to blacks in Jacksonville, Johnson left home to attend both secondary school and college at Atlanta University, where he earned his bachelor's degree in 1894. Johnson's mother had encouraged him to enjoy music, so from his childhood onward, he sang, played guitar, and performed songs. In Atlanta he appeared with the Atlanta University quartet, entertaining audiences with spirituals and lighter popular songs of the day. Johnson's involvement with music would eventually broaden his horizons and take him far from the dusty Southern city of his birth.

It was during his college years, as Johnson recalled in his autobiography, *Along This Way,* that he first became aware of the depth of the racial problem in the United States. Race questions were vigorously debated on campus, and Johnson's experience teaching black schoolchildren in a poor district of rural Georgia during two summers deeply impressed him with the need to improve the lives of his people. The struggles and aspirations of American blacks form a central theme in the thirty or so poems that Johnson wrote as a student.

Returning to Jacksonville in 1894, Johnson was appointed a teacher and principal of the Stanton School and managed to expand the curriculum to include high school-level classes. He also became an active local spokesman on black social and political issues and in 1895 founded the *Daily American*, the first black-oriented daily newspaper in the United States. During its brief life, the newspaper became a voice against racial injustice and served to encourage black advancement through individual effort—a "self-help" position that echoed the more conservative civil rights leadership of the day. Although the newspaper folded for lack of readership the following year, Johnson's ambitious publishing effort attracted the attention of such prominent black leaders as W.E.B. Du Bois and Booker T. Washington.

Composer, Diplomat, Author

Meanwhile, Johnson read law with the help of a local white lawyer, and in 1898 he became the first black lawyer admitted to the Florida Bar since Reconstruction. Johnson practiced law in Jacksonville for several years in partnership with a former Atlanta University classmate, while continuing to serve as the Stanton School's principal. He also continued to write poetry and discovered his gift for songwriting in collaboration with his brother Rosamond, a talented composer. Among other songs in a spiritual-influenced popular idiom, Johnson penned the lyrics to "Lift Every Voice and Sing," a tribute to black endurance, hope, and religious faith that was later adopted by the NAACP and dubbed "the Negro National Anthem."

In 1901, bored by Jacksonville's provincialism and disturbed by mounting incidents of racism there, the Johnson brothers set out for New York, NY to seek their fortune writing songs for the musical theater. In partnership with Bob Cole they secured a publishing contract paying a monthly stipend and over the next five years composed some two hundred songs for Broadway and other musical productions, including such hit numbers as "Under the Bamboo Tree," "The Old Flag Never Touched the Ground," and "Didn't He Ramble." The trio, who soon became known as "Those Ebony Offenbachs," avoided writing for racially exploitative minstrel shows but often found themselves obliged to present simplified and stereotyped images of rural black life to suit white audiences. But the Johnsons and Cole also produced works like the six-song suite titled *The Evolution of Ragtime* that helped document and expose important black musical idioms.

During this time James Weldon Johnson also studied creative literature formally for three years at Columbia University and became active in Republi-can party politics. He served as treasurer of New York's Colored Republican Club in 1904 and helped write two songs for Republican candidate Theodore Roosevelt's successful presidential campaign that year. When the national black civil rights leadership split into conservative and radical factions—headed by Booker T. Washington and W.E.B. Du Bois, respectively—Johnson backed Washington, who in turn played an important role in getting the Roosevelt Administration to appoint Johnson as United States consul in Puerto Cabello, Venezuela, in 1906. With few official duties, Johnson was able to devote much of his time in that sleepy tropical port to writing poetry, including the acclaimed sonnet "Mother Night" that was published in *The Century* magazine and later included in Johnson's verse collection *Fifty Years and Other Poems*.

The consul also completed his only novel, *The Autobiography of an Ex-Coloured Man*, during his three years in Venezuela. Published anonymously in 1912, the novel attracted little attention until it was reissued under Johnson's own name more than a decade later. Even then, the book tended to draw more comment as a sociological document than as a work of fiction. (So many readers believed it to be truly autobiographical that Johnson eventually wrote his real life story, *Along This Way*, to avoid confusion.)

The Autobiography of an Ex-Coloured Man bears a superficial resemblance to other "tragic mulatto" narratives of the day that depicted, often in sentimental terms, the travails of mixed-race protagonists unable to fit into either racial culture. In Johnson's novel, the unnamed narrator is light-skinned enough to pass for white but identifies emotionally with his beloved mother's black race. In his youth, he aspires to become a great black American musical composer, but he fearfully renounces that ambition after watching a mob of whites set fire to a black man in the rural South. Though horrified and repulsed by the whites' attack, the narrator feels an even deeper shame and humiliation for himself as a black man and he subsequently allows circumstances to guide him along the easier path of "passing" as a middle-class white businessman. The protagonist finds success in this role but ends up a failure in his own terms, plagued with ambivalence over his true identity, moral values, and emotional loyalties.

Early criticism of *The Autobiography of an Ex-Coloured Man* tended to emphasize Johnson's frank and realistic look at black society and race relations more than his skill as a novelist. Carl Van Vechten, for

At the turn of the nineteenth century Johnson began composing ragtime songs for Broadway musical productions similar to this film version of *Alexander's Ragtime Band*.

example, found the novel "an invaluable source-book for the study of Negro psychology," and the *New Republic*'s Edmund Wilson judged the book "an excellent, honest piece of work" as "a human and sociological document" but flawed as a work of literature. In the 1950s and 1960s, however, something of a critical reappraisal of the *Autobiography* occurred that led to a new appreciation of Johnson as a crafter of fiction. In his critical study *The Negro Novel in America*, Robert A. Bone called Johnson "the only true artist among the early Negro novelists," who succeeded in "subordinating racial protest to artistic considerations." Johnson's subtle theme of moral cowardice, Bone noted, set the novel far above "the typical propaganda tract of the day." In a 1971 essay, Robert E. Fleming drew attention to Johnson's deliberate use of an unreliable narrative voice, remarking that *The Autobiography of an Ex-Coloured Man* "is not so much a panoramic novel presenting race relations throughout America as it is a deeply ironic character study of a marginal

man." Johnson's psychological depth and concern with aesthetic coherence anticipated the great black literary movement of the 1920s known as the Harlem School, according to these and other critics.

In 1909, before the *Autobiography* had been published, Johnson was promoted to the consular post in Corinto, Nicaragua, a position that proved considerably more demanding than his Venezuelan job and left him little time for writing. His three-year term of service occurred during a period of intense political turmoil in Nicaragua, which culminated in the landing of U.S. troops at Corinto in 1912. In 1913, seeing little future for himself under President Woodrow Wilson's Democratic administration, Johnson resigned from the foreign service and returned to New York to become an editorial writer for the *New York Age*, the city's oldest and most distinguished black newspaper. The articles Johnson produced over the next ten years tended toward the conservative side, combining a strong sense of racial pride with a deep-rooted belief that blacks could individually improve their lot by means of self-education and hard work even before discriminatory barriers had been removed. This stress on individual effort and economic independence put Johnson closer to the position of black educator Booker T. Washington than that of the politically militant writer and scholar W.E.B. Du Bois in the great leadership dispute on how to improve the status of black Americans, but Johnson generally avoided criticizing either man by name and managed to maintain good relations with both leaders.

During this period Johnson continued to indulge his literary love. Having mastered the Spanish language in the diplomatic service, he translated Fernando Periquet's grand opera *Goyescas* into English and the Metropolitan Opera produced his libretto version in 1915. In 1917, Johnson published his first verse collection, *Fifty Years and Other Poems,* a selection from twenty years' work that drew mixed reviews. "Fifty Years," a sonorous poem commemorating the half-century since the Emancipation Proclamation, was generally singled out for praise, but critics differed on the merits of Johnson's dialect verse written after the manner of the great black dialect poet Paul Laurence Dunbar. The dialect style was highly popular at the time, but has since been criticized for pandering to sentimental white stereotypes of rural black life. In addition to his dialect work, Johnson's collection also included such powerful racial protest poems as "Brothers," about a lynching, and delicate lyrical verse on non-racial topics in the traditional style.

A Civil Rights Leader

In 1916, at the urging of Du Bois, Johnson accepted the newly created post of national field secretary for the NAACP, which had grown to become the country's premier black rights advocacy and defense organization since its founding in 1910. Johnson's duties included investigating racial incidents and organizing new NAACP branches around the country, and he succeeded in significantly raising the organization's visibility and membership through the years following World War I. In 1917, Johnson organized and led a well-publicized silent march through the streets of New York, NY to protest lynchings, and his on-site investigation of abuses committed by American marines against black citizens of Haiti during the U.S. occupation of that Caribbean nation in 1920 captured headlines and helped launch a congressional probe into the matter. Johnson's in-depth report, which was published by the *Nation* magazine in a four-part

series titled "Self-Determining Haiti," also had an impact on the presidential race that year, helping to shift public sentiment from the interventionist policies associated with the Wilson Democrats toward the more isolationist position of the Republican victor, Warren Harding.

Johnson's successes as field secretary led to his appointment as NAACP executive secretary in 1920, a position he was to hold for the next ten years. This decade marked a critical turning point for the black rights movement as the NAACP and other civil rights organizations sought to defend and expand the social and economic gains blacks had achieved during the war years, when large numbers of blacks migrated to the northern cities and found industrial and manufacturing jobs. These black gains triggered a racist backlash in the early years of the decade that found virulent expression in a sharp rise in lynchings and the rapid growth of the white supremacist Ku Klux Klan terror organization in the North as well as the South. Despite this violent reaction, Johnson was credited with substantially increasing the NAACP's membership strength and political influence during this period, although his strenuous efforts to get a federal anti-lynching bill passed proved unsuccessful.

Johnson's personal politics also underwent change during the postwar years of heightened black expectations. Disappointed with the neglectful minority rights policies of Republican presidents Harding and Calvin Coolidge, Johnson broke with the Republican party in the early 1920s and briefly supported Robert LaFollette's Progressive party. LaFollette also lost the NAACP leader's backing, however, when he refused to include black demands in the Progressives' 1924 campaign platform. Though frustrated in his political objectives, Johnson opposed Marcus Garvey's separatist "Back to Africa" movement and instead urged the new black communities in the northern cities to use their potentially powerful voting strength to force racial concessions from the country's political establishment.

Literary Success

Even with the heavy demands of his NAACP office, the 1920s were a period of great literary productivity for Johnson. He earned critical acclaim in 1922 for editing a seminal collection of black verse, titled *The Book of American Negro Poetry.* Johnson's critical introduction to this volume provided new insights into an often ignored or denigrated genre and is now considered a classic analysis of early black contributions to American literature. Johnson went on to compile and interpret outstanding examples of the black religious song form known as the spiritual in his pioneering *The Book of American Negro Spirituals* and *The Second Book of Negro Spirituals*. "It is ironic that Johnson, an avowed agnostic, contributed so significantly to increased respect for the soulful richness of black Christianity," noted Kinnamon in the *Dictionary of Literary Biography*. "Before collecting spirituals, he had paid tribute in 'O Black and Unknown Bards' to their creators. Religious themes appear elsewhere in his poetry, as in 'Prayer at Sunrise' and in the untitled envoi to *Fifty Years and Other Poems*. But these are overshadowed by the superb achievement of *God's Trombones*."

God's Trombones is a set of verse versions of rural black folk sermons that many critics regard as Johnson's finest poetic work. Based on the poet's recollections of the fiery preachers he had heard while growing up in Florida and Georgia, Johnson's seven sermon-poems about life and death and good and evil were deemed a triumph in overcoming the thematic and technical limitations of the dialect style while capturing, according to critics, a full resonant timbre. In *The Book of American Negro Poetry*, Johnson had compared the traditional Dunbar-style-dialect verse to an organ having only two stops, one of humor and one of pathos, and he sought with *God's Trombones* to create a more flexible and dignified medium for expressing the black religious spirit. Casting out rhyme and the dialect style's buffoonish misspellings and mispronunciations, Johnson's clear and simple verses succeeded in rendering the musical rhythms, word structure, and vocabulary of the unschooled black orator in standard English. Critics also credited the poet with capturing the oratorical tricks and flourishes that a skilled preacher would use to sway his congregation, including hyperbole, repetition, abrupt mood juxtapositions, an expert sense of timing, and the ability to translate biblical imagery into the colorful, concrete terms of everyday life. "The sensitive reader cannot fail to hear the rantings of the fire-and-brimstone preacher; the extremely sensitive reader may even hear the unwritten 'Amens' of the congregation," declared Eugenia W. Collier in a 1960 essay for *Phylon*.

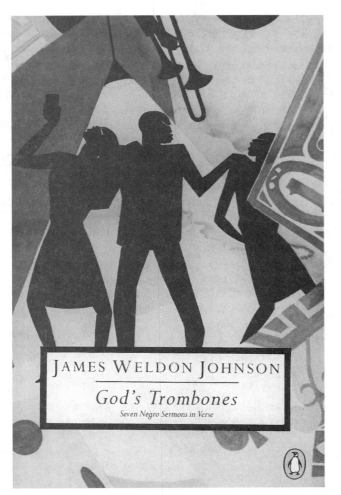

Breaking away from the use of dialect allowed Johnson to convey the dignity of the preachers who served as his inspiration for this work.

If you enjoy the works of James Weldon Johnson, you may also want to check out the following books:

Paul Laurence Dunbar, *Lyrics of Lowly Life*, 1896.
Jean Toomer, *Cane*, 1923.
Langston Hughes, *The Weary Blues*, 1926.

Johnson's efforts to preserve and win recognition for black cultural traditions drew praise from such prominent literary figures as H.L. Mencken and Mark Van Doren and contributed to the spirit of racial pride and self-confidence that marked the efflorescence of black music, art, and literature in the 1920s known as the Harlem Renaissance. This period of intense creative innovation forms the central subject of *Black Manhattan*, Johnson's informal survey of black contributions to New York's cultural life beginning as far back as the seventeenth century. The critically well-received volume focuses especially on blacks in the theater but also surveys the development of the ragtime and jazz musical idioms and discusses the earthy writings of Harlem Renaissance poets Langston Hughes, Countee Cullen, and Claude McKay. "*Black Manhattan* is a document of the 1920's—a celebration, with reservations, of both the artistic renaissance of the era and the dream of a black metropolis," noted critic Allan H. Spear in his preface to the 1968 edition of Johnson's book.

In December 1930, fatigued by the demands of his job and wanting more time to write, Johnson resigned from the NAACP and accepted a part-time teaching post in creative literature at Fisk University in Nashville, Tennessee. In 1933, he published his much-admired autobiography *Along This Way,* which discusses his personal career in the context of the larger social, political, and cultural movements of the times. Johnson remained active in the civil rights movement while teaching at Fisk, and in 1934 he published a book-length argument in favor of racial integration titled *Negro Americans, What Now?* The civil rights struggle also figures in the title poem of Johnson's last major verse collection, *Saint Peter Relates an Incident: Selected Poems.* Inspired by an outrageous act of public discrimination by the federal government against the mothers of black soldiers killed in action, Johnson's satirical narrative poem describes a gathering of veterans' groups to witness the Resurrection Day opening of the Tomb of the Unknown Soldier. When this famous war casualty is finally revealed, he turns out to be black, a circumstance that provokes bewilderment and consternation among the assembled patriots. Despite this original conceit, the poem is generally regarded as one of Johnson's lesser efforts, hampered by structural flaws and somewhat bland writing.

Johnson died tragically in June 1938 after a train struck the car he was riding in at an unguarded rail crossing in Wiscasset, Maine. The poet and civil rights leader was widely eulogized and more than two thousand mourners attended his Harlem funeral. Known throughout his career as a generous and invariably courteous man, Johnson once summed up his personal credo as a black American in a pamphlet published by the NAACP: "I will not allow one prejudiced person or one million or one hundred million to blight my life. I will not let prejudice or any of its attendant humiliations and injustices bear me down to spiritual defeat. My inner life is mine, and I shall defend and maintain its integrity against all the powers of hell." Johnson was buried in Brooklyn's Greenwood Cemetery dressed in his favorite lounging robe and holding a copy of *God's Trombones* in his hand.

Throughout his long and busy life, Johnson strove to end discrimination in America. By example and exhortation, he encouraged African Americans to become educated, to express themselves creatively, and to work hard for political power. Above all else, he was a staunch advocate of black pride, empowerment, and self-assertion, but he simultaneously called for interracial communication and cooperation. "Johnson was not the man to throw down the gauntlet to America," wrote Wagner. "He preferred to appeal to its reason and to persuade it that, since blacks and whites are irrevocably destined to live in association, the welfare of one group can only be maintained through assuring the welfare of another."

■ Biographical and Critical Sources

BOOKS

African American Writers, 2nd edition, Scribner's (New York, NY), 2001.

American Decades, Gale (Detroit, MI), 1998.

Baker, Houston A., Jr., *Singers of Daybreak: Studies in Black American Literature,* Howard University Press (Washington, DC), 1974.

Bell, Bernard W., *The Afro-American Novel and Its Tradition,* University of Massachusetts Press (Amherst, MA), 1987.

Bone, Robert A., *The Negro Novel in America,* Yale University Press (New Haven, CT), 1958.

Bronz, Stephen H., *Roots of Negro Racial Consciousness, the 1920s: Three Harlem Renaissance Authors,* Libra Publishers (New York, NY), 1964.

Contemporary Black Biography, Volume 5, Gale (Detroit, MI), 1993.

Dictionary of Literary Biography, Volume 51: *Afro-American Writers from the Harlem Renaissance to 1940,* Gale (Detroit, MI), 1987.

Egypt, Ophelia Settle, *James Weldon Johnson,* Crowell (New York, NY), 1974.

Encyclopedia of World Biography, 2nd edition, Gale (Detroit, MI), 1998.

Fleming, Robert E., *James Weldon Johnson,* Twayne (Boston, MA), 1987.

Fleming, Robert E., *James Weldon Johnson and Arna Wendell Bontemps: A Reference Guide,* G.K. Hall (Boston, MA), 1978.

Franklin, John Hope, and August Meier, editors, *Black Leaders of the Twentieth Century,* University of Illinois Press (Urbana, IL), 1982.

Gayle, Addison, Jr., *The Way of the New World: The Black Novel in America,* Doubleday (Garden City, NY), 1975.

Gloster, Hugh Morris, *Negro Voices in American Fiction,* University of North Carolina Press (Chapel Hill, NC), 1948.

Johnson, James Weldon, *Along This Way: The Autobiography of James Weldon Johnson,* Viking (New York, NY), 1933, Da Capo (New York, NY), 1973, reprinted with a new introduction by Sondra K. Wilson, 2000.

Kostelanetz, Richard, *Politics in the African-American Novel: James Weldon Johnson, W.E.B. Du Bois, Richard Wright, and Ralph Ellison,* Greenwood Press (New York, NY), 1991.

Levy, Eugene, *James Weldon Johnson: Black Leader, Black Voice,* Chicago University Press (Chicago, IL), 1973.

Notable Black American Men, Gale (Detroit, MI), 1998.

Novels for Students, Volume 22, Gale (Detroit, MI), 2005.

Poetry for Students, Volume 1, Gale (Detroit, MI), 1997.

Price, Kenneth M., and Lawrence J. Oliver, *Critical Essays on James Weldon Johnson,* G.K. Hall (Boston, MA), 1997.

Reference Guide to American Literature, 3rd edition, Gale (Detroit, MI), 1994.

Rubin, Louis D., Jr., and Blyden Jackson, *Black Poetry in America: Two Essays in Historical Interpretation,* Louisiana State University Press (Baton Rouge, LA), 1974.

St. James Encyclopedia of Popular Culture, St. James Press (Detroit, MI), 2000.

Stepto, Robert B., *From Behind the Veil: A Study of Afro-American Narrative,* University of Illinois Press (Urbana, IL), 1979.

Tolbert-Rouchaleau, Jane, *James Weldon Johnson,* Chelsea House (New York, NY), 1988.

Twentieth-Century Literary Criticism, Gale (Detroit, MI), Volume 19, 1986, Volume 175, 2006.

Wagner, Jean, *Black Poets of the United States: From Paul Laurence Dunbar to Langston Hughes,* translated by Kenneth Doublas, University of Illinois Press (Urbana, IL), 1973.

PERIODICALS

African American Review, spring, 1996, p. 17; summer, 1997, Robert E. Fleming, review of *The Selected Writings of James Weldon Johnson,* pp. 351-352; fall, 1999, John Sheehy, "The Mirror and the Veil," p. 401; Thomas L. Morgan, summer, 2004, "The City as Refuge," p. 213; fall, 2005, Michael Nowlin, "James Weldon Johnson's Black Manhattan and the Kingdom of American Culture," p. 315.

America, December 10, 1994, John W. Donohue, "Of Many Things," p. 2.

American Literature, March, 1971.

American Quarterly, winter, 1980, pp. 540-558.

CLA Journal, December, 1974, pp. 198-210; September, 1979, pp. 60-70.

Crisis, June, 1971.

Critique, December, 1971, pp. 5-14.

Jet, June 19, 1995, "James Weldon Johnson," p. 20; March 15, 2004, "James Weldon Johnson Remembered," p. 24.

Journal of Popular Culture, spring, 1968.

Nation, July 2, 1938.

Negro American Literature Forum, March, 1969, pp. 22-24, 29.

New Republic, February 1, 1928; February 21, 1934.

Newsweek, July 4, 1938.

Phylon, December, 1960; winter, 1971; winter, 1972, pp. 383-395.

Publishers Weekly, December 12, 1994, p. 61.

School Library Journal, May, 1994, p. 108; February, 1995, p. 92.

Southern Literary Journal, spring, 1979, pp. 43-55; spring, 1996, Martin Japtok, "Between 'Race' as Construct and 'Race' as Essence," p. 32.

Time, July 4, 1938.

Virginia Quarterly Review, summer, 1973, pp. 433-449.

ONLINE

Academy of American Poets Web site, http://www.poets.org/ (July 15, 2006), "James Weldon Johnson."*

William Kennedy

■ Personal

Born January 16, 1928, in Albany, NY; son of William J. (a deputy sheriff) and Mary Elizabeth (a secretary) Kennedy; married Ana Daisy (Dana) Sosa (a former actress and dancer), January 31, 1957; children: Dana Elizabeth, Katherine Anne, Brendan Christopher. *Education:* Siena College, B.A., 1949.

■ Addresses

Home—R.D. 3, Box 508, Averill Park, NY 12018. *Office*—Department of English, State University of New York at Albany, 1400 Washington Ave., Albany, NY 12222; NYS Writers Institute, Washington Avenue, Albany, NY 12222-0001. *Agent*—Liz Darhansoff, 1220 Park Ave., New York, NY 10028.

■ Career

Post Star, Glen Falls, NY, assistant sports editor and columnist, 1949-50; *Times-Union*, Albany, NY, reporter, 1952-56, special writer, 1963-70, and film critic, 1968-70; *Puerto Rico World Journal*, San Juan, assistant managing editor and columnist, 1956; *Miami Herald*, Miami, FL, reporter, 1957; correspondent for Time-Life publications in Puerto Rico, and reporter for Dorvillier (business) newsletter and Knight Newspapers, 1957-59; *Star*, San Juan, founding managing editor, 1959-61; full-time fiction writer, 1961-63; book editor of *Look* magazine, 1971. State University of New York at Albany, lecturer, 1974-82; New York State Writers Institute, founder and professor of English, beginning 1983; Writers Institute at Albany, founder, 1983, director, beginning 1984. Visiting professor of English, Cornell University, 1982-83. Cofounder, Cinema 750 (film society), Rennselaer, NY, 1968-70; organizing moderator for series of forums on the humanities lecturer and panelist. *Military service:* U.S. Army, 1950-52; sports editor and columnist for Army newspapers; became sergeant.

■ Member

Writers Guild of America, PEN, American Academy of Arts and Letters.

■ Awards, Honors

Award for reporting, Puerto Rican Civic Association (Miami, FL), 1957; Page One Award, Newspaper Guild, 1965, for reporting; New York State Publishers Award for Community Service (with staff of *Times-Union*), 1965, for series of articles on Albany's slums; National Association for the Advancement of Colored People award, 1965, for reporting; Writer of the Year Award, Friends of the Albany Public Library, 1975; National Endowment for the Arts fellowship, 1981; MacArthur Foundation fellowship, 1983; National Book Critics' Circle Award, 1983, and Pulitzer Prize for fiction, 1984, both for *Ironweed;* New York State Governor's Arts Award, 1984; honored by citizens of Albany and State University of New York at Albany with "William Kennedy's Albany" celebration, September 6-9, 1984; Before Columbus Foundation American Book Award, 1985, for *O Albany!;* Brandeis University Creative Arts Award, 1986; named commander, Order of Arts and Letters (France), 1993; PEN/Faulkner Award nomination, 2003, for *Roscoe;* L.H.D., Russell Sage College, 1980, Rensselaer Polytechnic Institute, 1987, Fordham University, 1992, and Trinity College, 1992; Litt.D., Siena College, 1984, and College of St. Rose, 1985.

■ Writings

NOVELS

The Ink Truck, Dial (New York, NY), 1968, reprinted, Viking (New York, NY), 1984.

Legs (also see below), Coward (New York, NY), 1975.

Billy Phelan's Greatest Game (also see below), Viking (New York, NY), 1978.

Ironweed (also see below), Viking (New York, NY), 1983.

Quinn's Book, Viking (New York, NY), 1988.

Very Old Bones, Viking (New York, NY), 1992.

The Flaming Corsage, Viking (New York, NY), 1996.

The Albany Trilogy (contains *Legs, Billy Phelan's Greatest Game,* and *Ironweed*), Penguin (New York, NY), 1996.

Roscoe, Viking (New York, NY), 2002.

SCREENPLAYS

(With Francis Ford Coppola and Mario Puzo) *The Cotton Club* (produced by Orion Pictures, 1984), St. Martin's Press (New York, NY), 1986.

Ironweed (based on Kennedy's novel), Tri-Star Pictures, 1987.

Also author of screenplay *Legs* for Gene Kirkwood and *Billy Phelan's Greatest Game* for Pepper-Prince Company.

OTHER

Getting It All, Saving It All: Some Notes by an Extremist, New York State Governor's Conference on Libraries, 1978.

(Contributor) *Gabriel García Márquez* (criticism), Taurus Ediciones, 1982.

O Albany!: An Urban Tapestry (nonfiction), Viking (New York, NY), 1983, published as *O Albany!: Improbable City of Political Wizards, Fearless Ethnics, Spectacular Aristocrats, Splendid Nobodies, and Underrated Scoundrels,* Penguin (New York, NY), 1985.

(With son, Brendan Kennedy) *Charlie Malarkey and the Belly-Button Machine* (juvenile), illustrated by Glen Baxter, Atlantic Monthly Press (Boston, MA), 1986.

(Author of introduction) *The Making of Ironweed,* Penguin (New York, NY), 1988.

Riding the Yellow Trolley Car: Selected Nonfiction, Viking (New York, NY), 1994.

(With Mary Lynch Kennedy and Hadley M. Smith) *Writing in the Disciplines: A Reader for Writers,* Prentice Hall (Englewood Cliffs, NJ), 1996.

Conversations with William Kennedy, edited by Neila C. Seshachari, University Press of Mississippi (Jackson, MS), 1997.

Also author of unpublished novel *The Angels and the Sparrows,* and of monographs and brochures for the New York State Department of Education, New York State University System, New York Governor's Conference on Libraries, Empire State College, Schenectady Museum, and New York State Library. Contributor of short fiction to journals, including *San Juan Review, Epoch,* and *Harper's;* contributor of articles, interviews, and reviews to periodicals, including *New York Times Magazine, National Observer, New York Times Book Review, Washington Post Book World, New Republic,* and *Look.*

■ Adaptations

The Ink Truck (audiocassette; includes *Legs, Billy Phelan's Greatest Game,* and *Ironweed*), American Audio Prose, 1984; *Ironweed* was adapted for audiocassette, Books on Tape, 1986, and a film starring Jack Nicholson and Meryl Streep, Taft Barish, 1987; *Legs* was adapted for audiocassette, Books on Tape, 1986; *Billy Phelan's Greatest Game* was adapted for audiocassette, Books on Tape, 1986.

■ Sidelights

William Kennedy rose from literary obscurity to national renown with the publication in 1983 of his novel *Ironweed.* With his first three novels failing to attract much interest from readers or critics, Kennedy was known primarily as a respected and versatile journalist who had worked for Albany, New York's *Times-Union*, the *Miami Herald*, and San Juan, Puerto Rico's *Star* newspapers. *Columbia Journalism Review* writer Michael Robertson cited former editor William J. Dorvillier's comment that Kennedy was "one of the best complete journalists—as reporter, editor, whatever—that I've known in sixty years in the business."

Not surprisingly, when Kennedy's *Ironweed* won the Pulitzer Prize, his three early novels were reissued and became best sellers. A regionalist, his gritty, downbeat fiction forms an intricate cycle spanning the history of his native Albany, New York. Like William Faulkner, who set his writings in Mississippi's imaginary Yoknapatawpha County, Kennedy sets his fiction in an Albany of the past which combines elements from both history and his own imagination.

A Roll of the Dice

Kennedy was born in Albany, New York, in 1928 to William Joseph and Mary Elizabeth McDonald Kennedy. He told Curt Suplee in the *Washington Post:* "I grew up in a very isolated pocket of Albany called the North End. . . . My father was involved in politics and wound up as deputy sheriff. . . . My mother worked all her life as a secretary. I'm just an only child—the only child in practically the whole family. It was that phenomenon that made me want to write my first novel—what happened to this family, why are there no kids." As a child, Kennedy's idols were hustlers and baseball players; he hung out in pool halls and bowling alleys and was an avoid movie goer. To broaden the boy's experiences, his father took him to political clubs and gaming rooms. Speaking to Margaret Croyden in the *New York Times Magazine*, Kennedy remembered: "Everyone was involved in some kind of gambling, including me when I was a kid. As soon as you were old enough to go to a candy store by yourself, you could play the punchboard. If you had an extra penny, you took a chance and you won something—a nickel, a dime, a quarter. Baseball pools were one of the biggest enterprises; I ran a football pool when I was in college. It was an accepted part of life. It was normal."

According to Edward C. Reilly in the *Dictionary of Literary Biography,* while growing up in Albany, Kennedy was "introduced to Irish-Democratic politics, most notably the United States' first Irish-Democratic political machine, which was organized and perpetuated by Daniel Peter O'Connell, whom Kennedy fictionalizes in *Billy Phelan's Greatest Game* as political boss Patsy McCall. In addition, "Big Jim" Carroll, Kennedy's great-grandfather, was an influential political leader in Albany's Ninth Ward; William Kennedy, Sr., was a deputy sheriff who worked the polls. On his mother's side, uncles Coop and Jim McDonald were political appointees." Kennedy wrote in *O Albany!* that "it was a common Albany syndrome for children to grow up obsessed with being a Democrat. Your identity was fixed by both religion and politics, but from the political hierarchy came the way of life: the job, the perpetuation of the job, the dole when there was no job, the loan when there was no dole, the security of the neighborhood, the new street-light, the new sidewalk, the right to run your bar after hours or to open a cardgame on the sneak. These things came to you not by right of citizenship. Republicans had no such rights. They came to you because you gave allegiance to Dan O'Connell and his party."

Kennedy served as an altar boy and attended the Christian Brothers Academy in Albany. In the sixth grade he began to play with a toy printing press, which led to his thinking about writing for a newspaper as a career. By the time he went to Siena College, a small Catholic school near Albany, Kennedy had set his sights on becoming a journalist and became editor of the Siena College newspaper. With his bachelor's degree in English, Kennedy secured a job as a sportswriter for the Glens Falls, New York *Post-Star*. His new career was interrupted when he was drafted into the U.S. Army at the start of the Korean War. While stationed in Europe, Kennedy realized that he was not interested in being a sportswriter. Even more important, he realized he did not want to stay in Albany. "I felt I had probably outgrown Albany, the way you outgrow childhood," he told Susan Chira in the *New York Times.*

Moves South to Puerto Rico

In 1956 Kennedy moved to Puerto Rico, where he was given the chance to help start the Puerto Rico *World Journal*. In a few months time, he had become the newspaper's assistant managing editor, but the paper encountered distribution and advertising problems and ceased publication soon after. The experience in Puerto Rico resulted in one happy event for Kennedy: he met and married his wife, Dana. The couple moved to Miami, where Kennedy worked for the *Miami Herald* for about a year before they moved back to Puerto Rico. In 1959, Kennedy and several other journalists founded the successful *San Juan Star*. Two years later, he had his fill of

Kennedy poses next to a poster displaying the cover of *Ironweed*, his Pulitzer Prize-winning 1983 novel.

journalism and quit, recalling to Suplee: "The shine wore off. I didn't aspire to any higher job and I knew I wanted to be a writer."

Kennedy decided to enroll in a writing workshop taught by Saul Bellow at the University of Puerto Rico. "He confirmed my belief that I had something to say. He was very, very encouraging, and helped me get an agent," Kennedy explained to Joseph Barbato in *Publishers Weekly*. Speaking to Peter Prescott in *Newsweek*, Kennedy remembered: "Bellow talked about character. I stewed on that for years. He would never tell me precisely what that meant. He said: 'Talent goes a certain distance; the rest of the writer's life has to be carried forward by character.' For me, character has come to mean pursuit of the art—refusal to yield to failure." Under Bellow's guidance, Kennedy finished his first novel, *The*

Angels and the Sparrows. "It was once again one of those downbeat books that publishers say they can't use," Kennedy told Suplee, "but a success of a high order for me—that I could write a serious novel."

In 1963 Kennedy returned to Albany to care for his ailing father. He explained to Suplee: "My mother had died, he was alone, and he was really a stubborn Irishman, wouldn't pay attention to anybody. Well, we got him straight and then I decided I'd have to come back to keep him straight for a while." Kennedy took a part-time job as a feature writer for the Albany *Times-Union*. "Send me anywhere. I'd do anything for $100," he told Suplee. In 1965, Kennedy was nominated for a Pulitzer prize for a series of articles he had written for the *Times-Union* on the city's slums.

From Journalism to Fiction

A strike at the newspaper inspired Kennedy's first published novel, *The Ink Truck*, a surreal story of a man's bizarre leadership during a prolonged newspaper strike. Reilly noted that, though based on a real-life newspaper strike, "the facts of the strike are transformed into fiction. As the novel opens, the strike has dragged on for a year—the actual strike lasted eighteen days—and most of the Newspaper Guild members have either capitulated or have been wooed back to work by the various absurd, and often nefarious, schemes that Stanley, the newspaper's manager, concocts. For example, Stanley promises raises, but, when most of the financially strained workers return, he cuts their pay. He offers all-expense-paid vacations at the newspaper's Florida resort, and many of the winter-weary strikers accept the offer." One of the few remaining holdouts is Bailey, described by *Time* reviewer R.Z. Sheppard as "a highly sexed free spirit with a loud checkered sports jacket, a long green scarf and a chip on his shoulder as big as the state capitol." *The Ink Truck*, Sheppard related, culminates in "a poignant conclusion, yet it does not show Kennedy at his full spellbinding power. Much of the book is inspired blarney, fun to read and probably fun to write." In *Library Journal*, Dorothy Curley remarked that Kennedy's "aims and characters are sympathetic" and recommended *The Ink Truck* as an "intriguing first novel." Shane Stevens, writing in the *Washington Post*, praised the novel as "inventive, circular, and multi-layered," with characters "as real as they are symbolic, the scenes as much reality as fantasy." Stevens concluded that "Kennedy has been able to confine his wickedly surrealist imagination within a well-told tale. The result is a Dantean journey through the hells of existence."

Kennedy left his part-time job at the *Times-Union* in 1970 to devote all of his time to writing. "I think it may have come, in part, from the fact that I had discovered that I could go so far and no farther in journalism; and that was why I quit to write fiction," he told Kay Bonetti in an interview for the American Audio Prose Library Web site. "From then on it was a matter of deciding how to discover what was really going on inside my mind, inside your mind, and I wasn't ever able to go back to that mundane world of realism. . . . I didn't need that

Jack Nicholson stars as Francis Phelan, a man haunted by the ghosts of his past, in the 1997 film adaptation of *Ironweed*.

much money. I didn't aspire to Bestsellerdom. I didn't aspire to big movie money or anything like that. I hoped for it. All I wanted to do was have a way of life and be able to write some fiction. And it was very, very difficult and it got increasingly more difficult. The better I got the more difficult it became."

Kennedy published the historical novel *Legs* in 1975. In preparation, he did extensive research on the gangster era of the 1920s and 1930s. *Legs,* according to Suplee, is a "fictional biography" of Jack "Legs" Diamond, the "vicious Irish-American gangster-bootlegger" who in 1931 was finally shot to death at an Albany rooming house. Kennedy's novel chronicles "Legs' attempts to smuggle heroin, his buying of politicians, judges and cops," and his womanizing, related W.T. Lhamon in the *New Republic.* A bully and a torturer who frequently betrayed associates, Diamond made many enemies. Several attempts were made on his life, and to many people, he seemed unkillable. Though vicious, Diamond was also a glamorous figure. *Listener* critic Tony Aspler indicated that writer F. Scott Fitzgerald met the gangster on a transatlantic crossing in 1926, and in the words of *Times Literary Supplement* writer Philip French, Diamond "may have been the model" for Fitzgerald's character Jay Gatsby. Legs Diamond, pointed out Suplee, "evolved into a national obsession, a godsend for copy-short newsmen, a mesmerizing topic in tavern or tearoom. Yet profoundly evil."

Billy Phelan's Greatest Game is based in part on an actual kidnapping. The book follows Billy Phelan, a small-time Albany gambler living in the 1930s who becomes caught up in the kidnapping of the nephew of the city's political boss. The plot of the novel is related by reporter Martin Daugherty. Through his eyes, wrote Suplee, "we watch Billy—a pool shark, bowling ace and saloon-wise hustler with a pitilessly rigid code of ethics—prowl among Albany's night-town denizens. But when kidnappers abduct the sole child of an omnipotent clan (patterned on the family of the late Dan O'Connell, of Albany's Democratic machine), Billy is pushed to turn informer, and faces competing claims of conscience." Kennedy told Bonetti: "Basically, Billy Phelan is a political novel. It is all about the power of a few politicians to control everybody's life, right down into the lowly hustler on the street (Billy Phelan) who all he wants to do is play pool and cards and they can lock him out of every bar in town just by putting the word out . . . that despotism, that kind of life existed here and doesn't exist any more." *Billy Phelan's Greatest Game* received a smattering of mildly favorable critical attention but did not sell particularly well; all three of the author's earlier novels sold only a few thousand copies.

Ironweed

Kennedy's novel *Ironweed* was originally accepted by Viking but later lost the vital support of the company's marketing department. In 1979 Kennedy agreed it would be best to submit the novel elsewhere. It was rejected twelve more times, and the author was disillusioned—past fifty and in debt—when Saul Bellow wrote to Viking, admonishing them for slighting Kennedy's talent and asking them to reconsider their decision not to publish *Ironweed.* Margaret Croyden, writing in the *New York Times Magazine,* quoted Bellow as saying: "These Albany novels will be memorable, a distinguished group of books. That the author of Billy Phelan should have a manuscript kicking around looking for a publisher is disgraceful." Viking ultimately published *Ironweed,* along with *Legs* and *Billy Phelan's Greatest Game* as an "Albany cycle." Kennedy explained in *Newsweek:* "The notion of a cycle of novels has been mine for more years than I can remember. I chose the word because what I propose to write is an uncertain number of inter-related novels."

Ironweed is set in Albany during the 1930s and centers on Francis Phelan, an ex-baseball player who returns to his hometown after twenty-two years on the road as a bum. Once Phelan ran from Albany after he threw a rock at a scab and killed the man during a trolley strike, setting off a riot; he was later in the habit of leaving the town and his family to play in the leagues every baseball season. When he accidentally dropped his newborn son—breaking the infant's neck and killing him—Francis ran from town and abandoned his family for good. Following an unsuccessful stint working for a local politician stuffing ballot boxes, he takes a job in the cemetery where his young son is buried. There he encounters the spirit of his child, who tells him he is about to undergo a process of "expiation." Francis decides to rejoin the family he abandoned years before, and on his way home he encounters the ghosts of several other significant persons in his past. Though his welcome is warm and he is invited to stay, he ultimately returns to a hobo jungle, where tragedy strikes. Discussing *Ironweed,* Kennedy told Bonetti: "I thought that it was my best book. I felt that I really knew what I was doing in structuring that book and it was the best language I could bring to bear on the story. I also felt that I was more able to penetrate deeply into Francis Phelan's soul than I was in any other work."

Kennedy judged *Ironweed* to be the best of his novels, and many critics agreed. In his *New Republic* review, William H. Pritchard claimed that *Ironweed* is the "best" of Kennedy's novels and "should bring

Kennedy, Francis Ford Coppola, and Mario Puzo coauthored the screenplay for the 1984 film *The Cotton Club*, starring Gregory Hines.

this original and invigorating novelist to the attention of many new readers, especially since it is written in a language that is vital throughout." Speaking of all the Albany novels, Paul Gray in *Time* stated: "Those who wish to watch a geography of the imagination take shape should read all three and then pray for more." As Prescott concluded: "Kennedy has written good fiction before, which has largely gone unnoticed. This novel . . . should place him among the best of our current American novelists. In its refusal to sentimentality, its freshness of language and the originality with which its author approaches scenes well worn before his arrival, *Ironweed* has a sense of permanence about it."

Ironweed sold more than 100,000 copies in the first two years following publication. Its success helped to sell the previous novels as well. Herbert Mitgang, writing in the *New York Times Book Review*, commented: "When *Ironweed* came out, the good response to the other books was as if they never had been published before." Kennedy told Joseph Barbato in *Publishers Weekly:* "What a coup that turned out to be. I couldn't imagine the kind of response the whole thing got when it was looked at

as a body of work. Almost everybody reviewed all three books. It was amazing." *Ironweed* went on to win both the National Book Critics Circle Award and the Pulitzer Prize for Fiction. Kennedy was also awarded a Macarthur Foundation grant for 264,000 dollars, to be paid out over a period of five years.

Kennedy's *O Albany!: An Urban Tapestry*, published the same year, is a collection of essays on his home town, part history and part autobiography. "It is the task of this and other books I have written, and hope to write," Kennedy writes in the collection, "to peer into the heart of this always shifting past, to be there when it ceases to be what it was, when it becomes what it must become under scrutiny, when it turns so magically, so inevitably, from then into now." Reilly explained that "although they need not be read to understand Kennedy's fiction, the *O Albany!* essays augment the reader' understanding of the works."

Kennedy's next novel, *Quinn's Book,* set in pre-U.S. Civil War Albany, begins another cycle centered on residents of New York's capitol city. Young narrator Daniel Quinn, an orphan working on a canal boat, rescues Maud Fallon from drowning in the Hudson River. After her rescue, Maud makes Quinn promise that he will someday rescue her from the dreary life she lives. This promise leads Daniel on a lifelong quest. "The end is a whirl of events that include sketches of high life in Saratoga and accounts of horse races, boxing matches and a draft riot," Richard Eder related in the *Los Angeles Times Book Review.* He continued: "Daniel shocks a fashionable audience with a bitterly realistic account of his Civil War experiences. Hillegond is savagely murdered; her murderer is killed by two owls jointly and mysteriously controlled by Maud and a magical platter owned by Daniel. The two lovers are lushly and definitively reunited." With these events, said Eder, *Quinn's Book* "elevates portions or approximations of New York history—Dutch, English, Irish—into legend."

"While there is a wealth of historical detail in this novel," wrote a contributor to *Contemporary Novelists,* "it is the apocalyptic opening—as Albany experiences freak disasters of fire and flood—and the surreal tinge to the events which imaginatively fire the narrative. Kennedy evokes a spirit world which shadows the lives of his characters providing sometimes comic, sometimes frightening perspectives on the past, present, and future. A sense of prescience grips the narration as Daniel grows to become the journalist-writer who views his life as a 'great canvas of the imagination.' As in his earlier novels, Kennedy intermingles fact and fantasy, but is perhaps more ambitious with his historical sweep, constructing a phantasmagoria of human actions and desires."

Although George Garrett, writing in Chicago's *Tribune Books,* called *Quinn's Book* "one of the most bloody and violent novels" he has read, the gore is necessary to tell the whole truth about life in Albany, the critic added. In this regard, Garrett elaborated, the author's "integrity is unflinching. Yet this is, too, a profoundly funny and joyous story, as abundant with living energy as any novel you are likely to read this year or for a long time to come." T. Coraghessan Boyle, writing in the *New York Times Book Review,* noted that "Kennedy does indeed have the power to peer into the past, to breathe life into it and make it indispensable, and Quinn's battle to control his destiny and win Maud is by turns grim, amusing and deeply moving. In an era when so much of our fiction is content to accomplish so little, *Quinn's Book* is a revelation. Large-minded, ardent, alive on every page with its author's passion for his place and the events that made it, it is a novel to savor." Concluded Toronto *Globe and Mail* reviewer H.J. Kirchhoff: "This is historical fiction suffused with mysticism and myth. . . . *Quinn's Book* is superlative fiction."

"Albany" Saga Continues

In *The Flaming Corsage* Kennedy covers the twenty-eight years between 1884 and 1912, concentrating on the marriage between Edward Daugherty, an Irish-American playwright, and Katrina, the daughter of a patrician family that traces its roots back to English Puritan revolutionary Oliver Cromwell. In tracing the course of this marriage, Kennedy dramatizes the conflict between Irish immigrants and the culture they struggled to adopt. Michael Gorra, writing for the *New York Times,* noted that never "before have we seen so clearly the degree to which Mr. Kennedy is not only a regional writer but an ethnic one. In the past, almost all his characters have been Irish Catholics, but here that's underlined by Edward's pursuit of the Episcopalian Katrina, a pursuit that offers a fuller sense of the society against which Irish America is defined." James B. Denigan, writing in *America,* called *The Flaming Corsage* "a complex, subtly sequenced novel that, in a florid tapestry of linguistic virtuosity, buttonholes readers with a compelling tale of guile, shame and conflict. In his novels, with their physical strength and vitality, obsession with capricious success and faith in a willful democracy hell-bent on denying class identity, Kennedy reconfirms that Albany is indeed a microcosm of America."

Kennedy's fascination with Albany continues in *Roscoe.* Although a fictional story about Roscoe Conway, a Democratic party boss immediately after World War II, *Roscoe,* like many of Kennedy's "Albany" novels, has a factual basis. With a Republican governor and an ongoing corruption investigation, Conway must put out a number of political fires surrounding the current Democratic leader in order to keep the peace and the power, while maintaining secrets that could rock the boat if uncovered. The death of Conway's long-time friend, Elisha Fitzgibbon, clears the way for him to resume his pursuit of his true love, his wife, Veronica. Noting Kennedy's talent for portraying Irish Americans who, while "self-destructive and melancholic, . . . are also wildly comic and vibrantly alive," David W. Madden added in his *Review of Contemporary Fiction* appraisal that in *Roscoe* the author "has created a rich tapestry of mid-twentieth-century America . . . home to schemers and swindlers, crooked politicians and charming rogues, the America often unacknowledged in the euphoria of the war years." Calling *Roscoe* the "most overtly political novel in Kennedy's Albany cycle," *Book* reviewer Don McCleese added that the novel eschews formal conventions for vitality. "As the author approaches his mid-seventies," the critic explained, "he plainly has plenty on his mind and little patience with formalistic conventions. . . . Kennedy is less concerned with dotting 'i's and crossing 't's than with letting the reader know how things really work—in Albany, on earth, in heaven."

If you enjoy the works of William Kennedy, you may also want to check out the following books:

John Steinbeck, *The Grapes of Wrath*, 1939.
E. L. Doctorow, *Billy Bathgate: A Novel*, 1989.
Richard Russo, *Empire Falls*, 2001.

Making use of an additional grant made available under the MacArthur Foundation, Kennedy created and became director of the New York State Writers Institute at Albany. The organization's aim is to provide aspiring writers with workshops and lectures given by well-known authors. The governor of New York signed a bill that granted the institute 100,000 dollars a year in support.

Kennedy and his wife, Dana, live in a nineteenth-century farm house in an Albany suburb. They have two daughters, one son, a grandson born the evening Kennedy won the Pulitzer Prize for *Ironweed*, and a granddaughter born two years later. Kennedy also owns a two-storey landmark building in located in downtown Albany. This former rooming-house, in which he has his office, is where the real-life gangster Legs Diamond was murdered.

■ Biographical and Critical Sources

BOOKS

Contemporary Literary Criticism, Gale (Detroit, MI), Volume 6, 1976, Volume 28, 1984, Volume 34, 1985, Volume 53, 1989.
Contemporary Novelists, 7th edition, St. James Press (Detroit, MI), 2001.
Dictionary of Literary Biography, Volume 143: *American Novelists since World War II, Third Series*, Gale (Detroit, MI), 1994.
McCaffery, Larry, and Sinda Gregory, *Alive and Writing: Interviews with American Authors of the 1980s*, University of Illinois Press (Champaign, IL), 1987.

Reilly, Edward C., *William Kennedy*, Twayne (New York, NY), 1991.
Van Dover, J.K., *Understanding William Kennedy*, University of South Carolina Press (Columbia, SC), 1991.

PERIODICALS

America, May 19, 1984; November 21, 1992, p. 410; January 29, 1994, James E. Rocks, review of *Riding the Yellow Trolley Car*, p. 29; September 14, 1996, p. 28.
American Film, January-February, 1988, "(Re)creating Ironweed," p. 18.
Atlantic Monthly, June, 1978.
Book, January-February, 2002, Don McCleese, review of *Roscoe*, p. 64.
Booklist, January 1, 2003, review of *Roscoe*, p. 792.
Chicago Tribune, January 23, 1983.
Christianity Today, May 13, 1988, p. 63.
Classical and Modern Literature, summer, 1988, pp. 247-263.
Commonweal, October 13, 1978; September 9, 1983; May 20, 1988, p. 308; May 19, 1989, p. 298; May 22, 1992, p. 28; September 13, 1996, Daniel M. Murtaugh, review of *The Flaming Corsage*, p. 36.
Critique, spring, 1986, pp. 167-184.
Detroit News, January 30, 1983; February 26, 1984.
Economist, March 2, 2002, review of *Roscoe*.
Entertainment Weekly, April 24, 1992, p. 60; July 9, 1993, p. 45; June 17, 1994, p. 66.
Esquire, March, 1985.
Film Comment, March-April, 1985, David Thomson, "The Man Has Legs."
Gentleman's Quarterly, June, 1993, p. 47.
Globe and Mail (Toronto, Ontario, Canada), September 1, 1984; December 15, 1984; May 21, 1988.
Horizon, December, 1987, Jay Parini, "Man of Ironweed," p. 35.
Hudson Review, summer, 1983.
Library Journal, October 1, 1969, William Kennedy, "On 'The Ink Truck'"; February 1, 1970, Dorothy Curley, review of *The Ink Truck*; April 15, 1996, p. 122; September 1, 1996, p. 228.
Life, January, 1985, William Kennedy, "How Winning the Pulitzer Has Changed One Writer's Life."
Listener, May 6, 1976.
Los Angeles Times, December 14, 1984.
Los Angeles Times Book Review, December 26, 1982; September 23, 1984; May 22, 1988.
National Review, August 9, 1985, Nichols Loxley, "William Kennedy Comes of Age," p. 46.
New Republic, May 24, 1975; February 14, 1983, William H. Pritchard, review of *Ironweed*; June 27, 1988, p. 41.

New Statesman & Society, June 17, 1988, p. 44.

Newsweek, June 23, 1975; May 8, 1978; January 31, 1983, Peter Prescott, review of *Ironweed;* February 6, 1984, Peter Prescott, "Having the Time of His Life"; May 9, 1988, p. 72.

New York, May 23, 1988, p. 93.

New Yorker, February 7, 1983; January 11, 1988, p. 78; April 27, 1992, p. 106; January 21, 2002, review of *Roscoe,* p. 83.

New York Review of Books, March 31, 1983; August 13, 1992, p. 54.

New York Times, January 10, 1983; September 17, 1983, Susan Chira, "Rogues of the Past Haunt an Author's Albany"; December 23, 1983; September 6, 1984, Harold Farber, "Albany Honoring a Native Literary Son for Four Days"; September 22, 1984; March 12, 1987; July 19, 1987; September 18, 1987; December 13, 1987; May 16, 1988; May 2, 1996, pp. B5, C19.

New York Times Book Review, January 23, 1983; November 13, 1983, Herbert Mitgang, "Inexhaustible Albany"; January 1, 1984; April 8, 1984, Evan Hunter, "Why Authors Are Singing the Mid-List Blues"; September 30, 1984; October 2, 1986; January 25, 1987, p. 3; May 22, 1988, p. 1; May 20, 1990, p. 1; May 10, 1992, p. 1; May 16, 1993, p. 11; May 19, 1996, p. 7; May 4, 1997, p. 32; June 1, 1997, p. 52.

New York Times Magazine, August 26, 1984, Margaret Croyden, "The Sudden Fame of William Kennedy."

Observer (London, England), October 20, 1969.

Paris Review, fall, 1989, pp. 35-59.

People, December 24, 1984; January 18, 1988, M. Ryan, "The Making of 'Ironweed'"; May 25, 1992, p. 31; June 24, 1996, p. 29.

Playboy, June, 1988, p. 22.

Poets & Writers, March-April, 1994, pp. 42-49.

Publishers Weekly, December 9, 1983, Joseph Barbato, "Man of *Ironweed*"; February 17, 1984, John F. Baker and Madalynne Reuter, "NBCC Awards"; July 5, 1985, "William Kennedy and Son Do Children's Book"; January 3, 1986; May 18, 1988, p. 71; February 3, 1992, p. 62; March 15, 1993, p. 76; June 6, 1994, p. 64; March 4, 1996, p. 52; March 17, 1997, p. 81.

Review of Contemporary Fiction, summer, 2002, David W. Madden, review of *Roscoe,* p. 227.

Rolling Stone, September 30, 1993, p. 18.

Saturday Review, April 29, 1978.

Time, January 24, 1983, Paul Gray, review of *Ironweed;* October 1, 1984, R.Z. Sheppard, "A Winning Rebel with a Lost Cause"; December 17, 1984; May 16, 1988, p. 92; April 27, 1992, p. 68; May 13, 1996, p. 92.

Times Literary Supplement, October 5, 1984.

Tribune Books (Chicago, IL), May 8, 1988.

Twentieth Century Literature, spring, 1999, Brock Clarke, "'A Hostile Decade': The Sixties and Self-Criticism in William Kennedy's Early Prose," p. 1.

Voice Literary Supplement, February, 1983; October, 1984.

Washington Post, October 5, 1969, Shane Stevens, review of *The Ink Truck;* May 18, 1975; December 28, 1983, Curt Suplee, "William Kennedy."

Washington Post Book World, January 16, 1983; January 29, 1984; October 14, 1984; May 8, 1988.

World Literature Today, summer, 1994, Marvin J. LaHood, review of *Riding the Yellow Trolley Car,* p. 580; spring, 1997, Marvin J. LaHood, review of *The Flaming Corsage,* p. 386.

OTHER

Kay Bonetti, *William Kennedy* (recording), American Audio Prose Library, 1984.*

Personal

Name is pronounced "Im-RAY KERtez"; born November 9, 1929, in Budapest, Hungary.

Addresses

Home—Budapest, Hungary. *Agent*—c/o Author Mail, Northwestern University Press, 625 Colfax St., Evanston, IL 60208-4210; c/o Magveto Press, 1055 Budapest, Balassi B. u. 7, Hungary. *E-mail*—magveto@mail.datanet.hu.

Career

Deported to Auschwitz, Poland, 1944, and Buchenwald, Germany, 1945; Vilagossag, Budapest, Hungary, journalist, 1948-51; writer and translator, 1950—.

Awards, Honors

Brandenburg Literary Prize, 1995; Leipzig Book Prize, 1997, for Diary of a Slave; Welt Prize, 2000; Nobel Prize for Literature, Swedish Academy, 2002.

Imre Kertesz

Writings

Sorstalansag: regeny, Szepirodalmi Konyvkiado (Budapest, Hungary), 1975, translation by Christopher C. Wilson and Katharina M. Wilson published as *Fateless,* Northwestern University Press (Evanston, IL), 1992, translation by Tim Wilkinson published as *Fatelessness,* Harvill (London, England), 2005.

A nyomkeresoe: ket regeny (title means "The Pathfinder"), Szepirodalmi Konyvkiado (Budapest, Hungary), 1977.

A kudarc: regeny (title means "Fiasco"), Szepirodalmi Konyvkiado (Budapest, Hungary), 1988.

Kaddis a meg nem szuletetett gyermekert, Magveto (Budapest, Hungary), 1990, translation by Christopher C. Wilson and Katharina M. Wilson published as *Kaddish for a Child Not Born,* Hydra Books (Evanston, IL), 1997.

Az angol lobogo (title means "The English Flag"), (Budapest, Hungary) 1991.

Galyanaplo (titles means "Galley Diary"), (Budapest, Hungary), 1992.

A holocaust mint kultura: harom eloeadas (title means "The Holocaust as Culture"), Szazadveg (Budapest, Hungary), 1993.

Jegyzokönyv, Magveto (Budapest, Hungary), 1993.

Valaki mas: A valtozas kronikaja (title means "I-Another: Chronicle of a Metamorphosis"), (Budapest, Hungary), 1997.

A gondolatnyi csend, amig a kivegzoeosztag ujratolt (title means "Moments of Silence While the Execution Squad Reloads"), (Budapest, Hungary), 1998.

A szamuezoett nyelv (title means "The Exiled Language"), (Budapest, Hungary), 2001.
Liquidation, Knopf (New York, NY), 2004.

Author of short stories, essays, and plays. Translator of literature and philosophy from German to Hungarian.

■ Adaptations

Fateless has been commissioned to be made into a film, financed by the Hungarian government.

■ Sidelights

When Hungarian writer Imre Kertesz won the Nobel Prize for Literature in 2002, the Swedish Academy praised him for "writing that upholds the fragile experience of the individual against the barbaric arbitrariness of history." According to Dva Forgacs in the *Dictionary of Literary Biography,* Kertesz is "a strong, independent voice in contemporary Hungarian literature. He is also a witness to the Holocaust, having survived the Auschwitz and Buchenwald concentration camps. His novels and essays fathom the Holocaust from the perspective of European historical, philosophical, and literary traditions." He became the first Hungarian writer to win the Nobel Prize for Literature, even though his works were not widely known in his native country, or in the English-speaking world. At the time he won the prize, only two of Kertesz's books had been translated into English. Kertesz attributes his neglect in Hungary to an unwillingness among the Hungarian people to acknowledge the Holocaust as well as to his own unwillingness to conform to the literary status quo during the decades Hungary suffered under Soviet oppression. "There is no awareness of the Holocaust in Hungary," Leonard Doyle quoted Kertesz as saying in the London *Independent.* "I hope in light of this recognition, they will face up to it more than until now." His books have been popular in Germany, and in a press conference covered by the Hungarian News Agency, Kertesz commented, "Here, my books are fulfilling the kind of mission a writer dreams of all his life."

Kertesz was born in Budapest, Hungary, on November 9, 1929, to a Jewish family. It was, as John Banville explained in the *Nation,* "a Jewish family so

Kertesz, who draws on his experiences as a concentration camp survivor in his works, received the Nobel Prize for Literature in 2002.

deeply assimilated into Hungarian society that they did not even consider themselves to be Jews." His father was a timber merchant; his mother worked as a clerk. When he was still a baby, his parents divorced. Kertesz was sent to a boarding school as soon as he was old enough to go. He then attended the Madsch Gymnasium in Budapest in 1940. In 1944, he was deported to the Auschwitz concentration camp and then taken to the camp at Buchenwald. Kertesz was still a teenager when he was liberated from Buchenwald in 1945 and returned to Hungary. His father had been killed during the war, as had his maternal grandparents. Following the war, Kertesz became a journalist but lost his job when the Communist party assumed power and turned his newspaper into a propaganda publication. For many years, he earned a living as a translator of literary and philosophical works, introducing works by Sigmund Freud, Ludwig Wittgenstein, and Friedrich Nieztsche to Hungarian readers. His first novel, *Fateless,* took ten years to find a publisher, and though it was initially praised in literary circles, it was not widely read. It was never banned by the government, but Kertesz's steadfast refusal to join the Communist party's official writer's association ensured that his works would never enjoy literary prominence in Hungary as long as the regime was in power.

With the collapse of the Soviet Union in the late 1980s, Hungary transitioned away from Communism peacefully, and by 1989 Kertesz's novels had gained a wider audience. A loyal following developed, particularly in Sweden and Germany, where his novels were readily available, and winning several prestigious literary prizes, including the Brandenburg Prize and the Leipzig Book Prize, strengthened his reputation.

Through his novels, Kertesz explores his belief that the Holocaust, and the kinds of torture inflicted in concentration camps, are not an aberration of history, but a state of normalcy. As Ruth Franklin put it in the *New York Times Book Review:* "Each of Kertesz's works of fiction—full-length novels and compact dramatic monologues—constitutes a building block in the unified edifice that is his great literary project." His most well-known works, *Sorstalansag* (published in English translation as both *Fateless* and *Fatelessness*), *A kudarc, Kaddis a meg nem sz'letetett gyermekert* (published in English translation as *Kaddish for a Child Not Born*), and *Felszamolas*, translated into English as *Liquidation*, form a semi-autobiographical saga in which Kertesz examines the horror and degradation visited upon the individual as a result of human animosity fueled by political power and religious intolerance. "As a Jew persecuted by the Nazis, and then a Hungarian writer living under a communist regime, Kertesz experienced some of the most acute suffering of the twentieth century," commented a writer for the Glasgow *Herald.* Thane Rosenbaum of the *New York Times* commented, "Kertesz's books are reflections on the nature of survival and the impact of the Holocaust on those who must reconcile themselves to living in a world of madness and mass death." In acknowledging Kertesz's first-hand experience with one of the greatest horrors of modern history, the Swedish Academy concluded that "for him, Auschwitz is not an exceptional occurrence. The shocking credibility of the description derives perhaps from this very absence of any element of the moral indignation or metaphysical protest that the subject cries out for." "A large corpus of writings by and about Holocaust survivors now exists," wrote Alvin H. Rosenfeld in the *New Leader.* "Rarely, however, does one encounter in this literature books as harrowing as [Kertesz's novels]—or, it should be added, as thoughtful and challenging."

In *Fateless,* written in 1965 but not published until 1975, the fifteen-year-old narrator, Gyorgy Koves, is

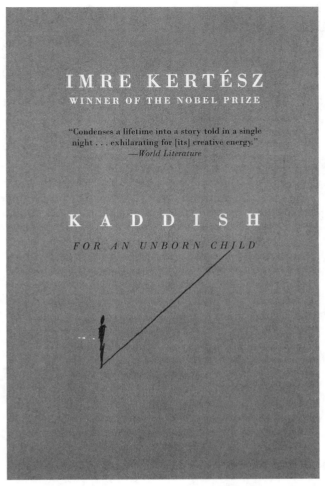

IMRE KERTÉSZ
WINNER OF THE NOBEL PRIZE

"Condenses a lifetime into a story told in a single night . . . exhilarating for [its] creative energy."
—*World Literature*

KADDISH
FOR AN UNBORN CHILD

The narrator of this story mourns for his unborn children, children he has refused to have after experiencing the horrors of the Holocaust.

taken to Buchenwald and learns to survive amid the starvation and boredom that fill his endless days. In the camp, Gyorgy is ostracized by the other Jews because he knows neither Hebrew nor Yiddish and becomes an outsider among outsiders. In order to cope in such an absurd world, Gyorgy rationalizes everything, and eventually he comes to believe that Buchenwald is a beautiful place. The concentration camp is not an aberration in his mind; it is a normal place, and Gyorgy does not bother to protest his treatment or contemplate the indignities he suffers. A reviewer for *Publishers Weekly* praised "Kertesz's spare, understated prose," noting that the novel's intensity "will make it difficult to forget." His next novel, *A kudarc,* is also narrated by Gyorgy, who is now a middle-aged novelist detailing his concentration camp experiences for a book. Upon completing the novel, Gyorgy prepares himself for rejection, but to his surprise the novel is published. He receives no solace, however, when the book is released and he continues to suffer the sadness and desolation that have plagued his entire life. "Straightforward the book may be," Banville wrote, "but it is also an extraordinary and devastating testament to the banality of evil . . . for what gives the book much of its peculiar power is the plodding doggedness of Gyorgy's effort to report accurately what happened to him, and to make sense of it."

Kertesz confronts his Jewish heritage in *Kaddis a meg nem sz'letetett gyermekert,* translated into English as *Kaddish for a Child Not Born.* Despite the book's title, Kertesz considers himself a nonbelieving Jew, even though much of his identity is tied inextricably to the religion. The book's title refers to the Jewish prayer for the dead, which in this case is said for

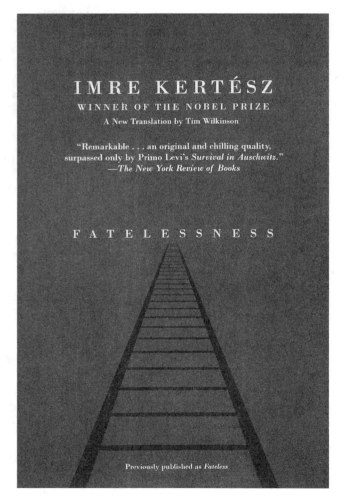

IMRE KERTÉSZ

WINNER OF THE NOBEL PRIZE

A New Translation by Tim Wilkinson

"Remarkable . . . an original and chilling quality, surpassed only by Primo Levi's *Survival in Auschwitz.*"
—*The New York Review of Books*

FATELESSNESS

Previously published as *Fateless*

Through teen narrator, Gyorgy Koves, Kertesz shows the ways the mind rationalizes things as a way of coping with life in a concentration camp.

the children the narrator could not bring himself to father, despite his wife's wishes for a family. Distrust, fear, and a Jewish identity are only three of the factors that torment the novel's narrator, a middle-aged translator and Holocaust survivor, who is eventually deserted by a loving wife because he cannot cast out his demons and live a "normal" life. The narrator hints at horrors other than the Holocaust that led to his neurosis. A traumatic childhood in Budapest, complete with the humiliating rigors of boarding school, pre-date his time in Auschwitz. These combined atrocities have left him pessimistic and faithless, circumstances under which he is not willing to create life. The sadness caused by his decision not to have children in turn leads him to mourn the absence of these children. In this cyclical despair, the Kaddish prayer becomes "a cry for death," wrote M. Anna Falbo in the *Library Journal.*

Kertesz's writing has been described as dense, and *Kaddish for a Child Not Born* is no exception. The short novel does not contain chapters, and one paragraph comprises nearly a quarter of the text. The story itself, according to Robert Murray Davis in *World Literature Today,* is similarly complex: "Part meditation, part memoir, part highly abstract and achronic narrative in the first person, part transcriptions from drafts of earlier work, part circling around a series of scenes, images, and issues without reaching any conclusion except the fact that it stops with a prayer to cease forever." Likewise, a reviewer for *Publishers Weekly* commented that the strength of the novel is the strength of the narrator, noting that "the reader is carried along on his desperate, nihilistic tirade." The novel tells of a narrator named B., who has gotten divorced from his wife when he tells her that he does not want to have a child. Having survived a period in a concentration camp, B. does not want to bring into the world a child who may have to suffer the same torments he did. "Most of all, perhaps, he feels he is illegally, unrightfully alive and, as someone who should be dead—who even thinks of himself as dead—cannot, intellectually or physically, conceive of himself as a father," according to Kelly Cherry in the *Hollins Critic.* "Kertesz," M. Anna Falbo concluded in the *Library Journal,* "has re-created a memorable, frail life in a slender work that is occasionally rambling but always compelling in its exploration of identity and the will to survive."

In 2002, Kertesz finished his novel *Felszamolas,* translated into English as *Liquidation.* The story is set in 1990, after the collapse of communism in Eastern Europe. According to Forgacs in the *Dictionary of Literary Biography,* the novel's "protagonist is B., the writer, who not only commits suicide but makes sure that his life's work, a novel, will be

Lajos Koltai directs Marceli Nagy on the set of *Fateless,* the 2005 film adaptation of Kertesz's acclaimed novel.

incinerated by his former wife. Whereas the hero of *Kaddis a meg nem sz'letetett gyermekert,* does not go beyond negating the possibility of having a child and lives to see his divorced wife having children in her second marriage, B. takes his own life and has the power over his former wife to make her execute his spiritual suicide, too."

If you enjoy the works of Imre Kertesz, you may also want to check out the following books:

Elie Wiesel, *Night,* 1960.
Thomas Keneally, *Schindler's List,* 1982.
W. G. Sebald, *The Emigrants,* 1996.

Despite the somber tone of his writing, Kertesz himself does not wallow in the mire that often traps his narrators. Alan Riding of the *New York Times*

quoted literary critic Hermann Tertsch as describing Kertesz as "a person who has created literature and culture where others would find only desolation and neurosis. . . . His smile is a permanent gesture of conciliation toward a world that at no moment deceives him. And his amiable nature seems like a generous revenge for the cruelties and miseries he has known."

■ Biographical and Critical Sources

BOOKS

Dictionary of Literary Biography, Volume 299: *Holocaust Novelists,* Gale (Detroit, MI), 2004.
Novels for Students, Volume 23, Gale (Detroit, MI), 2006.
Vasvari, Louise O., and Steven Totosy de Zepetnek, editors, *Imre Kertesz and Holocaust Literature,* Purdue University Press (West Lafayette, IN), 2005.

PERIODICALS

Daily Telegraph (London, England), October 11, 2002, Nigel Reynolds, "Holocaust Survivor Wins Nobel Prize for Literature."

Herald (Glasgow, Scotland), October 11, 2002, Thane Rosenbaum, "Survivor of Auschwitz Wins Nobel Prize; Writer's Work Looks at Ability of Man to Overcome Barbaric Forces."

Hollins Critic, April, 2005, Kelly Cherry, reviews of *Liquidation* and *Kaddish for a Child Not Born,* p. 15.

Hungarian News Agency, October 11, 2002, "Nobel Prize Winner Imre Kertesz Holds International News."

Hungarian Quarterly, winter, 2002, Peter Nadas, "Imre Kertesz's Work and His Subject," pp. 38-40; autumn, 2004, Gyorgy Dalos, "Parallel Lives," pp. 34-47.

Independent (London, England), October 11, 2002, Leonard Doyle, "Auschwitz Survivor Wins Nobel Prize for Literature."

Library Journal, June 1, 1997, M. Anna Falbo, review of *Kaddish for a Child Not Born,* p. 149.

Los Angeles Times, October 11, 2002, David Holley, "Hungarian Holocaust Survivor Is Awarded Nobel in Literature," p. A3.

Manchester Guardian, October 11, 2002, "Hungarian Camp Survivor Wins Literature Nobel."

Nation, January 31, 2005, John Banville, "Beyond Good and Evil," p. 29.

New England Review: Middlebury Series, Volume 25, 2004, Gary Adelman, "Getting Started with Imre Kertesz," pp. 261-278.

New Hungarian Quarterly, winter, 1991, Zoltan Andras Ban, "A Trilogy of Fatelessness," pp. 36-41.

New Leader, November-December, 2004, Alvin H. Rosenfeld, "The Auschwitz Disease," p. 30.

New York Times, October 10, 2002, "Hungarian Author Wins Nobel Prize in Literature"; October 11, 2002, Alan Riding, "Hungarian Novelist Wins Nobel Prize in Literature," p. A1; October 12, 2002, Thane Rosenbaum, "The Survivor Who Survived."

New York Times Book Review, December 19, 2004, Ruth Franklin, "The Inhuman Condition," p. 24.

Publishers Weekly, August 24, 1992, review of *Fateless,* p. 73; May 19, 1997, a review of *Kaddish for a Child Not Born,* p. 63.

World Literature Today, winter, 2002, Robert Murray Davis, review of *Kaddish for a Child Not Born,* p. 205.

ONLINE

BBC News, http:// news.bbc.co.uk/ (October 11, 2002), "Imre Kertesz: Literary Survivor."

National Public Radio, http://www.npr.org/ (October 10, 2002), "2002 Nobel Prize Winners."

Nobel e-Museum, http: / /www.nobel.se/ (October 10, 2002), "The Nobel Prize in Literature 2002."*

Jeph Loeb

producer, 2001-02; *Smallville* (television series), Warner Brothers, consulting producer, writer of numerous episodes, 2002-05; *Lost,* ABC-TV, writer and producer, 2004—. Awesome Entertainment, cofounder and publisher.

■ Personal

Born January 29, 1958, in Stamford, CT; married; wife's name, Christine; children: Sam, Audrey. *Education:* Columbia University, B.A., M.A.

■ Addresses

Agent—c/o Author Mail, DC Comics, 1700 Broadway, New York, NY 10019.

■ Career

Writer, screenwriter, comics creator, producer, and publisher. Film credits (as Joseph Loeb III) include *Teen Wolf,* screenplay, 1985; *Commando,* story, 1985; *Burglar,* screenplay, 1987; *Teen Wolf Too,* story and producer; 1987, *Firestorm,* producer, 1998. Television credits include *Model by Day* (television series), writer, 1994; *Maurice Sendak's Seven Little Monsters* (television series), Public Broadcasting Service (PBS), writer and producer, 2000; *Buffy the Vampire Slayer*(-unaired animated television series), executive

■ Awards, Honors

Eisner Award, 1999, for *Batman: The Long Halloween;* winner of two other Eisner Awards and five Wizard Awards.

■ Writings

COMICS PLOTS AND SCRIPTS

Batman: Haunted Knight: The Legends of the Dark Knight Halloween Specials: Three Tales of Halloween in Gotham City (contains *Batman: Legends of the Dark Knight Halloween Special, Batman: Madness: Legends of the Dark Knight: A Tale of Halloween in Gotham City,* and *Batman: Ghosts: A Tale of Halloween in Gotham City, Inspired by Charles Dickens' A Christmas Carol*), DC Comics (New York, NY), 1995.

X-Men: The Age of Apocalypse, Marvel (New York, NY), 1995.

X-Men: Dawn of the Age of Apocalypse, Marvel (New York, NY), 1996.

Onslaught: To the Victor, Marvel (New York, NY), 1997.

Wolverine Gambit Victims, Marvel (New York, NY), 1997.

Batman: The Long Halloween (contains thirteen issues of the miniseries), DC Comics (New York, NY), 1998.

Superman for All Seasons, DC Comics (New York, NY), 1999.

Superman: No Limits, DC Comics (New York, NY), 2000.

The Witching Hour, DC Comics (New York, NY), 2000.

Batman: Dark Victory, DC Comics (New York, NY), 2001.

Superman: Endgame, DC Comics (New York, NY), 2001.

Superman: 'Til Death Do Us Part, DC Comics (New York, NY), 2002.

Superman: Our Worlds at War, DC Comics (New York, NY), 2002.

Superman: The Ultimate Guide, DK Publishing (New York, NY), 2002.

Superman: President Lex, DC Comics (New York, NY), 2003.

Daredevil: Yellow, Marvel (New York, NY), 2003.

Spider-Man: Blue, Marvel (New York, NY), 2003.

Batman: Hush, DC Comics (New York, NY), Volume 1, 2003.

Batman: Hush, DC Comics (New York, NY), Volume 2, 2004.

Hulk: Gray, Marvel (New York, NY), 2004.

Challengers of the Unknown Must Die, DC Comics (New York, NY), 2004.

Catwoman: When in Rome, DC Comics (New York, NY), 2005.

Superman/Batman, Volume 1: *Public Enemies*, DC Comics (New York, NY), 2005, Volume 2: *Supergirl*, 2005, Volume 3: *Absolute Power*, 2005, Volume 4: *Vengeance*, 2005.

Supergirl: Power, DC Comics (New York, NY), 2006.

Writer for additional graphic novels and comic books for series and miniseries, including *Batman, Superman, The Avengers, Captain America, Coven, Daredevil, Fighting American, Generation X, The Savage Hulk, Kaboom, Spiderman, Wolverine, X-Force, X-Men, Challengers of the Unknown, Heroes Reborn* and *The Ultimates*.

■ Work in Progress

Onslaught Reborn, a five-art miniseries, with Rob Liefield; *Herobear and the Kid,* feature film, Universal, executive producer and writer (with creator, Mike Kunkel).

■ Sidelights

Jeph Loeb is a comic book writer best known for his work on *Superman* and *Batman* comics. Loeb, however, got his start in writing as a screenwriter, on such movies as *Teen Wolf* and *Commando,* films featuring Michael J. Fox and Arnold Schwarzenegger respectively. He has also written for and helped produce television shows such as *Smallville* and *Lost.* In his writing for comics, he has provided new aspects and dimensions to superheroes, including Batman, Superman, Spider-Man, and the Hulk, and his mini-series have been collected into numerous graphic novels. "I don't really have a niche that I like to put myself in," Loeb explained in a *BBC Online* interview. "That's what's led me through my career—not quite wanting to stay in any one place at any one time."

Gaga over Comics

Born Joseph Loeb III in 1958, Loeb was nicknamed Jeph by his mother, who did not want two Joes in the house and the ensuing confusion that would cause. He lived near New York, NY and then moved to Boston as a youth. At an early age he was an avid comic-book fan, so enthusiastic that he convinced his father to purchase a comic book collection which included every issue of the Marvel Comics published from 1961 until the late 1970s. As he noted on *BBC Online:* "I started collecting rather obsessively at the age of ten and now have this collection where my garage is supposed to be, much to the chagrin of my wonderful wife."

The move to Boston occurred when his mother remarried; his new step-father was the vice president of Brandeis University. A student at that university, Elliot Maggin, was already making a name for himself as a writer for *Superman,* and would go on to become the principle scriptwriter on that comic book from the 1970s to the mid-1980s. Knowing Loeb was a fan of the comics, the stepfather invited Maggin to dinner and he helped inspire the fourteen-year-old Loeb to write his first

Loeb, a screenwriter, producer, and comics creator, has received three Eisner Awards and five Wizard Awards for his creative achievements in comic books.

script for Superman, a story in which the superhero begins to doubt if he is doing the right thing by saving lives; perhaps these people were meant to die. When Loeb showed the story to Maggin, the older youth praised the story idea, but noted that Loeb had borrowed the ending of a *Spider-Man* comic. As Loeb noted in an interview on the Web site *Superman through the Ages,* "The fact that [Maggin] responded was thrilling, and the fact that he'd caught my hand in the cookie jar made me stop and think—'Okay. I have to figure out what comics are all about.'" That investigation would, however, be put on hold for another decade.

Meanwhile, Loeb attended Columbia University, where he earned both a bachelor's and a master's degree, the latter in film. At Columbia he studied with instructors and professional directors such as Milos Forman and Paul Schrader. Out of college,

Loeb began crafting screenplays, working with a writing partner, Matthew Weisman. Their first success was the 1985 film *Teen Wolf,* in which Michael J. Fox plays a teenager who discovers that he is a werewolf, a condition that, ironically, finally wins him popularity at school. Leonard Maltin, writing in *Leonard Maltin's 1996 Movie & Video Guide,* found this an "anemic comedy," and "pleasant at best." The film was popular enough at the box office, however, to spawn an animated television series as well as a 1987 sequel, *Teen Wolf Too,* with story and characters by Loeb. Also produced in 1985 was the Loeb and Weisman story (with a screenplay by Steven E. de Souza), *Commando,* in which Schwarzenegger plays a retired special agent forced back into activity when criminals kidnap his daughter. For Maltin, this was an "exceptionally noisy comic book yarn," a prescient remark, as Loeb had not yet considered writing for comics. The 1987 movie *Burglar,* adapted from a Lawrence Block novel, stars Whoopi Goldberg as a cat burglar who sees a murder in the course of her work, and then decides to solve the crime.

Turns to Comics

Loeb was working on a movie adaptation of the comic book superhero Flash, the fastest man alive, when an opportunity presented itself to write for comics. The Flash movie was a joint production with Warner Bros. and DC Comics, but the film was never produced. Instead, the publisher of DC at that time, Jeanette Kahn, asked Loeb if he would like to do a comic for the publishing concern. A neophyte at the industry, he immediately requested a Superman story, not knowing that there was a regular team that worked on that ever-popular superhero. In the event, his first comic book production was for the book *Challengers of the Unknown.* With that first production, he teamed up with illustrator Tim Sale, with whom Loeb has collaborated on numerous other projects. He also began working with Maggin, now an editor at DC. This was all like a dream come true for Loeb. As he noted in an interview with Sean Kleefeld for *FFPlaza.com:* "I think first and foremost I'm a comic book *fan.* I've read comics, Marvels and DC since I was a kid and now that I get to actually write them—it's just too good to be true. It's like playing sandlot ball and waking up one day and finding out you get to pitch for the Yankees."

This first comic book tale, appearing in 1991, caught the attention of fans and publishers alike, and Loeb was suddenly in demand for works with both DC and Marvel Comics, working on characters from Superman to Batman, Iron Man, Avengers, Fantastic Four, and X-Men. Speaking with the *BBC Online,* Loeb noted that he and Sale were "probably best known for *Batman: The Long Halloween,* a year-long detective serial we did for DC featuring Batman. It won numerous awards, including the Eisner, which in the world of comic books is equivalent to an Emmy. We also did *Superman for All Seasons,* which was a graphic retelling of the Superman origin in a pulp-spun Norman Rockwellian kind of way. Between those two things, while I was still writing and producing movies and television, I suddenly had a new career in the comic book industry."

With *Batman: The Long Halloween,* Loeb revamped characters from writer Frank Miller's time on the Batman character, including gangsters such as Carmine "The Roman" Falcone and the minor villain Solomon Grundy. Batman is caught up in the murders of mafia crime family members who are killed on holidays during every month of the year by a killer dubbed "Holiday." Reviewing *Batman: The Long Halloween* for *11th Hour* online, Yannick Belzil wrote that it is "the prime example of how a storyline should treat Batman, by putting him in his natural element: a mystery. . . . Writer Jeph Loeb has crafted a story that is unique to the characters. It's a complex murder mystery, but it's also a Batman story. It couldn't have been done with another character or setting—it belongs solely to the Caped Crusader." Belzil felt that "we're not often treated to the emotional side of Batman, other than the personal tragedy that took his parents away, but this story reveals his feelings about his city and the people that surround him."

In *Superman for All Seasons,* Clark Kent has recently arrived in Metropolis from Smallville and is at the beginning of his career. His story is told through several narrators, including his father, Lois Lane, Lex Luthor, and Lana Lang. Tom Knapp reviewed the book for *Rambles* online, commenting that this "is a pleasant, low-key book which, in the end, will likely stick with you far longer than the usual book about supervillains and massive brawls." Reviewing the same work for *11th Hour,* Belzil added further praise, noting: "The key ingredient to a solid comic script is heart, and Loeb's passion for the characters is obvious." Belzil further commented: "This is a great book. It's a good story with beautiful, uncluttered art—very easy to read and accessible to someone who's never read a Superman comic (or any comic, for that matter)."

Speaking with Patrick M. Gerard for the *Unofficial Golden-Age Superman Site,* Loeb noted the importance of Superman as a comic book hero: "He is so simple to identify with—you put on a cape and you fly around the house. Great stuff. All comics lead from that single point of creation. He's important!" Loeb further noted: "The one thing that makes him Superman is really Clark. That's an interesting character. He has two wonderful parents who instill in him a spark of goodness, but even after he leaves, he uses his powers to help others."

With *Batman: Dark Victory,* Batman is the Dark Knight in a story that begins where *Batman: The Long Halloween* ends and is set in Gotham City during the period in which such Batman opponents as the Joker are gaining a foothold. The character of Robin/Dick Grayson is not introduced until the end, a move that *Counterculture*'s Sion Smith said "gives the pacing a much-needed depth and a slant on the story that makes it so much fresher than its predecessors." Smith praised the characterizations of the Riddler, Two Face, and Albert the butler, adding that "this has all the look and feel of a real labor of love."

MARVEL

JEPH **LOEB** TIM **SALE**

SPIDER-MAN:
BLUE

Spider-Man battles the Green Goblin and other villians to get to Gwen Stacy, his first love.

Superheroes and Television

Batman: Hush, Volume 1, collects the first installments of a twelve-part series that brings together Loeb, illustrator Jim Lee, and inker Scott Williams. Batman's opposition includes Poison Ivy and Killer Croc, and at the same time, he pursues the luscious Catwoman. Other DC characters, including Superman, make appearances, but all are being subtly controlled by a mysterious manipulator. *Booklist* contributor Gordon Flagg felt the book did not live up to its publicity hype, writing that it is basically a "just-above average superhero saga." Other critics, however, had a more positive assessment. A *Publishers Weekly* contributor, reviewing *Batman: Hush,* Volume 1, wrote that "Loeb is especially talented at underwriting, not crowding the page full of long explanations and snappy patter; after all, readers have known these characters for years." *Library Journal* reviewer Steve Raiteri also felt that the book "makes good use of Batman's comrades." The second half of the twelve-issue miniseries was

published as *Batman: Hush,* Volume 2, in 2004. Flagg, writing in *Booklist,* felt that "few young superhero fans will resist this compelling rendition."

Meanwhile, Loeb continued to write and produce for television, including *Maurice Sendak's Seven Little Monsters* for public television, a children's show by the creator of *Where the Wild Things Are.* Loeb's television credits also include the animated version of *Buffy the Vampire Slayer,* which ultimately never found a network home and was left unaired. Thereafter, he became consulting producer for *Smallville,* a show that, in the words of *Hollywood Reporter* John Anderson, "placed mild-mannered Clark Kent in rural Kansas, where he would face off against the perils of a 'super-adolescence'—including dating, exams and x-ray vision." Aimed at the teenage demographic, the show, which debuted in 2001, became a "stalwart" for the WB Network, according to Anderson, "delivering solid ratings despite time-slot shifts and executive turnover." By its third season, the show was attracting over eight million viewers. Jennifer Armstrong, reviewing the DVD of the first season of *Smallville* for *Entertainment Weekly,* praised the "meaty characters, real relationships" and "addictive mix of supernatural thrills and typical teen angst." Loeb was with *Smallville* for several years, both as script writer and producer, leaving it to write and produce for a new ABC series, *Lost.*

Loeb continues also to be active in the world of comics. He and Sale collaborated on several modern treatments of the early years of various Marvel Comics superheroes, titling each of the works after the color of the costume each hero wears. In *Spider-Man: Blue,* Loeb reworks a story from the 1960s, a book that looks at a sad result of Peter Parker's heroism, when his girlfriend dies shortly after a battle. *Hulk: Gray* goes back to the color of that character's costume in his debut issue of 1962. A *Publishers Weekly* contributor commented that Loeb "deftly builds on the classic work of the past without making major revisions, reinterpreting it to expose and illuminate its underlying psychological depths."

If you enjoy the works of Jeph Loeb, you may also want to check out the following graphic novels:

John Byrne, *Superman: The Man of Steel,* 1991.
Frank Miller, *Batman: Year One,* 1997.
Brian Michael Bendis, *Ultimate Spider-Man,* 2002.

For DC Comics, Loeb also continued to work on various mini-series. In 2004, he revisited the quartet of superheroes with whom he got his start in comics. His *Challengers of the Unknown Must Die* is actually the work he and Sale did together in 1991, but only collected a dozen years later. It finds the four men in retirement after a tragic accident, with the remaining members having assumed aliases. But the arrival of a former enemy forces them back into action in an offering which, according to *Booklist* contributor Flagg, "demonstrates that Loeb's capacity to effectively reimagine hoary concepts and Sale's clean art and imaginative storytelling were there from the beginning."

Loeb pairs Superman and Batman in an ongoing series, the first of whose collections was *Superman/Batman* Volume 1: *Public Enemies*. In this tale Krypton, Superman's home planet, threatens Earth, and superheroes are called in to put matters right. Flagg, writing in *Booklist*, noted, "Loeb crafts a generally typical, if uncommonly elaborate story." In *Superman/Batman* Volume 3: *Absolute Power*, Loeb retells the origins of the both Superman and Batman. Loeb has also tackled female superheroes, in his tales of Supergirl, and with his 2005 *Catwoman: When in Rome*. Reviewing the latter title in *Rambles*, Knapp called the book "another winner from team Loeb and Sale." Knapp also noted that "Loeb's writing is more noirish and character-driven than the average superhero comic; he doesn't shy away from a little mayhem here and there, but it's not the central motivation of his work."

Finding a Balance

Instead of finding film and television work a jarring contrast to his work in comics, Loeb feels they feed off each other. Speaking with Daniel Robert Epstein on *UnderGroundOnline,* Loeb explained the synchronicity of his two writing styles: "My background is as a screenwriter. As such, when I started writing comics, I only had a screenwriting program on my computer, so I wrote the scripts to look like movie and television scripts. The descriptions of each panel isn't all that different from describing what is happening in a scene. Dialogue needs to be paced for film—as it does in comics. So, my artists, when they get the scripts often comment that they don't look like the 'typical' comic book script. They look like screenplays and teleplays."

Loeb explained to Mark Salisbury in *Writers on Comics Scriptwriting* how he adapted his method of writing films to writing comics: "I was taught by Paul Schrader . . . that fifty things happen in a movie. Not fifty scenes, fifty *things*. So, you number one-to-fifty on your pad and you write bullets of what's happening in the story: John meets Mary, Mary loses her leg, John goes off to war, that kind of thing. And those can be one act, one scene or they can be a whole group of scenes. By the time you get to the end of the story you've written out a whole plot. I adopted that for comics."

A test to Loeb's buoyancy came in 2005, when his seventeen-year-old son, Sam, died after a three-year battle with cancer. Sam, a promising young comic book writer himself, proved an inspiration for his father and all those he met. As Loeb commented on *Newsarama.com:* "We would often talk about the stupidity of Life—the great silliness that we all have inherited at work, at school, or in our relationships. No matter how big a problem you have or how mighty you think you are, there's still a banana peel out there waiting for you or a pie in the face. What Sam understood was that those bananas and pies weren't always literally there—they sometimes came in the form of finding yourself in a situation, whether it was about love, creativity, purpose, where you're just screwed and your only choice is to laugh."

■ Biographical and Critical Sources

BOOKS

Maltin, Leonard, *Leonard Maltin's 1996 Movie 5-Video Guide,* Signet (New York, NY), 1995.
Salisbury, Mark, *Writers on Comics Scriptwriting,* Titan Books (London, England), 1999.

PERIODICALS

Booklist, July, 2003, Gordon Flagg, review of *Batman: Hush,* Volume 1, p. 1856; April 1, 2004, Gordon Flagg, review of *Batman: Hush,* Volume 2, p. 1358; September 1, 2004, Gordon Flagg, review of *Superman/Batman* Volume 1: *Public Enemies,* p. 77; December 1, 2004, Gordon Flagg, review of *Challengers of the Unknown Must Die,* p. 643; December 15, 2005, Gordon Flagg, review of *Catwoman: When in Rome,* p. 32.
Entertainment Weekly, September 26, 2003, Jennifer Armstrong, review of *Smallville: The Compete First Season,* p. 80.
Hollywood Reporter, February 6, 2003, Scott Collins, "WB's 'Smallville' Flies High," p. 4; January 26, 2006, John Anderson, "Small Wonder," p. 23.

Library Journal, September 1, 2003, Steve Raiteri, review of *Batman: Hush,* Volume 1, p. 142.

Publishers Weekly, July 21, 2003, review of *Batman: Hush,* Volume 1, pp. 176-177; September 29, 2003, review of *Superman: President Lex,* pp. 45-46; August 9, 2004, review of *Hulk: Gray,* p. 234.

School Library Journal, July, 2004, Steve Weiner, "The Superhero Next Door," review of *Spider-Man: Blue,* p. 21; November, 2005, John Leighton, review of *Superman/Batman* Volume 3: *Absolute Power,* p. 178.

ONLINE

11th Hour, http://www.the11thhour.com/ (June 11, 2006), Yannick Belzil, review of *Batman: The Long Halloween* and *Superman for All Seasons.*

BBC Online, http://www.bbc.co.uk/ (October 22, 2001), interview with Jeph Loeb.

Comic Book Resources, http://www.comicbook-resources.com/ (May 1, 2000), Bill Baker, "A Scribe for All Seasons: Interview with Jeph Loeb"; (July 10, 2003), Arune Singh, "Don't Mess with the 'S': Jeph Loeb Talks Superman/Batman" (interview); (March 18, 2004), Arune Singh, "Super-Stars (Part 3): Jeph Loeb Talks 'Superman/Batman.'"

Counterculture, http://www.counterculture.co.uk/ (June 11, 2006), Sion Smith, review of *Batman: Dark Victory.*

FFPlaza.com, http://www.ffplaza.com/ (September 26, 2000), Sean Kleefeld, "Interview: Jeph Loeb."

KryptonSite, http://www.kryptonsite.com/ (June 11, 2006), Craig Byrne, "Jeph Loeb Talks 'Insurgence'" (interview with Jeph Loeb).

Newsarama.com, http://www.newsarama.com/ (June 11, 2006), "Jeph Loeb on 'Sam's Story.'"

Rambles, http://www.rambles.net/ (June 11, 2006), Tom Knapp, review of *Superman for All Seasons* and *Catwoman: When in Rome.*

Silver Bullet Comics Online, http://www.silverbulletcomics.com/ (October 23, 2005), Tim Harnett, review of *Superman/Batman* Volume 3.

Superman-Comics.com, http://superman.ws/superman-comics/ (August 13, 2003), Jeph Loeb, "About *Superman for All Seasons.*"

Superman Home Page, http://www.superman-homepage.com/ (September 22, 2004), Steven Younis, "Exclusive Interview with Jeph Loeb."

Superman through the Ages, http://www.theages.superman.ws/ (June 11, 2006), "Jeph Loeb and Superman."

UnderGroundOnline, http://www.ugo.com/ (June 11, 2006), Daniel Robert Epstein, "Jeph Loeb."

Unofficial Golden-Age Superman Site, http://www.superman.ws/ (October 22, 1999), Patrick M. Gerard, interview with Jeph Loeb.*

Joe Mantello

■ **Personal**

Born December 27, 1962, in Rockford, IL; partner, Jon Robin Baitz, 1990-2002. *Education:* Attended North Carolina School of the Arts.

■ **Addresses**

Agent—Creative Artists Agency, 9830 Wilshire Blvd., Beverly Hills, CA 90212.

■ **Career**

Actor, director. Stage appearances: *Crackwalker,* off-Broadway production, 1987; (as Joseph Mantello) Ticket inspector, gymnast, and second reporter, *The Visit,* Courtyard Playhouse, New York City, 1989; Stan, *Walking the Dead,* Circle Repertory Company, New York City, 1991; Third man, *The Baltimore Waltz,* Circle Repertory Company, 1992; Louis Ironson, *Angels in America: Millennium Approaches,* Center Theatre Group/Mark Taper Forum, Los Angeles, 1992-1993, then Walter Kerr Theatre, New York City, 1993-1994; Louis Ironson and Sarah Ironson, *Angels in America: Perestroika,* Center Theatre Group/Mark Taper Forum, 1992-1993, then Walter Kerr Theatre, 1993-1994; *Easter Bonnet Competition: Back to Basics,* Palace Theatre, New York City, 1995; also appeared in *Progress.* Stage director: *Imagining Brad,* Circle Repertory Theatre, New York City, 1989; *Nebraska,* Naked Angels Theatre, New York City, 1991; *Coq au Vin,* Naked Angels Theatre, 1991; *Babylon Gardens,* Circle Repertory Company, 1991; *The Innocents' Crusade,* Long Wharf Theatre, New Haven, CT, 1991-1992; *Three Hotels,* Circle Repertory Company, New York City, 1993; *Fat Men in Skirts,* Naked Angels Theatre, 1994; *What's Wrong with the Picture?,* Brooks Atkinson Theatre, New York City, 1994; *Three Hotels,* Centre Theatre Group, Mark Taper Forum, Los Angeles, 1994-1995; *Love! Valour! Compassion!,* Manhattan Theatre Club, Stage I, New York City, 1994-1995, then Walter Kerr Theatre, 1995, later Geffen Playhouse, Los Angeles, 1996-1997; *Blue Window,* Manhattan Theatre Club, Stage I, 1996; *The Santaland Diaries,* Atlantic Theatre, New York City, 1996; *God's Heart,* Lincoln Center, New York City, 1997; *Proposals,* Broadhurst Theatre, New York City, 1997; *Mizlansky/Zilinsky or "Schmucks,"* Manhattan Theatre Club, 1998; *Lillian,* New Theatre Wing, New York City, 1998; *House,* Bay Street Theatre, Sag Harbor, NY, 1998; *Corpus Christi,* Manhattan Theatre Club, 1998; *Bash,* 1999; *The Mineola Twins,* Laura Pels Theatre, New York City, 1999-2000; *The Vagina Monologues,* Westside Theater (Downstairs), New York City, 1999-2003; *Another American: Asking & Telling,* 1999; *Dead Man Walking,* San Francisco Opera, 2000; *Design for Living,* Roundabout Theatre Company, 2001; *Assassins,* Music Box Theatre, New York City,

2001, Studio 54, New York City, 2004; *Take Me Out*, Donmar Warehouse, London, then Walter Kerr Theatre, New York City, 2002; *Frankie and Johnny in the Clair de Lune*, Belasco Theater, New York City, 2002; *A Man of No Importance*, Mitzi Newhouse Theater, New York City, 2002; *Wicked*, Gershwin Theatre, New York City, 2003; *Pacific Overtures*, Studio 54, New York City, 2004; *Laugh Whore*, Cort Theatre, New York City, 2004; *Glengarry Glen Ross*, Royale Theatre, New York City, 2005; *The Odd Couple*, Brooks Atkinson Theatre, New York City, 2005; *Three Days of Rain*, Bernard B. Jacobs Theatre, New York City, 2006; also directed *Snakebit*, New York Stage and Film; *Three Hotels*, Bay Street Theatre Festival, Sag Harbor, NY. Film appearances: Dominick, *Cookie*, Warner Bros., 1989; *Showbusiness: A Season to Remember*, 2005. Film director: *Love! Valour! Compassion!*, Fine Line Cinema, 1997. Television appearances: *Three Hotels*, 1990; public defender, "Confession," *Law and Order*, NBC, 1991; Adam Oldenberg, "Moving Pictures," *Sisters*, NBC, 1992; *In the Wings: Angels in America on Broadway*, PBS, 1993; Ian Walker, *Central Park West*, CBS, 1995; Philip Marco, "Tabloid," *Law and Order*, NBC, 1998. Television director: *Bash: Latterday Plays*, Showtime, 2000; (and executive producer) *New Year* (pilot), TNT, 2000; *The Vagina Monologues*, HBO, 2002; *And Then One Night: The Making of 'Dead Man Walking,'* PBS, 2002. Cofounder, Edge Theatre, New York, NY.

■ Awards, Honors

Joe A. Callaway Award; Helen Hayes Award; Clarence Derwent Award, Tony Award nomination for Best Featured Actor in a Play, and Drama Desk Award for Outstanding Featured Actor in a Play, all 1993, and all for *Angels in America: Millennium Approaches*; Tony Award nomination for Best Director of a Play, and OBIE Award for Direction, both 1995, for *Love! Valour! Compassion!*; OBIE Award citation, 2000, for *Another American: Asking and Telling* (shared with actor Marc Wolf); Drama Desk nomination for Best Director of a Musical, for *A Man of No Importance*; Lucille Lortel Award for Outstanding Director, Drama Desk nomination for Best Director of a Play, Outer Critics Circle Award for Best Director of a Play, Drama League's Julia Hansen Award for Excellence in Directing, and Tony Award for Best Director of a Play, all 2003, and all for *Take Me Out*; Drama Desk Award for Outstanding Director of a Musical, and Outer Critics Circle Award for Outstanding Direction of a Musical, both 2004, for *Wicked*; Tony Award for Best Direction of a Musical, 2004, for *Assassins*; Drama Desk Award nomination for Outstanding Direction of a Play, Outer Critics Circle Award nomination for Outstanding Direction

of a Play, and Tony Award nomination for Best Director of a Play, all 2005, for *Glengarry Glen Ross*; Apple Award, New York Casting Society of America, for significant contribution to the New York theatre community, 2006.

■ Writings

Contributor of articles to periodicals and online journals.

■ Work in Progress

Blackbird, director of stage play, Manhattan Theatre Club, New York, NY, 2007.

■ Sidelights

Joe Mantello is, in the words of a *Vogue* contributor, "the most protean, accomplished theater director of his generation, heir to a line descended for Elia Kazan and Mike Nichols." *Variety* critic David Rooney praised Mantello as "the most versatile talent in New York theatre." Such versatility is shown not only in the range of genres he has directed, but also in the "Mount Rushmore of contemporary dramatists" whose work he has staged, as the critic for *Vogue* noted. These include writers from the humorists Neil Simon, Noel Coward, and David Sedaris, to the dramas of Jon Robin Baitz, Richard Greenberg, David Mamet, and Terrence McNally, and to the musical works of Stephen Sondheim. His directorial works include searing and comic monologues, such as *The Vagina Monologues* and *The Santaland Diaries*, to mordant and witty duologues, such as *Frankie and Johnny in the Clair de Line*, and offbeat musicals, such as *Assassins* and *Wicked*. "If there's a pattern there, it's unknown to me," Mantello told Rooney. "I learned a while back simply to follow my instincts. I just try to take everything on its own terms. For me, it's also about having a good time."

Beginning his theatrical career as an actor, Mantello made his first Broadway breakthrough with the 1995 production of *Love! Valour! Compassion!*, a trenchant comedy about eight gay men who, sharing a summerhouse, reconsider their lives in the time of AIDS. Mantello, himself gay, made his acting breakthrough in Tony Kushner's *Angels in America*. In all his work,

Mantello directed both the stage version and the 1997 film adaptation of Terrence McNally's *Love! Valour! Compassion!*

Mantello has, as the reviewer for *Vogue* observed, "shown a particular gift for capturing the Darwinian group dynamics of men thrown together by choice or by chance."

Both Sides of the Stage

The oldest of three boys, Mantello was born in Rockford, Illinois, in 1962. Though his family was long assimilated, Mantello retained much of the Italian temperament of his heritage. "Here I was in the suburbs," he told *Los Angeles Times* writer Patrick Pacheco, "with the Smiths and the Jones, and my temperament was very Mantello, very Italian. . . . I wasn't in sync with them. . . . I was always rather outspoken. . . . I worried about what people thought of me but there wasn't room for a lot of self-doubt." For a time, Mantello considered art as a career, but finally settled on theater, attending the North Carolina School of Arts. He thought that this would lead to acting in regional theater, but a senior class trip to New York secured him an agent. Without graduating, Mantello migrated to New York, where, with fellow classmates including Peter

Hedges and Mary-Louise Parker, he founded the Edge Theater. These early days in repertory theater gave him an insight into the relationship between actor and audience which he has carried with him ever since. By 1989, he had become associated with Circle Repertory Company, acting in plays such as *The Baltimore Waltz* by Paula Vogel, and began directorial duties with 1990's *Imagining Brad.* Of his performance in *The Baltimore Waltz*, Thomas M. Disch, writing in the *Nation,* praised Mantello's "zest and drollery." He also had his first film acting role in Susan Seidelman's comedy *Cookie.*

Mantello went on to join the experimental theater company Naked Angels, and auditioning for Kushner, he began a three-year association with that playwright's groundbreaking *Angels in America,* as Louis Ironson, "a sensitive portrayal of the tortured soul who abandons his dying lover," as Pacheco commented. A contributor for *Hollywood.com* felt that Mantello "demonstrated impressive range and likability" in this role for which he earned a Tony nomination.

Focuses on Directing

Until the mid-1990s, directing was a secondary career for Mantello. However, with his production of *Three Hotels,* by Baitz, who was Mantello's partner for a dozen years, his directing career took off. Bruce Weber of the *New York Times* praised Mantello's "subtle threading together of the play's three main monologues" in this work. But it was Mantello's work on *Love! Valour! Compassion!* that established him as a new and exciting director in New York. Premiering off-Broadway in 1994, the play, by Terrence McNally, proved so popular that it moved to Broadway in 1995, and was filmed, with direction by Mantello, in 1997. Stefan Kanfer, reviewing the stage play, found Mantello's direction "unfailingly lucid." Lisa Schwarzbaum, writing in *Entertainment Weekly,* also commended Mantello's "graceful stage direction." The play earned Mantello a Tony nomination for best director and an OBIE for best director. Reviewing the feature film, *New York Times* critic Stephen Holden observed that what makes the story "so moving is that this complicated group portrait never loses its slippery emotional footing." With the theater production of *Love! Valour! Compassion!,* Mantello, just thirty-two at the time, was dubbed "one of the new Young Turks of theater," by Pacheco

Love! Valour! Compassion! was the first in a long line of plays written by McNally for which Mantello provided the direction. Perhaps most controversial

In 2003 Mantello received his first Tony Award for his directorial efforts on the Broadway play *Take Me Out.*

of these was the 1998 *Corpus Christi*, with, as Lloyd Rose noted in the *Washington Post,* "the Christ figure as a picked-on gay kid from Texas." Religious groups and free-speech groups battled one another outside the New York theater where the production opened, and critics also differed on their views of both play and director. Lloyd found both "self-consciously arty," while *Variety* critic Charles Isherwood felt the play did not "live up to the promise of its vision," yet called Mantello's staging "continually inventive." Similarly, Robert Brustein, writing in the *New Republic,* called *Corpus Christi* "show biz at its most pretentious," while at the same time commenting that "Mantello has guided his thirteen actors through this modern misery play with considerable grace." Further collaborative efforts with McNally include the offbeat unsentimental romance, *Frankie and Johnny in the Clair de Lune* and *A Man of No Importance,* an unpretentious musical about a Dublin bus conductor in 1964. For *Variety* critic Isherwood, Mantello "proves a perfect fit" for *A Man of No Importance.*

Mantello also made a name for himself as the director of numerous one-person plays, including *The Vagina Monologues* (for which he also directed the

HBO television production), *Lillian, Another American: Asking & Telling, The Santaland Diaries,* and *Laugh Whore.* Writing in *Variety,* Robert Hofler noted in 2000 that "Mantello is giving one-person shows a good name." Similarly, Raymond M. Lane, reviewing the *The Santaland Diaries* in the *Washington Post,* noted that Mantello's adaptation of Sedaris's confessional humor "has become a seasonal cottage industry, running on college campuses and at regional theaters across the country."

Of Baseball and Witches

Mantello won his first Tony Award for best director for the 2002 production *Take Me Out.* Written by Richard Greenberg, the play tells the story of a baseball superstar who comes out of the closet. Writing in *Variety,* Isherwood called it a "heady, heartfelt and enormously appealing romance spliced into a sprawling comedy." Isherwood also felt that Mantello "has nicely fine-tuned the work of his excellent cast." Reviewing *Take Me Out* in the *New York Times,* Ben Brantley observed that Mantello "has sensibly chosen to emphasize the play's less ponderous aspects." The following year, Mantello scored another success with *Wicked,* a musical adaptation of the book by the same title by Gregory Maguire, a retelling of the *Wizard of Oz.* Writing in *Time* magazine, Richard Zoglin noted that the musical works so well because it presents "a story that adults can take seriously." Zoglin further praised Mantello's "assured direction." *Wicked* earned Mantello a Drama Desk Award for Outstanding Direction of a Musical.

Mantello followed up this success with work in 2004 that saw three of his plays on Broadway: *Assassins,* a dark musical about Americans and their obsessive dreams of the assassinations of famous people, from a book by John Weidman and music and lyrics by Sondheim; *Pacific Overtures,* a revival of the 1976 Sondheim musical; and the one-man show, *Laugh Whore.* The most successful of these was *Assassins,* for which Mantello earned his second Tony. Originally written by Sondheim in the late 1980s, the play did poorly with its first run. However, "Joe Mantello's new production liberates the show from its own hokey pageantry and airs out the genius within," according to *Entertainment Weekly* contributor Scott Brown. Isherwood, writing in *Variety,* had similar praise: "Joe Mantello's flawless production makes your skin crawl even as it seduces you." Joe Calarco, writing in the *Washington Post,* found Mantello's 2004 staging of *Assassins* "breathtaking."

The ever-busy Mantello turned to two veterans of the American stage for 2005 productions: David Mamet's *Glengarry Glen Ross* and Neil Simon's *The Odd Couple.* Mantello had, in 1997, directed the Simon play *Proposals,* and was in fact the personal choice of the playwright. In his 2005 revival of *The Odd Couple,* he paired Nathan Lane and Matthew Broderick, who had made a sensation in the Broadway production of *The Producers.* While critical response for the Simon revival was mixed, the praise for Mantello's direction of *Glengarry Glen Ross* was largely positive. Rooney, reviewing the Mamet play in *Variety,* wrote: "This smart, energetic revival continues the formidable run of Mantello, whose work . . . confirms an astonishing range, consistency and implicit trust in his material."

Mantello directed the 2005 revival of *Glengarry Glen Ross,* David Mamet's powerful drama about greed and corruption.

If you enjoy the works of Joe Mantello, you may also want to check out the following plays:

Tennessee Williams, *A Streetcar Named Desire*, 1947.
Neil Simon, *The Sunshine Boys*, 1972.
Stephen Sondheim, *Sweeney Todd,*, 1989.

Speaking with Rooney, Mantello noted that he had no idea where his career would take him next: "I don't think of my career, I just think of what's the next thing that catches my eye. . . . You have to accept that [directing is] a roller coaster and not get morally bankrupt by constantly asking 'How am I doing?'"

■ Biographical and Critical Sources

BOOKS

Contemporary Theatre, Film, and Television, Volume 53, Gale (Detroit, MI), 2004.

PERIODICALS

Los Angeles Times, November 14, 1992, Karen Fricker, "Joe Mantello's Many Choices," p. F2; March 19, 1995, Patrick Pacheco, "Mr. Mantello's Wild Ride," p. 7; July 13, 1997, Sean Mitchell, "The Unlikely Couple," p. 3.
Nation, March 23, 1992, Thomas M. Disch, review of *The Baltimore Waltz,* p. 389.
New Leader, June 14, 1993, review of *Angels in America,* p. 22; December 13, 1993, Stefan Kanfer, review of *Angels in America,* p. 22; February 13, 1995, Stefan Kanfer, review of *Love! Valour! Compassion!,* p. 23; December 1, 1997, Stefan Kanfer, review of *Proposals,* p. 22.
New Republic, November 30, 1998, Robert Brustein, review of *Corpus Christi,* p. 34.
Newsweek, March 2, 1998, Jack Kroll, review of *Mizlansky/Zilinsky, or "Schmucks,"* p. 80.
New York, February 16, 1998, Judith Stone, "Playmates," p. 36.
New Yorker, November 10, 2003, John Lahr, review of *Wicked,* p. 126; May 3, 2004, John Lahr, review of *Assassins,* p. 98; November 7, 2005, John Lahr, review of *The Odd Couple,* p. 144.

New York Times, October 30, 1994, Bruce Weber, "Couple of the Moment in New York Theater," p. A1; February 15, 1995, Vincent Canby, review of *Love! Valour! Compassion!,* p. C9; May 16, 1997, Stephen Holden, review of *Love! Valour! Compassion!* (film); September 3, 1998, Robin Pogrebin, "Play That Stirred Outcry Prepares for Its Opening," p. E1; February 28, 2003, Ben Brantley, review of *Take Me Out,* p. E1; October 28, 2005, Ben Brantley, review of *The Odd Couple,* p. E1.
Nine, fall, 2005, Mary Groebner, review of *Take Me Out,* p. 189.
Time, November 23, 1992, William A. Henry, III, review of *Angels in America,* p. 72; May 17, 1993, William A. Henry, III, review of *Angels in America,* p. 62; November 17, 2003, Richard Zoglin, review of *Wicked,* p. 143.
Variety, February 3, 1997, Emanuel Levy, review of *Love! Valour! Compassion!* (film), p. 45; November 10, 1997, Greg Evans, review of *Proposals,* p. 51; February 23, 1998, Greg Evans, review of *Mizlansky/Zilinsky, or "Schmucks,"* p. 185; June 22, 1998, Robert L. Daniels, review of *Lillian,* p. 63; August 31, 1998, Charles Isherwood, review of *House,* p. 102; October 19, 1998, Charles Isherwood, review of *Corpus Christi,* p. 84; February 22, 1999, Charles Isherwood, review of *The Mineola Twins,* p. 159; January 10, 2000, Robert Hofler, review of *Another American: Asking & Telling,* p. 118; February 14, 2000, Matt Wolf, review of *Bash,* p. 49; March 19, 2001, Charles Isherwood, review of *Design for Living,* p. 39; October 14, 2002, Charles Isherwood, review of *A Man of No Importance,* p. 37; March 3, 2003, Charles Isherwood, review of *Take Me Out,* p. 52; June 16, 2003, Dennis Harvey, review of *Wicked,* p. 37; April 26, 2004, Charles Isherwood, review of *Assassins,* p. 54; April 26, 2004, Matt Wolf, "Wicked His Way Comes," p. A6; May 9, 2005, David Rooney, review of *Glengarry Glen Ross,* p. 47; June 20, 2005, David Rooney, "'Couple' Continues Mantello Hot Streak," p. 39; October 31,, 2005, David Rooney, review of *The Odd Couple,* p. 47;
Vogue, October, 2005, "Master Class," p. 254.
Washington Post, October 14, 1998, Lloyd Rose, review of *Corpus Christi,* p. C1; December 23, 2005, Raymond M. Lane, review of *The Santaland Diaries,* p. T20; June 6, 2006, Peter Marks, review of *Assassins,* p. C1.

ONLINE

Broadway.com, http://www.broadway.com/ (June 15, 2006), "Joe Mantello."
BroadwayWorld, http://www.broadwayworld.com/ (May 30, 2006), "Joe Mantello to Direct MTC's Blackbird, Opening in April."

CurtainUp, http://www.ccurtainup.com/ (October 3, 1999), Les Gutman, review of *Vagina Monologues;* (December 17, 1999), Les Gutman, review of *Another American: Asking & Telling.*

Entertainment Weekly Online, (May 23, 1997), Lisa Schwarzbaum, review of *Love! Valour! Compassion!* (film); (November 8, 2002), Lawrence Frascella, review of *Take Me Out;* (November 21, 2003, Alice King, review of *Wicked;* (May 7, 2004), Scott Brown, review of *Assassins;* (June 25, 2004), "Joe Mantello"; (May 16, 2005), Scott Brown, review of *Glengarry Glen Ross;* (October 28, 2005), Scott Brown, review of *The Odd Couple;* (April 21, 2006), Scott Brown, review of *Three Days of Rain.*

Hollywood.com, http://hollywood.com/ (June 15, 2006), "Joe Mantello."

Internet Broadway Database, http://www.ibdb.com/ (June 15, 2006), "Joe Mantello."

Internet Movie Database, http://www.imdb.com/ (June 15, 2006), "Joe Mantello."

MusicalSingers.com, http://www.musicalsingers.com/ (June 15, 2006), Carol de Giere, "Director Joe Mantello's Audition Tips."

NYTheatre.com, http://www.nytheatre.com/ (April 18, 2006), Martin Denton, review of *Three Days of Rain.*

Playbill, http://www.playbill.com/ (June 15, 2006), "Joe Mantello."*

Elizabeth Moon

■ Personal

Born March 7, 1945, in McAllen, TX; daughter of Dorothy (Jamerson) Norris; married Richard Sloan Moon, November 1, 1969; children: Michael Edwin. *Education:* Rice University, B.A. (history), 1968; University of Texas, B.A. (biology), 1975; graduate study at University of Texas at San Antonio, 1975-77. *Religion:* Episcopal.

■ Addresses

Home—Florence, TX. *Agent*—JABberwocky Literary Agency, P.O. Box 4558, Sunnyside, NY 11104. *E-mail*—emoon1@earthlink.net.

■ Career

Worked as draftsman and sign painter; freelance math tutor, 1974-79; writer, 1981—. Former elected member of McAllen, TX, city council; former president, Chamber of Commerce; former member of library board. *Military service:* U.S. Marine Corps, 1968-71.

■ Member

Science Fiction Writers of America, Austin Writers League.

■ Awards, Honors

Compton Crook Award, 1988, for *Sheepfarmer's Daughter;* Hugo Award nomination, 1997, for *Remnant Population;* Arthur C. Clarke Award nomination, 2003, and Nebula Award for best novel, 2003, both for *The Speed of Dark.*

■ Writings

"PAKSENARRION" SERIES

Sheepfarmer's Daughter, Baen (New York, NY), 1988.
Divided Allegiance, Baen (New York, NY), 1988.
Oath of Gold, Baen (New York, NY), 1989.
Surrender None: The Legacy of Gird, Baen (New York, NY), 1990.
Liar's Oath, Baen (New York, NY), 1992.
The Deed of Paksenarrion, Baen (New York, NY), 1992.
The Legacy of Gird (contains *Surrender None: The Legacy of Gird* and *Liar's Oath*), Baen (New York, NY), 1996.

"PLANET PIRATES" SERIES

(With Ann McCaffrey) *Sassinak,* Baen (New York, NY), 1990.
(With McCaffrey) *Generation Warriors,* Baen (New York, NY), 1991.
(With McCaffrey and Jody Lynn Nye) *The Planet Pirates* (contains *Sassinak, Generation Warriors,* and *Death of Sleep*), Baen (New York, NY), 1993.

"SERRANO LEGACY" SERIES

Hunting Party, Baen (New York, NY), 1993.
Sporting Chance, Baen (New York, NY), 1994.
Winning Colors, Baen (New York, NY), 1995.
Once a Hero, Baen (New York, NY), 1997.
Rules of Engagement, Baen (New York, NY), 1998.
Change of Command, Baen (New York, NY), 1999.
Against the Odds, Baen (New York, NY), 2000.
Heris Serrano (contains *Hunting Party, Sporting Chance,* and *Winning Colors*), Simon & Schuster (New York, NY), 2000.

"VATTA'S WAR" SERIES

Trading in Danger, Del Rey (New York, NY), 2003.
Marque and Reprisal, Del Rey (New York, NY), 2004.
Engaging the Enemy, Del Rey (New York, NY), 2006.
Command Decision, Del Rey (New York, NY), 2007.

OTHER

Lunar Activity (story collection), Baen (New York, NY), 1990.
Remnant Population, Baen (New York, NY), 1996.
Phases (story collection), Baen (New York, NY), 1997.
The Speed of Dark, Del Rey (New York, NY), 2003.

Contributor to anthologies, including *Sword and Sorceress III,* DAW Books (New York, NY), 1986; *New Destinies IX,* Baen (New York, NY), 1990; and *Siege of Arista,* ROC, 1991. Contributor to magazines, including *Analog, Magazine of Fantasy and Science FIction, Amazing Stories,* and *Ellery Queen's Mystery Magazine.* Moon's novels have been translated into Norwegian, Russian, French, Polish, Spanish, German, and Italian.

■ Adaptations

The Speed of Dark has been adapted as an audiobook.

■ Sidelights

Popular fantasy and science fiction writer Elizabeth Moon is the creator of several bestselling series, often concerning members of the military of the future. According to Cynthia Ward in *Science Fiction Weekly,* Moon has created "some of the most believable soldiers and most interesting universes to grace SF and fantasy."

Moon was born on March 7, 1945, in McAllen, Texas. She told *Authors and Artists for Young Adults* (*AAYA*): "I grew up on the Texas-Mexico border, an only child in a one-parent family. Until I was nine, my mother worked in a hardware store on Main Street, and I spent hours in the store and also exploring other stores. After that, my mother worked for a small oil company, doing drafting. (She was an engineer, but women couldn't easily get work in engineering after World War II.) This was a great background for a writer. Not only is that area multi-cultural, the Main Street experience developed an understanding of how a mercantile community works—the social ecology of a healthy agricultural and merchant economy. Later, when my mother was working for the oil company, I got an inside look at how the energy industry views itself. I had the chance to go along on business trips and observe and learn about everything from travel in private planes to petroleum geology, law as it relates to subsurface property rights, and political pressures on (and by) energy suppliers. This would not have been possible if she'd worked for a larger company."

Moon began to write early on: "According to family stories, I started writing very early; I remember trying to write a book when I was six or seven, about our dog (it was so boring that I never finished it.) I started reading very early (preschool); my mother was an avid reader and I caught the bug from her. I used to spend my whole allowance on books, and books were the usual birthday and Christmas presents." Her favorites were "horse books and dog books, at first. Marguerite Henry's books, the Black Stallion and Island Stallion books, Terhune's books about collies, Col. S.P. Meeks' books about dogs and horses. I didn't like series books as much (Bobbsey Twins, Nancy Drew) because I figured out the formula and that took the fun out of it. (Yes, the Black Stallion books had a formula, but the horses made it more palatable.) By the middle grades, I was reading my mother's books as well (historical novels, short stories, etc.), magazine fiction (the *Saturday Evening Post* and other general magazines of that period had fiction in every issue) and nonfiction (especially *National Geographic*) and moved from that into reading history (especially military history and aviation history) and other fiction and nonfiction from the local library, and in 9th grade I discovered science fiction. If this sounds like I always had my nose in a book, that's about right."

"My first job was painting the fence around the hardware store parking lot; I was seven. I used the money to buy a hunting knife. Later, I did lettering and drafting work in high school and college. When I went in the military, I was assigned to data processing, and learned computer programming. After that, I did freelance tutoring in math, painted signs for a stable, and finally moved into writing for publication."

Moon's "Paksenarrion" series recounts the exploits of the title character, a woman warrior in a land of enchantment and violence. "In many ways, the [Paksenarrion] novels seem like standard fantasies, set in a faraway medieval land inhabited by humans, elves, dwarves, orcs, and various practitioners of good and evil magic," reported Gary Westfahl in the *St. James Guide to Fantasy Writers.* But he added that Moon's fiction is distinguished from other fantasy works by its similarities to an unlikely volume, *The Lives of the Saints.* "It is almost as if Moon consciously reached back to *The Lives of the Saints* to provide a modernized role model for young female readers," wrote Westfahl, who described Paksenarrion as "a woman who could outfight any man while maintaining higher moral standards in her adventures."

The "Paksenarrion" series began in 1988 with *Sheepfarmer's Daughter.* Enraged with her father for arranging a marriage for her with a neighboring farmer, Paksenarrion leaves home to join a band of mercenaries. She quickly becomes a hardened warrior. Her violent adventures with the band transform her into a hero, chosen by the gods to restore a lost ruler to his throne. Christopher Ware, reviewing the book for *SFFWorld.com,* believed that "brilliantly developed and engaging characters, great narration, and an exciting story all add up to take the reader on a thoroughly rousing ride."

In the next volume of the series, *Divided Allegiance,* Paksenarrion breaks from her fellow mercenaries, whose gruesome deeds have finally grown unacceptable to her, and she pledges herself to Gird, an ancient saint. In her consequent training to better serve Gird, Paksenarrion runs afoul of black magic, which leaves her, in Westfahl's words, "a pathetic wanderer." But in *Oath of Gold,* Paksenarrion regains her courage, and in an ensuing conflict she undergoes various tortures and degradations while fighting to restore a duke to his proper kingdom.

Moon recounts Gird's own exploits in an ensuing novel set five hundred years in the past, *Surrender None: The Legacy of Gird,* which relates Gird's lead-

Sheepherder's Daughter, the first volume in this trilogy, won the Compton Crook Award as the best first novel in 1989.

ing role in a peasant revolt. The aristocracy, descended from overseas invaders, has become increasingly cruel and tyrannical. Eventually, Gird is pressed too far and joins the dispossessed and rebellious outlaws in the forest. Gird puts his military training to good use to organize the outlaws, and develops plans for removing the aristocracy and instituting more compassionate and equitable rule.

Liar's Oath reveals that, following the revolution led by Gird, the mageborn are forbidden to use their magic on common folk and no longer rule. Tempted by his discovery of a new land accessible through magic, Luap ignores his oath to Gird and seeks to establish himself as leader of the mageborn in the new land. The hidden powers seeking to control Luap delight in the broken oath, which they see as reflecting additional weakness which they may employ to their own evil ends.

The "Serrano Legacy" series begins with *Hunting Party*, which tells of Heris Serrano, a disgraced Space Service officer who leaves the military to work as space yacht commander for a wealthy older woman. The crew proves generally lazy and poorly trained and the passengers are spoiled rich kids, but the ship inspections seem current so the *Sweet Delight* departs for Sirialis despite Captain Serrano's well-founded reservations. The series is set in the future when longevity drugs are extending the lifespans of people beyond the norm and long-distance space travel is thus feasible. In the novel *Once a Hero*, Esmay Suiza faces a military court-martial after she leads a mutiny on a starship. Having saved the planet Xavier from invasion after preventing her captain from giving their ship to the enemy Bloodhorde, Esmay stands trial for mutiny. Cleared by the Military Board for acting as captain and cleared by the court martial for mutiny, Esmay is assigned to the starship *Koskiusko,* where she must prevent a traitor from giving their ship to the Bloodhorde for longevity drugs. A *Publishers Weekly* critic proclaimed that "this is a satisfying read, full of the finely detailed settings and excitement that Moon's readers have come to expect." In *Rules of Engagement*, Suiza interrupts her training as a star fleet commander and determines to rescue a rival in romance. A *Publishers Weekly* critic praised the story's "smart pacing" and "lively characters." In a review for the *SF Site*, Peter D. Tillman maintained that, "as usual, Moon's fast-&-furious action, meticulous military-medical backgrounding, and formidable storytelling skills carry the day."

Change of Command continues the intergalactic epic as Esmay and Barin Serrano find romance while embroiled in labyrinthine political plottings among the ruling Familias Regnant. "The novel moves slowly at times," commented a *Publishers Weekly* reviewer, "and may appeal more to readers who appreciate romance than space opera." *Booklist* contributor Roland Green, however, deemed it a "thoroughly excellent adventure."

Mutiny threatens the Familias Regnant in *Against the Odds,* in which the married Lieutenant Esmay Suiza-Serrano finds herself removed without explanation from the Familias Regnant's Space Fleet following her rescue of a council member who lives on the Fleet's home planet, Castle Rock. At odds with Admiral Vida Serrano over that and her marriage to Vida's nephew Barin Serrano, Esmay must nonetheless journey to Castle Rock to seek reinstatement. She teams up with civilian trader Goonar and encounters mutineers and social upheaval over the use of rejuvenating drugs. Then she is again summoned for duty to track down a possible traitor. A reviewer for *Publishers Weekly* enjoyed its memorable descriptions of a "deeply layered

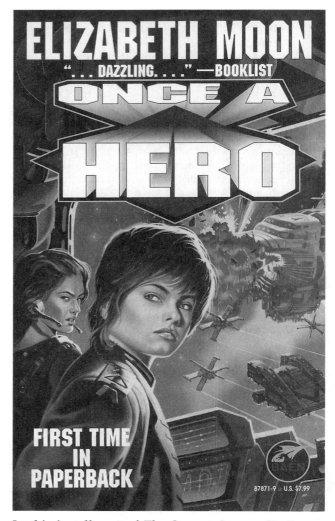

In this installment of The Serrano Legacy, Lt. Esmay Suiza learns a secret from her childhood and ends up on trial for mutiny.

political and military culture" and its "twisting, thorny" plot. *Kliatt* reviewer Liz LaValley concluded that *Against the Odds* was "a beautifully constructed tapestry of interwoven events and charming people that spins faster and tighter to satisfying endings."

With the "Vatta's War" series, Moon chronicles the saga of the Varras, a wealthy trading family. In *Trading in Danger*, Ky Vatta leaves the family business to join the space fleet, but she is kicked out of the academy and her dreams of a military command are shattered. "Returning home to her wealthy family's influential interstellar shipping firm," T.M. Wagner explained in his review for *SF Reviews.net*, "she finds herself placed in the captain's chair of one of their older and more decrepit freighters, the *Glynnis Jones*, on what is meant to be its final voyage to the scrapyard." This humiliating assignment leads Ky into unexpected adventure as she tries to help a planet of colonists obtain badly-needed agricultural equipment and runs into ruthless rivals in the process. "*Trading in Danger* has a libertarian slant, a compelling plot, an emphasis on military virtue and personal honor and a competent and sympathetic young hero," wrote Cynthia Ward in *Science Fiction Weekly*. She concluded: "*Trading in Danger* is a superior novel." Christine C. Menefee, writing in the *School Library Journal*, believed that, for most readers, "the human interest, well-wrought story, humor, and rich world-building will more than satisfy."

The Vatta saga continues in *Marque and Reprisal*, when the family and its far-flung business become the targets of criminal attack. Many of the Vatta family are killed, and Ky finds herself in desperate straits as she tries to determine just who the enemy is and how to stop them. A critic for *Kirkus Reviews* found that the novel's "excellent plotting and characters support the utterly realistic action sequences: swift, jolting, confusing, and merciless." Menefee maintained that "the universe of the Vattas is freshly imagined and abundant in believable detail and exotic possibility." According to a critic for *Publishers Weekly, Marque and Reprisal* is a "rip-roaring sequel."

Engaging the Enemy finds Ky and her cousin Stella trying to run what remains of the family business when their livelihood is threatened by a gang of space pirates. Before engaging in battle, however, Ky must hire a dependable crew, avoid assassins, raise much-needed financial backing, and even convince some important figures that she really is a surviving member of the Vatta family. "If you enjoy military science fiction," Wagner wrote, "then you will most likely enjoy this as Moon keeps things moving right along and manages to throw a number of problems in front of her characters for them to solve, sometimes in unorthodox ways." Jackie Cassada in the *Library Journal* found that this third novel in the series "excels in character development as well as in its fast-paced action sequences and intricate plotting."

Moon's descriptions of military activities in many of her novels are grounded in personal experience. A U.S. Marine Corps veteran who achieved the rank of first lieutenant, Moon acquired what she described in an *Adventures in Crime & Space* interview as an "understanding of relationships between enlisted and officer, sergeant and private, colonel and lieutenant, to the constants of military life. . . . I also have direct first-person experience with several varieties of civilian/military interaction,

from the anti-military civilian who wants you dead, to the politican who wants some dirt on another politician's relative in service." In addition, Moon observed, the Marine Corps gave her "a better understanding of myself" that she believes also shows up, though indirectly, in her work.

Taking a break from her popular series' novels, Moon has also written two stand-alone novels: *Remnant Population* and *The Speed of Dark. Remnant Population* tells of seventy-year-old Ofelia, a widow on a space colony established on another planet. When Sims Bancorp loses their franchise to the colony and pulls everyone out, Ofelia hides and stays behind, content to finally have a chance to live by herself. Ofelia happily maintains the crops and livestock left behind, as well as the power plant and radio. But when a new colony unexpectedly tries to land about forty miles away, Ofelia overhears its total destruction by previously unknown intelligent natives. Ultimately, the natives meet and come to accept Ofelia and the other colonists. The role that elderly people play in modern society is an underlying theme in the story. Duncan Hunter, writing in the Zone, pointed out that "humanity's contempt for the wisdom of its elders and caregivers and its obsession with power through the pursuit of academic, commercial and military status is thrown into stark contrast against the 'natural' values of the alien people." *Booklist* reviewer Carl Hays described *Remnant Population* as "a fascinating adventure of interspecies contact," while the critic for *Publishers Weekly* called it a "well-written, original novel." Kim Fawcett, in her review for the *SF Site*, called *Remnant Population* "a great story and a well-written book. Beyond that, it accomplishes what too few books, science fiction and otherwise, fail to do—it raises bigger questions that don't necessarily have neat answers."

Set several decades into the future, *The Speed of Dark* tells of Lou Arrendale, a middle-aged man who is autistic and has trouble functioning in the normal world. He works at a corporation where his advanced sense of pattern recognition is put to good use, but he and the company's other autistics can only do their work thanks to a number of special conditions. Without those conditions, they would be unable to do their jobs. When a new manager comes along, he sees the autistics only as a group of sick people who cost the company extra money for privileges they could do without. There is a technique to treat autism that has been developed, after all, and they could be made "normal." Lou must decide whether he wants to give up a life he has grown accustomed to or venture into a frightening but completely independent new life. "Moon's novel," wrote Margaret Gunning in *January Magazine*, "underscores a powerful truth—that sometimes the supposedly handicapped can make leaps of perception (not to mention compassion) far beyond the tedious bounds of 'normal.'" Pauline Finch of *Book Reporter* believed that, with *The Speed of Dark,* "Moon has formed and sculpted a heroic plotline from seemingly mundane ingredients, taking the reader into fictional, ethical and even spiritual realms that have rarely been so memorably blended." *The Speed of Dark,* according to John Grant in a review for *Infinity Plus,* "is one of those exceptionally rare novels that has the power to alter one's entire worldview, and reading it is a profoundly rewarding and enriching experience."

Moon told *AAYA* how she writes her books: "In the very early stages, I'm working on the production phase of the previous book (which overlaps the start of a new book by several months) and also doing research and brainstorming on the new one. So I start the day with production work (which is always on a tight deadline), then work on the new book—looking up what I need to look up, making notes, and thinking about it. It doesn't look much like writing, at this stage. When the real writing starts, I prefer to do first-drafting in the morning. So I get up, eat breakfast, and sit down to write for several hours. If it's going well, I may be writing for four or more hours, and produce about 2,000 words. If it's not, I will quit at lunchtime or when I have 1,000 words, whichever comes first. The afternoon may be either writing-related work (correspondence, reading up on something for the story) or work on the land, depending on weather and other circumstances. I don't edit during the main creative phase. This may be interrupted by domestic crises, illness, or travel. I try to schedule the book so that these breaks don't push the deadline.

"After finishing the main draft, the book goes to my alpha readers and I start revision, and this has a different schedule. I divide the book into big sections (this varies with the book—if it's a multi-viewpoint book, every viewpoint is a section; if it's a one-viewpoint book, then a section is several chapters in a lump) and try to do revision on each section in one or two days. So I would spend all day (with only brief breaks) on one section, then the next day on the next, and so forth. Revision is a three-stage process, working from the book's skeleton on up, working from beginning to end each time, and revising only the things that belong to that level. Some people hate revision, but I enjoy it, because I can see the story clarifying with each level. When traveling, I take along either the laptop computer or a thick pad of paper, and make notes or actually write (depends on where I am on the project) every day. Travel (especially overseas) offers new experiences, including the chance to walk over landscapes very different from home. I take extensive notes (and, when possible, photographs) of landscapes, plants, buildings, etc."

If you enjoy the works of Elizabeth Moon, you may also want to check out the following books:

Lois McMaster Bujold, *Brothers in Arms,* 1989.
David Eddings, *The Sapphire Rose,* 1991.
Melanie Rawn, *The Ruins of Ambrai,,* 1994.

When not writing, Moon enjoys a number of other activities: "We are doing wildlife management and prairie restoration on our land, so some of my non-writing time is spent working on the land—mowing grassland with tractor and shredder, pruning brush, grubbing out invasive cactus, checking wildlife water sources, putting out supplementary feed as needed, and so forth. I also do nature photography. Then there's music—I sing in a choir and play the piano for fun. Reading is mostly work these days, but I still enjoy it. Horses, travel, cooking, Renaissance-style fencing (rapier and dagger) and entertaining friends are some of the other activities that fill my time."

Speaking of the writing life, Moon once commented: "Writing science fiction and fantasy requires both self-discipline and a sense of play—an ability to turn the internal editor off and on at will. One of the best things about it is getting to use everything I've learned, and all my interests—from archaeology to zoology—in the service of the story. It's not only a 'what if?' working environment, but also 'why not?' I have a perfect excuse for looking up anything, learning anything, trying anything."

■ Biographical and Critical Sources

BOOKS

St. James Guide to Fantasy Writers, St. James Press (Detroit, MI), 1996.

PERIODICALS

Booklist, April 15, 1996, Carl Hays, review of *Remnant Population,* p. 1425; February 1, 1997, Dennis Winters, review of *Once a Hero,* p. 929; November 1, 1998, Roland Green, review of *Rules of Engagement*, p. 478; November 15, 1999, Roland Green, review of *Change of Command*, p. 609; December 1, 2000, Roland Green, review of *Against the Odds*, p. 698; February 1, 2003, Meredith Parets, review of *The Speed of Dark*, p. 972; September 1, 2003, Roland Green, review of *Trading in Danger*, p. 75; September 1, 2004, Roland Green, review of *Marque and Reprisal*, p. 75; March 1, 2006, Roland Green, review of *Engaging the Enemy*, p. 77.

Bookseller, December 9, 2005, review of *Engaging the Enemy*, p. 31.

Entertainment Weekly, October 29, 2004, Noah Robischon, review of *Marque and Reprisal*, p. 71.

Kirkus Reviews, November 1, 2000, review of *Against the Odds*, p. 1523; November 1, 2002, review of *The Speed of Dark*, p. 1559; July 15, 2003, review of *Trading in Danger*, p. 944; July 15, 2004, review of *Marque and Reprisal*, p. 666.

Kliatt, March, 2002, Liz LaValley, review of *Against the Odds*, p. 24; September, 2003, Nancy C. Chaplin, review of *The Speed of Dark* audiobook, p. 58.

Library Journal, May 15, 1996, Sue Hamburger, review of *Remnant Population*, p. 86; March 15, 1997, Susan Hamburger, review of *Once a Hero*, p. 93; December 1999, Jackie Cassada, review of *Change of Command*, p. 192; December, 2000, Jackie Cassada, review of *Against the Odds*, p. 197; January, 2003, Corey Seeman, review of *The Speed of Dark*, p. 157; August, 2003, Jackie Cassada, review of *Trading in Danger*, p. 142; March 15, 2006, Jackie Cassada, review of *Engaging the Enemy*, p. 67.

Publishers Weekly, February 9, 1990, Penny Kaganoff, review of *Sassinak*, p. 56; April 22, 1996, review of *Remnant Population*, p. 63; February 24, 1997, review of *Once a Hero*, p. 69; November 23, 1998, p. 63; November 23, 1998, review of *Rules of Engagement*, p. 63; November 29, 1999, review of *Change of Command*, p. 56; November 20, 2000, review of *Against the Odds*, p. 51; December 16, 2002, review of *The Speed of Dark*, p. 45; September 29, 2003, review of *Trading in Danger*, p. 48;

August 2, 2004, review of *Marque and Reprisal*, p. 56; January 16, 2006, review of *Engaging the Enemy*, p. 41.

School Library Journal, January 1997, Pam Johnson, review of *Remnant Population*, p. 140; January, 2004, Christine C. Menefee, review of *Trading in Danger*, p. 163; May, 2005, Christine C. Menefee, review of *Marque and Reprisal*, p. 169.

ONLINE

Adventures in Crime & Space, http://www.crimeandspace.com/ (January 6, 2001), author interview.

Book Reporter, http://www.bookreporter.com/ (July 7, 2006), Pauline Finch, review of *The Speed of Dark*.

Elizabeth Moon's Home Page, http://www.sff.net/people/Elizabeth.Moon (July 2, 2006).

Infinity Plus, http://www.infinityplus.co.uk/ (July 7, 2006), John Grant, review of *The Speed of Dark*, and John Toon, review of *Remnant Population*.

January Magazine, http://www.janmag.com/ (April, 2003), Margaret Gunning, review of *The Speed of Dark*.

Science Fiction Weekly, http://www.scifi.com/ (July 7, 2006), Cynthia Ward, review of *Trading in Danger*.

SFFWorld.com, http://www.sffworld.com/ (May 15, 2001), Christopher Ware, reviews of *Sheepfarmer's Daughter*, *Divided Allegiance*, and *Oath of Gold*.

SFReader.com, http://www.sfreader.com/ (May 19, 2006), Steven Sawicki, review of *Engaging the Enemy*.

SF Reviews.net, http://sfreviews.net/index.html/ (July 7, 2006), T.M. Wagner, reviews of *Trading in Danger* and *Marque and Reprisal*.

SF Site, http://www.sfsite.com/ (July 7, 2006), Kim Fawcett, review of *Remnant Population*, and Peter D. Tillman, review of *Rules of Engagement*.

Zone, http://www.zone-sf.com/ (July 7, 2006), Duncan Hunter, review of *Remnant Population*.

Henry Moore

■ Personal

Born July 30, 1898, in Castleford, Yorkshire, England; died August 31, 1986, in Much Hadham, Hertfordshire, England; son of Raymond Spencer (a coal miner) and Mary Moore; married Irina Radetsky (a painter), July 27, 1929; children: Mary Spencer Moore Danovsky. *Education:* Attended Leeds School of Art, 1919-21, and Royal College of Art, 1921-25.

■ Career

Sculptor, 1922-86; Royal College of Art, London, England, instructor in sculpture, 1925-32; Chelsea School of Art, London, instructor in sculpture, 1932-39. Established department of sculpture at the Chelsea School of Art, 1932; served as official war artist in London, 1940-45; trustee of the Tate Gallery, London, 1941-48, 1949-56, and of the National Gallery, London, 1955-63, 1964-74; member of the Art Panel of the British Council, 1945, of the Royal Fine Art Commission, 1947-71, and of the Arts Council of Great Britain, 1963-67; formed Henry Moore Foundation, 1977. First solo show at the Warren Gallery, London, 1928; first American museum show at the Museum of Modern Art, New York, NY, 1946.

Major works include the *Reclining Figure*, 1929, *Mother and Child*, 1931, *Three Standing Figures*, 1947-48, the bronze *Draped Reclining Figure* for the *Time-Life* building in London, 1952-53, and *King and Queen*, 1952-53. *Exhibitions:* Individual exhibitions include, Warren Gallery, London, England, 1928; Leicester Galleries, London, England, 1931; Leicester Galleries, London, England, 1933; Zwemmer Gallery, London, England, 1935; Leicester Galleries, London, England, 1936; Mayor Gallery, London, England, 1939; Temple Newsam, Leeds, Yorkshire, England, 1941; Buchholz Gallery, New York, NY, 1943; Berkeley Galleries, London, England, 1945; Leicester Galleries, London, England, Phillips Memorial Gallery, Washington, DC, Museum of Modern Art, New York, NY, 1946; Art Institute of Chicago, IL (traveled to the San Francisco Museum of Art), National Gallery of New South Wales, Sydney, Australia (toured Australia), 1947; Arts Council Gallery, Cambridge, England, Galleria d'Arte Moderna, Milan, Italy, Roland Browse and Delbanco, London, England, 1948; Wakefield City Art Gallery, Yorkshire, England, Galerie de Arte Mexicano, Mexico City, Mexico, 1949; Tate Gallery, London, England, Leicester Galleries, London, England, Haus am Waldsee, Berlin, Germany, Bucholz Gallery, New York, NY, Albertina, Vienna, Austria, 1951; National Gallery of South Africa, Cape Town, South Africa, Academian, Stockholm, Sweden (toured Europe), Neue Galerie der Stadt, Linz, Austria, Boymans-van Beuningen Museum, Rotterdam, Netherlands, Institute of Contemporary Arts, London, England, Comite voor Artisticke Werking, Antwerp, Belgium, Kestner Gesellschaft, Hannover, West Germany (toured West Germany), Galerie

Welz, Salzburg, Austria (with Mario Marini and Fritz Wotruba), 1953; Leicester Galleries, London, England, Kunsthalle, Mannheim, West Germany (toured West Germany), Stadverwaltung, Goettingen, West Germany, Curt Valentin Gallery, New York, NY, 1954; Leicester Galleries, London, England, Kunsthalle, Basel, Switzerland, University of Colorado, Boulder (toured the United States), Museum of Fine Arts, Montreal, Canada (toured Canada and New Zealand), 1955; Hatton Gallery, Newscastle upon Tyne, England, Marlborough Fine Art, London, England, Ashmolean Museum, Oxford, England, 1958; Palacio Foz, Lisbon, Portugal (toured Spain), Metropolitan Art Gallery, Tokyo, Japan (toured Japan), Middelheim Park, Antwerp, Belgium, Marlborough Fine Art, London, England, Zachenta Gallery, Warsaw, Poland (toured Poland), 1959; Kunsthalle, Hamburg, West Germany (toured West Germany), 1960; Arts Council Gallery, Cambridge, England, Marlborough Fine Art, London, England, 1962; Marlborough Fine Art, London, England, Wakefield City Art Gallery, Yorkshire, England, Ferens Art Gallery, Hull, Yorkshire, England, La Jolla Art Center, CA (toured California), 1963; Marlborough Fine Art, London, England, Palacio de Bellas Artes, Mexico City, Mexico (toured South America), 1964; Marlborough Fine Art, London, England, Orleans Gallery, New Orleans, LA, Marlborough Galleria d'Arte, Rome, Italy, University of Arizona Art Gallery, Tucson, AZ, Arkansas Art Center, Little Rock, AK, Museum des 20 Jahrhunderts, Vienna, Austria (with Jean Dubuffet and Mark Tobey), 1965; Marlborough Fine Art, London, England, City Museum and Art Gallery, Folkstone, Kent, England (traveled to the Museum and Art Gallery, Plymouth, Devon, England), Philadelphia College of Art, PA, Israel Museum, Jerusalem, Israel, Sala Delles, Bucharest, Romania (toured Eastern Europe), Cordova Museum, Lincoln, NE, Sheffield Art Gallery and Museum, Yorkshire, England, Trinity College, Dublin, Ireland, Smithsonian Institution, Washington, DC, 1966; Marlborough Fine Art, London, England, 1967; Tate Gallery, London, England, Rijksmuseum Kroeller-Mueller, Otterlo, Netherlands (toured West Germany and the Netherlands), 1968; National Museum of Modern Art, Tokyo, Japan (toured Japan and traveled to Hong Kong), York University, England, Norwich Castle Museum, Norfolk, England, 1969; Marlborough Gerson Gallery, New York, NY, Knoedler Gallery, New York, NY, Galerie Beyeler, Basel, Switzerland, Galerie Cramer, Geneva (toured Europe and traveled to New York), Marlborough Fine Art, London, England (with Pablo Picasso and Graham Sutherland), 1970; Forte di Belvedere, Florence, Italy, 1972; Fischer Fine Art, London, England, 1973; Los Angeles County Museum of Art, CA, Wilhelm Lehmbruck Museum, Duisburg, West Germany (toured West Germany and Belgium), 1974; Zuercher Forum, Zurich, Switzerland, Imperial War Museum, London, England, Scottish National Gallery of Modern Art, Edinburgh, Scotland (with Kenneth Martin), Fischer Fine Art, London, England, Grafton Gallery, Bury St. Edmonds, Suffolk, England, Lillian Heidenberg Gallery, New York, NY, 1976; Orangerie des Tuilleries, Paris, France, Bibliotheque Nationale, Paris, France, Gracefield Arts Centre, Dumfries, Scotland, Art Gallery of Ontario, Toronto, Canada (toured Japan and traveled to London 1977-78), 1977; Cartwright Hall and Lister Park, Bradford, Yorkshire, England, Serpentine Gallery, London, England, Tate Gallery, London, England, Bayerischen Staatsgemaldesammlungen, Munich, West Germany, Galeria Joan Prats, Barcelona, Spain, Festival Gallery, Aldeburgh, Suffolk, England, Gallery Kasahara, Osaka, Japan, Stiftung Landis und Gyr, Zug, Switzerland, Schossgut Wolfsberg, Ermstigen, Switzerland, Galeria Pieter Coray, Lugano, Switzerland, 1978; Prince Henry's High School, Evesham, Worcestershire, England, Wildenstein Gallery, New York, NY, Jersey Museum, Channel Islands, Bundeskanzleramt, Bonn, West Germany (traveled to William Hack Museum, Ludwigshafen, West Germany), Umetnosti Pavilijon, Slovenj Gradec, Yugoslavia (traveled to the Serbian Academy, Belgrade), 1979; Il Bisonte, Florence, Italy, Victoria and Albert Museum, London, England, Galerie Levy und Forderkreis, Hamburg, West Germany, Campus West Library, Welwyn Garden City, Hertfordshire, England, Fishcer Fine Art, London, England, Galerie Patrick Cramer, Geneva, Switzerland, 1980; 125 Raskowsky, Sofia, Bulgaria, Retire Park, Madrid, Spain, Gulbenkian Foundation, Lisbon, Portugal, Royal Museum, Folkestone, England, Galleria Bergamini, Milan, Italy, Wildenstein Gallery, London, England, Contemporary Sculpture Center, Tokyo, Japan, Gallery Welz, Salzburg, Austria, Alex Rosenberg Gallery, New York, NY, 1981; Joan Miro Foundation, Barcelona, Spain, Fine Arts Center, Colorado Springs, CO, Galleria Comunale, Forte dei Marmi, Italy, Hoam Art Museum, Seoul, Korea, Durham Light Infantry Museum, County Durham, England, Fischer Fine Art, London, England, Linda Goodman Gallery, Sandton, South Africa, 1982; Galerie Maeght, Paris, France, Alex Rosen Gallery, New York, NY, 1983; Marlborough Fine Art, London, England, Marlborough Graphics, London, England, Kunstmuseum, Herning, Denmark, Columbus Museum of Art, OH, 1984; San Francisco Museum of Modern Art, CA, Art Gallery of Ontario, Toronto, Canada, 1985; Kent Fine Art, New York, NY, Galerie Patrick Cramer, Geneva, Switzerland, Thomas Gibson Fine Art, London, England, 1986; Marlborough Fine Art, London, England, Fischer Fine Art, London, England, Vallecchi Editore, Florence, Italy, Hofstra University, Hempstead, NY; 1987; Art Gallery of

Ontario, Toronto, Canada, Marlborough Fine Art, London, England, 1989; Mead Gallery, Coventry, England, 1990; Gosudarstvennyi Muzei Al.S. Pushkina, Moscow, Russia, 1991; Art Gallery of New South Wales, Sydney, Australia, Waddington Galleries, London, England, Didier Imbert Fine Art, Paris, France, 1992; Galeria BWA, Cracow, Poland, Waddington Galleries, London, England, Grosvenor Gallery, London, England, 1995; Berkeley Square Gallery, London, England, Brighton Museum and Art Gallery, Brighton, England, Yorkshire Sculpture Park, West Bretton, England, Philadelphia Museum of Art, PA, Hirshhorn Museum and Sculpture Garden, Washington, DC, 1998; "Henry Moore: Sculpting the 20th Century," Dallas Museum of Art, TX, Palace of the Legion of Honor, San Francisco, CA, National Gallery of Art, Washington, DC, 2001-02; "Henry Moore," Dulwich Picture Gallery, London, England, 2003; "Henry Moore: Imaginary Landscapes," Frederik Meijer Gardens and Sculpture Park, Grand Rapids, MI, 2005. Permanent collections include, Tate Gallery, London, England; Victoria and Albert Museum, London, England; Henry Moore Foundation, Much Hadham, Hertfordshire, England; Stedelijk Museum, Amsterdam, Netherlands; National Gallery of Victoria, Melbourne, Australia; Art Gallery of Ontario, Toronto, Canada; Hirshhorn Museum and Sculpture Garden, Washington, DC; Museum of Modern Art, New York, NY; Experimental Museum, Mexico City, Mexico. *Military service:* British Army, Civil Service Rifles, 1917-19; bayonet instructor.

■ Member

British Academy (fellow), American Academy of Arts and Sciences (foreign honorary member), Akademie der Kunste (Berlin; foreign honorary member), Swedish Royal Academy of Fine Arts (foreign member), Academie des Beau-Arts (Paris; foreign corresponding member), Academie des Lettres et Beaux-Arts (Belgium; foreign corresponding member), Academie Flamande des Sciences (foreign corresponding member), Weiner Secession (Vienna; honorary member), Royal Institute of British Architects (honorary associate), Churchill College, Cambridge (honorary fellow).

■ Awards, Honors

International Prize for Sculpture from the twenty-fourth Venice Biennale, 1948; International Sculpture Prize from the second Biennale of Sao Paulo, 1953; named Companion of Honour, 1955; Stefan Lochner Medal from the city of Cologne, 1957; second prize for sculpture from the Carnegie International, Pittsburgh, PA, 1958; International Sculpture Prize from the Feltrinelli Foundation, Milan, Italy, 1963; named to British Order of Merit, 1963; Gold Medal from the city of Florence, 1967; Erasmus Prize, 1968; Einstein Prize, 1968; Commemorative Award for the Arts from Yeshiva University, New York, 1968; named to Order of Merit (Federal Republic of Germany, Bonn), 1968, (Italy), 1972; medal from the Royal Canadian Academy of Arts, 1972; named Commandeur de l'Ordre des Arts et des Lettres (France), 1973; Biancoumano Prize, 1973; Goslar Prize, 1975; Decoration of Honour for Science and Art (Austria), 1978; Grand Cross of the Order of Merit (Federal Republic of Germany), 1980; Order of the Aztec Eagle (Mexico), 1984. Twenty honorary degrees from colleges and universities in United States, England, Canada, and Germany, including Leeds University, London University, University of Oxford, Royal College of Art, Harvard University, Yale University, University of Toronto, and Technische Hochschule, Berlin; honorary professor emeritus of sculpture, Carrara Academy of Fine Arts.

■ Writings

Shelter Sketch Book, Editions Poetry London, 1940, Marlborough Fine Art (London, England), 1967, published as *London's War, The Shelter Drawings of Henry Moore,* edited by Julian Andrews, Lund Humphries (London, England), 2003.

Heads, Figures, and Ideas, with commentary by Geoffrey Grigson, New York Graphic Society (New York, NY), 1958.

Henry Moore on Sculpture: A Collection of the Sculptor's Writings and Spoken Words, edited with an introduction by Philip James, MacDonald & Co. (London, England), 1966, Viking (New York, NY), 1967, revised and expanded edition, Viking (New York, NY), 1971.

Henry Spencer Moore, edited and photographed by John Hedgecoe, Simon & Schuster (New York, NY), 1968.

(Author of introduction and collaborator on photographs with Ilario Bessi) Michael Ayrton, *Giovanni Pisano: Sculptor,* Thames & Hudson (London, England), 1969.

(Illustrator) Constantine Fitz Gibbon, *The Blitz,* MacDonald & Co. (London, England), 1970.

Energy in Space (text in English, French, and German), photographs by John Hedgecoe, German translation by Renate Zauscher, French translation by Emmanuela de Nora, New York Graphic Society (New York, NY), 1973.

(Illustrator) *Auden Poems, Moore Lithographs,* British Museum Publications (London, England), 1974.

(Author of commentaries) David Finn, *Henry Moore: Sculpture and Environment,* Abrams (New York, NY), 1976.

(Author of introduction) Stephen Spender, *Sculptures in Landscape,* photographs and forward by Geoffrey Shakerley, Studio Vista (London, England), 1978, C.N. Potter (New York, NY), 1979.

(With Kenneth Clark) *Henry Moore's Sheep Sketch Book,* Thames & Hudson (London, England), 1980.

(Author of comments) David Mitchinson, editor, *Henry Moore Sculpture,* Rizzoli (New York, NY), 1981.

Large Two Forms: A Sculpture, preface by Clark, introduction by William T. Ylvisaker, photographs by Finn, Abbeville Press (New York, NY), 1981.

Henry Moore at the British Museum, photographs by Finn, British Museum Publications (London, England), 1981, Abrams (New York, NY), 1982.

(Author of commentary) *Henry Moore: Wood Sculpture,* photographs by Gemma Levine, Universe Books (New York, NY), 1983.

Henry Moore: The Reclining Figure, Columbus Museum of Art (Columbus, OH), 1984.

(With John Hedgecoe) *Henry Moore: My Ideas, Inspiration, and Life as an Artist,* edited by Suzanne Webber, photographs by Hedgecoe, Chronicle Books (San Francisco, CA), 1986.

Henry Moore: Sketch-models and Working-models, The Centre (London, England), 1990.

Henry Moore, 1898-1986, Art Gallery of New South Wales (Sydney, Australia), 1992.

Henry Moore: disegni, sculture, grafica, Electa (Milan, Italy), 1993.

Henry Moore: A Sculptor's Drawings: December 3, 1993-January 15, 1994, Pace Gallery (New York, NY), 1993.

Henry Moore: sculture, disegni, incisioni, arazzi, Electa (Milan, Italy), 1995.

Henry Moore, Animals, Gerhard Marcks-Stiftung (Bremen, Germany), 1997.

Celebrating Moore: Works from the Collection of the Henry Moore Foundation, University of California Press (Berkeley, CA), 1998.

Henry Moore: In the Light of Greece, E. Goulandris Foundation (Andros, Greece), 2000.

Henry Moore: Writings and Conversations, University of California Press (Berkeley, CA), 2002.

Contributor of articles to periodicals, including *Architectural Association Journal, Listener, Transformation, Ark,* and *Art News.*

■ Sidelights

Superlatives generally describe the career of British sculptor Henry Moore. Writing in the *Christian Science Monitor,* Jerome Tarshis, for example, called Moore "arguably the greatest sculptor of the 20th century." Writing in *Grove Art Online,* Alan G. Wilkinson observed: "Generally acknowledged as the most important British sculptor of the 20th century, [Moore] took the human figure as his central subject-matter throughout his career." During the course of his long career he continually reverted to explorations of three main themes: the "reclining figure, the mother and child, and the interior and exterior form," as a critic for *International Dictionary of Art and Artists* noted. Influenced by non-European sculpture, including Egyptian, Sumerian, African, and the pre-Columbian Toltec-Maya or Aztec style known as Chacmool, Moore blended such influences into an abstract art which viewers and critics at first ridiculed, but later warmly responded to. His signature large-scale works in bronze and carved marble ultimately took abstraction to new heights of popularity; many is the town or city that has a Moore statue gracing the outside of an office building, university, or church. By the later part of his career, he was acknowledged a modern master, and was much sought after for commissions.

However, Moore's very popularity acted against him with some critics who found his art, as David Peters Corbett noted in the *Journal of British Studies,* "easy to dismiss . . . as the artistic equivalent of the postwar 'New Towns' (the sites of many of his sculptures), an insipid amalgam of tradition and modernity that neglected the real complexities of British culture and twentieth century art." Similarly, Blake Gopnik, writing in the *Washington Post* in 2001 on the advent of a large Moore retrospective exhibition, commented: "Moore's exemplary Moore-ness also works against him. There is an undeniable sameness to his work that can easily come off as shtick. It can seem as though he's more interested in deploying the formula he's found for making successful art than in carrying on with the experimental process that led him to it." In fact, years after his death in 1986, his reputation still "bobs like a cork on the sea of twentieth-century art," according to Richard Shone in *Artforum International.* "Innovator or magpie? Last of the greats or a grandiose bore in his later years?" John Russell, writing in the *New York Times* at the time of Moore's death, however, had a more measured assessment of the artist: "In a world at odds with itself, his sculptures got through to an enormous constituency as something that stood for breadth and generosity of feeling. They also suggested that the human body could be the measure of all things, for it was in terms of head, shoulder, breast, pelvis, thigh, elbow and knee that Mr. Moore set the imagination free to roam across a vast repertory of connotations in myth and symbol." Moore himself best summed up

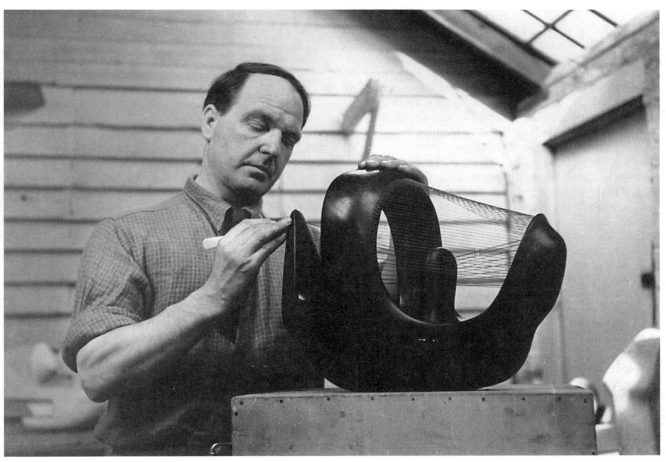

Moore, at work in his studio in 1945, is widely regarded as one of the most important sculptors of the twentieth century.

his own career. In the inscription to his *Henry Moore: My Ideas, Inspiration, and Life as an Artist* he wrote: "I would like my work to be thought of as a celebration of life and nature."

Humble Origins

The seventh of eight children of Raymond Spencer Moore, a miner, and his wife, Mary Baker, Henry Spencer Moore was born on July 30, 1898, in the small coalmining town of Castleford in the English district of Yorkshire. The father was widely read, though self-educated, and was determined that his children should gain an education and not work in the mines. The mother was a strong influence on Moore's development, an affectionate woman who also suffered from arthritis. It was Moore's duty as a young boy growing up to rub her back with liniment in the evening, a ritual which some feel provided the future sculptor's hands with a familiar-

ity in the body contours. Moore attended grammar school and secondary school in Castleford. As a young boy, Moore was already carving in wood and modeling clay. Then, when he was eleven, he was inspired to become a sculptor, hearing of the work of Michelangelo from his Sunday school teacher. When he told his father of his plans in art, the boy was not discouraged in his ambitions, but was counseled to first be trained as a teacher. In secondary school, to which he won a scholarship, Moore was further encouraged in his artistic endeavors by the art teacher, and was chosen to carve the wooden memorial scroll to commemorate alumni who enlisted in the army to fight in the First World War. After finishing his teacher training in 1915, Moore taught for a time in his old grammar school in Castleford, but in 1917 he joined the Fifteenth London Regiment and was shipped off to France, where he fought in the battle of Cambrai. There he came under gas attack, and was sent back to England to recuperate. After spending two months in hospital, Moore became an instructor for the remainder of the war, leaving the army in 1919 and returning home to Yorkshire.

His war experiences convinced Moore that he needed to take his life in his own hands now. He decided not to return to teaching, but to follow his dreams to become a great sculptor. Applying for and being granted an ex-serviceman's grant for education, he became the first sculpture student at the Leeds School of Art. There, while still living at home, he completed courses in drawing and sculpting, finishing the coursework in half the time usually required. An important influence from this time was Roger Fry's *Vision and Design,* which introduced Moore to non-Western sculpture. Like one of his fellow students at Leeds, Barbara Hepworth, Moore too won a scholarship to the Royal College of Art's Sculpture School in London. However, as Wilkinson pointed out, "his weekly visits to the British Museum were far more influential on his early development than his academic course work." Moore concentrated on the work of Africa, the South Pacific, and pre-Columbian Mexico instead of ancient Greece, the tradition most artists of the time were trained in. This emphasis, however, he had to reserve for weekends and holidays, the rest of the time keeping to the academic agenda of the Royal College.

Cast in bronze, Moore's 1953 work *Three Standing Figures* reflects his interest in the human form.

Develops His Own Style

Like other modern masters such as Constantin Brancusi and Amedeo Modigliani, Moore "believed passionately in direct carving and in 'truth to materials,' respecting the inherent character of stone or wood," according to Wilkinson. One of his earliest works, the stone *Mother and Child* of 1924, set a lifelong theme for the artist. Though his primitivist style did not always find acceptance at the Royal College, he was ultimately appointed a lecturer in sculpture and won traveling scholarships to France, where he became familiar with the work of the transplanted Brancusi, and to Italy, where he was particularly drawn to the volumetric paintings of Giotto and Massaccio, as well as the late work of his inspiration, Michelangelo. Back in England, he had his first one-person show, in 1928, at London's Warren Gallery. The following year he married a student of painting at the Royal College, Irina Radetsky, who acted as a model for many of his sculptures. That same year he carved his first *Reclining Figure,* taking as his inspiration the chunky solidity of the pre-Columbian reclining warrior priest in the sculpture *Chacmool,* a picture of which he had once seen in an

art book. This *Reclining Figure,* like his *Mother and Child,* provided another lifelong theme for Moore. It was, as Wilkinson noted, "the first of many sculptures in which the female figure became a metaphor for landscape." Moore also sculpted the concrete *Mask,* from 1929, which also emphasized pre-Columbian motifs. The year 1928 additionally proved something of a turning point in Moore's career, as he earned his first major public commission, for the London Transport headquarters. The subsequent *West Wind Relief* was his first effort at making public art, and his first possibility to work out his ideas on a more monumental scale.

The decade of the 1930s saw Moore finding his own sculptural idiom, and becoming less dependent on such non-Western sources. For a time he was influenced by cubism, and worked such influences into his reclining figures, creating smoother and more flowing lines, as in his 1930 *Reclining Woman.* His wooden *Two Forms* was shown in New York's Museum of Modern art, and he began to find an audience for his work outside of England. Slowly during the course of this decade his work took on more of an abstract quality, as in *Reclining Figure*

Fourpieces, and *Reclining Figure* of 1935 and 1938, as well as *Recumbent Figure,* from 1938. He also began to experiment with an exterior-interior image, as found in *The Helmet,* from 1939, and with stringed sculpture, and began exhibiting with Surrealists. During this time he lived in Hampstead, London, near other artists such as Hepworth, Ben Nicholson, and Piet Mondrian, and there was mutual influence between them.

Gains Acceptance

Despite sales and public commissions, Moore had still not found popularity. In fact, his works were as often ridiculed as they were praised. For example, as he increasingly used a hollowed space to interrupt or break up the volumes of his large wooden, metal, or stone sculptures, some critics derisively

One of Moore's major works, *Draped Reclining Figure* was inspired by the classical sculptures he viewed on a trip to Greece.

called him "the sculptor of the hole." Others complained of his primitivism. A more realistic phase of his work took place during the Second World War, and public acceptance came with it. With the outbreak of war, Moore's London studio was damaged by bombs, and he and his wife moved to Perry Green, Much Hadham, about thirty miles from the capital. Appointed Official War Artist, he began a series of drawings of Londoners taking shelter from German air raids in the Underground. These realistic sketches became known as his Shelter Drawings, and, as Wilkinson commented, "with their almost visionary intensity and sense of shared danger, are Moore's greatest achievement as a draughtsman." Tarshis also called these drawings "the greatest works of his career." He created the realistic *Madonna and Child,* 1943, for the church of St. Matthew in Northampton, England, too.

With the end of the war, Moore returned to the motif of the reclining figure, sculpting in marble and metal for places as varied as the UNESCO headquarters in Paris and New York's Lincoln Center. He also returned to the mother and child motif in *Family Group,* from 1946, and further explored his interior-exterior theme in *Internal External Forms.* The family continued to live in Much Hadham, where Moore could work on his monumental sculptures, eventually building nine studios on the property for drafting, photographing, printmaking, casting small bronzes, drawing, and sculpting. His international reputation was secured in 1948 with the winning of the Sculpture Prize of the Venice Biennale. Commissions worldwide followed.

Throughout the course of his long career, Moore was credited with 919 sculptures, 5,500 drawings, and 717 graphics. Exhibitions of his work were mounted worldwide, one of the most acclaimed being the 1972 exhibit in Florence at Michelangelo's Forte di Belvedere, with 289 exhibits and 345,000 visitors over the course of the four-month exhibit. Moore became a wealthy man, but continued to live simply. He contributed major pieces to museums around the world and established the Henry Moore Foundation in 1977, to promote arts and sculpture in particular. Even in his declining years, he continued to explore the possibilities of the reclining figure and the mother and child theme, combining them to produce *Draped Reclining Mother and Baby* in 1984.

With his death in 1986, Moore was celebrated for his ability to blend the human form with landscape, and for the vitality of his sculpture. Much of his work is on display at his former home, Perry Green, in Much Hadham. Unfortunately, thieves were able to steal one of his monumental sculptures from that location in late 2005. They loaded the 4,600-pound bronze onto the back of a truck and drove away. Though worth an estimated five million dollars, the sculpture was destined, police feared, to be melted down for the bronze, worth about 9,000 dollars. Happily, there are many more sculptures by Moore in the world, and his influence in art and sculpting lives on. Tarshis called him "a modern-day colossus among English artists." Though there was some criticism of his latter work and its somewhat staid quality, Moore is, as Scarlet Cheng noted in the *Los Angeles Times,* "generally regarded as one of the greatest sculptors of the 20th century." As Morgan Falconer noted in the *New Statesman:* "If, today, Moore looks antique, we perhaps forget that he is older than he seems. His moment of popular triumph might have been in the 1970s, but critics have long recognized that he produced his best work in the 1930s and 1940s."

If you enjoy the works of Henry Moore, you may also want to check out the following:

The art of Romanian sculptor Constantin Brancusi (1876-1957), Russian sculptor Naum Gabo (1890-1977), and British sculptor Barbara Hepworth (1903-1975).

Again Moore, one of the most articulate of artists, and one who wrote widely on his art, was able to

Moore's sculptures can often be found in public settings, gracing university campuses or park grounds.

Moore standing next to his 1957 piece *Seated Nude*.

sum up his career and its inspiration best in his own words. As he wrote in the essay "The Hidden Struggle," collected in *Henry Moore: Writings and Conversations:*"There is one quality I find in all the artists I admire most. . . . I mean a disturbing clement, a distortion, giving evidence of a struggle or some sort. . . . I personally believe that all life is a conflict; that's something to be accepted. . . . One must try to find a synthesis, to come to terms with opposite qualities. Art and life are made up of conflicts. . . . I think really that in great art, i.e., in the art I find great, this conflict is hidden, it is unsolved."

■ **Biographical and Critical Sources**

BOOKS

Beckett, Jane, and Fiona Russell, editors, *Henry Moore: Critical Essays*, Ashgate (Burlington, VT), 2003.

Berthoud, Roger, *The Life of Henry Moore*, Faber and Faber (London, England), 1987, revised edition, Giles de la Mare Publishers (London, England), 2003.

Bowness, Alan, editor, *Henry Moore: Sculpture and Drawings*, five volumes, Lund, Humphries (London, England), 1977.

Clark, Kenneth, *Henry Moore Drawings*, Harper (New York, NY), 1974.

Contemporary Artists, fifth edition, St. James Press (Detroit, MI), 2001.

Davis, Alexander, compiler and editor, *Henry Moore Bibliography*, Henry Moore Foundation (Much Hadham, England), 1994.

Hall, Donald, *Henry Moore: The Life and Work of a Great Sculptor*, Harper (New York, NY), 1966.

Hedgecoe, John, *A Monumental Vision: The Sculpture of Henry Moore*, Stewart, Tabori & Chang (New York, NY), 1998.

Gardner, Jane Mylum, *Henry Moore: From Bones and Stones to Sketches and Sculptures*, Four Winds (New York, NY), 1993.

Garrould, Ann, editor, *Henry Moore: Complete Drawings,* Henry Moore Foundation (Much Hadham, England), 1996.

International Dictionary of Art and Artists, St. James Press (Detroit, MI), 1990.

Levine, Gemma, *With Henry Moore: The Artist at Work,* Sedgwick & Jackson (London, England), 1978.

Mitchinson, David, *Henry Moore: Unpublished Drawings,* Abrams (New York, NY), 1972.

Mitchinson, David, and Julian Stallabrass, *Henry Moore,* Rizzoli (New York, NY), 1992.

Moore, Henry, *Henry Moore on Sculpture: A Collection of the Sculptor's Writings and Spoken Words,* edited with an introduction by Philip James, MacDonald & Co. (London, England), 1966.

Moore, Henry, and John Hedgecoe, *Henry Moore: My Ideas, Inspiration, and Life as an Artist,* Chronicle Books (San Francisco, CA), 1986.

Read, Herbert, *Henry Moore: A Study of His Life and Work,* Praeger (London, England), 1966.

Sylvester, David, editor, *Henry Moore: Complete Sculpture,* Lund Humphries (London, England), 1988.

Teague, Edward H., *Henry Moore Bibliography and Reproductions Index,* McFarland & Co. (Jefferson, NC), 1981.

Wilkinson, Alan G., *The Drawings of Henry Moore,* Borden Publishing (Los Angeles, CA), 1970.

PERIODICALS

American Artist, April, 2005, "Frederik Meijer Gardens Celebrates 10th Anniversary with Henry Moore Exhibition," p. 10.

Apollo, March, 2006, James Hall, "Moore and His Mother," p. 82.

Art Business, January, 2002, "Moore Retrospective Shows Range of Artist's Work," p. 68.

Artforum International, January, 2001, Richard Shone, review of "Henry Moore: Sculpting the 20th Century," p. 47.

Christian Science Monitor, August 20, 2001, Jerome Tarshis, "Sorting Out the Best of Henry Moore," p. 18.

Contemporary Review, November, 2003, review of *London's War: The Shelter Drawings of Henry Moore,* p. 315.

Journal of British Studies, July, 2005, David Peters Corbett, review of *Henry Moore: Critical Studies,* p. 646.

Library Journal, August, 1998, Jack Perry Brown, review of *A Monumental Vision: The Sculpture of Henry Moore* and *Celebrating Moore: Works from the Collection of the Henry Moore Foundation,* p. 82; December, 2003, Martin R. Kalfatovic, review of *The Life of Henry Moore,* p. 104.

Los Angeles Times, July 15, 2001, Scarlet Cheng, "Henry Moore, Without the Preconceptions," p. 1; December 20, 2005, John Daniszewski, "Thieves Lift a 4,600-Pound Moore Statue," p. A3.

New Criterion, December, 2002, Eric Gibson, review of *Henry Moore: Writings and Conversations,* p. 41.

New Statesman, May 17, 2004, Morgan Falconer, "The Last Primitivist," pp. 38-39.

Sculpture, July-August, 2001, Brian McAvera, "The Enigma of Henry Moore."

Spectator, June 26, 2004, Andrew Lambirth, "Enlightened by Moore," p. 42.

Wall Street Journal, September 1, 1998, Eric Gibson, "Moore and Moore," p. 1; May 1, 2001, Eric Gibson, "Searching for Moore," p. A24.

Washington Post, October 20, 2001, Blake Gopnik, "Henry Moore, Seen from Many Angles," p. C1; October 26, 2001, "Less Is Moore," p. T54.

ONLINE

Artchive, http://www.artchive.com/ (June 19, 2006), "Henry Moore."

Artcyclopedia, http://www.artcyclopedia.com/ (June 19, 2006), "Henry Moore."

Grove Art Online, http://www.groveart.com/ (June 19, 2006), Alan G. Wilkinson, "Moore, Henry (Spencer)."

Henry Moore Foundation Web site, http://www.henry-moore-fdn.co.uk (June 19, 2006).

OBITUARIES

PERIODICALS

New York Times, September 1, 1986, John Russell, "Henry Moore, Sculptor of an Age, Does at 88," p. 1.*

Terry Moore

◼ Personal

Born 1954; married; wife's name, Robyn.

◼ Addresses

Office—Abstract Studio, Inc., P.O. Box 271487, Houston, TX 77277-1487. *E-mail*—SIPnet@strangers inparadise.com.

◼ Career

Cartoonist. Author of the comic book series "Strangers in Paradise," first as a three-issue mini-series for Antarctic Press, 1993, then self-published under Abstract Studio, also self-publishing eight issues for Homage Comics. Founder, Abstract Studio; co-founder, Homage Comics, 1996. Television editor.

◼ Member

American Society of Composers, Authors, and Publishers (ASCAP).

◼ Awards, Honors

Eisner Award for Best Continuing Series, 1996, Ruben Award, National Cartoonists Society, for Best Comic Book of 1997, and GLAAD Award, Best Comic Book, 2001, all for *Strangers in Paradise.*

◼ Writings

"STRANGERS IN PARADISE" SERIES

I Dream of You, Abstract Studio (Houston, TX), 1996.
It's a Good Life, Abstract Studio (Houston, TX), 1997.
Love Me Tender, Abstract Studio (Houston, TX), 1997.
Immortal Enemies, Abstract Studio (Houston, TX), 1997.
High School!, Abstract Studio (Houston, TX), 1999.
Sanctuary, Abstract Studio (Houston, TX), 1999.
My Other Life, Abstract Studio (Houston, TX), 2000.
Child of Rage, Abstract Studio (Houston, TX), 2001.
Tropic of Desire, Abstract Studio (Houston, TX), 2001.
Brave New World, Abstract Studio (Houston, TX), 2002.
Heart in Hand, Abstract Studio (Houston, TX), 2003.
Flower to Flame, Abstract Studio (Houston, TX), 2003.
David's Story, Abstract Studio (Houston, TX), 2004.
Tomorrow Now, Abstract Studio (Houston, TX), 2004.
Molly and Poo, Abstract Studio (Houston, TX), 2005.

Tattoo, Abstract Studio (Houston, TX), 2005.
Love & Lies, Abstract Studio (Houston, TX), 2006.

Strangers in Paradise has been translated into seven languages.

COLLECTIONS

The Collected Strangers in Paradise: Volume I (contains the first three issues of *Strangers in Paradise*) Abstract Studio (Houston, TX), 1995.

The Complete Strangers in Paradise: Volume II, Abstract Studio (Houston, TX), 2000.

The Complete Strangers in Paradise: Volume III, Part 1, Abstract Studio (Houston, TX), 2000.

The Complete Strangers in Paradise: Volume III, Part 2, Abstract Studio (Houston, TX), 2000.

The Complete Strangers in Paradise: Volume III, Part 3, Abstract Studio (Houston, TX), 2001.

The Complete Strangers in Paradise: Volume III, Part 4, Abstract Studio (Houston, TX), 2002.

The Complete Strangers in Paradise: Volume III, Part 5, Abstract Studio (Houston, TX), 2003.

The Complete Strangers in Paradise: Volume III, Part 6, Abstract Studio (Houston, TX), 2004.

Strangers in Paradise: Treasury Edition, Perennial Currents (New York, NY), 2004.

Strangers in Paradise: Pocket Book 1, Abstract Studio (Houston, TX), 2005.

Strangers in Paradise: Pocket Book 2, Abstract Studio (Houston, TX), 2005.

Strangers in Paradise: Pocket Book 3, Abstract Studio (Houston, TX), 2005.

Strangers in Paradise: Pocket Book 4, Abstract Studio (Houston, TX), 2005.

Strangers in Paradise: Pocket Book 5, Abstract Studio (Houston, TX), 2005.

"PARADISE TOO" SERIES

Drunk Ducks, Abstract Studio (Houston, TX), 2003.
Checking for Weirdos, Abstract Studio (Houston, TX), 2003.

OTHER

(With David Mack) *Kabuki Volume 3: Masks of the Noh TP,* Image Comics (Berkeley, CA), 1999.

(With Tony Millionaire and Andi Watson) *Star Wars: Tales, Volume 2,* Dark Horse Comics (Milwaukie, OR), 2002.

(With Amber Benson and Christopher Golden) *Buffy the Vampire Slayer: Willow & Tara,* Dark Horse Comics (Milwaukie, WI), 2003.

(With Brian Michael Bendis) *Ultimate Marvel Team-up,* Marvel Comics (New York, NY), 2004.

(With Malcolm Bourne and Mike Alfred) *Tales of Ordinary Madness,* Oni Press (Portland, OR), 2004.

■ **Adaptations**

Strangers in Paradise has been optioned for a film by HBO.

■ **Work in Progress**

Final issues of *Strangers in Paradise;* a syndicated comic strip.

■ **Sidelights**

American comic book author and illustrator Terry Moore is the creator of the popular *Strangers in Paradise,* a series that began in 1993 and was set for conclusion in 2007. The black-and-white comic, also known as "SiP," follows the adventures and misadventures of three main characters: Helen Francine Peters, known as Francine, Katina Marie Choovanski, known as Katchoo, and their friend David Qin. The relationships between these three forms "the Bermuda Triangle of love triangles," according to George A. Tramountanas, writing for *Comic Book Resources.* While Francine considers Katchoo her best friend, Katchoo is in love with Francine. To complicate matters further, David is in love with Katchoo. More complications are added by a thriller plot element, involving the character Darcy Parker, who is attempting to control the political system through highly trained and skilled call girls. A contributor to *Publishers Weekly* described the plot of the ongoing series as a "soap-operatic serial about two women's love for each other, and the various men, philosophical debates and globe-trotting assassins who get in its way."

The comic, an issue of which is written, illustrated, and self-published by Moore every six weeks, has been collected in a number of graphic novels, and has won a prestigious Eisner Award, as well as critical acclaim from fellow comics writers and reviewers alike. As quoted on *Dragon*Con,* graphic novelist Neil Gaiman noted: "What most people don't known about love, sex, and relations with other human beings would fill a book. *Strangers in Paradise* is that book." Gaiman went on to call the work "delightful," and dubbed Moore a "fun writer and a fine cartoonist." For *Booklist* contributor Tina Coleman, *Strangers in Paradise* "is one soap opera no one should miss." In a *CSIndy* online article, Moore is quoted as saying: "I think of [*Strangers in Paradise*] as a modern-day *Archie and Veronica*. . . . It's more of a condensation of life." In this updated relationships comic, Moore explores such issues as homosexuality and the role of religion in the modern world. It appeals to an audience not usually attracted to comic books; more than fifty percent of its readership is female. Moore's non-linear approach to story-telling—going back and forth in time throughout the course of the story arc—and his finely-tuned line drawings have attracted readers around the world.

Finds a Niche in Comics

Born in 1954, Moore spent his first eleven years in Texas, Panama, Mississippi, Arkansas, and Africa. He told *Authors and Artists for Young Adults* (*AAYA*): "I was born in Texas but moved immediately to Panama because my very young father was in the Air Force. After that we lived all over the south until I was ten years old when we moved to Africa. My youngest of two sisters was born there, in Dar es Salaam, East Tanzania. My mother tells me I was given a child's drawing table and art supplies when I was two and that I went right to work. Growing up, my mother was the one who encouraged me to do something with my talent. I don't recall my father ever even commenting on anything I drew or wrote. I love reading and always have. I remember going to the first day of school and telling my younger sister I would learn to read for the both of us so I could read our story books to her. My mother loved to read also, so we always had plenty of books around the house. She read fiction about the human stuggle; my father read macho fiction such as Ian Fleming and Hemingway. Between the two I grew up with a diverse interest that followed me into my own works. My favorite stories as a boy were Ian Fleming's James Bond series and Enid Blyton's Mallory Towers series. Both were British, one was macho fiction, the other a young reader's series about a girls boarding school." As he explained to Dirk Deppey of *Comics Journal*, these were the only books available at the time, so he read them and "loved them both." Moore further commented: "Years later, I came out with my own series, and it really is just drawing from these two diverse influences in my life. I think I got inspiration from both of them. I've enjoyed that dichotomy of entertainment my whole life."

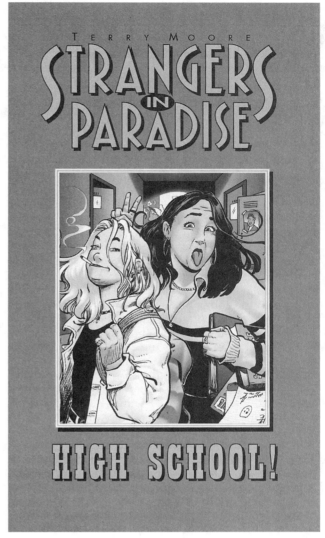

This volume tells of the High School exploits of Francine and Katchoo.

The Moore family eventually had to make a rapid departure from war-torn Tanzania. Back in the United States, Moore as a teenager had dreams of becoming a rock star, playing guitar for a band. However, he found a home in television for some years, working as an editor of documentaries, music videos and advertisements. It was not a job that suited him well, and he finally decided to turn his talents to illustration and writing.

Speaking of this period in his life, Moore told *AAYA:* "I left college to become a working musician, so I never had a steady job until I quit music several years later to become a television video editor. All through school and my music career I was writing short stories and fantasy novellas, just to amuse myself. During my editing career I focused more on the visual arts and my drawing skills. It wasn't until I had decided to leave editing that I returned to writing and began the long process of working my brain back into shape. I had been editing for a little over ten years and was tired of the routine, wondering what I could do, when I developed the very strong desire to write my own stories and publish them. I believe that, while I had always written and created stories for my own enjoyment, it wasn't until I was approaching middle-age that I realized my stories would never be read by anybody if I didn't get serious and do something to get them out to the public. The simplest way for me to publish my work seemed to be in comic books, so I began writing, drawing and publishing my own comic, *Strangers in Paradise*."

Moore visited comic book stores and researched the medium, finding that there was a new wave of small press publishers in the early 1990s enjoying modest success in the comic book field, many of them focusing on reality-based stories instead of men in tights. He spent a year studying the business and at the same time began writing the first issue of *Strangers in Paradise,* a title he took from the Tony Bennett ballad. Moore explained to *Sequential Tart* contributor Katherine Keller the inspiration for his tale: "I was looking for this story, I wanted to read it, but I couldn't find it so I just started making it myself for my own entertainment." Explaining his focus on females in the comic book, he further noted to Keller: "I thought, well, if I'm going to have to obsess as an artist over somebody, I'd rather it be a woman than a man. So . . . I really did it for very male chauvinistic reasons. . . . I was just more interested in drawing women than men. . . . My goal was to write about people we would sit next to on the train, or the plane, or the car, or the cab, or stand next to on the sidewalk, or sit next to at the restaurant. I wanted to write about people that we really could meet." At heart, Moore's *Strangers in Paradise* is a love story. "Love is a surprise and you have no say so over where you will find it," Moore told Keller. "In my comic I'm trying to give the characters just enough realism in there so that you feel more like a fly on the wall—that you really are listening to real conversation, and we know we're not supposed to be eavesdropping."

Speaking with Tramountanas, Moore observed that *Strangers in Paradise* was conceived of as a three-part mini-series. That series was published beginning in 1993 by Antarctic Press. "I hoped it would be a good way to break into the business," Moore told Tramountanas. "Then I realized most creators dreamed of having their own book, so I decided to stay with 'SiP' and run with it as a series—see how far I could go before I had to give it up and go to

mainstream." In 1994, Moore began self-publishing the comic through his own Abstract Studio imprint. The first mini-series focused on Francine and Katchoo and their boyfriends, suitors, love, and jealousy. With the second installment, collected as the graphic novel *I Dream of You,* the story is "darker," according to Sara Lipowitz writing for the online *Seized by the Tale.* Here Moore brings in the darkness of Katchoo's past: the victim of child abuse who ran away from home and became a high-priced prostitute for a criminal organization run by Darcy Parker. This Mafia-like organization has been on the hunt for Katchoo ever since she disappeared from her work as a call girl, for a sizeable amount of money went missing at the same time. The art student David is also developed in the second installment; overall the series takes on a more noirish feel with *I Dream of You,* which earned an Eisner Award in 1996 as Best Continuing Series. Lipowitz praised the intricate tangle of lives that Moore had created: "These people are so wound around each other they could be a human pretzel, and it doesn't look like anything's going to be straightened out among them for a long time. Lucky for us."

The Series Stretches to Ninety Issues

In 1996, Moore teamed up with other comic book creators, including Jim Lee, Kurt Busiek, and James Robinson, to start a new imprint, Homage Comics. Moore began a new story arc to launch *Strangers in Paradise* under the Homage imprint, releasing eight issues, which began Volume 3 of the collected *Strangers in Paradise,* in which the author returned to more relationship-oriented issues, downplaying the thriller aspect for a time. After eight issues under the Homage imprint, however, Moore returned to the Abstract Studio imprint, under which the comic has been appearing regularly, with the ongoing Volume 3, and set to reach the climax of the story with issue 90 in 2007.

Along the way, Moore also produced additional comic book tales, songs, sketches, and cartoons, published in the "Paradise Too" books. Additionally, Moore hired out his illustrating talents to Dark Horse Comics, Marvel Comics, and DC Comics. However, most of his creative energy has been placed in the ongoing *Strangers in Paradise.* In 2005, Moore began collecting the tales in pocket books. Reviewing *Strangers in Paradise: Pocket Book 1, Booklist* contributor Coleman noted that his story "has an epic feel but never loses the details of the characters' lives." For Coleman, this was a "sophisticated must-read." *Strangers in Paradise: Book 2* opens a decade later with Francine married and filled with boredom, Katchoo a successful artist, and David out of the picture for the time being. Moore then provides flashbacks to show the reader how his characters arrived at this place, including the unraveling of David's own dark past. "The particular beauty of Moore's graphic storytelling shows in its seamless welding of the events of everyday life and extraordinary underworld/Mafia plot," wrote Coleman in a *Booklist* review of this installment. Reviewing *Strangers in Paradise: Book 4,* Coleman, again writing in *Booklist,* called the series "comfort-food comics." Coleman also commended its creator: "Moore's writing takes us into the inner lives of his characters, while his crisp, vibrant artwork expertly depicts emotion and humor." In *Strangers in Paradise: Book 5,* David's involvement with the yazuka underground is explored more fully.

In 2006, Moore announced on his Web site that he would finally be concluding his series. "'SiP' is a story and, like all stories, must come to an end," Moore wrote. "I think the story needs a strong ending to be a definitive statement," Moore told Daniela Zeta in a *Yattaaa!* interview. "If I let it go till it fizzles out, all those years of work will amount to nothing more than a rambling monologue." Speaking with Jennifer M. Contino for *COMICON.com,* Moore noted: "I'm grateful for the way 'SiP' has touched people's lives. I never expected that, of course. . . . I know the story has value to the general public. Once I've finished the work it will be marketed and pushed to the public. Time will tell what will become of it. I am apprehensive about that, the long-term future of my baby. . . . Over time, if the work is worthy, a much broader audience can be found."

If you enjoy the works of Terry Moore, you may also want to check out the following graphic novels:

Craig Thompson, *Blankets,* 2003.
Adrian Tomine, *Summer Blonde,,* 2003.
Jaime Hernandez, *Locas: A Love and Rockets Book,* 2004.

"My typical day," Moore told *AAYA,* "begins around 9:30 or 10 when I go to a nearby bagel shop, read the paper, do the crossword puzzle and drink my iced green tea. I'm in the studio usually by 10:30 where I answer my email and phone messages. Ro-

byn always has some things for me to do, such as pull art that has been sold or sign books that have been ordered. When I finally get to my drawing board I read the previous day's work and either polish what I have or begin another page. Once I sit down to the table, I will work until midnight or so, with breaks for lunch and dinner. I do this six days a week. On the seventh day I skip the email part."

Speaking of his future plans, Moore explained: "I try to attend as many conventions as I can each year, and meet with the fans. I am always grateful to them for supporting my work and allowing me to have this wonderful career. As far as the web goes, I have a website for *Strangers in Paradise* where I post the latest updates on books and appearances. I'm also developing a site separate from SiP where I will feature my other work and future projects, along with a blog that will, hopefully, put me more in touch with people interested in following my crazy trail."

As for what he hopes to accomplish through his work, Moore explained: "I hope my books depict the stories of people who bravely get up every day and give it their best shot, whatever their circumstances. I hope to convey the appeal of every person through the things we all have in common, our hearts, our minds, our feelings, our desires."

■ **Biographical and Critical Sources**

PERIODICALS

Booklist, February 1, 2003, review of *Strangers in Paradise,* p. 986; March 15, 2005, Tina Coleman, review of *Strangers in Paradise: Pocket Book 1,* p. 1280; June 1, 2005, Tina Coleman, review of *Strangers in Paradise: Pocket Book 2* and *Strangers in Paradise: Pocket Book 3,* p. 1771; September 1, 2005, Tina Coleman, review of *Strangers in Paradise: Pocket Book 4,* p. 77; April 1, 2006, Tina Coleman, review of *Strangers in Paradise: Pocket Book 5,* p. 30.

Comics Journal, May, 2006, Dirk Deppey, "Terry Moore Interview."

Library Journal, February 1, 2002, review of *I Dream of You,* p. 57.

Los Angeles Times, January 10, 1998, Paul Iorio, "The Next Wave," p. F1.

Publishers Weekly, October 18, 2004, "'Strangers' Due from Harper," p. 26; November 15, 2004, review of *Strangers in Paradise: Treasury Edition,* p. 43.

School Library Journal, December, 2003, Christine C. Menefee, review of *Buffy the Vampire Slayer: Willow and Tara*, p. 179.

ONLINE

Comic Book Resources, http://www. comicbookresources.com/ (November 15, 2002), Arune Singh, "Keeping It 'Real'"; (March 17, 2006), George A. Tramountanas, "Strangers No More, as Moore Brings 'Strangers in Paradise' to an End."

COMICON.com, http://www.comicon.com/ (April 26, 2006), Jennifer M. Contino, Terry Moore interview.

CSIndy, http://www.csindy.com/ (May 19, 2005), "Reality Bites: Comic Creator Terry Moore Gets Down and Dirty."

Dragon*Con, http://www.dragoncon.org/ (June 21, 2006), "Terry Moore."

Lambiek.net, http://www.lambiek.net/ (June 21, 2006), "Terry Moore."

Seized by the Tale, http://www.flowerfire.com/ (June 21, 2006), Sara Lipowitz, review of *Strangers in Paradise*.

Sequential Tart, http://www.sequentialtart.com/ (October, 1999), Katherine Keller, "A Quiet, Soft Spoken Man"; (May, 2001), Adrienne Rappaport, "Strangers No More."

Strangers in Paradise Official Web site, http://www. strangersinparadise.com (June 21, 2006).

Yattaaa!, http://www.yattaaa.net/ (June 21, 2006), Daniela Zeta and others, "Yattaaa Interview: Terry Moore."

Louise Plummer

■ Personal

Married Tom Plummer (a professor); children: Jonathon, Edmund, Charles, Samuel. *Education:* University of Minnesota, M.A. *Religion:* Mormon

■ Addresses

Home—Provo, UT. *Office*—Department of English, Brigham Young University, Provo, UT 84602. *E-mail*—Louise Plummer@byu.edu.

■ Career

Writer, educator. Brigham Young University, Provo, UT, associate professor of English.

■ Awards, Honors

Honorable mention, Delacorte Press First Young Adult Novel Contest, 1987, Children's Choice Book, New York Public Library and International Reading Association, for *The Romantic Obsessions and Humiliations of Annie Sehlmeier;* ALA Best Book, *School Library Journal* Best Book, Utah Arts Council Best Young Adult Novel, Association of Mormon Letters Best Young Adult Novel, and New York Public Library Children's Choice Book, all for *My Name Is Susa5an Smith. The 5 Is Silent;* ALA Best Book, *School Library Journal* Best Book, Association of Mormon Letters Best Young Adult Novel, all for *The Unlikely Romance of Kate Bjorkman;* ALA Best Book, for *A Dance for Three.*

■ Writings

JUVENILE

A Walk to Grow On, Parker Bros. (Beverly, MA), 1985.

The Romantic Obsessions and Humiliations of Annie Sehlmeier, Delacorte Press (New York, NY), 1987.

My Name Is Susa5an Smith. The 5 Is Silent, Delacorte Press (New York, NY), 1991.

The Unlikely Romance of Kate Bjorkman, Delacorte Press (New York, NY), 1995.

A Dance for Three, Delacorte Press (New York, NY), 2000.

OTHER

Thoughts of a Grasshopper: Essays and Oddities, Deseret Book Co. (Salt Lake City, UT), 1992.

Author of introduction, *Eating Chocolates and Dancing in the Kitchen: Sketches of Marriage and Family* (sound recording), by Tom Plummer, Deseret Book Co. (Salt Lake City, UT), 1998; contributor to periodicals, including *LDS Living*.

■ **Adaptations**

Thoughts of a Grasshopper was adapted for audio cassette, Deseret Book Co., 1992.

■ **Work in Progress**

Finding Daddy, a mystery, for Delacorte Press.

■ **Sidelights**

Louise Plummer is the award-winning author of several young adult novels that explore the humorous and painful ups and downs of teenage romance and coming-of-age angst. An associate professor of English at Brigham Young University, Plummer also occasionally blends Mormon themes into her work, as in her 1991 novel, *My Name Is Susa5an Smith. The 5 Is Silent,* in which the precocious female narrator comes from a Mormon family. However, as the Association for Mormon Letters awards committee noted on its Web site, "Louise Plummer never intrudes into the novel, never preaches. Susan and her family are LDS but not obtrusively so." Other award-winning titles from Plummer include *The Unlikely Romance of Kate Bjorkman* and the 2000 novel *A Dance for Three*.

Young Adults in Utah

Plummer's first young adult title, *The Romantic Obsessions and Humiliations of Annie Sehlmeier*, draws on the author's own history. Plummer's mother emigrated from the Netherlands to Utah, where she raised her family. In her book, Plummer features teenaged Annie Sehlmeier, who makes a similar voyage, immigrating from the Netherlands to Salt Lake City with her parents, grandmother, and sister. While Annie is the reserved one in the family, her younger sister, Henny, is more outgoing. However, this changes somewhat when Annie meets good-looking fellow student Tom Wooley. Though she

In this 1987 novel, a teenage girl emigrates with her family from Holland to Utah, where she develops a crush on a handsome high school boy.

prides herself on being calm and collected, underneath, Annie becomes obsessed with Tom, and that frightens her, because Annie knows that sometimes obsessions make people do silly and even dangerous things. Reviewing the work in the *School Library Journal*, Therese Bigelow concluded that "romantic obsessions have not been as well covered in other young adult novels as in this first novel."

Plummer's second novel, *My Name Is Susa5an Smith. The 5 Is Silent,* is also set in Utah. The protagonist, seventeen-year-old Susan, is an aspiring artist. She uses the silent 5 in her name in order to set herself apart from the rest of her Mormon family. A gifted painter, she feels circumscribed at home; she hangs on to a romantic and early attachment for her Uncle Willy, who left her aunt. As she notes in the book: "When Uncle Willy left, I was Susan Smith. Now, ten years later, I am Sus5an Smith. The 5 is silent. It's a silence that drives certain members of my family up the wall, but I figure if you're going to have the last name of Smith, then your first name should be more exotic than Susan or Sue or even Sioux." Life in Springfield, Utah, is not very stimulating for Susan; her Uncle Willy represents far-off, exotic locales. For this year's student art show, Susan is painting a family portrait, and one that still includes Uncle Willy, who is persona non grata with the rest of the family. Though she wins first prize for the portrait, her family is more embarrassed than elated. The summer after high school graduation, she sets out into the world to make her way as an artist. She goes to Boston to live with another aunt, who introduces her to a bigger world. There she meets an eccentric woman who lives next door, encounters another young artist, and also finally finds her long-lost Uncle Willy. She idolizes him and actually falls in love with the older man, hoping that he will marry her. Uncle Willy, however, proves to be a scoundrel, stealing all Susan's possessions, even her paintings, as well as other contents of her aunt's apartment. This event in turn proves an inspiration for Susan to make peace with her family. In the end, she decides to remain in Boston and study art, rather than attend college in Utah.

This second novel brought mostly positive reviews for Plummer. Though a reviewer for *Publishers Weekly* thought the novel was "predictable," other critics found more to like. Ellen Ramsay, reviewing the novel in *School Library Journal,* praised the "considerable wit" Plummer employed, which "furthers the plot rather than being gratuitous." *Horn Book* contributor Maeve Visser Knoth called this second novel "lively," and concluded that Plummer's tale is a "careful and compelling portrait of a young woman on the brink of maturity." For the Association for Mormon Letters awards committee, which presented Plummer with the Best Young Adult Novel Award for 1991, Susan is "one of the most delightful characters in young adult literature."

Joys and Pains of Romance

Plummer's third young adult novel, *The Unlikely Romance of Kate Bjorkman,* moves away from the familiar territory of Utah and is set in the freezing winter of Minnesota. This tale of a Christmas romance is narrated by an intelligent teen. Six-foot-tall Kate Bjorkman has an I.Q. that spirals off the charts, and she wears thick enough glasses to qualify her as something of a "geek." However, this "charismatic, lighthearted, and irresistible" protagonist, as *School Library Journal* reviewer Alice Casey Smith described Kate, "proves that true love awaits

even the gawkiest, most socially inept teen." Kate narrates her story in the faux language of a romance writer's manual, playing with and at times making fun of the literary traditions of that genre. The story revolves around Kate's love for her brother's friend, Richard, who comes to visit one Christmas. Her love is complicated by Fleur, a California beauty who Kate initially mistakes for Richard's girlfriend, and by Kate's supposed best friend, Ashley, who goes in pursuit of Richard despite Kate's confession that he is the man of her dreams. "The heroine, of course, vanquishes her enemy in the end and wins the hero's heart, but not without some hurt," observed *Horn Book* critic Lauren Adams. Kate alternates her romance-novel chapters with her own revision notes dealing with previous chapters.

Again, Plummer earned awards and critical praise for her work in *The Unlikely Romance of Kate*

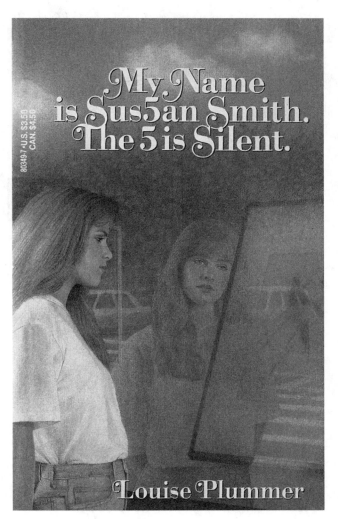

A gifted seventeen-year-old painter leaves her Mormon family behind to study art in Boston in this 1991 work.

In this humerous novel, Kate tells the story of how she overcame misunderstandings and betrayal to capture the man of her dreams.

Bjorkman. Smith noted Plummer's "witty, keen writing" and called the work a "fast-paced, refreshing book with lots of appeal." For another *School Library Journal* contributor, Luann Toth, the same novel was a "good-natured spoof." Similarly, Jeri Drew, writing in the *Book Report*, concluded that the novel provides a "fresh twist" to the usual teenage romance book. Likewise, for Adams, "the holiday cheer, the appealing protagonist, and the happy ending are sure to evoke the simple pleasures of popcorn and cocoa on a cold winter's day."

Plummer investigates the costs of teenage love in *A Dance for Three,* a study of teen pregnancy. Hannah is a fifteen year old who fantasizes about marrying her boyfriend, Milo, the most popular boy in school and son of a wealthy family. However, in Hannah's case, there is more than fantasy to her dreams, for she is pregnant with his child. In her daydreams, she thinks that Milo will be overjoyed when he hears that he is to become a father; instead he hits her, calls her names, and denies that the baby is his. Hannah's mother is not much help, either, for she has become helpless after the death of Hannah's father, and accuses her daughter of being insane just like one of the grandmothers. Over time, Hannah in fact gives in to these thoughts of madness, breaking down and finally getting counseling help that saves her and convinces her to give her child up for adoption.

If you enjoy the works of Louise Plummer, you may also want to check out the following books:

Richard Peck, *Unfinished Portrait of Jessica,* 1991.
Randy Powell, *Is Kissing a Girl Who Smokes Like Licking an Ashtray?,* 1992.
Joan Bauer, *Thwonk,* 1995.

Writing in *Horn Book,* Christine Hepperman noted that such a synopsis could sound "grim." However, as Hepperman further stated: "Hannah's dry wit and unique perspective save her story from becoming just another morality tale." For Hepperman, *A Dance for Three* is "smart, witty, and affecting." *Book Report* contributor Melinda Elzinga felt that "readers will need a full box of tissues." Higher praise came from a *Publishers Weekly* critic who commended Plummer's "sharply etched characters" and "uncanny ability to project details and human idiosyncrasies" into them. For this same reviewer, *A Dance for Three* contained "memorable" characters and conflicts. Similarly, *Booklist* contributor Frances Bradburn thought that the "beautifully depicted multidimensional adults, and Hannah herself, are the strength of the novel." *School Library Journal* writer Francisca Goldsmith likewise noted: "In a crowded genre, this story excels in character development, plot devices, and underlying themes." Goldsmith concluded: "Plummer has succeeded in displaying the other side of the pregnant teen coin."

■ **Biographical and Critical Sources**

BOOKS

Plummer, Louise, *My Name Is Susa5an Smith. The 5 Is Silent,* Delacorte Press (New York, NY), 1991.

PERIODICALS

Booklist, May 1, 2000, Frances Bradburn, review of *A Dance for Three,* p. 1660.

Book Report, January-February, 1996, Jeri Drew, review of *The Unlikely Romance of Kate Bjorkman,* p. 46; September-October, 2000, Melinda Elzinga, review of *A Dance for Three,* p. 60.

English Journal, July, 2002, John Bennion, "Austen's Granddaughter: Louise Plummer Re(de)fines Romance," pp. 44-50.

Horn Book, July-August, 1991, Maeve Visser Knoth, review of *My Name Is Susa5an Smith. The 5 Is Silent,* pp. 464-465; March-April, 1996, Lauren Adams, review of *The Unlikely Romance of Kate Bjorkman,* p. 213; March-April, 2000, Christine Hepperman, review of *A Dance for Three,* p. 199.

Publishers Weekly, June 7, 1991, review of *My Name Is Susa5an Smith. The 5 Is Silent,* p. 66; February 14, 2000, review of *A Dance for Three,* p. 201.

School Library Journal, December, 1987, Therese Bigelow, review of *The Romantic Obsessions and Humiliations of Annie Sehlmeier,* p. 104; June, 1991, Ellen Ramsay, review of *My Name Is Susa5an Smith. The 5 Is Silent,* p. 127; October, 1995, Alice Casey Smith, review of *The Unlikely Romance of Kate Bjorkman,* p. 160; December, 1995, Luann Toth, "SLJ's Best Books 1995," p. 22; February, 2000, Francisca Goldsmith, review of *A Dance for Three,* p. 124.

ONLINE

Association for Mormon Letters Web site, http://www.aml-online.org/ (September 19, 2003), "1991 AML Award for Young Adult Literature Presented to: Louise Plummer."

Brigham Young University English Department Web site, http://english.byu.edu/ (June 22, 2006), "Louise Plummer."

Deseret Book Web site, http://deseretbook.com/ (June 22, 2006), "Louise Plummer."*

Robert J. Sawyer

■ Personal

Born April 29, 1960, in Ottawa, Ontario, Canada; son of John Arthur (a professor of economics) and Virginia (a statistician; maiden name, Peterson) Sawyer; married Carolyn Joan Clink (a poet), December 22, 1984. *Education:* Ryerson Polytechnical Institute, B.A.A., 1982. *Politics:* Liberal. *Hobbies and other interests:* Reading.

■ Addresses

Home and office—4470 Tucana Ct., No. PH2, Mississauga, Ontario, Canada L5R 3K8. *Agent*—(Literary) Ralph M. Vicinanza Ltd., 303 West 18th St., New York, NY 10011; fax: 212-691-9644; (Film and television) Vincent Gerardis, Created By, 1041 N. Formosa Ave., West Hollywood, CA 90046; fax: 323-850-3554. *E-mail*—robertj@sfwriter.com.

■ Career

Freelance writer, Toronto, Ontario, Canada, 1983—. Teaching assistant, Ryerson Polytechnical Institute, Toronto, 1982-83; consultant to business and govern-

mental agencies on communications issues and public relations, Toronto, 1983-89; freelance radio documentary writer and narrator, Canadian Broadcasting Corporation (CBC), 1984—; @discovery.ca, Discovery Channel, monthly columnist, 1997-98; Science FACTion, CBC, Toronto, weekly syndicated radio columnist, 2002—; editor, Robert J. Sawyer Books (an imprint of Red Deer Press), Calgary, Alberta, Canada, 2004—. Writer-in-residence, "Wired Writers" program (electronic residence), 1991, Maclean's Online (electronic residence), 1997, Richmond Hill Public Libraries, Richmond Hill, Ontario, Canada, 2000, and Merrill Collection of Science Fiction, Toronto Public Library, Toronto, 2003. Frequently appears on television and radio programs, including Newsworld Day; narrated special *Inventing the Future: 2000 Years of Discovery*, Discovery Channel Canada, 2000. Frequently speaks at conferences, gives readings and lectures, leads workshops and writing classes, and judges writing contests.

■ Member

Science Fiction and Fantasy Writers of America (Canadian regional director, 1992-95, president, 1998), Crime Writers of Canada, Writers Union of Canada (membership committee, 1996-97), Writers Guild of Canada, Horror Writers Association.

■ Awards, Honors

Critic's Choice, Best Science Fiction Novel of the Year, *Magazine of Fantasy and Science Fiction*, 1991, and Aurora Award, Canadian Science Fiction and

Fantasy Association (CSFFA), 1992, both for *Golden Fleece*; Best Books for the Teen Age citation, New York Public Library, 1992, and HOMer Award, CompuServe Science Fiction and Fantasy Forum, 1993, both for *Far-Seer*; HOMer Award, CompuServe Science Fiction and Fantasy Forum, 1993, for *Fossil Hunter*; Aurora Award for best English short story, CSFFA, 1993, and Arthur Ellis Award, Crime Writers of Canada, 1993, both for "Just Like Old Times"; Aurora Award for best English short story, CSFFA, 1996, for "Peking Man," 1999, for "Stream of Consciousness," and 2002, for "Ineluctable"; writer's reserve grant, Ontario Arts Council, 1993, Aurora Award, CSFFA, 1995, and Nebula Award for Best Novel, Science Fiction and Fantasy Writers of America (SFWA), 1995, all for *The Terminal Experiment*; Seiun Award (Japan) for best foreign science fiction novel, 1996, for *End of an Era*, 2000, for *Frameshift*, and 2003, for *Illegal Alien*; finalist for Nebula Award for Novel, SFWA, 1996, for *Starplex*; Grand Prix de l'Imaginaire (France) for best foreign science fiction short story, 1996, for "You See but You Do Not Observe"; nomination, Hugo Award for Best Novel, World Science Fiction Society, 1996, for *The Terminal Experiment*, 1997, for *Starplex*, 1998, for *Frameshift*, 1999, for *Factoring Humanity*, 2001, for *Calculating God*, and 2003, for *Hominids*; best Canadian mystery novel, *Globe and Mail*, 1997, for *Illegal Alien*; Primio Universitat Polit[0088]cnica de Catalunya de Ciencia Ficción (Spain), 1997, for *Factoring Humanity*, and 1998, for *Flashforward*; writer of the month, *USA Today* Online, 1998; Reader Award for best short story, *Science Fiction Chronicle*, 1998, for "The Hand You're Dealt"; Aurora Award, CSFFA, 1999, for *Flashforward*; travel grant, Canada Council for the Arts, 1999; writing grant, Canada Council for the Arts, 2001; Ryerson University Alumni Award of Distinction, 2002; Established Literary Artist Award, Mississauga (Ontario) Arts Council, 2002; Collectors Award for Most Collectible Author of the Year, Barry R. Levin, Science Fiction & Fantasy Literature, 2003; Hugo Award for Best Novel, 2003, for *Hominids*; nominated for Hugo Award for Best Novel, 2004, for *Humans*.

■ **Writings**

SCIENCE FICTION

Golden Fleece, Warner (New York, NY), 1990.
End of an Era, Berkley/Ace (New York, NY), 1994.
The Terminal Experiment, HarperPrism (New York, NY), 1995.
Starplex, Ace Books (New York, NY), 1996.

Frameshift, Tor (New York, NY), 1997.
Illegal Alien, Ace Books (New York, NY), 1997.
Factoring Humanity, Tor (New York, NY), 1998.
Flashforward, Tor (New York, NY), 1999.
Calculating God, Tor (New York, NY), 2000.
Iterations (short stories), Quarry (Kingston, Ontario, Canada), 2002.
Mindscan, Tor (New York, NY), 2005.
Rollback, Tor (New York, NY), 2007.

"QUINTAGLIO ASCENSION" TRILOGY

Far-Seer, Berkley/Ace (New York, NY), 1992.
Fossil Hunter, Berkley/Ace (New York, NY), 1993.
Foreigner, Berkley/Ace (New York, NY), 1994.

"NEANDERTHAL PARALLAX" TRILOGY

Hominids, Tor (New York, NY), 2002.
Humans, Tor (New York, NY), 2003.
Hybrids, Tor (New York, NY), 2003.

EDITOR

(With wife, Carolyn Clink) *Early Harvest Magazine: Young Adult Collection of Short Stories and Poetry*, 1994 edition, Vaughan Public Library Board (Vaughan, Ontario, Canada), 1994.
(With wife, Carolyn Clink) *Early Harvest Magazine: Young Adult Collection of Short Stories and Poetry*, 1995 edition, Vaughan Public Library Board (Vaughan, Ontario, Canada), 1995.
(With wife, Carolyn Clink) *Tesseracts 6: The Annual Anthology of New Canadian Speculative Fiction*, Tesseract Books (Edmonton, Alberta, Canada), 1997.
(With David Skene Melvin) *Crossing the Line: Canadian Mysteries with a Fantastic Twist*, Pottersfield (East Lawrencetown, Nova Scotia, Canada), 1998.
(With Peter Sellers) *Over the Edge: The Crime Writers of Canada Anthology*, Pottersfield (East Lawrencetown, Nova Scotia, Canada), 2000.
(With David Gerrold) *Boarding the Enterprise: Transporters, Tribbles, and the Vulcan Death Grip in Gene Roddenberry's Star Trek*, BenBella Books (Dallas, TX), 2006.

OTHER

Relativity (stories and essays), ISFiC Press (Chicago, IL), 2004.

(With Michael Lennick) *Birth* (radio drama), Canadian Broadcasting Corporation (CBC) Radio, first broadcast, July, 2005.

Also author of short stories "Just Like Old Times," "Peking Man," "Stream of Consciousness," "You See but You Do Not Observe," and "The Hand You're Dealt." Author and narrator of five one-hour documentaries on speculative fiction for Canadian Broadcasting Corporation (CBC) Radio's Ideas series, 1986, 1990. Author of commissioned series bibles for *Exodus: Mars*, Nelvana, 2000; *Charlie Jade*, CHUM Television, 2002; and *Robotech Revival*, Harmony Gold USA, 2003. Contributor of articles on science fiction to *The Canadian Encyclopedia* and *The Canadian Writer's Guide: Official Handbook of the Canadian Authors Association.* Contributor of short fiction to numerous periodicals, including *Canadian Fiction Magazine, Village Voice*, and *Globe and Mail.* Short stories included in numerous anthologies. Contributor of nonfiction to numerous periodicals, including *Toronto Star, Books in Canada, New York Review of Science Fiction*, and *Quill & Quire*; contributor of business journalism to periodicals, including *Financial Post, Financial Times of Canada, Report on Business Magazine, Your Money, InfoAge*, and *Broadcaster.* Columnist for *On Spec*, 1995-97. Editor of feature supplements for *Financial Times of Canada*, 1988 and 1990; editor of special reports for *Playback: Canada's Broadcast and Production Journal*, 1987.

■ Work in Progress

Identity Theft, a collection of stories.

■ Sidelights

The novels of Canadian science fiction writer Robert J. Sawyer have dealt with computers running amok, dinosaurs reliving the Age of Enlightenment, time-traveling paleontologists, and space-age detectives. Austin Booth, writing in the *Dictionary of Literary Biography*, explained that "Sawyer is a hard-science-fiction writer whose work is influenced by the novels of Arthur C. Clarke and the character-driven stories of Frederik Pohl. His fiction documents conflicts between science and superstition; in Sawyer's world, science is singularly able to explain or reveal truth—the mechanisms of this apparently chaotic and random universe are revealed to the reader through well-explained scientific fact." More than that, Sawyer's writings are, R. John Hayes

wrote in *Quill & Quire*, "not just wonderful SF, [but] wonderful fiction." According to Mark Grahm in the *Rocky Mountain News*, "Sawyer is just about the best science fiction writer out there these days: compelling stories, believable scenarios, science and fiction that really interact."

Sawyer was born on April 29, 1960, in Ottawa, Ontario, Canada. His father, John Arthur Sawyer, was a professor of economics and his mother, Virginia Sawyer, was a statistician. Sawyer told *Authors and Artists for Young Adults* (*AAYA*): "My parents both taught at the University of Toronto: my father taught economics and my mother taught statistics. I was born in 1960, and, back then, it was unusual to have a mother who worked outside the home, even more so to have one who was in a prestige profession. This doubtless led to the many strong, professional female characters in my books: Molly Bond in *Frameshift*, Heather Davis in *Factoring Humanity*, Mary Vaughan in *Hominids* and its sequels, Karen Bessarian in *Mindscan*, and Sarah Halifax in *Rollback*. Still, I wish I'd had a sister in addition to my two brothers; when I was young, I had a hard time understanding or relating to girls, probably because there weren't any in my home.

Sawyer showed an early interest in writing stories. "The oldest stories I can remember writing." he told *AAYA*, "date back to Grade Two; my mother still has copies of some of these—I suspect they'll show up on eBay some day! One of my very first was actually a science-fiction story, about a spaceship I called the *Stargazer.* Thirty years later, I was amused when, on *Star Trek: The Next Generation*, it turned out that Captain Picard's previous command had been called the *Stargazer*, too. I was always interested in science fiction, mostly from TV shows, and fooled around a lot drawing pictures of spaceships and aliens, and writing stories about them. My parents, and a couple of my teachers, very much encouraged my writing—in particular, the teacher I had in both grade five and grade six, who, by coincidence, was the same woman, Miss Matthews."

"I was a chubby kid, uncoordinated, and lousy at sports," Sawyer went on. "I suspect that's one of the reasons I spent so much time reading. Fortunately, my parents were very supportive of that. My father used to read to me every night when I was very young, and when I was growing up I had to wait for my birthday or Christmas for new toys, but could always have any new book I wanted." As a child, Sawyer read widely, but when he first discovered a book on dinosaurs, he became truly hooked. "My favorite book when I was a kid was *The Enormous Egg* by Oliver P. Butterworth. It was the story of a young boy in New Hampshire whose hen laid—you guessed it—an enormous egg, and out of that egg came a baby dinosaur! I totally loved dinosaurs, then and now, and read this book over and over again. One of the things that captivated me was that even though the premise was silly, Butterworth took pains to make it realistic. I was also thrilled in the book to see that the world's greatest expert on dinosaurs was a Canadian, from Toronto! We Canadians are so used to growing up reading and hearing only about Americans, so this was just wonderful, and I suspect it's why so many of my own books ended up having fictional scientists from Toronto being the world's top specialists in their fields."

Television was the conduit for Sawyer's first experiences with science fiction. Because he lived in Canada, he was exposed to both British and American sci-fi television, including the original *Star Trek* series and the British series *Fireball XL5* and *Thunderbirds.* From television science fiction, Sawyer soon moved to the masters of the printed form: Isaac Asimov, Robert Silverberg, Arthur C. Clarke, and Lester del Rey. Sawyer commented: "I also remember reading with great pleasure short stories by Isaac Asimov and Arthur C. Clarke—and some of the nicest praise I've had as a writer myself is in being compared to them."

This reading was the one bright spot for Sawyer throughout much of his early school life. It was not until grade six that he felt challenged by his classes, when his teacher gave him independent work. He fit in well socially, and by high school he was a high achiever: president of the student council and editor of the school paper. But most importantly, he founded a science fiction club, finding other people who shared his interest in the genre. It was in high school, also, that Sawyer began writing short stories, and vacations in Italy and Greece when he was sixteen and seventeen gave him a new perspective with which to view the world. But, as graduation approached, his investigations of a future career as a paleontologist bore discouraging fruit.

To that end, Sawyer attended Ryerson Polytechnical Institute in Toronto, where he studied script writing and broadcasting. After graduating, Sawyer stayed on as a teaching assistant for a year while his high school sweetheart, Carolyn Joan Clink, was finishing her degree. They married in 1984, and Sawyer never looked back to academe. He set up as a freelance writer until 1989, working with businesses and publishers in Toronto, doing everything from corporate newsletters to radio broadcasts. This apprenticeship taught him the value of deadlines and of the need to produce daily, as well as some of the fundamentals of good writing, such as voice and narrative technique.

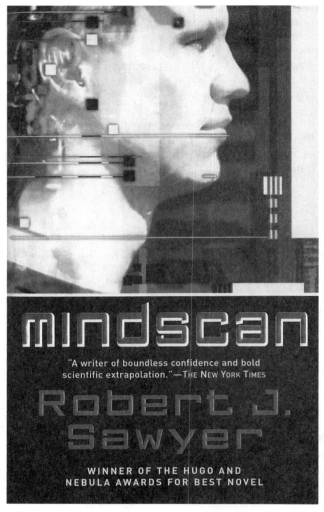

A human discards his physical body and uploads his consciousness into an android form in this 2005 work.

Sawyer remembered those days: "I've been extremely lucky: I've been a full-time writer since I was 23. In the early days, I mostly did nonfiction: articles for newspapers and magazines, corporate newsletters, brochures, speeches, and so on. Although that was indeed writing, it wasn't creative, and I wasn't fulfilled. And so, when I was 28, I decided to set all that aside and gamble on writing my first novel, even though it meant making almost no money for a few years. The lesson, of course, is simple: you only get one shot at life, so take risks, and don't be afraid to go after the things you want."

Sawyer turned in the completed manuscript of the novel *Golden Fleece* to his agent, who sold it within six weeks. *Golden Fleece* is a science fiction mystery narrated from the point of view of a sentient computer named Jason. Reminiscent of HAL, the computer in Arthur C. Clarke's *2001*, Jason kills a member of the crew who was jeopardizing the ship's forty-seven-light-year mission. Most of the narration and the subsequent unraveling of the death is told through the computer's numerous lenses aboard the ship. "The result," wrote Gordon Graham in *Quill & Quire*, "is a well-paced page-turner replete with hard science." Writing in *Books in Canada*, Gary Draper thought that Sawyer's first novel was done "with wit and imagination."

Though the reviews for *Golden Fleece* were mostly positive and the book garnered the prestigious Aurora Award, sales were poor. For his next novel, Sawyer had to go hunting for a new publisher. With *Far-Seer*, he turned to a staple that had been nourishing him for many years: dinosaurs. Inverting the acronym of his old high school science fiction club, he came up with the name Afsan for his protagonist, a dinosaur in a world in which such creatures—known as Quintaglios—have evolved sophisticated intellects comparable to human consciousness. In the Quintaglio civilization, there are cities, religions,

rulers, and a budding science. Afsan is an apprentice to the court astrologer, and on a voyage to pay homage to the god of their religion, he discovers—with the aid of a new invention called the far-seer or telescope—that his world is not the center of the universe after all. He learns, in fact, that the Quintaglio world is only a moon which eventually will crash into the planet it orbits. This Copernican discovery, described in minute detail, is bound to make Afsan a pariah to court and priests alike, much as it did for the historical astronomers Copernicus and Galileo in their time. Afsan's attempts to convince others of the truth of his scientific discoveries and the need for resettlement of the Quintaglios provides the engine for the novel that Graham described in another *Quill & Quire* review as "refreshingly original."

Far-Seer was submitted to Sawyer's agent, Richard Curtis, who immediately saw the possibilities of a book series developing from the idea and convinced Sawyer not to kill off Afsan in the first volume. After a touch of rewriting, the book was auctioned to publishers with options for the remaining volumes. This time the sales were on a par with the reviews: "A tour de force," wrote a critic in *Isaac Asimov's Science Fiction Magazine*, adding that the book is "vastly enjoyable, beautifully realized." The book also earned positive reviews in the mainstream press. A contributor to the Toronto Star reported that "without question, *Far-Seer* will be remembered as one of the year's outstanding books." And for the first time, young adult reviewers were looking at Sawyer's work. Katharine L. Kan, writing in the *Voice of Youth Advocates*, termed the book "an enjoyable read, especially for dinosaur fans," while a reviewer in *Kliatt* wrote that "this is a truly great piece of fantasy SF."

While he admits that his favorite of his own books changes from time to time, Sawyer told *AAYA* that "these days I'm feeling quite fond of *Far-Seer*, which is a novel about a world of intelligent dinosaurs—going right back to my childhood, my interest in dinosaurs from then, and *The Enormous Egg*. And my favorite character would have to be the hero of that book, Afsan. He's bright, loyal, and kind—the kind of friend I think anyone would be proud to have."

Sawyer continued the trilogy with *Fossil Hunter*, in which the son of Afsan, Toroca, continues where his father has left off. In searching for minerals necessary for the space-flight evacuation of the Quintaglios from their world, he uncovers their fossil record. Like Darwin, Toroca must come to terms with the implications of such a record. He concludes that the Quintaglios developed elsewhere and were

Sawyer standing next to a display of his paperback novels at the World Biggest Bookstore.

transplanted onto the moon they call home. Meanwhile, an element of murder mystery creeps into Sawyer's story, for with the deaths of two of Afsan's children, the old dinosaur sets out to find the culprit. It is a blend of genres to which Larry D. Condit, writing in the *Voice of Youth Advocates*, responded positively: "Sawyer . . . has done an admirable job and has developed a world into which YA science fiction and dinosaur [fans] will enjoy a brief escape." "The characterization is brilliant," wrote Hayes in *Quill & Quire*, "the plotting enviable, and the narrative technique tight and fast-paced." A *Toronto Star* critic gave it a thumbs up, calling *Fossil Hunter* "a superlative science-fiction novel."

The final book in the trilogy, *Foreigner*, was published in 1994. Afsan, now an old and venerated astronomer, again plays a key role in the action, as does a female dinosaur named Mokleb, who becomes a saurian Freud, examining the aggressiveness and intense feeling of territoriality that makes it so difficult for the Quintaglios to work together. Reviewers again commended Sawyer on his blend of science and action. Writing in *Booklist*, Carl Hays noted that Sawyer "deftly combines well-reasoned hard-science speculation with psychology, imaginative anthropology, and even linguistics." Hayes of *Quill & Quire* wrote that *Foreigner* was "a fine end to a brilliant series, one that should vault Sawyer into the first rank of science fiction writers."

In *Calculating God,* a spaceship lands outside the Royal Ontario Museum in Toronto. An eight-legged alien emerges from the craft and goes inside. He insists on seeing the head of the paleontology department. Dr. Tom Jericho is called out to meet the alien, named Hollus, who wants to examine the fossil record on Earth to prove the existence of God. The novel "smoothly combines ethical questions and comical dialogue in a highly absorbing tale," Roberta Johnson wrote in *Booklist.* "Much of the novel is relatively cerebral, as Jericho and Hollus argue over the scientific data they've gathered in support of God's existence," explained a *Publishers Weekly* reviewer, who went on to call *Calculating God* "unusually thoughtful SF." The atheist Jericho's newfound interest in religious matters is strengthened by the knowledge that he is dying: years of breathing rock dust have given him terminal lung cancer. "It sounds like a recipe for a rather depressing book," Margaret Mackey commented in *Resource Links*, "but in fact it is engaging and stimulating."

Sawyer's "Neanderthal Parallax" trilogy is set in a parallel universe where Neanderthals, not Homo sapiens, became the sole intelligent species. In *Hominids,* the first novel in the trilogy, one of these Neanderthals, scientific researcher Ponter Boddit, accidentally finds himself in real-world, modern Canada when he slips through some sort of portal. Boddit must now adapt to the foreign ways of the human world, while in his home universe, his research partner must defend himself from charges that he murdered Boddit. Roberta Johnson in *Booklist* called *Hominids* "an engaging, thought-provoking story." A critic for *Publishers Weekly* noted that "the author's usual high intelligence and occasionally daunting erudition are on prominent display."

In the second book of the trilogy, *Humans,* Boddit persuades a Canadian scientist, Mary Vaughan (whom he befriended in the first book), to come visit his universe. Now it is her turn to be perplexed by an unfamiliar society, one which is highly advanced, technologically and culturally, but which

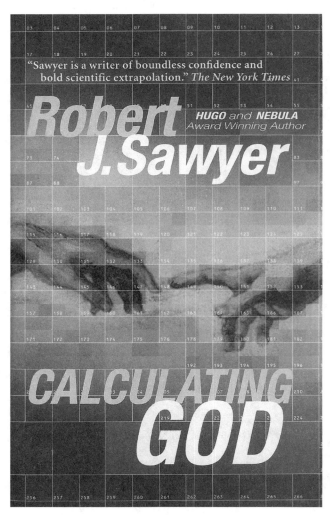

In this novel, an alien being comes to Earth to study critical extinction events in order to prove the existence of God.

never adopted agriculture. The *Publishers Weekly* reviewer dubbed the title to be "extremely well done." The trilogy is completed with *Hybrids,* in which Vaughan and Boddit decide to conceive a child together, which forces them to face the implications of the genetic engineering necessary to make such a child viable, while also fighting off various humans who want to exploit the trusting Neanderthals and plunder their world's wealth. The critic for *Publishers Weekly* called the novel "some of the most outrageous, stimulating speculation since Robert Heinlein's *Stranger in a Strange Land.*" Johnson found that "a fine combination of love story, social commentary, and ecothriller closes a terrific series with a bang."

If you enjoy the works of Robert J. Sawyer, you may also want to check out the following:

Octavia E. Butler, *Dawn,* 1987.
Terry Bisson, *Virtuosity,* 1995.
Alan Dean Foster, *Parallelities,* 1998.

In *Mindscan,* Sawyer tells of Jake Sullivan, who pays to have his mind scanned by the Immortex company and uploaded into an android body. By leaving behind his human body, he hopes to avoid sickness, pain, and eventual death. But trouble soon develops. Jake's old body is sent to the moon while his android lives on Earth. On the moon, the old Jake discovers there is a new cure for old age and death that does not involve using androids. Can he retrieve himself from his other body? Meanwhile, the android Jake has found a new love in Karen, who is also an android. Karen's original body has died and her android is being sued by her son, who claims that she is legally dead; he wants to collect his inheritance. Regina Schroeder in *Booklist* called *Mindscan* "a good story that is a new meditation on an old sf theme, the meaning of being human." A critic for *Publishers Weekly* concluded that *Mindscan* provides "plenty of philosophical speculation on the ethics of bio-technology and the nature of consciousness."

Sawyer explained to *AAYA* his process for developing the characters in his books: "I never base a character directly on anyone. First, that can get you in trouble: even if you change the name and identifying physical characteristics, the real person

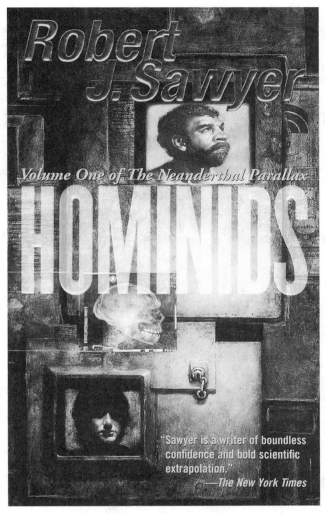

In this 2002 novel a Neanderthal from a parallel universe finds himself accidentally transported to present-day Canada.

can sue if he thinks other people will recognize that the character is him, and the portrayal is unflattering. Of course, I do take little bits and pieces of real people, and jumble them together: a mannerism from one person, a way of dressing from another, the sense of humor from a third. But most of my characters are just made up: they aren't real people, although they're supposed to seem like they are. People who don't write often don't understand that: they lack the imagination to create a person, and they can't conceive of others being able to do that. But writers do, all the time. To create a character, I come up with the situation I want to explore first, and then devise a person who is going to have a challenging time in that situation."

When asked what advice he gives budding writers, Sawyer explained: "I always tell them that making it in writing takes three things: talent, luck, and perseverance. Talent you either have or you don't, and if you don't, you won't make it. That's a hard one for some people to swallow—but no one would expect to be able to be a rock star or a baseball player without talent, and the same thing is true for writing. Luck is also a hard one, because sometimes it comes your way, and sometimes it doesn't. But perseverance you control completely: so stick with it. In the end, it's only 10% talent and 10% luck—the other 80% is keeping at it. I also tell them that not everyone is going to like their work—and that's okay. Your job as a writer isn't to be blandly acceptable to everyone; rather, it's to be the favorite author of a narrow segment of the population. If you try to please everybody, you'll end up pleasing no one. And, most of all, you should try to please yourself."

■ Biographical and Critical Sources

BOOKS

Dictionary of Literary Biography, Volume 251: *Canadian Science-Fiction and Fantasy Writers*, Gale (Detroit, MI), 2002.

St. James Guide to Science Fiction Writers, 4th edition, St. James Press (Detroit, MI), 1996.

Science Fiction and Fantasy Literature, 1975-1991, Gale (Detroit, MI), 1992.

Van Belkom, Edo, *Northern Dreamers: Interviews with Famous Science Fiction, Fantasy, and Horror Writers*, Quarry Press (Kingston, Ontario, Canada), 1998.

PERIODICALS

American Way (American Airlines in-flight magazine), January 15, 2006, profile of Sawyer.

Analog Science Fiction & Fact, December 15, 1990, Tom Easton, review of *Golden Fleece*, pp. 179-180; June, 1992, Tom Easton, review of *Far-Seer*, pp. 164-165; August, 1993, Tom Easton, review of *Fossil Hunter*, pp. 164-165; March, 1994, Tom Easton, review of *Foreigner*, p. 161; October, 1994, Tom Easton, review of *End of an Era*, p. 163; December 15, 1994, Jay Kay Klein, "Biolog: Robert J. Sawyer," pp. 69-70; May, 1997, Tom Easton, review of *Frameshift*, pp. 146-147; January, 1998, Tom Easton, review of *Illegal Alien*, p. 145; September, 1998, Tom Easton, review of *Factoring Humanity*, pp. 133-134; September, 1999, Tom Easton, review of *Flashforward*, pp. 132-137.

Booklist, March 15, 1994, Carl Hays, review of *Foreigner*, p. 1333; October 15, 1994, Carl Hays, review of *End of an Era*, p. 405; October 15, 1996, Roland Green, review of *Starplex*, p. 408; April 15, 1997, William Beatty, review of *Frameshift*, p. 1387; May 15, 1998, John Mort, review of *Factoring Humanity*, pp. 1606-1607; May 15, 1999, John Mort, review of *Flashforward*, p. 1682; April 15, 2000, Roberta Johnson, review of *Calculating God*, p. 1534; June 1, 2002, Roberta Johnson, review of *Hominids*, p. 1698; January 1, 2003, Roberta Johnson, review of *Humans*, p. 862; September 1, 2003, Roberta Johnson, review of *Hybrids*, p. 75; March 15, 2005, Regina Schroeder, review of *Mindscan*, p. 1276.

Books in Canada, March, 1991, Gary Draper, review of *Golden Fleece*, p. 56; March, 1993, interview with Sawyer, pp. 22-25.

Calgary Herald (Calgary, Alberta, Canada), July 21, 1998, interview with Sawyer, p. B5.

Canadian Literature, spring, 2001, Douglas Ivison, "Knights and Alien Signals," pp. 163-165.

Challenging Destiny, January, 1999, James Schellenberg and David M. Switzer, "Interview with Robert J. Sawyer," pp. 32-44.

Columbus Dispatch (Columbus, OH), October 6, 1999, p. C10.

Edmonton Journal (Edmonton, Alberta, Canada), April 16, 1997, p. B6.

Entertainment Weekly, April 22, 2005, Noah Robischon, review of Mindscan, p. 67.

Financial Post, November 23, 1996, p. 35.

Globe and Mail (Toronto, Ontario, Canada), July 22, 2000, review of *Calculating God*, p. D10; June 8, 2002, review of *Hominids*, p. D19; November 22, 2003, review of *Hybrids*, p. D22; June 11, 2005, Shlomo Schwartzberg, review of *Mindscan*, p. D10.

Halifax Chronicle-Herald (Halifax, Nova Scotia, Canada), September 20, 1996, p. D2.

Interzone, November, 1999, David Mathew, "Beyond Humanity," pp. 27-31.

Isaac Asimov's Science Fiction Magazine, June, 1992, review of *Far-Seer*, p. 170.

Kirkus Reviews, May 15, 2002, review of Hominids, p. 712; December 1, 2002, review of *Humans*, pp. 1741-1742; March 1, 2005, review of Mindscan, p. 268.

Kliatt, April, 1991, p. 21; September, 1992, review of *Far-Seer*, p. 23; September, 1993, p. 22.

Library Journal, November 15, 1990, Jackie Cassada, review of *Golden Fleece*, p. 95; April 15, 1993, Jackie Cassada, review of *Fossil Hunter*, p. 130; August, 1996, Susan Hamburger, review of *Starplex*, p. 120; May 15, 1997, Susan Hamburger, review of *Frameshift*, p. 106; June 15, 1998, Jackie Cassada, review of *Factoring Humanity*, p. 111; April 15, 2000, Jackie Cassada, review of *Calculating God*, p. 126; March 15, 2005, Jackie Cassada, review of *Mindscan*, p. 75.

Locus, August, 1990, p. 21; January, 1991, p. 58; January, 1992, p. 19; June, 1993, p. 31; February, 2003, interview with Sawyer, pp. 92-94.

Maclean's, August 19, 1996, "A Canadian Writer's Newfound Respect, "p. 53; June 21, 1999, interview with Sawyer; October 7, 2002, Robert J. Sawyer, "Privacy: Who Needs It?, "p. 44.

Magazine of Fantasy and Science Fiction, December, 1990, Orson Scott Card, review of *Golden Fleece,* pp. 89-90; May, 1991, p. 50; December, 1994, Charles de Lint, review of *End of an Era,* pp. 30-31; October-November, 1996, Charles de Lint, review of *The Terminal Experiment,* pp. 61-62.

Metro Pulse (Knoxville, TN), November 25-December 3, 1998, p. 17.

Mystery Review, spring, 1999, interview with Sawyer.

Ottawa Citizen (Ottawa, Ontario, Canada), May 26, 1998, interview with Sawyer, p. C7; July 5, 1998, p. C3; March 9, 2003, profile of Sawyer; September 4, 2003, interview with Sawyer, pp. A1-A2.

Publishers Weekly, May 4, 1992, review of *Far-Seer,* p. 54; November 10, 1997, review of *Illegal Alien,* p. 59; May 25, 1998, review of *Factoring Humanity,* p. 70; April 19, 1999, review of *Flashforward,* p. 66; March 20, 2000, review of *Calculating God,* p. 75; June 17, 2002, review of *Hominids,* p. 48; January 13, 2003, review of *Humans,* pp. 45-46; September 1, 2003, review of *Hybrids,* p. 69; January 24, 2005, review of *Mindscan,* p. 226.

Quill & Quire, July, 1990, Gordon Graham, review of *Golden Fleece,* p. 55; July, 1992, Gordon Graham, review of *Far-Seer,* p. 37; May, 1993, R. John Hayes, review of *Fossil Hunter,* p. 26; January, 1994, R. John Hayes, review of *Foreigner,* p. 33; May, 2000, Meredith Renwick, review of *Calculating God,* pp. 29-30; July, 2002, Robert Wiersema, review of *Hominids,* p. 35.

Resource Links, October, 2001, Margaret Mackey, review of *Calculating God,* p. 57.

Rocky Mountain News (Denver, CO), July 9, 2000, review of *Calculating God,* p. 4E.

St. Catharines Standard (St. Catharines, Ontario, Canada), June 28, 1997, p. B1.

Science Fiction Chronicle, September, 1993, interview with Sawyer; October, 1994, review of *End of an Era,* p. 38; June-July, 2000, interview with Sawyer.

Tennessean (Nashville, TN), January 11, 1998, p. K1.

Toronto Star (Toronto, Ontario, Canada), August 22, 1992, interview with Sawyer and review of *Far-Seer,* p. H14; July 3, 1993, review of *Fossil Hunter,* p. H14; December 3, 1994, review of *End of an Era,* p. SS2; August 1, 1998, interview with Sawyer, p. K4; August 6, 2000, review of *Calculating God,* p. F8; August 31, 2003, profile of Sawyer.

Toronto Sun (Toronto, Ontario, Canada), September 11, 2002, "Career Connection, "p. 4.

Voice of Youth Advocates, October, 1992, Katharine L. Kan, review of Far-Seer, pp. 242-243; August, 1993, Larry D. Condit, review of *Fossil Hunter,* p. 170.

Winnipeg Free Press (Winnipeg, Manitoba, Canada), October 16, 1997, interview with Sawyer, p. 14.

ONLINE

Meme Therapy, http://memetherapy.blogspot.com/ (June 12, 2006), interview with Sawyer.

Robert J. Sawyer's Blog, http://www.sfwriter.com/ blog.htm (July 6, 2006).

Robert J. Sawyer Home Page, http://www.sfwriter. com/ (July 6, 2006).

OTHER

In the Mind of Robert J. Sawyer (one-hour television special), 2003.

Gary D. Schmidt

■ Personal

Born April 14, 1957, in Massapequa, NY; son of Robert H. (a bank vice president) and Jeanne A. (a teacher) Schmidt; married Anne E. Stickney (a writer), December 22, 1979; children: James, Kathleen, Rebecca, David, Margaret, Benjamin. *Education:* Gordon College, B.A., 1979; University of Illinois at Urbana-Champaign, M.A., 1981, Ph.D., 1985. *Religion:* Christian Reformed. *Hobbies and other interests:* Gardening.

■ Addresses

Home—Alto, MI. *Office*—Department of English, Calvin College, Grand Rapids, MI 49546. *E-mail*—schg@calvin.edu.

■ Career

Writer, educator. Calvin College, Grand Rapids, MI, professor of English, 1985—, department head, 1991-97.

■ Member

Children's Literature Association, Early English Text Society, Phi Kappa Phi, Phi Alpha Chi.

■ Awards, Honors

Honorable mention, Children's Literature Association, 1993, for *Robert McCloskey;* Best Books for Young Adults citation, American Library Association, 1997, for *The Sin Eater; Booklist* "10 Best Historical Fiction Novels," 2001, for *Anson's Way;* Newbery Medal Honor Book, Printz Honor Book, *Booklist* Top Ten Historical Fiction for Youth list, all 2005, and all for *Lizzie Bright and the Buckminster Boy.*

■ Writings

JUVENILES

John Bunyan's Pilgrim's Progress, illustrated by Barry Moser, Eerdmans (Grand Rapids, MI), 1994.

Robert Frost, illustrated by Henri Sorensen, Sterling Publishing (New York, NY), 1994.

The Sin Eater (novel), Dutton (New York, NY), 1996.

The Blessing of the Lord: Stories from the Old and New Testaments, illustrated by Dennis Nolan, Eerdmans (Grand Rapids, MI), 1997.

William Bradford: Pilgrim of Answerable Courage, Eerdmans (Grand Rapids, MI), 1997.

Anson's Way (novel), Clarion Books (New York, NY), 1999.

William Bradford: Plymouth's Faithful Pilgrim, Eerdmans (Grand Rapids, MI), 1999.

Saint Ciaran: The Tale of a Saint of Ireland, illustrated by Todd Doney, Eerdmans (Grand Rapids, MI), 2000.

(Editor, with Frances Schoonmaker Bolin and Brod Bagert) *The Blackbirch Treasury of American Poetry,* Blackbirch Press (Woodbridge, CT), 2001.

(As Gary Schmidt) *Mara's Stories: Glimmers in the Darkness* (novel), Henry Holt (New York, NY), 2001.

Straw into Gold (novel), Clarion Books (New York, NY), 2001.

(As Gary Schmidt) *The Wonders of Donal O'Donnell: A Folktale of Ireland* (picture book), Henry Holt (New York, NY), 2002.

(As Gary Schmidt, reteller) Nathaniel Hawthorne, *The Great Stone Face* (picture book), illustrated by Bill Farnsworth, Eerdmans (Grand Rapids, MI), 2002.

Lizzie Bright and the Buckminster Boy (novel), Clarion Books (New York, NY), 2004.

(As Gary Schmidt) *First Boy* (novel), Henry Holt (New York, NY), 2005.

(As Gary Schmidt, with Lawrence Kushner) *In God's Hands* (picture book), Jewish Lights Pub. (Woodstock, VT), 2005.

FOR ADULTS

Supplementary Essays for College Writers, Prentice-Hall (Englewood Cliffs, NJ), 1988.

(Editor, with Charlotte F. Otten) *The Voice of the Narrator in Children's Literature: Insights from Writers and Critics,* Greenwood Press (Westport, CT), 1989.

Robert McCloskey, Twayne (Boston, MA), 1990.

Hugh Lofting, Macmillan (New York, NY), 1992.

(Editor, with Donald R. Hettinga) *Sitting at the Feet of the Past: Retelling the North American Folktale for Children,* Greenwood Press (Westport, CT), 1992.

(Editor, with William J. Vande Kopple) *Communities of Discourse: The Rhetoric of Disciplines* (includes instructor's manual), Prentice-Hall (Englewood Cliffs, NJ), 1993.

Katherine Paterson, Macmillan (New York, NY), 1994.

The Iconography of the Mouth of Hell: Eighth-Century Britain to the Fifteenth Century, Susquehanna University Press (Cranbury, NJ), 1995.

(Editor, with Donald R. Hettinga) *British Children's Writers, 1914-1960,* Gale (Detroit, MI), 1996.

Robert Lawson, Macmillan (New York, NY), 1997.

(With Carol Winters) *Edging the Boundaries of Children's Literature,* Allyn & Bacon (Boston, MA), 2001.

(Editor as Gary Schmidt, with Susan M. Felch) *Winter: A Spiritual Biography of the Season,* illustrated by Barry Moser, SkyLight Paths Pub. (Woodstock, VT), 2003.

(Editor as Gary Schmidt, with Susan M. Felch) *Autumn: A Spiritual Biography of the Season,* illustrated by Mary Azarian, SkyLight Paths Pub. (Woodstock, VT), 2004.

(Editor as Gary Schmidt, with Susan M. Felch) *Summer: A Spiritual Biography of the Season,* illustrated by Barry Moser, SkyLight Paths Pub. (Woodstock, VT), 2005.

(Editor as Gary Schmidt, with Susan M. Felch) *Spring: A Spiritual Biography of the Season,* illustrated by Mary Azarian, SkyLight Paths Pub. (Woodstock, VT), 2006.

OTHER

Contributor to books, including *Text and Matter: New Critical Perspectives of the Pearl Poet,* edited by Robert J. Blanch, Miriam Miller, and Julian Wasserman, Whitston (Troy, NY), 1991. Contributor of articles, essays, stories, poems, and reviews to journals, including *Christian Home and School, Lion and the Unicorn, Studies in American Humor, Christian Educators Journal,* and *Martha's KidLit Newsletter.* Guest editor, *Children's Literature Association Quarterly,* 1989.

■ Adaptations

Lizzie Bright and the Buckminster Boy and *First Boy* were adapted for audio cassette, Listening Library, 2005.

■ Sidelights

Winner of a Printz Honor Book award and a Newbery Honor Medal for his young adult novel *Lizzie Bright and the Buckminster Boy,* American writer Gary D. Schmidt has blended an academic career as an English professor with writing for both adults and juveniles. His adult works include biographies of children's writers and spiritual evocations of the seasons, as well as professional critical works. Writing for younger readers, Schmidt has created tales from picture books to middle grade and young

Gary Schmidt onstage with Katherine Paterson at Calvin College's Faith and Writing Festival.

adult novels. Among the latter are *The Sin Eater, Anson's Way, Straw into Gold, Mara's Stories: Glimmers in the Darkness, Lizzie Bright and the Buckminster Boy,* and *First Boy.* In other works, such as *The Blessing of the Lord: Stories from the Old and New Testaments, William Bradford: Plymouth's Faithful Pilgrim, Saint Ciaran: The Tale of a Saint of Ireland,* and *In God's Hands,* Schmidt blends religious themes, biography, and narrative, while in *John Bunyan's Pilgrim's Progress, Old Stone Face,* and *The Wonders of Donal O'Donnell: A Folktale of Ireland,* Schmidt acts as a reteller.

Begins with Adult Works

Born in New York state in 1957, Schmidt received his doctorate from the University of Illinois at Urbana-Champaign in 1985. Thereafter, he began teaching as a professor of English at Calvin College in Grand Rapids, Michigan. His earliest works dealt with children's literature, critical books for an adult audience. For example, his *Robert McCloskey,* for the Twayne series on writers, looks at the life and works of this recipient of the Caldecott Medal. *Horn Book* critic Ethel L. Heins praised Schmidt for working with "unstinting effort, making exhaustive use of both published and archival material." Reviewing his *Katherine Paterson, Booklist* contributor Ilene Cooper commented that Schmidt does "an excellent job of chronicling" the life of this two-time Newbery Award winner." Similarly, Margaret W. Bird, writing in *Book Report,* felt "this volume will enhance a school library's collection of critical material on authors." Schmidt does a similar job for another well-known children's author in his *Robert Lawson,* and for the nineteenth-century writer, Hannah Adams. His *A Passionate Usefulness: The Life and Literary Labors of Hannah Adams* details the life and work of this pioneering female writer. Writing in *Legacy: A Journal of American Women Writers,* Michael

Everton commented, "Schmidt meticulously canvases Adams's sources to assemble a cogent portrait of her ideological positions" to create an "essential biography." Working with Susan M. Felch as coeditor, Schmidt also prepared the four season volumes of *A Spiritual Biography of the Seasons*. Collecting inspirational works from many sources, these anthologies celebrate the wheel of the year. Reviewing *Spring: A Spiritual Biography of the Season*, a *Publishers Weekly* contributor concluded: "Through poetry, prose, hymns and essays, this collection joyfully celebrates the glories of the season."

Schmidt turned his hand to children's books with the 1994 work *Robert Frost*, a book in the "Poetry for Young People" series. Meg Stackpole, writing in *School Library Journal*, felt this overview of the famous American poet "satisfies in every way." His next children's work was the retelling of the seventeenth-century allegory *Pilgrim's Progress*, by

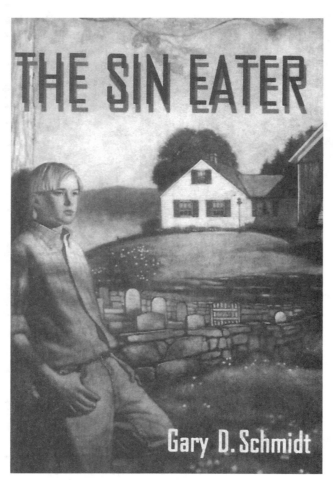

After his mother's death, a teenage boy returns to the family farm to start a new life with his father and grandparents in this 1996 novel.

John Bunyan, in his own *John Bunyan's Pilgrim's Progress*. Schmidt once noted: "*Pilgrim's Progress* had been with me some fifteen years before I finally turned to a retelling. It seemed to me that there were strong reasons why children would have turned this into a child's story back in the seventeenth and eighteenth centuries, and I was not convinced that those reasons no longer pertained in the late twentieth century. I wrote the retelling thinking of my own early responses to the book, cutting out the parts that bored and that struck discordant notes." Schmidt's retelling of *Pilgrim's Progress* "is much more accessible than the original version," according to *School Library Journal* contributor Kate Hegarty Bouman, who also noted that Schmidt's "mix of both historical periods and ethnic groups is a fascinating way to extend the text spatially and temporally." A reviewer for *Publishers Weekly* similarly praised Schmidt's "masterly rendition" as "a treasure sure to delight young and old."

Further retellings from Schmidt include both religious and folk tales. *The Blessing of the Lord: Stories from the Old and New Testaments* includes retellings from "unusual perspectives," as Shelley Townsend-Hudson commented in *Booklist*. Schmidt retells the stories of Jonah, Deborah, Barak, Peter, and others, with a twist that gives the "often tired old tales . . . new life," according to Townsend-Hudson. Maeve Visser Knoth, writing in *Horn Book Guide*, felt that Schmidt emphasized "the humanity of the characters," while a *Publishers Weekly* reviewer praised the "dramatic spin" Schmidt gave to these tales. Reviewing the same work in *School Library Journal*, Patricia Pearl Dole praised the "short, creative, insightful, and moving accounts" in these twenty-five biblical adaptations. Another retelling of a religious folktale is Schmidt's 2005 picture book, *In God's Hands*, authored with Lawrence Kushner.

With *The Great Stone Face*, Schmidt retells a Nathaniel Hawthorne story with a text that is "clear and succinct," and with a "stately rhythm that lends itself to reading aloud," according to *Booklist* critic Kay Weisman. For Grace Oliff, writing in *School Library Journal*, "This thoughtful look at what it means to live a good life is as relevant today as when first written." Schmidt's *The Wonders of Donal O'Donnell* retells four Irish folktales, blending them into one to "emphasize a particular theme: loss, grief and healing," as a reviewer for *Publishers Weekly* observed. Marie Orlando, writing in *School Library Journal*, called this picture book "beautiful."

Further religious and spiritual matters are served up in *William Bradford: Plymouth's Faithful Pilgrim* and *Saint Ciaran: The Tale of Saint of Ireland*. The former biography, intended for older readers, looks at the guiding light of the Plymouth Colony, painting "a warm and cohesive picture of William Bradford's role in that colony's foundation and growth," as a critic for *Kirkus Reviews* observed. Bradford, an orphan from early childhood, embraced Puritan ideals as a teenager and ultimately led a group of Separatists on a perilous mission to found a colony in the New World. Schmidt uses Bradford's own writings as well as contemporary journals and prints to take the reader back into the religious beliefs of those early colonists. "The author clearly presents Bradford's religious views and shows how those beliefs affected his life and actions and those of the Pilgrims," wrote Elaine Fort Weischedel in a *School Library Journal* review.

Schmidt's *Saint Ciaran* is another picture book intended for older readers. "In mouth-filling cadences of Gaelic . . . Schmidt tells the story of the sixth-century Irish saint," noted GraceAnne A. De-Candido in *Booklist.* Growing up a spiritual child, Ciaran went to Rome and discovered religion in the city's churches. Sent back to Ireland by St. Patrick, he founded a religious community that attracted members from all over the island. DeCandido felt that this was a "beautiful picture book for older children," and Kathleen Kelly MacMillan, writing in *School Library Journal,* similarly thought the book was a "gently moving tribute to a lesser-known saint."

Novels for Young Readers

Though he is the author a wide range of works, Schmidt is best known for his novels for middle grade and young adult readers. Schmidt's first young adult novel was *The Sin Eater,* in which middle-schooler Cole and his father move in with Cole's maternal grandparents in rural New Hampshire after Cole's mother dies of cancer. Cole delights in their new surroundings and in the village lore and tales of ancestry told him by his grandparents and other locals. Cole's father, however, remains grief-stricken and ultimately commits suicide. "A work laden with atmosphere and meaning, this is a promising debut from an author who captures with admirable accuracy both the dark and light of life," asserted a *Kirkus Reviews* critic. A *Publishers Weekly* reviewer also found Schmidt's *Sin Eater* an "engrossing first novel," adding that the plot forms a "point of departure for a profound and lyrical meditation on life and the importance of shared history."

Set in the eighteenth-century Ireland, this 1999 work concerns a young drummer boy who questions his loyalty to the King's army after he witnesses several acts of violence committed by British soldiers.

Schmidt demonstrates the variety of his prose styles and themes in two further novels, *Anson's Way* and *Straw into Gold.* Again using Ireland for a setting, this time in the eighteenth century, Schmidt features a young Anson Granville Staplyton who follows his family calling and joins the Staffordshire military, the Fencible. Dreaming of glory, he is sent to Ireland as a mere drummer to help keep the peace. When he sees fellow soldiers persecuting the locals, he begins to have mixed loyalties. He meets an Irish hedge master, a person who illegally teaches the Irish their forbidden language and culture, and he soon befriends some of the Irish rebels. Ultimately, Anson is forced to choose between his comrades in arms and his new Irish friends. This book "realistically portrays not only the tragedies of war but also the battle between heart and mind of a young soldier," as *Booklist* writer Shelle Rosenfeld remarked. Janice M. Del Negro, reviewing the title in *Bulletin of the Center for Children's Books,* also praised this "complex action/adventure novel" with its "shifting moral center." For Hilary Crew in *Voice of Youth Advocates,* the same novel was "replete with drama and action . . . [and] presents a side of Irish history that is frequently marginalized in textbooks." And for Starr E. Smith, reviewing the work in *School Library Journal, Anson's Way* was a "first-rate historical novel," with a "tense, exciting story people with lively characters moving through glorious Irish landscapes, all depicted movingly."

In his middle-grade novel *Straw into Gold,* Schmidt spins a new twist in the old Rumpelstiltskin tale, extending it to see what could have happened. In Schmidt's rendering, young Tousle leaves his forest cottage with his magical father, Da, to travel to the city and view the king's procession. He becomes separated from his father and then surprises himself by calling out for mercy for some rebels facing execution. One other voice raised against the execution is that of the queen herself. The king will spare the lives only if Tousle and a blind young rebel, Innes, are able solve the riddle the king sets for them about what fills a hand fuller than a skein of gold. "So begins a suspenseful quest that adds surprising twists and turns to the traditional fairy tale," wrote *Booklist* critic Frances Bradburn. *School Library Journal* reviewer Ginny Gustin also reacted positively to the tale, calling it a "fantasy-flavored quest."

Schmidt tells tales of a much different sort in *Mara's Stories,* supposedly first told by a young concentration camp inmate during the Holocaust. Mara uses twenty-two Jewish tales to entertain the other women and children in her barracks. Roger Sutton, writing in *Horn Book,* noted that these tales "flicker across a spectrum from transcendent hope to the absolute bleakness of a universe deserted by God." Similarly, a *Reading Today* contributor felt the "stories celebrate the resilience of the human spirit," and are a "testament to truth and a promise to remember."

Schmidt's award-winning 2004 title, *Lizzie Bright and the Buckminster Boy,* is a "haunting combination of fact and fiction," according to *Booklist* reviewer Hazel Rochman. Set in 1912 on the Maine coast, the tale involves a minister's son, who has just moved to Maine from Boston, and his friendship with a young black girl, Lizzie Bright Griffin, a resident of nearby Malaga Island, which was settled by freed

Schmidt won the Newberry Honor for this novel dealing with prejudice in Maine in 1912.

slaves. Lizzie makes Turner Buckminster feel more at home in Maine, teaching him the ins and outs of Maine baseball, among other things, and when the town leaders decide to clear the nearby island of its occupants to make way for the tourist trade, Turner tries to help his new friend, but to no avail. She, along with the other residents, are sent to a home for the mentally ill. Schmidt's historical novel received critical acclaim upon publication. *School Library Journal* contributor Connie Tyrrell Burns noted that "Schmidt's writing is infused with feeling and rich in imagery." Burns further praised the "memorable characters . . . [in this] fascinating, little-known piece of history." Similarly, a critic for *Kirkus Reviews* concluded: "There can be no happy ending to this story, but the telling is both beautiful and emotionally honest, both funny and piercingly sad." And for Beverly Vaughn Hock, writing in *Library Media Connection,* "This shameful incident is recounted with sensitivity and humor."

If you enjoy the works of Gary D. Schmidt, you may also want to check out the following books:

Robin McKinley, *The Door in the Hedge,* 1981.
Donna Jo Napoli, *Song of the Magdalene,* 1996.
Pete Hautman, *Godless,* 2004.

Schmidt followed up this success with the 2005 young adult novel *First Boy,* set in contemporary New Hampshire and "blending political farce with a poignant account of one boy's search for home," according to *Booklist* contributor Rochman. Cooper is orphaned at fourteen, when his grandfather dies, but he wants to stay on the family dairy farm. The neighbors help out, but he is suddenly plagued by mysterious fires in the barn and by men in dark suits prowling the countryside in large sedans. Cooper was abandoned by his parents, and has no idea who they are, but soon his secrets become caught up in the U.S. presidential race, for the challenger believes the female incumbent may be Cooper's birth mother and hopes for a scandal. Ultimately Cooper is kidnapped and comes face to face with the female president, but Schmidt never reveals if, in fact, Cooper is her son, for the president refuses a DNA test. For Burns, writing in *School Library Journal, First Boy* was a "fast-paced tale" in which "Cooper's grief, solitude, and loneliness are poignantly and realistically drawn." *Horn Book* critic Vicky Smith was also moved by Schmidt's characterization, calling Cooper "an entirely appealing protagonist." And a *Kirkus Reviews* critic dubbed the work a "suspenseful, surprisingly over-the-top novel" which ultimately demonstrates that "love conquers all."

Schmidt, who lives on a farm in Michigan with his wife and six children, is an author who graphs the full texture of life in his universal tales that show the ups and downs of life. As he once noted: "In thinking about my own work in children's literature, it seems to me that I am interested in showing the beatific and terrible complexities of our lives. I have had one reader tell me that *The Sin Eater* was sadder and funnier than he thought it would be. It seems to me that our lives are just that: often sadder and funnier than we ever thought they would be. They are also more beatific than we have any reason to expect, and my hope is to show that in the context of a world that is often dark."

■ Biographical and Critical Sources

PERIODICALS

Booklinks, January, 2005, review of *Lizzie Bright and the Buckminster Boy,* p. 13.
Booklist, April 1, 1990, p. 1563; May 1, 1994, Ilene Cooper, review of *Katherine Paterson,* p. 1611; November 1, 1994, p. 1611; December 1, 1994, Hazel Rochman, review of *Robert Frost,* p. 669; November 1, 1996, Ilene Cooper, review of *The Sin Eater,* p. 491; November 1, 1997, Shelley Townsend-Hudson, review of *The Blessing of the Lord: Stories from the Old and New Testaments,* p. 469; April 1, 1999, Shelle Rosenfeld, review of *Anson's Way,* p. 1428; April 1, 2000, GraceAnne A. DeCandido, review of *Saint Ciaran,* p. 1459; August, 2001, Frances Bradburn, review of *Straw into Gold,* p. 2108; October 1, 2002, Kay Weisman, review of *The Great Stone Face,* p. 327; January 1, 2003, GraceAnne A. DeCandido, review of *The Wonders of Donal O'Donnell: A Folktale of Ireland,* pp. 885-886; May 15, 2004, Hazel Rochman, review of *Lizzie Bright and the Buckminster Boy,* pp. 1629-1630; May 15, 2005, Hazel Rochman, "Top 10 Historical Fiction for Youth," p. 1675; September 15, 2005, Hazel Rochman, review of *First Boy,* p. 60; October 1, 2005, Ilene Cooper, review of *In God's Hands,* p. 70, Lolly Gepson, review of *Lizzie Bright and the Buckminster Boy* (audiobook), p. 78; February 15, 2006, Lolly Gepson, review of *First Boy* (audiobook), p. 118.
Book Report, September-October, 1994, Margaret W. Bird, review of *Katherine Paterson,* p. 55; March-April, 1997, Carol A. Burbridge, review of *The Sin Eater,* p. 41; November-December, 1999, review of *Anson's Way,* p. 66; December, 2001, Charlotte Decker, review of *Straw into Gold,* p. 66.
Bulletin of the Center for Children's Books, May, 1994, p. 306; November, 1996, p. 114; May, 1999, Janice M. Del Negro, review of *Anson's Way,* pp. 327-328.
Christian Century, May 16, 2006, review of *Summer: A Spiritual Biography of the Season,* p. 41.
Horn Book, July, August, 1990, Ethel L. Heins, review of *Robert McCloskey,* p. 476; January-February, 2002, Roger Sutton, review of *Mara's Stories: Glimmers in the Darkness,* p. 89; November-December, 2004, Betty Carter, review of *Lizzie Bright and the Buckminster Boy,* pp. 717-718; September-October, 2005, Vicky Smith, review of *First Boy,* p. 589.
Horn Book Guide, spring, 1997, p. 84; spring, 1998, Maeve Visser Knoth, review of *The Blessing of the Lord,* p. 96; fall, 1998, Tanya Auger, review of *William Bradford: Plymouth's Faithful Pilgrim,* p. 416.
Journal of English and Germanic Philology, July, 1997, Thomas H. Ohlgren, review of *The Iconography of the Mouth of Hell: Eighth-Century Britain to the Fifteenth Century,* p. 434.

Kirkus Reviews, September 1, 1996, review of *The Sin Eater,* p. 1328; June 1, 1998, review of *William Bradford,* p. 816; November 15, 2002, review of *The Wonders of Donal O'Donnell,* p. 1702; May 1, 2004, review of *Lizzie Bright and the Buckminster Boy,* p. 448; August 1, 2005, review of *In God's Hands,* p. 852; September 1, 2005, review of *First Boy,* p. 982.

Legacy: A Journal of American Women Writers, June, 2005, Michael Everton, review of *A Passionate Usefulness: The Life and Literary Labors of Hannah Adams,* p. 203.

Library Media Connection, April-May, 2005, Beverly Vaughn Hock, review of *Lizzie Bright and the Buckminster Boy,* p. 79.

New York Times Book Review, November 13, 1994, Tom Ferrell, "Make Way for Allegories," review of *John Bunyan's Pilgrim's Progress,* p. 30.

Publishers Weekly, December 19, 1994, review of *John Bunyan's Pilgrim's Progress,* pp. 54-55; October 14, 1996, review of *The Sin Eater,* p. 84; August 25, 1997, review of *The Blessing of the Lord,* p. 66; March 1, 1999, review of *Anson's Way,* p. 70; April 10, 2000, review of *Saint Ciaran,* p. 95; November 4, 2002, review of *The Wonders of Donal O'Donnell,* p. 84; January 16, 2006, review of *First Boy* (audiobook), p. 68; January 30, 2006, review of *Spring: A Spiritual Biography of the Season,* p. 66.

Reading Today, February-March, 2002, review of *Mara's Stories,* p. 32.

School Library Journal, December, 1994, Kate Hegarty Bouman, review of *Pilgrim's Progress,* p. 130; February, 1995, Meg Stackpole, review of *Robert Frost,* p. 104; January, 1997, John Peters, review of *The Sin Eater,* p. 116; October, 1997, Patricia Pearl Dole, review of *The Blessing of the Lord,* p. 154; April, 1999, Starr E. Smith, review of *Anson's Way,* p. 142; June, 1999, Elaine Fort Weischedel, review of *William Bradford,* p. 153; August, 2000, Kathleen Kelly MacMillan, review of *Saint Ciaran,* p. 175; August, 2001, Ginny Gustin, review of *Straw into Gold,* p. 188; December, 2001, Amy Lilien-Harper, review of *Mara's Stories,* p. 143; November, 2002, Grace Oliff, review of *The Great Stone Face,* p. 135; December, 2002, Marie Orlando, review of *The Wonders of Donal O'Donnell,* p. 129; May, 2004, Connie Tyrrell Burns, review of *Lizzie Bright and the Buckminster Boy,* pp. 157-158; October, 2005, Rachel Kamin, review of *In God's Hands,* p. 118, Connie Tyrrell Burns, review of *First Boy,* p. 173; February, 2006, Jane P. Fenn, review of *First Boy* (audiobook), p. 73.

Teacher Librarian, February, 2005, Kathleen Odean, review of *Lizzie Bright and the Buckminster Boy,* p. 10; October, 2005, Betty Winslow, review of *Straw into Gold,* p. 18.

Voice of Youth Advocates, August, 1994, p. 176; June, 1998, Kathleen Beck, review of *The Sin Eater,* p. 103; August, 1999, Hilary Crew, review of *Anson's Way,* pp. 185-186.

ONLINE

Calvin College Web site, http://www.calvin.edu/ (January 12, 1999), "Of Duchesses and Sin Eaters: The Patterns of Story."

Houghton Mifflin Web site, http://www. houghtonmifflinbooks.com/ (June 23, 2006), "Gary D. Schmidt."*

Jim Shepard

■ Personal

Born December 29, 1956, in Bridgeport, CT; son of Albert R. and Ida (Picarazzi) Shepard; married; wife's name Karen; children: Aidan, Emmett. *Education:* Trinity College, B.A., 1978; Brown University, M.F.A., 1980.

■ Addresses

Home—132 White Oaks Rd., Williamstown, MA 01267. *Office*—Department of English, C-19 Stetson Hall, Williams College, Williamstown, MA 01267. *Agent*—Peter Matson, Sterling Lord Literistic, 65 Bleecker St., New York, NY 10012. *E-mail*—James.R. Shepard@Williams.edu.

■ Career

Writer. University of Michigan, Ann Arbor, MI, lecturer in creative writing, 1980-83; Williams College, Williamstown, MA, 1983—, began as assistant professor, became J. Leland Miller Professor of English.

■ Member

Phi Beta Kappa.

■ Awards, Honors

Transatlantic Review Award, Henfield Foundation, 1979, for "Eustace"; Alex Award, Margaret Alexander Edwards Trust, 2005, for *Project X.*

■ Writings

FICTION

Flights (novel), Knopf (New York, NY), 1983.
Paper Doll: A Novel, Knopf (New York, NY), 1987.
Lights Out in the Reptile House: A Novel, Norton (New York, NY), 1990.
Kiss of the Wolf (novel), Harcourt, Brace (New York, NY), 1994.
Battling against Castro: Stories, Knopf (New York, NY), 1996.
Nosferatu: A Novel, Knopf (New York, NY), 1998, published with an introduction by Ron Hansen, University of Nebraska Press (Lincoln, NE), 2005.
Love and Hydrogen: New and Selected Stories, Vintage Contemporaries (New York, NY), 2004.
Project X: A Novel, Knopf (New York, NY), 2004.

WITH WILLIAM HOLINGER; UNDER JOINT PSEUDONYM SCOTT ELLER

Short Season, Scholastic (New York, NY), 1985.
21st Century Fox, Scholastic (New York, NY), 1989.

"THE JOHNSON BOYS" SERIES FOR YOUNG ADULTS; UNDER JOINT PSEUDONYM SCOTT ELLER

The Football Wars, Scholastic (New York, NY), 1992.
First Base, First Place, Scholastic (New York, NY), 1993.
That Soccer Season, Scholastic (New York, NY), 1993.
Jump Shot, Scholastic (New York, NY), 1994.

NONFICTION

(Editor, with Ron Hansen) *You've Got to Read This: Contemporary American Writers Introduce Stories That Held Them in Awe*, HarperPerennial (New York, NY), 1994.
(Editor, with Amy Hempel) *Unleashed: Poems by Writers' Dogs*, Crown (New York, NY), 1995.
(Editor) *Writers at the Movies: Twenty-six Contemporary Authors Celebrate Twenty-six Memorable Movies*, Perennial (New York, NY), 2000.

OTHER

Contributor to periodicals, including *Atlantic Monthly, Esquire, Harper's, New Yorker, Paris Review, Triquarterly, South Atlantic Quarterly, Doubletake,* and *Playboy.*

■ Sidelights

Dubbed "something of a patron saint of the maladapted" by *BookForum* critic Art Winslow, and a "pointillist master of middle-American disaffection" by *Village Voice* reviewer Michael Atkinson, American author Jim Shepard has created a body fiction that appeals to both adults and young adult readers. In many of his novels, such as *Flights, Lights Out in the Reptile House: A Novel, Kiss of the Wolf,* and *Project X: A Novel,* the protagonist is a teenager or adolescent. Indeed, the last-named novel won a 2005 Alex Award for the top adult books for teenagers. *Antioch Review* contributor Kyle Minor placed Shepard, regardless of his intended audience, in the select company of other "virtuosic writers," including Jonathan Lethem and Michael Chabon, whose work "blurs the line between literary fiction and genre fiction." And for a *Kirkus Reviews* critic, reviewing his 2004 *Love and Hydrogen: New and Selected Stories,* Shepard is "one of the most interesting of all contemporary American writers." For his part, Shepard noted to Robert Birnbaum of *IdentityTheory.com,* that he has been "dealing with adolescence in fiction for a long time." Shepard further noted: "I started with adolescence, . . . it helps to actually have some sort of mineral and unteachable adolescent built in me somewhere. . . . It also helps to have always been fascinated with the cardinal struggles that all adolescents have. That sense, for example, of not having the words for feelings—that sense of an intensity that is kind of inchoate. That sense of being attracted to and repelled by one's own passivity."

Starting with Adolescence

Born in 1956, in Bridgeport, Connecticut, Shepard grew up Catholic among Italian relatives. "Individual responsibility versus passivity is an issue I grew up with," Shepard told Amanda Smith in a *Publishers Weekly* profile. "I was always being raised in both implicit and explicit ways by my education in a Catholic school, and by family, too." Shepard ultimately rendered the theme of how passivity allows good people to do bad things in several of his later novels and short stories. Shepard was the first in his family to dream of a writing career. Initially discouraged by a writing instructor at Trinity College, where he did his undergraduate work, Shepard ultimately won the same instructor over with a short story in which he finally discovered his own voice. The professor encouraged him to send the story to the *Atlantic.* Though the editors did not take that story, they did take the next, a month later. "I had a four-week struggle to publish," Shepard told Smith. He was just nineteen at the time.

Graduating with a master's degree from Brown University in 1980, Shepard spent the next three years on the faculty of the University of Michigan, teaching creative writing and film theory. Thereafter, he joined the faculty of Williams College, in Williamstown, Massachusetts. Shepard explained to Smith that such a teaching career has proved a nice balance for him: "It's a wonderful way of having an irregular life, which is what most writers would like in terms of what hours you have to put in when. It's also a superb way of training yourself to be a better reader, which is what you have to do to be a better writer, anyway. Even if I were a zillionaire, I think I would work out some sort of thing where I taught half the year."

Shepard's first novel, *Flights,* was published in 1983. It is the story of the adolescent boy, Biddy Siebert, who lives in Connecticut. Biddy's life is lonely and unpleasant, with no lasting relationships, and the few friendships he has end when families move away. Neither does he find much solace at home, for his parents are given to tormenting each other. Judy, Biddy's mother, is weak and submissive to her husband, the domineering Walt. However, it is Biddy's father who becomes the catalyst for the boy's great adventure, for he encourages the youth's interest in airplanes. Walt Siebert brings his son books on aircraft and even takes Biddy along when his friend offers an airplane ride. Biddy, who sees himself as a failure, is inspired by the books and his flight and decides to steal the friend's plane and fly it. For Biddy, the theft and flight seem to be an opportunity for redemption. *Flights* was praised as a distinguished debut for its author. *Washington Post Book World* critic Tom Paulin deemed Shepard's work "subtle, brilliant,beautifully-wrought fiction." Further praise came from the author Frederick Busch, who described the novel in the *New York Times Book Review* as "well-made, well-written and splendidly imagined." For *Library Journal* contributor T.F. Smith, *Flights* was a "fine first novel," while for *School Library Journal* contributor Larry Domingues, the novel "dramatizes a modern adolescent experience to which many young adults will relate." Shepard also wrote for the young adult market directly under the joint pseudonym of Scott Eller, creating a number of sports stories with William Holinger.

Turns to Adult Fiction

Shepard's second novel, *Paper Doll: A Novel,* is about an American B-17 crew flying dangerous missions over Germany during World War II, told from the viewpoint of one of the plane's crew. James Lasdun, who reviewed the novel in the *New York Times Book Review,* called Shephard's historical recreation "minutely detailed" and went on to note: "Where his skills become most evident are the opportunities for descriptions of vividly heightened sensory experience afforded by a story about wartime flying. After the leisurely, earthbound opening, with its teasing series of delayed and aborted missions, the story at last becomes airborne, and the accumulation of detail suddenly comes into its own." *Library Journal* contributor Thomas L. Kilpatrick commented on Shepard's "commendable job of individual and collecting character development," but also complained that the "novel drags" as Shepard completes his set up.

For his third novel, Shepard returned to a teenage narrator. *Lights out in the Reptile House: A Novel,* tells about a youth's experiences in a country increasingly dominated by fascism. The novel's hero is fifteen-year-old Karel Roeder, who finds that his schoolwork is becoming more and more devoted to subjects extolling the virtues of fascism and the fascist state. The shy Karel, who works at a zoo's reptile house, is in love with the rebellious Leda, who defies the state in its institutionalization and impending execution of her dyslexic brother. State intrusion hits closer to home when Karel's father disappears and a soldier moves into the home. Matters spiral downward with the soldier becoming a personal enemy to Karel, leading to the burning of the reptile house. Dean Williams, reviewing the novel in *Library Journal,* found it a "winner," further observing that the work takes a "fresh, horrifying look at man's inhumanity to man." However, a reviewer for the *New York Times* gave the novel what Shepard described to Smith as a "horrifying review," and many other reviewers followed suit. His publishers cut back any advertising on the book thereafter, and Shepard was left without an adult publisher for a time. Thus, in the early 1990s, he concentrated on four sports books for Scholastic under the pseudonym Scott Eller.

Finally his fourth adult novel, *Kiss of the Wolf* found a home at Harcourt Brace. That novel saw Shepard further working toward a blending of genre with mainstream fiction. He mixes the terror and intrigue of the thriller novel with the psychological drama of the strained relationship between a boy and his mother. Eleven-year-old Todd and his mother, Joanie, are devastated when Todd's father, Gary, abandons them and moves west. Joanie finally begins to see a man named Bruno, a used car salesman and suspicious character who seems to have connections with several shady customers. Then, on the night of a party given for Todd, Joanie hits a pedestrian with her car. She panics and drives off without reporting the incident to the police. Unwilling to confess her crime, she also tries to persuade Todd to be quiet about what he has witnessed. "Altar boy Todd is deeply shocked by his mom's behavior and subsequent coverup," related a *Kirkus Reviews* contributor; "their rift is the heart of the novel." Further complications arise when it is learned that the victim was an associate of Bruno's, and that he was supposed to be carrying money that is now missing. Bruno begins to suspect Joanie, and he goes after her. Richard Bausch in the *New York Times Book Review* felt that *Kiss of the Wolf* succeeds not only as a thriller, but on other levels as well, commenting that "we go through all the stages of Joanie's guilt, we are privy to all the nuances of feeling between her and the boy as their understanding of what has happened changes them, and we come to see the story as a parable of responsibility and absolution." Similarly, a *Publishers Weekly* reviewer called the same work a "gritty, effective" novel, with a "grisly conclusion [that] is as gripping as any thriller's." For Jackie Gropman, writing in *School Library Journal, Kiss of the Wolf* was a "compelling and disturbing novel." *Booklist* critic Anne Gendler found the work a "spare, modern tale" that is "at once morbid and gripping." And writing in *Commonweal*, critic and author Ron Hansen called the novel "tight, tense, [and] chilling," as well as a "deft, funny, disquieting thriller."

Short Stories and Novels

Shepard turned to the short story form for his 1996 collection, *Batting against Castro: Stories,* in which a "memorable cast of characters faces various forms of alienation," according to a *Publishers Weekly* critic. The same critic noted the "astonishing assortment of utterly convincing voices" which Shepard, often writing in the first person, forges in these stories. Robert E. Brown, writing in *Library Journal*, found the same collection "intelligent and imaginative," while Kevin J. Bochynski, writing in *Magill Book Reviews*, thought *Batting against Castro* "is a memorable collection that captivates the reader and makes a lasting impression."

Shepard returned to the novel with *Nosferatu*, the protagonist of which is German film director F.W. Murnau, whose works include the German movie *Nosferatu.* He is considered by many to be the greatest of the silent filmmakers. Murnau's career ended in 1931 when, at age forty-two, he was killed in an automobile accident. The first part of Shepard's book follows Murnau's life, first as a student who falls in love with the poet Hans Ehrenbaum-Degele, then as a member of Max Reinhardt's theater school, and finally as a soldier during wartime, when he discovers that Hans has been killed at the front. The novel then goes forward in time to the making of the silent movie *Nosferatu,* the first great vampire film. Leslie Epstein, in the *New York Times Book Review,* praised Shepard's blend of historical research and fictional technique in his depiction of Murnau's filmmaking technique, noting that it is "as fine a realization of the creative process—of the struggle to bring to life an interior vision, to make it move—as exists in the literature of film." A *Publishers Weekly* reviewer called the work a "protean leap" as well as a "trenchant story," and concluded that "discriminating readers will appreciate Shepard's skill and integrity." And *Entertainment Weekly* contributor Michael Giltz called the same work "mordantly funny and moving."

In 2004, Shepard published both a collection of stories, *Love and Hydrogen: New and Selected Stories,* and the novel *Project X.* Again with his stories,

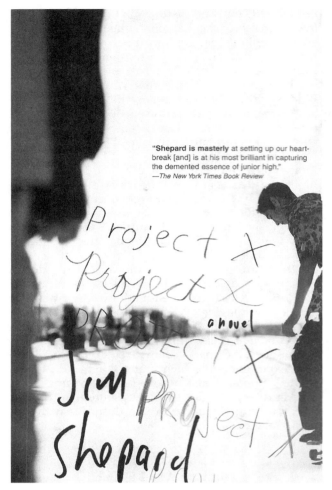

"Shepard is masterly at setting up our heartbreak [and] is at his most brilliant in capturing the demented essence of junior high."
—*The New York Times Book Review*

In this 2004 novel, a pair of outsiders plot a horrible revenge against their junior high classmates.

Shepard displayed a wide range of themes and voices, though some of the tales were reprints from his earlier *Batting against Castro.* A *Kirkus Reviews* critic called this collection of twenty-two tales a "first-rate gathering." Similarly Minor praised the "wonderful" stories in this collection, while *Booklist* contributor Donna Seaman called the tales "mordantly funny, unsettling, yet immensely gratifying," and concluded that "Shepard is breathtaking."

Shepard's *Project X: A Novel* is a depiction of school shootings such as that at Columbine High School in Colorado, looking at the background of the sort of young people that perpetrate such deeds. This particular school nightmare is hatched by Edwin, an eighth grader, who, like the actual perpetrators of the Columbine school shooting, is picked on and bullied. With another outsider friend, Flake, he plots his revenge. This "searing, startlingly real account," as *Booklist* critic Gillian Engberg described *Project X,* was actually based more on Shepard's own junior high experiences than it was on research into the Columbine shooting, but Shepard did also spend a good deal of time visiting schools in preparation for the novel. Numerous critics noted Shepard's fine ear for the speech and voice of adolescents. A critic for *Publishers Weekly,* for example, praised Shepard's "pitch-perfect feel for the flat, sardonic, . . . language of disaffected teens" in this "engrossing novel." Atkinson noted that Shepard's "portrait of traumatized, half-comprehended reality sounds like he'd held his ear to a real, acne-maimed 13-year-old's chest," while *Esquire* contributor Daniel Torday similarly commended Shepard's "feat of verisimilitude."

If you enjoy the works of Jim Shepard, you may also want to check out the following books:

George Orwell, *Animal Farm,* 1954.
Dorothy Allison, *Bastard out of Carolina,* 1992.
DBC Pierre, *Vernon God Little,* 2003.

Other reviewers noted the candor and sensitivity with which Shepard portrayed boys and adults in the work. For *School Library Journal* contributor Susanne Bardelson, *Project X* was a "heartbreaking and wrenching novel [that] will leave teens with plenty of questions and, hopefully, some answers." A *Kirkus Reviews* critic found the same work "vivid" and "frightening," concluding that it was a "bitter, gem-like work of art." *Booklist* contributor Seaman observed that Shepard "neatly and devastatingly explicates teenage alienation" in this "lean and stinging" work. *Salon.com* critic Stephanie Zacharek likewise concluded: "Shepard puts us into the shoes of two boys with murder on their minds but not in their hearts. His compassion for them rings out like a shout—the kind no one hears until it's too late."

Speaking with Smith, Shepard summed up one of the major motivations in his writing, as witnessed in books from his debut *Flights,* to the apocalyptic notions of *Project X.* "I am fascinated by the problem of evil, the issue of evil," he noted. "But I'm fascinated by evil figures in the context of the possibility of good."

■ Biographical and Critical Sources

BOOKS

Contemporary Literary Criticism, Volume 36, Gale (Detroit, MI), 1986.

PERIODICALS

Antioch Review, summer, 2004, Kyle Minor, review of *Love and Hydrogen: New and Selected Stories,* p. 580.
Booklist, January 15, 1994, Anne Gendler, review of *Kiss of the Wolf,* p. 901; October 1, 1994, Donna Seaman, review of *You've Got to Read This: Contemporary American Writers Introduce Stories That Held Them in Awe,* p. 230; June 1, 1995, Ray Olson, review of *Unleashed: Poems by Writers' Dogs,* p. 1721; March 1, 1998, Ray Olson, review of *Nosferatu,* p. 1096; January 1, 2004, Donna Seaman, reviews of *Love and Hydrogen* and *Project X: A Novel,* p. 828; January 1, 2005, review of *Project X,* p. 771; April 1, 2005, Gillian Engberg, "The Alex Awards, 2005," p. 1355.
Commonweal, December 2, 1994, Ron Hansen, review of *Kiss of the Wolf,* p. 30.
Dog World, August, 1999, Donald McCaig, review of *Unleashed,* p. 69.
Entertainment Weekly, April 17, 1998, Michael Giltz, review of *Nosferatu,* p. 68; December 8, 2000, Charles Winecoff, review of *Writers at the Movies: Twenty-six Contemporary Authors Celebrate Twenty-six Memorable Movies,* p. 92.
Esquire, February, 2004, Daniel Torday, review of *Project X,* p. 30.
Film Comment, November, 1998, Mark Harris, "Books Silents and Darkness," p. 67.
Kirkus Reviews, November 15, 1993, review of *Kiss of the Wolf,* p. 1419; November 15, 2003, review of *Project X* and *Love and Hydrogen,* p. 1337.
Library Journal, August, 1983, T.F. Smith, review of *Flights,* p. 1505; November 15, 1986, Thomas L. Kilpatrick, review of *Paper Doll: A Novel,* p. 111; February 15, 1990, Dean Williams, review of *Lights Out in the Reptile House: A Novel,* p. 213; December, 1993, Susan Clifford, review of *Kiss of the Wolf,* p. 177; October 1, 1994, Stephanie Furtsch, review of *You've Got to Read This,* p. 118; July, 1996, Robert E. Brown, review of *Battling against Castro: Stories,* p. 167; April 15, 1998, Susan Gene Clifford, review of *Nosferatu,* p. 116; January, 2004, Mark Andre Singer, review of *Project X,* p. 160.
Magill Book Reviews, September 1, 1996, Kevin J. Bochynski, review of *Batting against Castro.*
New York Times Book Review, October 9, 1983, Frederick Busch, review of *Flights,* pp. 15, 33; November 9, 1986, James Lasdun, "The Death of the Ball

Turret Gunner," p. 9; December 20, 1994, Richard Bausch, review of *Kiss of the Wolf,* p. 34; April 12, 1998, Leslie Epstein, "The Undead."

Publishers Weekly, November 15, 1993, review of *Kiss of the Wolf,* p. 69; January 31, 1994, Amanda Smith, "Jim Shepard," p. 64; April 29, 1996, review of *Battling against Castro,* p. 51; January 26, 1998, review of *Nosferatu,* p. 67; October 23, 2000, review of *Writers at the Movies,* p. 69; November 24, 2003, review of *Project X,* p. 41.

School Library Journal, February, 1984, Larry Domingues, review of *Flights,* pp. 87-88; August, 1994, Jackie Gropman, review of *Kiss of the Wolf,* p. 184; December, 1996, Karen Sokol, review of *Batting against Castro,* p. 152; May, 2004, Susanne Bardelson, review of *Project X,* p. 175.

Washington Post Book World, September 25, 1983, Tom Paulin, review of *Flights,* p. 4; February 11, 1990, p. 4; April 5, 1998, review of *Nosferatu,* p. 1.

ONLINE

5 Questions With, http://www.beatrice.com/ (March 17, 2004), "Jim Shepard."

BookForum, http://www.bookforum.com/ (June 26, 2006), Art Winslow, "Misfits on Main."

IdentityTheory.com, http://www.identitytheory.com/ (May 14, 2004), Robert Birnbaum, "Jim Shepard: Author of *Project X* Converses with Robert Birnbaum."

Salon.com, http://www.salon.com/ (February 4, 2004), Stephanie Zacharek, review of *Project X.*

Village Voice Online, http://www.villagevoice.com/ (February 4, 2004), Michael Atkinson, "Freaks and Geeks."

Williams College English Department Web site, http://www.williams.edu/ (June 25, 2006), "James R. Shepard."*

Mary Stewart

■ Personal

Born September 17, 1916, in Sunderland, Durham, England; daughter of Frederick Albert (a Church of England clergyman) and Mary Edith (Matthews) Rainbow; married Frederick Henry Stewart, 1945. *Education:* University of Durham, B.A. (first class honours), 1938, M.A., 1941. *Hobbies and other interests:* Music, painting, the theatre, gardening.

■ Addresses

Agent—c/o Author Mail, William Morrow & Co., 105 Madison Ave., New York, NY 10016. *E-mail*—

■ Career

University of Durham, Durham, England, lecturer, 1941-45, part-time lecturer, 1948-55; writer, 1954—. *Military service:* Royal Observer Corps, World War II.

■ Member

PEN, Royal Society of Arts (fellow).

■ Awards, Honors

British Crime Writers Association Silver Dagger Award, 1961, for *My Brother Michael*; Mystery Writers of America Edgar Award, 1964, for *This Rough Magic*; Frederick Niven Literary Award, 1971, for *The Crystal Cave*; Scottish Arts Council Award, 1975, for *Ludo and the Star Horse*; fellow, Newnham College, Cambridge, 1986.

■ Writings

Madam, Will You Talk? (also see below), Hodder & Stoughton (London, England), 1955.

Wildfire at Midnight (also see below), Appleton (New York, NY), 1956.

Thunder on the Right, Hodder & Stoughton (London, England), 1957.

Nine Coaches Waiting (also see below), Hodder & Stoughton (London, England), 1958.

My Brother Michael (also see below), Hodder & Stoughton (London, England), 1960.

The Ivy Tree (also see below), Hodder & Stoughton (London, England), 1961, Mill (New York, NY), 1962.

The Moon-Spinners (also see below), Hodder & Stoughton (London, England), 1962.

Three Novels of Suspense (contains *Madam, Will You Talk?*, *Nine Coaches Waiting*, and *My Brother Michael*), Mill, 1963.

This Rough Magic (Literary Guild selection; also see below), Mill, 1964.

Airs above the Ground (also see below), Mill, 1965.

The Gabriel Hounds (Doubleday Book Club selection; Reader's Digest Condensed Book Club selection; Literary Guild alternate selection; also see below), Mill, 1967.

The Wind Off the Small Isles, Hodder & Stoughton (London, England), 1968.

The Spell of Mary Stewart (contains *This Rough Magic, The Ivy Tree,* and *Wildfire at Midnight*), Doubleday (New York, NY), 1968.

Mary Stewart Omnibus (contains *Madam, Will You Talk?, Wildfire at Midnight,* and *Nine Coaches Waiting*), Hodder & Stoughton (London, England), 1969.

The Crystal Cave (Literary Guild selection; also see below), Morrow (New York, NY), 1970.

The Little Broomstick (juvenile), Brockhampton Press (Leicester, England), 1971.

The Hollow Hills (also see below), Morrow (New York, NY), 1973.

Ludo and the Star Horse (juvenile), Brockhampton Press, 1974.

Touch Not the Cat (also see below), Morrow (New York, NY), 1976.

Triple Jeopardy (contains *My Brother Michael, The Moon-Spinners,* and *This Rough Magic*), Hodder & Stoughton (London, England), 1978.

Selected Works (contains *The Crystal Cave, The Hollow Hills, Wildfire at Midnight,* and *Airs above the Ground*), Heinemann (London, England), 1978.

The Last Enchantment (Literary Guild selection; also see below), Morrow (New York, NY), 1979.

A Walk in Wolf Wood, Morrow (New York, NY), 1980.

Mary Stewart's Merlin Trilogy (contains *The Crystal Cave, The Hollow Hills,* and *The Last Enchantment*), Morrow (New York, NY), 1980.

The Wicked Day, Morrow (New York, NY), 1983.

Mary Stewart—Four Complete Novels (contains *Touch Not the Cat, The Gabriel Hounds, This Rough Magic,* and *My Brother Michael*), Avenel Books (New York, NY), 1983.

Thornyhold, Morrow (New York, NY), 1988.

Frost on the Window and Other Poems, Morrow (New York, NY), 1990.

The Stormy Petrel, Morrow (New York, NY), 1991.

The Prince and the Pilgrim, Morrow (New York, NY), 1995.

Rose Cottage, Morrow (New York, NY), 1997.

Also author of radio plays *Lift from a Stranger, Call Me at Ten-Thirty, The Crime of Mr. Merry,* and *The Lord of Langdale,* produced by British Broadcasting Corporation, 1957-58. Stewart's works have been translated into sixteen languages, including Hebrew, Icelandic, and Slovak. The National Library of Scotland houses Stewart's manuscript collection.

■ Adaptations

The Moon-Spinners was filmed by Walt Disney in 1964.

■ Sidelights

Mary Stewart's writing career divides into two distinct parts. In her first period, according to Kay Mussell in the *St. James Guide to Crime and Mystery Writers,* Stewart "wrote a remarkable series of 10 popular novels of romantic suspense. . . . In her later phase, beginning in the late 1960s, Stewart's novels have been concerned with history and frequently with the occult. Her best-known work from this period is her four-volume series about King Arthur and Merlin." In the words of a *National Observer* critic, Stewart writes "like a magician, she conjures exotic moods and mysteries from mere words, her only aim to entertain."

Stewart explained in an article for *Writer* magazine: "I am first and foremost a teller of tales, but I am also a serious-minded woman who accepts the responsibilities of her job, and that job, if I am to be true to what is in me, is to say with every voice at my command: 'We must love and imitate the beautiful and the good.' It is a comment on our age that one hesitates to stand up and say this aloud."

Stewart was born in 1916 in Sunderland, Durham, England. Her father, Frederick Albert Rainbow, was a clergyman in the Church of England and her mother, Mary Edith Rainbow, was a homemaker. Stewart attended the University of Durham, where she received her B.A. in 1938 and her M.A. in 1941. She went on to teach English literature until 1955. In 1945 Stewart married Frederick Henry Stewart, a renowned geologist who was knighted in 1974 for his devotion to science. In 1956 Stewart moved to Edinburgh, Scotland, where her husband accepted a professorship at the University of Edinburgh. It was then that Stewart decided to give up her own university career to concentrate on writing full time.

While "predictability" is not a quality most authors would strive for, a *Christian Science Monitor* reviewer felt that this very trait is the secret of Stewart's success. Prior to 1970, for example, her plots followed a fairly consistent pattern of romance and suspense set in such vividly depicted locales as Provence, the Isle of Skye, the Pyrenees, Delphi, and Lebanon. "One of Stewart's finest qualities as a writer," Mussell wrote, "is her extraordinary descriptive prose. Stewart's ability to evoke a highly specific time and place, through sensuous descriptions of locale, character, and food, provides an immediacy that is often lacking in mystery fiction." Furthermore, noted the *Christian Science Monitor* reviewer, "Mrs. Stewart doesn't pull any tricks or introduce uncomfortable issues. Attractive, well-brought-up girls pair off with clean, confident young men, always on the side of the angels. And when the villains are finally rounded up, no doubts disturb us—it is clear that the best men have won again." "Although Stewart's works may resemble the modern gothic formula," Mussell admitted, "they clearly transcend it. Thoroughly contemporary, her heroines innocently embark on an adventure that quickly turns sinister. Most often, the terrifying events occur while the protagonists are cut off from safety in an exotic locale."

Describing these early novels in *Twentieth-Century Romance & Historical Writers,* a contributor pointed out the special traits possessed by Stewart's characters: "Stewart's heroes and heroines are people of commitment, not just to each other as in many other romances, but especially to others and to abstract concepts of truth and justice. Their values may seem archaic in the modern world, but Stewart portrays them so sensitively that they remain believable. Without preaching or moralizing, she places her characters in situations of extreme danger where it would be acceptable for them to walk away from someone else's trouble. They do not, and her delineation of their motivation and personal growth is always crucial to understanding their stories."

Explaining the appeal of Stewart's suspense novels for younger people, a contributor to the *St. James Guide to Young Adult Writers* maintained: "For young adults the attraction of Stewart's romantic thrillers lies particularly in their use of a conventional romance framework to present a succession of intelligent and resourceful women who are fully equal to their male coadventurers in virtually every quality except brute muscular strength. Book after book ends with some impressive male chivalry, but one is often aware of a tongue-in-cheek quality in Stewart's depiction of these sexual partnerships, and when the story ends, as it invariably does, in the female protagonist's delighted surrender to protective marital union, the motive is clearly shown to be instinctive natural pleasure, not weakness or social necessity."

Stewart's first novel, *Madam, Will You Talk?,* tells of Charity Selborne, a young widow on vacation in Avignon, France, who forms a friendship with a young boy vacationing with his glamorous stepmother. According to the stepmother, the child is in danger from his father, who attempted to murder the boy. All is not as it seems, however, and Charity must ultimately rely on her wits to save the boy's life. James Sandoe of the *New York Herald Tribune Book Review* called *Madam, Will You Talk?* "a distinctly charming, romantic thriller. . . . [that is] intelligently soft-boiled, pittypat and a good deal of fun."

In *Thunder on the Right,* Stewart tells of Jennifer, who travels to France to find her cousin Gillian. Gillian has failed to write as promised in her last letter. Uneasy about Gillian for a number of reasons, including a recent illness, hints from Gillian that she is thinking about becoming a nun, and her failure to write, Jennifer is determined to make sure her cousin is well. When Jennifer arrives at the convent at which Gillian has been recuperating, she is told that Gillian is dead. Jennifer senses that all is not right at the convent and refuses to believe their story. Her search for the truth ultimately threatens her own life.

Stewart's *My Brother Michael* is set in Greece, where a vacationing young English woman joins a young man in his search for clues about the fate of his brother, who died near Delphi while on an undercover mission for the resistance during World War II. *My Brother Michael,* according to Francis Iles of the *Guardian,* is "the contemporary thriller at its very best." Speaking of the same novel, Christopher Pym of the *Spectator* commented: "Mary Stewart gives each of her admirable novels an exotically handsome (if somewhat rather travel-folderish) setting. . . . The Greek landscape and—much more subtle—the Greek character are splendidly done, in a long, charmingly written, highly evocative, imperative piece of required reading for an Hellenic cruise." Boucher, too, found the book to be worthy of praise: "This detective adventure, rich in action and suspense, is seen through the eyes of a characteristic Stewart heroine; and surely there are few more attractive young women in today's popular fiction. . . . These girls are as far removed as you can imagine from the Idiot Heroine who disfigures (at least for men) so much romantic fiction."

The Moon-Spinners is set on the Mediterranean island of Crete. Nicola Ferris, a secretary at the British Embassy in Athens, has arrived for her vacation in Agios Georgios on Crete a little earlier than she expected. When a sudden flight of fancy, in the guise of a very real white heron, seems to point her way to the famous White Mountains, Nicola is up to the adventure her extra time and beautiful setting seem to inspire. Harsh reality intrudes when Nicola stumbles across a wounded Englishman, Mark Langley. Her determination to help him leads to an adventure that includes murder, political treachery, and stolen jewels. In 1964, *The Moon-Spinners* was filmed by Walt Disney and starred Hayley Mills.

In 1970, Stewart turned to historical fiction based in England's legends of King Arthur, especially as seen through the eyes of Merlin the magician. Liz Holliday in the *St. James Guide to Fantasy Writers* believed Stewart's Merlin character to be "an intriguing mixture of pragmatist and fey, believer and agnostic. He has visions, true dreams in which he sees what is and what is to come. These, he believes, come from a god. . . . At the same time he is portrayed as a polymath, dedicated to understanding the world through scholarship in the fields of science, mathematics and engineering." "The Merlin of Mary Stewart's trilogy—*The Crystal Cave, The Hollow Hills,* and *The Last Enchantment*—is a man of many roles: prophet, prince, enchanter, king-maker, teacher, engineer, physician, poet, and singer," according to Jeanie Watson in *Arthurian Interpretations.* "But in all of these, he is first and foremost a man of power. Merlin's power is the power of knowledge, knowledge revealed progressively through active preparation and wise waiting."

Unlike most other authors who have written about the legends of Camelot in terms of the Middle Ages, Stewart places her story in more historically accurate fifth-century Britain. *The Crystal Cave,* the first of three books on Merlin, tells the story of King Arthur from the point of view of Myrddin, or Merlin, Arthur's legendary enchanter. The illegitimate son of a Welsh princess, Myrddin is born when Britain is being overrun by Saxon tribes from the continent. Gifted with the Sight, Myrddin sets out on a quest for knowledge, a quest which eventually leads him to his father and to great power. He uses his power to bring about the birth of Arthur, who is destined to be the saviour of Britain. A *Best Sellers* critic wrote: "Fifth century Britain and Brittany come to life in Miss Stewart's vigorous imagination. . . . Those who have read and enjoyed the many novels of Mary Stewart will not need to be told this is an expertly fashioned continually absorbing story, with a facile imagination fleshing out the legend of the parentage of the future King Arthur—and, too, of Merlin himself." A *Books and Bookmen* critic called it "a highly plotted and rattling good yarn. Mary Stewart's evocation of an era of magic, as well as of bloodletting, is magnificently done. Her writing is virile, and of a very high quality indeed. Her descriptions of the countryside are

often moving, also poetical." Martin Levin of the *New York Times Book Review,* after reminding readers that little is actually known of Merlin's life, noted that "the author obligingly expands [Merlin's] myth into a first person history. . . . Cheerfully disclaiming authenticity, Miss Stewart . . . lightens the Dark Ages with legend, pure invention and a lively sense of history."

Stewart's second book in the series, *The Hollow Hills,* follows Arthur from his conception to his crowning as king. Because of political danger and intrigue, Arthur is spirited away at birth and raised in obscurity. Always nearby is Merlin, Arthur's uncle, protector, and teacher, who narrates the story. A *Publishers Weekly* critic called the novel "romantic, refreshing and most pleasant reading. . . . Mrs. Stewart has steeped herself well in the folklore and known history of fifth century Britain and she makes of her feuding, fighting warlords lively and intriguing subjects." A *Best Sellers* critic concluded: "All in all, this makes a smashing good tale. The suspense is superb and the reader is kept involved in the unwinding of the plot. Miss Stewart has taken the main lines of the Arthurian legend and has developed the basic elements in a plausible way."

The Last Enchantment finds Arthur now King of Britain. When he sets out to drive the invading Saxons from his land, he must face domestic enemies as well, particularly his half-sister, Morgause, who seduced him into an incestuous affair, and Mordred, the child of that union. In the meantime the aging Merlin, his powers failing, finds an unexpected joy in the arms of his pupil, Nimue. Joseph McLellan of the *Washington Post Book World* found that, in this novel, Stewart "gives us . . . traditional materials, but the treatment is her own, the emphasis shifted for her purpose, which is not simply to recast old material but to bring alive a long-dead historical epoch—not the Middle Ages of Malory but the Dark Ages of the original Arthur. This she does splendidly. Fifth-century Britain is caught in these pages, and while it may lack some of the exotic glitter of the imaginary 12th-century Britain that Arthur usually inhabits, it is a fascinating place."

Stewart followed her Merlin Trilogy with one last book based on the Arthurian legends, *The Wicked Day,* a tale told by Arthur's bastard son, Mordred. According to Arthurian tradition, Mordred is the cause of Arthur's eventual downfall. He has a "bad reputation as Arthur's mean-spirited, traitorous, regicidal son," as Roy Hoffman explained in the *New York Times Book Review.*

If you enjoy the works of Mary Stewart, you may also want to check out the following books:

T. H. White, *The Once and Future King,* 1958.

Marion Zimmer Bradley, *The Mists of Avalon,* 1982.

Stephen R. Lawhead, *Arthur,* 1989.

But in Stewart's version of the story, Mordred is more a tragic figure in the drama than a conscious agent of destruction. A reviewer for *People* explained that Stewart "casts Mordred as a misunderstood hero." "Stewart," Hoffman wrote, "attempts to resurrect him as a compassionate young man who is helpless before fate." M. Jean Greenlaw in the *Journal of Reading* found that "Stewart shapes a sense of the inevitable doom of Camelot, not by Mordred's desire but by the fateful actions of many men and women." Mary Mills in the *School Library Journal* concluded that "Stewart has created flesh and blood characters out of legends, and in doing so has crafted a well-plotted and passionate drama." Holliday believed that "telling the tale from Mordred's point of view works splendidly. It allows his character to emerge as much more complex and sympathetic than it might otherwise have done. Here, Mordred is clearly as much a victim . . . as Arthur ever was, and his attempts to overcome the weakness of character that leads him to his final clash with his father make him an engaging, if not wholly likeable, character." "*The Wicked Day,*" wrote a contributor to the *St. James Guide to Young Adult Writers,* "has much to offer young adult readers and deserves to be widely known. . . . This is a fine piece of storytelling—immensely readable, full of action, incident, and suspense. It is extremely skilful in combining believable character, motive, and the actions of men in a stylised but intricate political world with the overarching sense of destiny and fatefulness which is true to the legend in all its classic forms."

In an article for *Philological Quarterly,* Maureen Fries compared Stewart's treatment of Arthurian legend with that of T.H. White, the author of *The Once and Future King.* "Of all literary genres," Fries begins, "romance is perhaps the most irrational, focusing as it does upon the strange, the marvelous, and the supernatural. And of all the 'matters' of romance, that of Britain contains the most irrationalities." But Fries concludes that "in making over medieval romance into modern novels, T.H. White and Mary Stewart have not only coped, mostly successfully, with the irrationality of the Matter of Britain. They have also grasped and translated into a convincing modern, if diverse, idiom that rational core of truth about human psychology, and the human condition, which constitutes not only the greatness of the Arthurian legend but also its enduring appeal to readers of all centuries and all countries, and to writers of every time and every literary persuasion."

Explaining her decision to switch from writing thrillers to historical fiction, Stewart once commented: "I always planned that some day I would write a historical novel, and I intended to use Roman Britain as the setting. This is a period that I have studied over many years. But then, quite by chance, I came across a passage in Geoffrey of Monmouth's *History of the Kings of Britain,* which described the first appearance of Merlin, the Arthurian 'enchanter.' Here was a new story, offering a new approach to a dark and difficult period, with nothing known about the 'hero' except scraps of legend. The story would have to come purely from imagination, pitched somewhere between legend and truth and fairy-tale and known history. The setting would be imaginary, too, a Dark Age Britain in the unrecorded aftermath of the Roman withdrawal. I had originally no intention of writing more than one volume, but the story seized my imagination. . . . It has been a tough job and a rewarding one. I have learned a lot, not least that the powerful themes of the Arthurian 'Matter of Britain' are as cogent and real today as they were fourteen centuries ago. And Merlin's story has allowed me to return to my first avocation of all, that of poet."

"Stewart defies categorization," a contributor to *Twentieth-Century Romance & Historical Writers* concluded. "Although her books may resemble those of other writers, she remains, even in her weaker books, a writer of uncommon originality and grace. She may work within a formula, but her scene is the larger setting of romance through centuries of literature, making her novels both rewarding and inimitable."

■ Biographical and Critical Sources

BOOKS

Contemporary Literary Criticism, Gale (Detroit, MI), Volume 7, 1977; Volume 35, 1985.

Contemporary Popular Writers, St. James Press (Detroit, MI), 1997.

Friedman, Lenemaja, *Mary Stewart,* Twayne (Boston, MA), 1990.

Gollnick, James, editor, *Comparative Studies in Merlin from the Vedas to C.G. Jung,* Mellen (Lewiston, NY), 1991.

Morse, Donald E., Marshall B. Tymn, and Csilla Bertha, editors, *The Celebration of the Fantastic: Selected Papers from the Tenth Anniversary International Conference on the Fantastic in the Arts,* Greenwood Press (Westport, CT), 1992.

Newquist, Roy, *Counterpoint,* Rand McNally, 1964.

St. James Guide to Crime and Mystery Writers, 4th edition, St. James Press (Detroit, MI), 1996.

St. James Guide to Fantasy Writers, St. James Press (Detroit, MI), 1996.

St. James Guide to Young Adult Writers, 2nd edition, St. James Press (Detroit, MI), 1999.

Twentieth-Century Romance & Historical Writers, 3rd edition, St. James Press (Detroit, MI), 1994.

PERIODICALS

Arthurian Interpretations, spring, 1987, Jeanie Watson, "Mary Stewart's Merlin: Word of Power," pp. 70-83.

Best Sellers, October 1, 1967; July 15, 1970; July 15, 1973; November, 1976, p. 250.

Booklist, April 15, 1992, p. 1547.

Books and Bookmen, August, 1970.

Books Magazine, November, 1995, review of *The Prince and the Pilgrim,* p. 24.

Book Week, November 21, 1965.

Christian Science Monitor, September 28, 1967; September 3, 1970.

Clues: A Journal of Detection, spring-summer, 2000, Kayla McKinney Wiggins, "'I'll Never Laugh at a Thriller Again': Fate, Faith, and Folklore in the Mystery Novels of Mary Stewart," pp. 49-60.

Guardian, February 26, 1960, Frances Iles, review of *My Brother Michael.*

Harper's, September, 1970.

Interpretations: A Journal of Ideas, Analysis, and Criticism, spring, 1984, Harold J. Herman, "The Women in Mary Stewart's Merlin Trilogy," pp. 101-114.

Journal of Reading, May, 1984, M. Jean Greenlaw, p. 741.

Kirkus Reviews, February 1, 1960, p. 107; August 1, 1983, p. 840; July 15, 1991, p. 887; August 15, 1997, p. 1255.

Library Journal, June 15, 1973.

National Observer, October 23, 1967.

New Statesman, November 5, 1965.

New York Herald Tribune Book Review, May 27, 1956, James Sandoe, review of *Madam, Will You Talk?;* October 5, 1958; March 8, 1959; March 4, 1962.

New York Times, March 18, 1956; September 9, 1956; May 18, 1958; January 18, 1959.

New York Times Book Review, April 10, 1960, Anthony Boucher, review of *My Brother Michael;* January 7, 1962; October 24, 1965, Anthony Boucher, review of *Airs above the Ground;* October 15, 1967; August 9, 1970, Martin Levin; July 29, 1973; September 2, 1979; January 1, 1984, Roy Hoffman, p. 20.

North American Review, spring, 1965, Mary Byerly, "Lucy in Corfu," pp. 55-56.

People, December 5, 1983, review of *The Wicked Day,* p. 22.

Philological Quarterly, spring, 1977, Maureen Fries, "The Rationalization of the Arthurian 'Matter' in T.H. White and Mary Stewart," pp. 259-265.

Publishers Weekly, May 28, 1973, review of *The Hollow Hills;* September 16, 1988; July 12, 1991.

San Francisco Chronicle, October 21, 1956; May 22, 1960.

School Library Journal, March, 1984, Mary Mills, p. 178.

Spectator, March 18, 1960, Chritsopher Pym, review of *My Brother Michael.*

Sunday Times Colour Supplement, June 13, 1976.

Time, January 5, 1968.

Times Educational Supplement, February 5, 1982, p. 28.

Times Literary Supplement, July 18, 1980, Mary Cadogan, p. 806.

Washington Post Book World, March 31, 1968; September 15, 1976; July 22, 1979, Joseph McLellan.

Writer, May, 1970, pp. 9-12, 46.

ONLINE

The Camelot Project Web site, http://www.lib.rochester.edu/camelot/cphome.stm/ (July 3, 2006), Raymond H. Thompson, "Taliesin's Successors: Interviews with Authors of Modern Arthurian Literature."*

Mary Stolz

■ Personal

Born March 24, 1920, in Boston, MA; daughter of Thomas Francis and Mary Margaret (a nurse; maiden name, Burgey) Slattery; married Stanley Burr Stolz (a civil engineer), January, 1940 (divorced, 1956); married Thomas C. Jaleski (a physician), June, 1965; children: (first marriage) William. *Education:* Attended Birch Wathen School, Columbia University Teacher's College, 1936-38, and Katharine Gibbs School, 1938-39. *Politics:* "Liberal Northern Democrat." *Hobbies and other interests:* Social and environmental issues, ballet, baseball, cats, hard games of Scrabble, bird-watching, reading.

■ Addresses

Home—7095 Gulf of Mexico Dr., Periwinkle #24, Longboat Key, FL 34228. *Agent*—Roslyn Targ Literary Agency, 105 West Thirteenth St., Ste. 15E, New York, NY 10011.

■ Career

Writer of books for children and young adults. Worked variously as a bookstore clerk and secretary.

■ Member

Authors League of America.

■ Awards, Honors

Notable Book citation, American Library Association (ALA), 1951, for *The Sea Gulls Woke Me*; Children's Book Award, Child Study Children's Book Committee at Bank Street College, 1953, for *In a Mirror*; Spring Book Festival Older Honor Award, *New York Herald Tribune*, 1953, for *Ready or Not*, 1956, for *The Day and the Way We Met*, and 1957, for *Because of Madeline*; ALA Notable Book citation, 1961, for *Belling the Tiger*; Newbery Award Honor Book designation, 1962, for *Belling the Tiger*, and 1966, for *The Noonday Friends*; Junior Book Award, Boys' Club of America, 1964, for *The Bully of Barkham Street*; Honor List citation, *Boston Globe/Horn Book* and National Book Award finalist, Association of American Publishers, both 1975, for *The Edge of Next Year*; Recognition of Merit award, George G. Stone Center for Children's Books, 1982, for entire body of work; ALA Notable Book citation, 1985, for *Quentin Corn*; Children's Science Book Younger Honor Award, New York Academy of Sciences, 1986, for *Night of Ghosts and Hermits: Nocturnal Life on the Seashore*; German Youth Festival Award; ALA Notable Book citation, and Notable Children's Trade Books in Social Studies, Children's Book Council, both 1988, and Teacher's Choice citation, International Reading Association, 1989, all for *Storm in the Night*; numerous other ALA Notable Book citations; Kerlan Award, 1993, for body of work.

■ Writings

FOR YOUNG ADULTS

To Tell Your Love, Harper (New York, NY), 1950.

The Organdy Cupcakes, Harper (New York, NY), 1951.

The Sea Gulls Woke Me, Harper (New York, NY), 1951.

In a Mirror, Harper (New York, NY), 1953.

Ready or Not, Harper (New York, NY), 1953.

Pray Love, Remember, Harper (New York, NY), 1954.

Two by Two, Houghton (Boston, MA), 1954, revised edition published as *A Love, or a Season,* Harper (New York, NY), 1964.

Rosemary, Harper (New York, NY), 1955.

Hospital Zone, Harper (New York, NY), 1956.

The Day and the Way We Met, Harper (New York, NY), 1956.

Good-by My Shadow, Harper (New York, NY), 1957.

Because of Madeline, Harper (New York, NY), 1957.

And Love Replied, Harper (New York, NY), 1958.

Second Nature, Harper (New York, NY), 1958.

Some Merry-Go-Round Music, Harper (New York, NY), 1959.

The Beautiful Friend and Other Stories, Harper (New York, NY), 1960.

Wait for Me, Michael, Harper (New York, NY), 1961.

Who Wants Music on Monday?, Harper (New York, NY), 1963.

By the Highway Home, Harper (New York, NY), 1971.

Leap before You Look, Harper (New York, NY), 1972.

The Edge of Next Year, Harper (New York, NY), 1974.

Cat in the Mirror, Harper (New York, NY), 1975.

Ferris Wheel, Harper (New York, NY), 1977.

Cider Days, Harper (New York, NY), 1978.

Go and Catch a Flying Fish, Harper (New York, NY), 1979.

What Time of Night Is It?, Harper (New York, NY), 1981.

Ivy Larkin: A Novel, Harcourt (San Diego, CA), 1986.

Tales at the Mouse Hole, illustrated by Pamela Johnson, D. Godine (Boston, MA), 1991.

Stealing Home, HarperCollins (New York, NY), 1992.

Cezanne Pinto: A Memoir, Knopf (New York, NY), 1994.

Coco Grimes, HarperCollins (New York, NY), 1994.

The Weeds and the Weather, pictures by N. Cameron Watson, Greenwillow Books (New York, NY), 1994.

A Ballad of the Civil War, illustrated by Sergio Martinez, HarperCollins (New York, NY), 1997.

Casebook of a Private (Cat's) Eye, Front Street/Cricket Books (New York, NY), 1999.

FOR CHILDREN

The Leftover Elf, illustrated by Peggy Bacon, Harper (New York, NY), 1952.

Emmett's Pig, illustrated by Garth Williams, Harper (New York, NY), 1959, published with illustrations by Williams and watercolors by Rosemary Wells, HarperCollins (New York, NY), 2003.

A Dog on Barkham Street (also see below), illustrated by Leonard Shortall, Harper (New York, NY), 1960.

Belling the Tiger, illustrated by Beni Montresor, Harper (New York, NY), 1961, published with new illustrations by Pierre Pratt, Running Press (Philadelphia, PA), 2004.

The Great Rebellion (also see below), illustrated by Beni Montresor, Harper (New York, NY), 1961.

Fredou, illustrated by Tomi Ungerer, Harper (New York, NY), 1962.

Pigeon Flight, illustrated by Murray Tinkelman, Harper (New York, NY), 1962.

Siri, the Conquistador (also see below), illustrated by Beni Montresor, Harper (New York, NY), 1963.

The Bully of Barkham Street (also see below), illustrated by Leonard Shortall, Harper (New York, NY), 1963.

The Mystery of the Woods, illustrated by Uri Shulevitz, Harper (New York, NY), 1964.

The Noonday Friends, illustrated by Louis S. Glanzman, Harper (New York, NY), 1965.

Maximilian's World (also see below), illustrated by Uri Shulevitz, Harper (New York, NY), 1966.

A Wonderful, Terrible Time, illustrated by Louis S. Glanzman, Harper (New York, NY), 1967.

Say Something, illustrated by Edward Frascino, Harper (New York, NY), 1968, revised edition illustrated by Alexander Koshkin, 1993.

The Story of a Singular Hen and Her Peculiar Children, illustrated by Edward Frascino, Harper (New York, NY), 1969.

The Dragons of the Queen, illustrated by Edward Frascino, Harper (New York, NY), 1969.

Juan, illustrated by Louis S. Glanzman, Harper (New York, NY), 1970.

Land's End, illustrated by Dennis Hermanson, Harper (New York, NY), 1973.

Cat Walk, illustrated by Erik Blegvad, Harper (New York, NY), 1983.

Quentin Corn, illustrated by Pamela Johnson, David Godine (New York, NY), 1985.

The Explorer of Barkham Street (also see below), illustrated by Emily Arnold McCully, Harper (New York, NY), 1985.

Night of Ghosts and Hermits: Nocturnal Life on the Seashore (nonfiction), illustrated by Susan Gallagher, Harcourt (San Diego, CA), 1985.

The Cuckoo Clock, illustrated by Pamela Johnson, David Godine (Boston, MA), 1986.

The Scarecrows and Their Child, illustrated by Amy Schwartz, Harper (New York, NY), 1987.

Zekmet, the Stone Carver: A Tale of Ancient Egypt, illustrated by Deborah Nourse Lattimore, Harcourt (New York, NY), 1988.

Storm in the Night, illustrated by Pat Cummings, Harper (New York, NY), 1988.

Pangur Ban, illustrated by Pamela Johnson, Harper (New York, NY), 1988.

Barkham Street Trilogy (contains *A Dog on Barkham Street, The Bully of Barkham Street,* and *The Explorer of Barkham Street*), Harper (New York, NY), 1989.

Bartholomew Fair, Greenwillow (New York, NY), 1990.

Tales at the Mousehole (contains revised versions of *The Great Rebellion, Maximilian's World,* and *Siri, the Conquistador,* illustrated by Pamela Johnson, David Godine (Boston, MA), 1990.

Deputy Shep, illustrated by Pamela Johnson, Harper-Collins (New York, NY), 1991.

King Emmett the Second, illustrated by Garth Williams, Greenwillow (New York, NY), 1991.

Go Fish, illustrated by Pat Cummings, HarperCollins (New York, NY), 1991.

The Weeds and the Weather, HarperCollins (New York, NY), 1994.

OTHER

Truth and Consequence (adult novel), Harper (New York, NY), 1953.

Stolz has also contributed short stories to periodicals, including *Cosmopolitan, Cricket, Good Housekeeping, Ladies' Home Journal, McCall's, Redbook, Seventeen, Woman's Day,* and *The Writer.* Her books have been published in over twenty-five languages; several have been made available in Braille editions. Stolz's manuscripts are included in the Kerlan collection at the University of Minnesota, Minneapolis, and the de Grummond Collection at the University of Southern Mississippi.

■ Adaptations

"Baby Blue Expression" (short story; first published in *McCall's*) was adapted for television by Alfred Hitchcock; *The Noonday Friends* was recorded by Miller-Brody, 1976.

■ Sidelights

Mary Stolz is the author of novels and short stories for children and young adults. Noted for her eloquence and sensitivity to the everyday events that shape the lives of her characters, her books for teenage readers, including *The Noonday Friends, The Edge of Next Year,* and *Go and Catch a Flying Fish,* were among the first to be recognized for their accurate representation of the emotional concerns of adolescence. She has written on such subjects as divorce, family relationships, social problems, and the growth towards adulthood, all with a characteristic respect for the sensitivity and maturity of her young readers. According to a contributor in the *St. James Guide to Young Adult Writers,* "Stolz's work is particularly noteworthy for her strong characterization. Her characters are well-rounded and introspective. They observe and analyze their own behavior and feelings as well as the actions and emotions of family and friends."

Stolz was born in Boston, Massachusetts, into a family with strong Irish traditions. Together with her sister Eileen and cousin Peg, she moved to New York, NY, where the three girls were raised. Stolz developed a love for books early in her childhood, and was encouraged in her reading by her Uncle Bill. He bought her volumes of literature over the years, including works by such authors as A.A. Milne, Kenneth Grahame, Ernest Thompson Seton, Emily Dickinson, Jane Austen, and John Keats. "They instructed—without scaring me witless—amused, saddened, puzzled, delighted, enriched. Opened worlds, lighted corners. They sustained me," she wrote in *Children's Book Council: 1975.* Her love of reading has oftentimes extended into the lives of her characters and much of her writing is interspersed with literary allusion.

"As a girl I was flighty, flirtatious, impulsive, self-involved, and not very thoughtful," Stolz once commented. "Then I read *Pride and Prejudice* and fell in love with Elizabeth Bennet. To me, she's the loveliest female in fiction, as Rochester is the most captivating male. I used to think they should have married each other. Anyway, I tried to model myself after Elizabeth Bennet, so you can see how much the book affected me. It worked, too. Sort of. My manners improved, even my deportment changed. I think I became more considerate. And *Little Women* . . . I don't know if anyone still reads it. I hope so. The book has such warmth and closeness—the closeness of family and friends. The death of Beth March was devastating to me. I used to go back and start over again, actually almost thinking that the next time it would turn out differently. But that book showed how a family faced a loss so great, and survived it, and went on, and even knew happiness again. Quite a lesson to learn from a book."

An Early Interest in Literature

Stolz's love of reading soon transformed itself into a love of writing. Stolz's prolific outpouring of stories extended into her teenage years, and she wrote constantly while a student at the Birch Wathen School in New York, NY. The unstructured academic environment of this progressive school allowed her the freedom to both read and write material of her own choosing. Stolz recalled in *Something about the Author Autobiography Series (SAAS)*, "I always wanted to be a writer, a real, published writer—the way other girls at school wanted to become actresses. A few of them did become actresses, and here am I, a writer."

Stolz went on to study at Columbia University Teacher's College, followed by a year at the Katharine Gibbs School, where she learned typing skills that allowed her to get a secretarial position at Columbia as well as aiding her in her own written effort. When she was eighteen years old, Stolz left her job and married Stanley Burr Stolz. She and her husband had a son, William, who kept her busy and away from writing for several years. However, in 1950, after suffering a great deal of physical pain which necessitated her undergoing an operation, Stolz found herself confined to her home during her recovery. Her physician, Dr. Thomas Jaleski (who later was to become her second husband), encouraged her to occupy herself with something during her recuperation. As she recalled in *SAAS*, "I told him that when I was in school (not so awfully far in the past) I'd liked to write. 'Well, that's excellent,' he said. 'My advice is that you write something that will take you a long time. Write a novel.'" Stolz bought a secondhand typewriter, a ream of yellow paper, and started writing. Her efforts paid off when the manuscript was accepted by the first publisher she sent it to. *To Tell Your Love* was published in 1950.

"It is sometimes said that the first novel is written some ten years back in a writer's life," Stolz wrote in *SAAS*. "This probably isn't a rule, but I followed it, writing about a fifteen-year-old girl who falls in love and loses her love, which probably should, or anyway does, happen to most fifteen-year-old girls. It had happened to me, and it was easy to recall the disbelief, the *pain* of having to accept that a boy who had seemed to love me, who had *said* he loved me, no longer did. Creating a family, adding some relatives, putting in my cat, July, I simply wrote my own story and sent the book to Harper's."

Stolz developed a strong relationship with her editor at Harper's over the many years since she began her writing career, and once stated, "The matchless Ursula Nordstrom supported, inspired, and *put up* with me over many, many years. When she died in 1988, I wrote an essay in her memory, in her honor. . . . She was the finest children's book editor ever, the trail blazer, and all her artists and writers would say the same. When I finish a book, or when working on one, I actually ache, knowing she will not see it."

Life Experiences Inform Works

Much of Stolz's writing is a patchwork of memories of people, places, and circumstances from her own life. *Ready or Not* is the story of the Connor family, who live in a low-income housing project in New York, NY and try to get by on a small income. The book centers around the eldest daughter, Morgan Connor, and her efforts to help sustain the family through their rough times with her warmth and mature wisdom. *Ivy Larkin: A Novel* is also set in New York, NY, and takes place during the Depression era when Stolz herself was a young girl. The protagonist, fourteen-year-old Ivy, faces the isolation of being a scholarship student from a poor family at an exclusive private school catering to the children of wealthy parents. The book tells how Ivy overcomes her fear of being an outsider, her worries when her father loses his job, and her resentments of the snobbishness of the other students.

Stolz credits the daily experience of life with providing the inspiration for her writing. Asked where the ideas from her stories come from, she once replied, "From living, and looking, and being curious, and eavesdropping, and caring about nearly everything. From reading." Stolz is adamant about the importance of books to the developing writer: "Reading has been my university, my way of living in history, prehistory, the present, the future. I mean that reading has made me know and understand more people than one person ever could know, or possibly understand, in seven lifetimes. I mean that to me, and to most writers, I think, reading has been as necessary as taking nourishment, sleeping, loving. I mean that to me a life without books would not be worth living." She discussed the development of her characters, "Fictional characters are an amalgam of the real, the imagined, the dreamed-of. They are mosaics—bits of a nephew, a stranger, a beloved poet, a character in someone else's fiction (I think that I put a little of Elizabeth Bennet in my heroines). All these, and more, are put together, pulled apart, shuffled, and altered until, on paper, there is someone not to be recognized as that nephew, that woman seen on a subway and never seen again, that reclusive poet, *or* Jane Austen's perfect young lady."

In an article in *Writer*, Stolz commented, "On the whole, it is my belief—and I have written from that belief—that after infancy there develops between children and adults (especially parents) an uneasiness, a withdrawal, a perplexity, sometimes hostility. In some cases, the feelings persist until the children are adults. Sometimes, between parents and children, it simply never stops. This tension, this loving and hating, this bafflement and struggle to understand is, in my opinion, the underpinning of all I've written." According to a contributor in the *St. James Guide to Young Adult Writers*, the conflicts that Stolz's face center on "the interactions of family members as they struggle to cope with some of the senseless suffering many people face."

The Noonday Friends, designated as a Newbery Honor Book in 1966, is written for the junior high school reader. The book tells the story of Franny Davis whose father is an out-of-work artist and whose mother must work to keep the family together. Eleven-year-old Franny develops a close friendship with Simone, a Puerto Rican girl she is only able to meet during school lunch period. The two friends have a great deal in common: they have to give up their social life for the responsibilities of baby-sitting for younger brothers and sisters and keeping house for their working mothers. Franny and Simone feel overwhelmed by their household chores but their friendship helps each girl learn to accept her family situation.

In *By the Highway Home*, thirteen-year-old Catty must deal with the death of her brother in the Vietnam War. When Catty's father loses his job, pressures mount on the family. "Catty's outburst, decrying her family's unrelenting sadness and despair, helps to break the hold of grief upon their lives," noted the *St. James Guide to Young Adult Writers*, contributor. An unexpected death changes the life of another teenager in *The Edge of Next Year*. After his mother is killed in a car accident, Orin takes charge of his younger brother, nurturing and caring for him even as their father descends into alcoholism. Orin also comes to terms with his ambivalent feelings toward his mother, whose unconventional behavior he both admired and disdained. In *Go and Catch a Flying Fish*, Taylor and Jim Reddick are raised by a nonconformist mother who alienates her family. "As the tensions between their parents rise, the children assume protective stances, attempting to defuse conflict between their parents," wrote the contributor in *St. James Guide to Young Adult Writers*. When their mother abandons them, the family members must fend for themselves. A sequel, *What Time of Night Is It?*, follows the story of the Reddick family as Taylor, Jim, and their father adjust to life without their mother.

Stolz's books are highly regarded as quality literature for young adult readers. *New York Times Book Review* critic Ellen Lewis Buell commented on the "wit, originality and a rare maturity" contained within Stolz's books. "Mary Stolz's remarkable empathy with the characters in her books is particularly important in her stories about older boys and girls," Ruth Hill Viguers wrote in *Margin for Surprise: About Books, Children, and Librarians*. "At a time when many teen-age stories are misleading, she always plays fair. The people of her books are alive, their world is the contemporary world, and their stories are told with truth and dignity." Stolz's more recent young-adult novels have been criticized by some as not "relevant" to today's teen-age reader; that her method of dealing with social problems faced by young people has not kept pace with changing times. Stolz agrees that today's high school student is more sophisticated than when she began writing. "I have not dealt with the drug scene. My characters . . . are not battered, they are not criminals, they are not homeless on the road," Stolz commented in *Writer*. "I know that many writers today . . . handle all these themes in their books. . . . But a writer can write only as he can write." Stolz recognizes her limitations in reflecting the issues of modern young people, "I don't understand the drug culture of today," she told Linda Giuca in the *Hartford Courant*. "You can't write about what you don't know." In the 1980s, Stolz shifted her energies to writing for younger children who still seem to grow up in much the same fashion as they did thirty years ago.

Although Stolz began her career writing primarily for teenage girls, she soon varied her audience by writing for pre-teens and younger children as well. When her son, Billy, was old enough to be read aloud to, he wanted his mother to write stories that he would enjoy. His insistence inspired her first book for young children, *The Leftover Elf*, which has been followed by many notable children's books, including *Belling the Tiger*, *The Bully of Barkham Street*, and *Emmett's Pig*. As with her books for teenagers, Stolz's stories for younger readers have emotional depth, as well as being entertaining. *King Emmett the Second*, the sequel to *Emmett's Pig*, deals with the adjustments that young Emmett must make, not only in moving from the city out to a new home in the country, but with the death of his beloved pet pig. Emmett learns to cope with loss and change and by story's end is able to accept a new pet, as well as a new home, into both his life and his heart.

Stolz has published four books about the adventures of Thomas, a young African American boy, and his grandfather who share a love of baseball. Beginning with *Storm in the Night*, these tales continue with *Go Fish*, *Stealing Home*, and the 1994 title, *Coco Grimes*.

In this last-named book, Thomas is excited at the prospect of meeting a former player from the Negro Leagues. However, when the meeting finally comes about, it is something of a disappointment for Thomas as Coco is old, forgetful, and rather cranky. A moment of epiphany does come however, when the two connect momentarily. "As always," noted *Booklist's* Hazel Rochman, "the real interest of the story is in the loving home that orphan Thomas shares with Grandfather. . . ." Rochman further concluded, "Stolz has the rare ability to write about happiness without being sentimental."

In *Cezanne Pinto: A Memoir,* Stolz provides a further connection to Thomas in the form of a fictional memoir of a runaway child slave who becomes a soldier, cowboy, and teacher. The story of Cezanne, the ancestor of Thomas from Stolz's previous books, is interwoven with the stories of actual historical personalities in the pages of this fiction: Frederick Douglass and Harriet Tubman among others. "Rarely does historical fiction achieve the immediacy and power of this exceptional novel," wrote a contributor for *Publishers Weekly* in a review of the book. The same reviewer concluded, "Stolz dazzles with the scope of her vision."

More history is served up in *A Ballad of the Civil War,* a tale of twins who grow up to fight on opposite sides in that bloody war. For this story, Stolz adapted an old Union Army song she often heard when growing up. A critic for *Publishers Weekly* wrote that Stolz's "pellucid, descriptive prose delivers a bite-size piece of history."

Writing in a lighter vein in the *Casebook of a Private (Cat's) Eye,* Stolz "adopts a Victorian voice and syntax for this eloquent tale of a resourceful sleuth," according to a contributor for *Publishers Weekly.* The sleuth is Eileen O'Kelly, a female, feline private detective. Told with tongue firmly in cheek, *Casebook of a Private (Cat's) Eye* provides a series of short mysteries complete in themselves which "will likely win over both beginning sleuths and lovers of language," as a reviewer for *Publishers Weekly* noted.

The Writer's Philosophy

Stolz once commented, "Many people who think they want to write want, actually, to have written something. This is not the same as writing, which is very disciplined work, and there are a lot of things to be doing that are simpler and, perhaps, more fun. So—reading, reading, reading . . . writing, writing, writing. When I say this sort of thing to groups of children, I can feel them thinking, 'Then what does she *do:* she reads things, and then she goes and writes something.' I had one child tell me right out that it sounded like a funny way to go about it. I tried to explain that, to me, the reading, in addition to everything else it is, is a form of going to school. It's not imitating, it's learning.

If you enjoy the works of Mary Stolz, you may also want to check out the following books:

Jill Paton Walsh, *A Pattern of Parcels,* 1983.
Brenda Wilkinson, *Not Separate, Not Equal,* 1987.
James Howe, *The Misfits,* 2001.

"There are books in which you lose yourself and there are books in which you find yourself. There's a place for both. Detective stories, for instance, are fine for getting lost in. But the great books are those in which you find yourself. And a great book needn't be a classic. It just needs to be the right book at the right time for the person who's reading it."

Stolz and Jaleski make their home in the Florida Keys, she once explained: "We live a shell's throw from the Gulf of Mexico, with nothing between us and the ocean but pale sand and sea oats," the author remarked. "Sunrise, sunset, seabirds, shorebirds, and the mockingbird who comes in early spring bringing us the songs of the north. It is not New England, and we shall always miss New England, but in its way this hurricane-threatened island where we live has us in thrall."

Stolz has always been very concerned about the role human beings have played in the custodianship of the earth. Quoting from her acceptance speech for the George C. Stone recognition of merit, Stolz said: "Perhaps the animals are planning some fine benign surprise for us. Maybe the whales and elephants with their massive brains are conspiring . . . with the eagles . . . and, of course, our pets, to lead us blunderers into respect for this small, shared planet. We seem unlikely to arrive at such an attitude on our own, but without it we won't need to wait for a cosmic finale to the earthly drama. We'll arrange one ourselves." Stolz considers young people best able to look ahead, to change the course of society. "Children do a lot of thinking," she wrote. "They continue to ask the simple-hard questions: What's the world about? Life about? What am I about? Or you? What's worth something? What's worth everything? Who *am* I and who are all these others and what are we going to do about *that?* From my mail, I know that there are many children still looking for answers in books. I used to, as a child. I still think something reassuring is to be found in them. If we read hard enough they can offer us at least part of a perspective. . . . Even with that . . . we could, possibly, still save our world. It's a hope." Stolz's faith and optimism in the possibilities of childhood have inspired her as a children's writer. Children, she explained, "are, at present, all we can hope through. Which is why I write for them."

■ Biographical and Critical Sources

BOOKS

Contemporary Literary Criticism, Volume 12, Gale (Detroit, MI), 1980.

Eakin, Mary K., *Good Books for Children*, 3rd edition, University of Chicago Press (Chicago, IL), 1966, pp. 318-319.

Fisher, Margerie, *Who's Who in Children's Books*, Holt (New York, NY), 1975.

Fuller, Muriel, editor, *More Junior Authors*, H.W. Wilson (New York, NY), 1963, pp. 195-196.

Hopkins, Lee Bennett, *More Books by More People: Interviews with Sixty-five Authors of Books for Children*, Citation (New York, NY), 1974.

St. James Guide to Young Adult Writers, 2nd edition, St. James Press, 1999.

Silvey, Anita, *Children's Books and Their Creators*, Houghton Mifflin (Boston, MA), 1995.

Something about the Author Autobiography Series, Volume 3, Gale (Detroit, MI), 1986, pp. 281-292.

Twentieth Century Children's Writers, 3rd edition, St. James Press (Detroit, MI), 1989, pp. 921-923.

Viguers, Ruth Hill, *Margin for Surprise: About Books, Children, and Librarians*, Little, Brown (Boston, MA), 1964, p. 107.

PERIODICALS

Atlantic Monthly, December, 1953.

Booklist, September 15, 1974; January 1, 1976, p. 628; November 1, 1988; January 15, 1994, p. 919; March 15, 1994, p. 1375; May 1, 1994, Hazel Rochman, review of *Coco Grimes*, p. 1602; October 1, 1997, p. 333; April 15, 1999, p. 1532; September 1, 2004, Carolyn Phelan, review of *Belling the Tiger*, p. 125; November 1, 2004, Carolyn Phelan, review of *Emmett's Pig*, p. 494.

Book Report, May-June, 1989, p. 47; March-April, 1991, p. 47; September-October, 1994, p. 46; September-October, 1999, p. 63.

Bulletin of the Center for Children's Books, November, 1965, pp. 50-51; May, 1969; December, 1969; July, 1979; July, 1981; July, 1983; October, 1985; May, 1988.

Chicago Sunday Tribune, August 23, 1953; November 6, 1960, p. 49.

Christian Science Monitor, November 11, 1971, p. B5.

Cricket, September, 1974.

English Journal, September, 1952; September, 1955; April, 1975; October, 1975; November, 1989, p. 82.

Hartford Courant, June 2, 1974, Linda Giuca, "Add Talent to Volumes of Reading, Writing."

Horn Book, December, 1953, pp. 469-470; April, 1957, p. 141; October, 1957, pp. 406-407; October, 1965; October, 1971; October, 1974; December, 1975, p. 598; April, 1981; November, 1985; January, 1986, p. 61; November-December, 1990, pp. 746-747; July-August, 1991, pp. 454-455; September, 2003, review of *Emmett's Pig*, p. 586.

Kirkus Reviews, October 15, 1974, pp. 111-112.

Language Arts, April, 1989, p. 456.

Los Angeles Times Book Review, July 28, 1985; April 20, 1986; May 3, 1987.

New York Herald Tribune Book Review, October 28, 1951; March 22, 1953, Ellen Lewis Buell, review of *Ready or Not*, p. 24; December 13, 1953; November 14, 1954; November 28, 1954; November 13, 1955; December 30, 1956.

New York Times Book Review, May 13, 1951; August 30, 1953, p. 15; September 26, 1954; April 22, 1956; May 18, 1958; November 13, 1960, p. 28; May 14, 1961; November 12, 1961; October 24, 1971, p. 81; September 3, 1972.

Psychology Today, July, 1975.

Publishers Weekly, July 12, 1985; August 9, 1985; September 20, 1985; September 26, 1986; October 9, 1987; January 15, 1988; February 12, 1988; August 26, 1988; August 31, 1990; January 10, 1994, review of *Cezanne Pinto: A Memoir*, p. 63; April 18, 1994, pp. 62-63; November 10, 1997, review of *A Ballad of the Civil War*, p. 74; April 26, 1999, review of *Casebook of a Private (Cat's) Eye*, p. 83; February 10, 2003, review of *Emmett's Pig*, p. 189.

School Library Journal, April, 1964; September, 1985; November, 1985; January, 1986; December, 1986; April, 1987; January, 1988; November, 1990;

October, 1991, pp. 105-106; March, 1993, p. 202; April, 1993, p. 102; December, 1993, p. 118; May, 1994, p. 105; June, 1994, p. 135; February, 1998, p. 110; June, 1999, pp. 137-138; September, 2004, Bina Williams, review of *Belling the Tiger,* pp. 181-182.

Times Literary Supplement, November 26, 1954.

Washington Post Book World, May 10, 1987; February 10, 1991.

Wilson Library Bulletin, September, 1953; September, 1991, p. 142.

Writer, October, 1980, Mary Stolz, "Believe What You Write About," pp. 22-23.*

Allan Stratton

■ Personal

Born 1951, in Stratford, Ontario, Canada. *Education:* University of Toronto, B.A., 1973, Graduate Centre for the Study of Drama, M.A.; studied at New York Actor's Studio.

■ Addresses

Home—248 Hiawatha Rd., Toronto, Ontario M4L 2Y4, Canada. *Agent*—Denise Bukowski, The Bukowski Agency, 14 Prince Arthur Ave., #202, Toronto, Ontario M5R 1A9, Canada. *E-mail*—allanstratton@sympatico.ca.

■ Career

Playwright. Etobicoke School of the Arts, Toronto, Ontario, Canada, former head of drama department.

■ Member

Writers' Union of Canada, Playwrights Guild of Canada.

■ Awards, Honors

Chalmers Award and Dora Mavor Moore Award, both 1981, and Canadian Authors' Association Award for best play, all for *Rexy!*; Chalmers Award, 1985, for *Papers*; Stephen Leacock Award of Merit, for *The Phoenix Lottery*; Best Books for Young Adults selection and Quick Picks for Reluctant Young Adult Readers selection, both American Library Association, both for *Leslie's Journal*; New York Public Library Books for the Teenage selection, Notable Book selection, International Readers Association, Best Books for Young Adults selection, Popular Paperbacks for Young Adults selection, and Michael L. Printz Honor Book award, all American Library Association, all 2005, all for *Chanda's Secrets*.

■ Writings

NOVELS

Leslie's Journal (young adult), Annick Press (Toronto, Ontario, Canada), 2000.

The Phoenix Lottery, Riverbank Press (Toronto, Ontario, Canada), 2000.

Chanda's Secrets (young adult), Annick Press (Toronto, Ontario, Canada), 2004.

PLAYS

72 under the O: A Farce (produced in Vancouver, British Columbia, Canada, 1977), Playwrights Co-op (Toronto, Ontario, Canada), 1978, revised and published as *Bingo!: A Comedy* (produced in Barrie, Ontario, Canada, 1985), Samuel French (New York, NY), 1987.

Nurse Jane Goes to Hawaii (produced in Toronto, Ontario, Canada, 1980), Playwrights Canada (Toronto, Ontario, Canada), 1981.

Rexy! (produced in Toronto, Ontario, Canada, 1981), Playwrights Canada (Toronto, Ontario, Canada), 1981, published in *Canada Split: Two Plays*, 1991.

Joggers (produced in Toronto, Ontario, Canada, 1982), Playwrights Canada (Toronto, Ontario, Canada), 1983, published in *Words in Play*, 1988.

Friends of a Feather (adaptation of *Célimare*, by Eugene Labiche and A. Delacour; produced in Toronto, Ontario, Canada, 1984), Playwrights Canada (Toronto, Ontario, Canada), 1984.

Papers (produced in Toronto, Ontario, Canada, 1985), Playwrights Canada (Toronto, Ontario, Canada), 1986, Samuel French (New York, NY), 1990.

The 101 Miracles of Hope Chance (produced in Winnipeg, Manitoba, Canada, 1987), published in *Words in Play*, 1991.

Words in Play: Three Comedies by Allan Stratton (includes *The 101 Miracles of Hope Chance* and *Joggers*), edited by Robert Wallace, Coach House Press (Toronto, Ontario, Canada), 1988.

Bag Babies: A Comedy of (Bad) Manners (produced in Toronto, Ontario, Canada, 1990), Coach House Press (Toronto, Ontario, Canada), 1991.

A Flush of Tories (produced in Winnipeg, Manitoba, Canada, 1991), Playwrights Canada (Toronto, Ontario, Canada), 1991, published in *Canada Split*, 1991.

Canada Split: Two Plays (contains *A Flush of Tories* and *Rexy!*), edited by Odette Dubé Nuage (Montreal, Quebec, Canada), 1991.

Dracula: Nightmare of the Dead (adaptation of the novel by Bram Stoker), produced in Toronto, Ontario, Canada, 1995.

The Phoenix Lottery (based on Stratton's novel), Playwrights Canada (Toronto, Ontario, Canada), 2001.

Also author of radio play *When Father Passed Away*.

■ Adaptations

A Flush of Tories and *Friends of a Feather* were adapted for television by Canadian Broadcasting Corporation (CBC); *The Rusting Heart*, first published in the magazine *Alphabet*, was adapted for CBC Radio in 1970.

■ Work in Progress

The Resurrection of Mary Mabel McTavish, a novel; *Chanda's War*, a young adult novel.

■ Sidelights

Allan Stratton is an award-winning Canadian playwright and author. He is well known for *Rexy!*, which received the Canadian Authors' Association Award for best play, *Papers*, which garnered the Chalmers Award, and *The Phoenix Lottery*, which earned the Stephen Leacock Award of Merit. Stratton has also published works for young adults, including *Leslie's Journal* and *Chanda's Secrets*, a Michael L. Printz Honor Book.

Stratton has been involved with the arts from a young age. Born in Stratford, Ontario, Canada, Stratton and his mother moved in with his grandparents when he was just a toddler. He spent his days listening to fairy tales and classical music on a record player, and he developed a passion for literature at a young age. Stratton's mother, a teacher, took her son to see a play by William Shakespeare when he was five years old; he soon organized his friends to produce backyard performances for an audience of doting parents. By the sixth grade, Stratton had written a fifteen-minute play about explorer Henry Hudson that was performed by his classmates. He was also a voracious reader. Before he graduated from elementary school, Stratton had read the complete works of Shakespeare in addition to the Narnia Chronicles, the Enid Blyton adventures and the Nancy Drew mysteries.

Stratton acted while in high school, and his play *The Rusting Heart* was produced for radio by the Canadian Broadcasting Corporation when Stratton was in twelfth grade. Stratton's interest in the roles people play was also influenced by his own sexual orientation. As a gay teenager, he felt compelled to hide his true self, yet he found the experience instructive. "You're very aware of playing roles," he told Jeffrey Canton of *Xtra*. "You play the role of a straight kid, aware that what you are presenting to the world is not what you are feeling on the inside."

Finds Success as Playwright

While working on an honors degree in English at the University of Toronto, Stratton performed with the Stratford Festival and the Huron County

While researching his young adult novel *Chanda's Secrets*, Stratton traveled to Malawi and other African nations.

Playhouse. Later, while earning a master's degree from the Graduate Centre for the Study of Drama, he acted with regional theatre troupes across the country. In 1977, his first professional stage play, *72 under the O: A Farce,* was produced at the Vancouver Playhouse. Eight years after the play was first produced, a revised form, titled *Bingo!,* was staged at the Gryphon Theatre in Barrie, Ontario, and since then, it has been produced at venues across Canada and the United States.

With the success of his next play, *Nurse Jane Goes to Hawaii,* a comedy about a writer of Harlequin romances, Stratton was able to write full-time. *Rexy!,* a satire about former Canadian Prime Minister William Lyon Mackenzie King, premiered in 1981 and was also hugely successful. Stratton spent several years in New York, beginning in 1982, and joined Lee Strasberg's Actor's Studio, but his plays have all premiered in Canada.

Joggers is a dark comedy about family and sexual repression, while *Friends of a Feather* is an adaptation of a French farce. The predicament of two lonely lovers who are unable to communicate is the focus of the romantic comedy *Papers,* and *The 101 Miracles of Hope Chance* is a satire about the exploitation of a believer by televangelists.

Stratton returned to Canada in the late 1980s and resettled in Montreal. His first production after returning was *Bag Babies: A Comedy of (Bad) Manners,* a comedy with a message about poverty and homelessness. Like so many of Stratton's plays, it received a number of award nominations and has since been performed in England, Scotland, and the United States. *A Flush of Tories* is a satire that examines the administration of Canadian Prime Minister John A. MacDonald and MacDonald's four Tory successors. *Dracula: Nightmare of the Dead* is an adaptation of the novel by Bram Stoker, featuring a female van Helsing, it is an examination of Victorian mores and the relationship between sex and death.

Stratton's novel *The Phoenix Lottery,* which the author also adapted as a stage play, focuses on Junior Beamish, who launches a lottery to raise money and plans to torch a painting by Vincent van

Gogh live on the Internet in order to sell the story. His dead father fights his scheming son from beyond the grave, and the Vatican sends a cardinal to oppose Junior on behalf of human civilization. The novel version of *The Phoenix Lottery* is an epic that takes place over fifty years, while the play version deals with the period immediately surrounding the actual lottery.

Delves into Young Adult Literature

Stratton briefly headed the drama department of the Etobicoke School of the Arts in Toronto, where he also taught playwriting, acting, and directing. His students benefited from his talent, earning several awards for their plays. He returned to writing full-time and several years later published his first young adult novel, *Leslie's Journal,* which *School Library Journal* reviewer Marilyn Payne Phillips felt "could be the *Go Ask Alice . . .* of this millennium." In the novel Leslie is not doing well in school. Her parents are divorced, her father has a live-in girlfriend, and Leslie cannot communicate with her mother. Her only friend is Katie, who sticks by Leslie and helps her out of the situation that is at the center of the story.

Leslie's English teacher has asked her students to write journals, which she keeps locked in a closet and promises to never read. When a substitute teacher who does not know about the agreement takes over, however, the startling revelations in Leslie's journal are exposed. Leslie is, in fact, having a relationship with wealthy, popular Jason, who raped her and took pictures of her after getting her drunk. As the teen confides in the pages of her journal, she attempted to break up with him, but he beat her and threatened to kill her. The substitute teacher takes the journal to the principal, but she believes Jason rather than Leslie. Jason stalks Leslie, who runs away, and it takes bravery and Katie's support before the resolution is reached. Phillips noted that "this cautionary tale is not easy to read; few of the characters are likable."

On his Web site, Stratton explained that his second young adult novel, *Chanda's Secrets,* grew "out of my experiences in Botswana, as well as the times

During his trips to Africa to research the AIDS pandemic, Stratton met with healthcare workers and educators.

I've spent as a caregiver for friends in the final stages of AIDS." While researching the work, Stratton traveled to South Africa, Botswana, and Zimbabwe, where frontline AIDS workers and agencies took him into homes, care centers, and mortuaries. "I'm fascinated by world cultures and at how similar we human beings are in matters of the heart, no matter what our social and cultural contexts," Stratton said in an interview on the *Children's Literature* Web site. "Television reports tend to portray Africa as this strange 'other' place. I wanted to write a book that would bring people into the human story of the African pandemic, to lower walls, and to make people think about Africa as 'here.'"

Chanda is a sixteen-year-old girl who, as *Chanda's Secrets* opens, is preparing the funeral of her younger sister. Chanda lost her father in a diamond-mining accident, and her first stepfather abused her. The second died of a stroke, and the current stepfather is now dying. The cause of his death and that of little Sara is the secret that can't be discussed. Chanda's mother is also sick, as is her best friend, who has turned to prostitution; Chanda, who has been raped, now fears that she might also be infected. When her mother is rejected by the family, Chanda cares for her until her death and overcomes her obsession with keeping the secret in favor of advocating for the truth as she takes on the responsibility of her siblings.

If you enjoy the works of Allan Stratton, you may also want to check out the following books:

Nancy Farmer, *A Girl Named Disaster*, 1996.
Stephen Chbosky, *The Perks of Being a Wallflower*, 1999.
Sonya Sones, *One of Those Hideous Books Where the Mother Dies*, 2004.

Chanda's Secrets earned a host of honors and garnered praise from critics. *Resource Links* contributor Anne Hatcher wrote that in *Chanda's Secrets* "Stratton brings the despair, overwhelming poverty and the impact of AIDS/HIV to life while at the same time depicting the strength of human character when faced with adversity." Kathleen Isaacs commented in *School Library Journal* that Stratton's description of life in sub-Saharan Africa is "convincing and smoothly woven into this moving story of poverty and courage, but the real insight for readers will be the appalling treatment of the AIDS victims." The proceeds from the sale of Stratton's novel are being used to fight AIDS. "At its core," Stratton stated in his interview on the *Children's Literature* Web site, "*Chanda's Secrets* is about the love of parents and children; the loyalty between friends; the pain of fear, shame, and stigma; and the courage it takes to live openly with truth." He concluded, "When people finish this book, I want them to imagine themselves in Chanda's shoes, and to keep her and her struggles in their hearts and minds."

■ Biographical and Critical Sources

PERIODICALS

Alliston Herald, June 20, 2003.

Booklist, July, 2004, Hazel Rochman, review of *Chanda's Secrets,* p. 1843.

Books In Canada, April, 1982, review of *Nurse Jane Goes To Hawaii* and *Rexy,* p. 10; March, 1987, review of *Papers,* p. 26; March, 1989, review of *Words in Play,* pp. 5-6; October, 1991, review of *Bag Babies: A Comedy of (Bad) Manners,,* p. 47.

Calgary Herald, February 12, 1994, p. F5.

Canada Newswire, March 22, 2004.

Canadian Children's Literature, fall, 2002, Judith P. Robertson and Kathleen M. Connor "Growing Up and the Work of Teen Narrative," pp. 69-71.

Canadian Literature, summer, 1992, Jill Tomasson Goodwin, review of *Words in Play: Three Comedies,* pp. 174-175; spring, 1993, review of *Bag Babies,* pp. 85-86.

Canadian Theatre Review, fall, 1990, review of *Words in Play,* pp. 87-89; spring, 1993, Jerry Wasserman, review of *Bag Babies,* pp. 167-169.

CM: Canadian Review of Materials, February 16, 2001, review of *Leslie's Journal.*

Eye Weekly, October 12, 1998.

Globe and Mail, April 22, 2004, p. R1.

Kirkus Reviews, May 15, 2004, review of *Chanda's Secrets,* p. 498.

Kliatt, July, 2004, KaaVonia Hinton, review of *Chanda's Secrets,* p. 24.

Montreal Gazette, August 9, 1991, p. C3.

Quill & Quire, September, 1986, review of *Papers,* p. 81; August, 2000, review of *The Phoenix Lottery,* p. 21; September, 2000, review of *Leslie's Journal,* p. 63.

Resource Links, December, 2000, review of *Leslie's Journal,* p. 30; June, 2004, Anne Hatcher, review of *Chanda's Secrets,* p. 27.

School Library Journal, April, 2001, Marilyn Payne Phillips, review of *Leslie's Journal,* p. 150; July, 2004, Kathleen Isaacs, review of *Chanda's Secrets,* p. 112.

Skipping Stones, May-August, 2005, Yvonne Young, review of *Chanda's Secrets,* p. 32.

Toronto Star, November 16, 1990, p. D8; November 18, 1990, p. F6; December 8, 1990, p. K8; May 28, 1992, p. NY8; July 14, 1995, p. B12.

University of Waterloo Imprint, December 1, 2000.

University of Western Ontario Gazette, January 12, 2001; January 16, 2001.

Voice of Youth Advocates, December, 2004, review of *Chanda's Secrets,* p. 397.

Windsor Star, September 28, 1990, p. C2.

Xtra, December 14, 2000.

ONLINE

Allan Stratton Home Page, http://www.allanstratton.com (July 20, 2006).

Children's Literature Web site, http://www.childrenslit.com/ (May 2, 2005), "A Question-and-Answer Session with Allan Stratton."*

Wendy Wasserstein

■ Personal

Born October 18, 1950, in Brooklyn, NY; died of cancer, January 30, 2006, in New York, NY; daughter of Morris W. (a textile manufacturer) and Lola (a dancer; maiden name, Schleifer) Wasserstein; children: Lucy Jane. *Education:* Mount Holyoke College, B.A., 1971; City College of the City University of New York, M.A., 1973; Yale University, M.F.A., 1976.

■ Career

Dramatist, actress, and screenwriter. Teacher at Columbia University and New York University, New York, NY. Actress in plays, including *The Hotel Play*, 1981. Member of artistic board of Playwrights Horizons; board member of WNET (public television affiliate) and MacDowell Colony.

■ Member

Dramatists Guild (member of steering committee and women's committee), British-American Arts Association (board member), Dramatists Guild for Young Playwrights.

■ Awards, Honors

Joseph Jefferson Award, *Dramalogue* Award, and Inner Boston Critics Award, all for *Uncommon Women and Others*; grant for playwriting, Playwrights Commissioning Program of Phoenix Theater, c. 1970s; Hale Mathews Foundation Award; Guggenheim fellowship, 1983; grant for writing and for studying theater in England, British-American Arts Association; grant for playwriting, American Playwrights Project, 1988; Pulitzer Prize for drama, Antoinette Perry ("Tony") Award for best play, League of American Theatres and Producers, Drama Desk Award, Outer Critics Circle Award, Susan Smith Blackburn Prize, and award for best new play, New York Drama Critics' Circle, all 1989, all for *The Heidi Chronicles*; Outer Critics Circle Award and Tony Award nomination for best play, both 1993, both for *The Sisters Rosensweig*.

■ Writings

PLAYS

Any Woman Can't, produced off-Broadway, 1973.
Happy Birthday, Montpelier Pizz-zazz, produced in New Haven, CT, 1974.
(With Christopher Durang) *When Dinah Shore Ruled the Earth,* produced in New Haven, CT, 1975.
Uncommon Women and Others (also see below; produced as a one-act in New Haven, CT, 1975; revised and enlarged two-act version produced off-Broadway, 1977), Avon (New York, NY), 1978.

Isn't It Romantic (also see below; produced off-Broadway, 1981; revised version produced off-Broadway, 1983), Doubleday (New York, NY), 1984.

Tender Offer (one-act), produced off-off-Broadway, 1983.

The Man in a Case (one-act; adapted from the short story by Anton Chekhov), written as part of *Orchards* (anthology of seven one-act plays adapted from short stories by Chekhov; produced off-Broadway, 1986), Knopf (New York, NY), 1986.

Miami (musical), produced off-Broadway, 1986.

The Heidi Chronicles (also see below; produced off-Broadway, 1988, produced on Broadway, 1989), Dramatists Play Service (New York, NY), 1990.

The Heidi Chronicles, and Other Plays (contains *Uncommon Women and Others, Isn't It Romantic,* and *The Heidi Chronicles*), Harcourt (San Diego, CA), 1990.

The Sisters Rosensweig (produced at Mitzi E. Newhouse Theater, Lincoln Center, 1992), Harcourt (New York, NY), 1993.

An American Daughter, Harcourt (New York, NY), 1997.

Seven One-Act Plays (includes *Bette and Me, Boy Meets Girl, The Man in a Case, Medea* [coauthored with Christopher Durang], *Tender Offer, Waiting for Philip Glass,* and *Workout*), Dramatist Play Service (New York, NY), 1999.

Old Money (produced at Mitzi E. Newhouse Theater, Lincoln Center, 2000), Harcourt (New York, NY), 2002.

Psyche in Love (one-act), produced at the TriBeCa Theater Festival (New York, NY), 2004.

Third (one-act), produced at the Mitzi E. Newhouse Theater, Lincoln Center, 2005.

Welcome to My Rash (one-act), produced at Theater J. Washington DC, 2005.

TELEVISION PLAYS

Uncommon Women and Others (adapted from Wasserstein's play), Public Broadcasting Service (PBS), 1978.

The Sorrows of Gin (adapted from the short story by John Cheever), PBS, 1979.

OTHER

Bachelor Girls (comic essays), Knopf (New York, NY), 1990.

Pamela's First Musical (children's picture book), illustrated by Andrew Jackness, Hyperion (New York, NY), 1996.

Shiksa Goddess; or, How I Spent My Forties: Essays, Knopf (New York, NY), 2001.

Sloth: The Seven Deadly Sins (comic essay), Oxford University Press (New York, NY), 2005.

Elements of Style (novel), Knopf (New York, NY), 2006.

Also author of television plays *"Drive," She Said,* PBS, *Sam Found Out: A Triple Play,* 1988, *Kiss-Kiss, Dahlings!,* 1992, *The Heidi Chronicles,* 1995, *An American Daughter,* 2000, *The Nutcracker* (commentary), 2001, and of sketches for *Comedy Zone* (series), Columbia Broadcasting System, Inc. (CBS), 1984. Author of *The Festival of Regrets,* libretto for one-act opera, 1999, and unpublished musical review *Smart Women/Brilliant Choices,* 1988. Author of unproduced film scripts, including (with Christopher Durang) *"House of Husbands,"* adapted from the short story "Husbands"; and a script adapted from the novel *The Object of My Affection* by Stephen McCauley. Contributor of articles to periodicals, including *Esquire, New York Times,* and *New York Woman.* Contributing editor, *New York Woman.*

■ **Sidelights**

The first woman playwright to win a Tony Award, Wendy Wasserstein became the voice for a generation of women "struggling," as Charles Isherwood noted in the *New York Times,* "to reconcile a desire for romance and companionship, drummed into baby boomers by the seductive fantasies of Hollywood movies, with the need for intellectual independence and achievement separate from the personal sphere." According to Mike Boehm of the *Los Angeles Times,* Wasserstein "secured her place in American theater with four consecutive plays [*Uncommon Women and Others, Isn't It Romantic, The Heidi Chronicles,* and *The Rosensweig Sisters*] that traced women's progress from college to middle age in the wake of the feminist revolution of the 1960s." Boehm further noted that "part of their strength and charm . . . was that they weren't sociological sketches of a generation, but highly personal stories anchored in her own experiences with family and friends." Peter Marks observed in the *Washington Post* at the time of Wasserstein's untimely death in 2006 at age fifty-five, that "feminism has never exactly been thought of as a laugh riot, but somehow Wendy Wasserstein managed to locate its funny bone. Not by mocking it—she was an ardent believer—but by making the intoxicating, bewildering choices it presented to women a natural ingredient of the human comedy." Similarly, a critic for *Contemporary Dramatists* noted that such works

An illustration by Andrew Jackness from Wasserstein's 1996 children's book *Pamela's First Musical.*

"placed [Wasserstein] in the slippery position of championing women's causes and feminists concerns." The same critic went on to comment: "The playwright, however, is more concerned with genetics than gender and more likely to employ humor than humanism in creating her female characters. . . . What unites and sustains her dramaturgy is Wasserstein's coy sense of humor, supported by keen observations of everyday life."

Writing in the *Chronicle of Higher Education,* Tamsen Wolff noted that Wasserstein took the Russian playwright Anton Chekhov "as her dramatic hero." In fact, as Wolff further observed, Wasserstein's play *The Sisters Rosensweig* "is a straightforward nod to [Chekhov's] *The Three Sisters,*" while her 1997 play, *An American Daughter,* "recalls [Chekhov's] *Uncle Vanya.*" However, as Wolff further noted, "Most of [Wasserstein's] plays are social comedies, distant cousins to the work of Phillip Barry, S.N. Behrman, George S. Kaufman, and Edna Ferber." In addition to her work in the theater, Wasserstein also proved herself as a writer of humorous essays and sketches, as seen in *Bachelor Girls* and *Shiksa Goddess; or, How I Spent My Forties,* and as a satirical novelist in her

2006 posthumously published first novel, *Elements of Style.* Isherwood noted that for Wasserstein herself, "as for many of her characters and fans, humor was a necessary bulwark against the disappointments of life, and a useful release vale for anger at cultural and social inequities." Isherwood felt that Wasserstein's work, including plays, essays, and a novel, "had a significant influence on depictions of American women in the media landscape over the years."

Where Are All the Girls?

Wasserstein was born in 1950, in Brooklyn, New York, the youngest child of Morris and Lola Wasserstein, Jewish immigrants from Central Europe. The father, the inventor of velveteen, developed a successful textile manufacturing industry, while the mother was both homemaker and avid dance student who attempted to impart her love of dance and theater to her youngest child. The family also placed a high value on achievement: Wasserstein's brother Bruce went on to become the chairman of the investment bank Lazard as well as the owner of *New York* magazine. In the early 1960s, the family moved from Brooklyn to affluent Upper East Side of Manhattan. Wasserstein's education was conservative: the product of an exclusive Manhattan prep school and the all-women Mount Holyoke College. She had considered a career in law, medicine, or business, but a major turning point came during her junior year when a friend recommended she take a summer playwriting course at Smith College. This experience encouraged her; she subsequently spent her junior year at Amherst College, involved in theater production. After graduation from Mount Holyoke, she studied creative writing at the City College of New York with novelist Joseph Heller and playwright Israel Horovitz. Her thesis play, *Every Woman Can't,* was produced off-Broadway in 1973. This debut play set the tone for much of the work to follow: a somewhat bitter comedy about a woman attempting to find success in a male-dominated field.

Wasserstein went on to attend the School of Drama at Yale University, where fellow classmates included actors Meryl Streep, Sigourney Weaver, Glenn Close, and Jill Elkenberry, and playwrights Christopher Durang and Albert Innaurato. She earned her M.F.A. in 1976, and during this time she learned to refine her broad humor, making her characterizations subtler. Among the student plays she wrote are *Happy Birthday, Montpelier,* set at a college party, and *When Dinah Shore Ruled the Earth,* which she authored with classmate Durang, a play that satirizes a beauty pageant. A major shift can be seen, however, with her thesis play, *Uncommon Women and Others.* First produced as a one-act, the play was later revised by Wasserstein, who after leaving Yale worked for the Eugene O'Neill Theater Center reviewing play submissions. After reading and viewing hundreds of plays, she began to realize that something was missing on the stage; namely "girls," as she was fond of calling female actors. She took it upon herself to create theatrical works with strong parts for women.

Uncommon Women and Others is set at a reunion of a group of former Mount Holyoke students six years after graduation. Through flashbacks, we learn what

Wasserstein speaking at a press conference for the 2004 Tribeca Theater Festival.

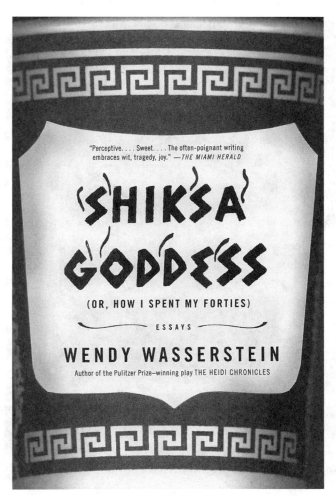

"Perceptive. . . . Sweet. . . . The often-poignant writing embraces wit, tragedy, joy." —THE MIAMI HERALD

SHIKSA GODDESS

(OR, HOW I SPENT MY FORTIES)

ESSAYS

WENDY WASSERSTEIN

Author of the Pulitzer Prize–winning play THE HEIDI CHRONICLES

Wasserstein discusses the difficult birth of her child, her relationship with her mother, and coming to terms with her sister's death in this 2001 collection of essays.

has happened to them since graduation. Products of feminist optimism, these women have suffered the ups and downs of such expectations. Nancy L. Bunge, writing in *Dictionary of Literary Biography*, found that "through the women's shared confusion, the play offers a kind of answer. The one thing that remains unambiguous to all of them is their love and support for one another. They care about and enjoy each other, despite the different paths they have taken."

Uncommon Women and Others was first presented at Yale in 1975. Then Wasserstein rewrote the play in a two-act version and prepared it for the professional stage. The finished work received widespread attention from reviewers when it premiered in 1977 under the auspices of Phoenix Theater, a troupe that spotlighted new American plays. While *Time* reviewer T.E. Kalem found Wasserstein's characters

"stereotypical," Richard Eder in the *New York Times* wrote that "if the characters . . . represent familiar alternatives and contradictions, Miss Wasserstein has made each of them most real." *New Yorker* contributor Edith Oliver dubbed the work "a collage of small scenes" rather than a play. Nonetheless, she found the result a "wonderful, original comedy" in which "every moment is theatrical," adding that "for all [the characters'] funny talk and behavior, they are sympathetically drawn." Oliver also called Wasserstein "an uncommon young woman if ever there was one." *Uncommon Women* soon reached national television as part of public television's *Theatre in America* series. College ties also figured in the casting of this play: fellow Yale classmates Elkenberry, Close, and Streep were all involved in either stage or television productions.

Continues Her Informal Series of Plays

Wasserstein continued to write from her own life and experiences in her next play, *Isn't It Romantic.* Approaching thirty, an age when most women are either already married or thinking about it, Wasserstein felt the usual biological pressures as well as her mother's expectations for her to marry. The result was the character Janie Blumberg in *Isn't It Romantic. Nation* contributor Elliott Sirkin described her as a "plump, emotionally agitated young Jewish woman, who insults herself with sophisticated quips." Meanwhile she attempts to resist the entreaties of an earnest but boring young doctor. Janie's mother, outgoing and energetic, urges her daughter to get married. In contrast to the Blumbergs are Janie's best friend, Harriet—an emotionally restrained Anglo-Saxon, more attractive and successful than Janie—and Harriet's mother, cooler and more successful yet. The play consists of many short scenes, abundant with comic one-liners, that explore how and why women choose a husband, a career, or a way of life. As the play ends, Janie, shocked to realize that Harriet is about to marry a man she does not love, pointedly refuses to move in with her own boyfriend. As Bunge noted, *Isn't It Romantic* "argues that women need to stop worrying about getting the right answer and having it all; instead, they need to focus on trusting their passions, wherever those take them."

Critical response to *Isn't It Romantic* focused largely on the fact that Wasserstein's episodic play was somewhat out of control: serious issues were obfuscated by too much humor. For example, *New York* magazine critic John Simon thought the first production was encumbered by "Yale Drama School . . . humor." Simon went on to note, however, that Wasserstein "has a lovely forte: the comic-wistful

A scene from the 1988 play *The Heidi Chronicles*, the play that cemented Wasserstein's fame.

line. . . . This could be a vein of gold, and needs only proper engineering to be efficiently mined." Seven rewritings later and reduced by forty-five minutes, *Isn't It Romantic* received a new production. Oliver, writing in the *New Yorker*, praised this version's sped up "momentum and . . . sense of purpose," further noting that the "troubling emotions that were an undercurrent the first time around have now been brought to the surface, and with any loss of humor."

Wasserstein began to write for other media in the 1980s, creating adaptations for her plays for television production, and writing essays for the *New York Times* and the *New Yorker*, among other periodicals. She also penned the one-act *Tender Offer* and the musical comedy *Miami*. But it was her next major play, *The Heidi Chronicles*, that cemented her fame.

The Heidi Chronicles was inspired by a single image in Wasserstein's mind: a woman speaking to an assembly of other women, confessing her growing sense of unhappiness. The speaker evolved into Dr. Heidi Holland, an art history professor who finds that her successful, independent life has left her alienated from men and women alike. Most of the play consists of flashbacks that capture Heidi's increasing disillusionment. Starting as a high-school student, she experiences, in turn, the student activism of the late 1960s, the feminist consciousness-raising of the early 1970s, and the tough-minded careerism of the 1980s. Friends disappoint her: a feminist activist becomes an entertainment promoter, valuing the women's audience for its market potential; a boyfriend becomes a manipulative and selfish magazine editor; a gay male friend tells her that in the 1980s, when gays are dying of AIDS, her unhappiness is a mere luxury. Heidi remains subdued until the play's climactic scene, when she addresses fellow alumnae from a private school for girls, complaining that she had thought the whole point of the feminist revolution was that women were all sisters and in it together. However, at her current point in life she feels abandoned by other women. At the end of the play Heidi adopts a baby and poses happily with the child in front of an exhibition of works by Georgia O'Keeffe, an acclaimed woman artist. Such an ending foreshadowed Wasserstein's own decision, at age 48, to have a child, and also drew considerable discussion and debate in feminist circles.

Reviewers debated how well the play reflects the reality of Heidi's—and Wasserstein's—generation. In the *Village Voice*, Alisa Solomon suggested that the playwright lacked sympathy with the aspirations of feminism. In *New York* John Simon felt the characters were oversimplified, noting that "Heidi's problem as stated—that she is too intellectual, witty, and successful for a mere hausfrau—just won't wash." Mimi Kramer, however, wrote in the *New Yorker* that "Wasserstein's portrait of womanhood always remains complex." Kramer found "generosity in the writing," contending that no character in the play "is made to seem ludicrous or dismissible." More praise came from *New York Times* critic Mel Gussow, who found the work an "enlightening portrait of [Wasserstein's] generation." Gussow went on to note: "The author looks beyond feminism and yuppie-ism to individualism and one's need to have pride of accomplishment. We are what we make of ourselves, but we keep looking for systems of support." Gussow also praised Wasserstein for "not settling for easy laughter," thus creating a "more penetrating play." *The Heidi Chronicles* became Wasserstein's first show to move to a Broadway theater, running for 622 performances. The play brought its author the Pulitzer Prize as well as a Tony Award.

The Sisters Rosensweig completes the informal cycle of plays begun with *Uncommon Women*. This play "looks at the lives of women who are weighing priorities and deciding which doors to open and deciding which gently to close," reported Linda Simon in the *Atlanta Journal-Constitution*. The play is set in London, where fifty-four-year-old Sara is celebrating her birthday with her two younger sisters. Twice divorced and having long since abandoned any hope of real romance in life, she is surprised when love suddenly seems possible after all. "With her focus on the hidden yearnings and emotional resistance of the women, . . . [Wasserstein's] obvious debt is to Noel Coward," Simon noted, adding that *The Sisters Rosensweig* "is very much a drawing room comedy." Gussow, in the *New York Times*, found echoes of Chekhov in Wasserstein's work: "Overlooking the play is the symbolic figure of Anton Chekhov, smiling. Although the characters do not directly parallel those in *The Three Sisters*, the comparison is intentional. . . . Wasserstein does not overstate the connection but uses it like background music while diverting her attention to other cultural matters."

Writing in Many Forms

In 1990, Wasserstein collected her essays written for the *New Yorker* and the *New York Times* in the book *Bachelor Girls*. In 1996, she published a children's book, *Pamela's First Musical*. The following year was the long-awaited premier of her play *An American Daughter*, in which she takes up political themes. At the center the play is the plight of Dr. Lyssa Dent Hughes, an upright feminist physician nominated to become the next U.S. surgeon general. Confirmation problems ensue when it is revealed that Hughes forgot to show up for jury duty some years before. Many reviewers found the play muddled, the comedy weighed down by political pretension. "Wasserstein has little to say, and that little is false," wrote Stefan Kanfer in the *New Leader*, deriding *An American Daughter* for what he saw as its shallow characters and "sitcom soul." The play's "brisk satire gives way to whiny venting and windy summations that have marred earlier Wasserstein plays," wrote *Seattle Times* contributor Misha Berson, who still found some of Wasserstein's political quipping trenchant and breezy. More positive in his evaluation was Michael Toscano, reviewing a 2001 production in Washington, DC, in the *Washington Post*. For Toscano, Wasserstein had become "a defining voice on conflicts between a woman's personal sense of fulfillment and fluctuating social expectations." Toscano praised the play's "witty dialogue and thought-provoking subject matter."

In 2001, Wasserstein published a further collection of her essays in *Shiksa Goddess*. Among other themes broached in the volume was the difficult birth of her child, her relationship with her mother, and coming to terms with her sister's death. These essays were deemed "highly readable" by Berson in the *Seattle Times*. Despite the serious nature of some of the topics in the book, Wasserstein writes in a "breezy, splashy style," noted Penelope Mesic in *Book Magazine*. "Mildly funny, good-natured and ephemeral, these essays reveal that Wasserstein's overwhelming strength and weakness is the same: She is totally in touch with contemporary society." Wasserstein gently pokes fun at prominent gentiles who discover their Jewish roots in the title piece, claiming to have found some Episcopalians in her past and exploring her newfound culture. While such pieces were deemed "silly" by Jack Helbig in *Booklist*, the critic went on to note that Wasserstein's reflections on fertility, family ties, and death are "riveting and sometimes searing," and her observations on the state of writing and theater are "sharp and pungent." A *Publishers Weekly* writer also found the author's writing on childbirth and death to be imbued "with notable humor and heartbreaking poignancy."

Wasserstein wrote the screenplay for the 1998 film *The Object of My Affection,* starring Jennifer Aniston and Paul Rudd.

Wasserstein also contributed an entry in the "Seven Deadly Sins" series from Oxford University Press. Her *Sloth: The Seven Deadly Sins* "offers a delightfully hilarious parody of the self-help genre," according to Lynne F. Maxwell, writing in *Library Journal.* In this send-up, she explains why sloth is important and explains techniques for maintaining sloth. Naomi Glauberman, writing in the *Los Angeles Times,* noted that Wasserstein's work "simultaneously parodies self-help books, notions of sin and the shibboleths of contemporary society." Several months after her death in 2006, Wasserstein's debut novel, *Elements of Style,* was published. In this work, which deals with the aftermath of the terrorist attacks on New York in 2001, "New York City's A-list socialites struggle to find meaning in their lives even while they continue to worry over what to serve at their dinner parties," wrote Joy Humphrey in a *Library Journal* review. Humphrey felt that Wasserstein did a "good job of simultaneously poking fun at high society and evoking the anxiety of maintaining a perfect image." Reviewing the novel in the *New York Times Book Review,* Caryn James

called it a "bright social comedy that takes a sudden, tragic turn." Janet Maslin, writing in the *New York Times,* found the novel "both a blithe, funny feat of escapism and a sobering reminder of the inescapable."

Wasserstein's last major theater production was *Third,* a play in which a "college professor's well-ordered life is thrown into chaos when she accuses a male student of plagiarism," as Joe Holley described it in the *Washington Post.* The play takes its title from a preppie male student named Woodson Bull III, son of privilege, for whom the left-leaning female professor develops an instant antipathy. When Third hands in a cogent, literate paper on Shakespeare's *King Lear,* she immediately accuses him of plagiarism, though she has no evidence to prove this. Reviewing the play in the *Washington Post,* Peter Marks felt that Wasserstein was on "interesting turf, writing about women of distinction on the downward slope, suddenly worrying about their failing bodies and passé ideas." Ben Brantley, reviewing the work for the *New York Times,* thought the comedy was both "thoughtful" and "imbalanced." Brantley commented on problems such as "an overly schematic structure" and a "sometimes artificial topicality and a reliance on famous names and titles as a shorthand for establishing character." However, Brantley also commented that *Third* "ultimately registers as more than the fractured sum of flawed parts. . . . Ms. Wasserstein is politely asking audiences who have grown older with her to acknowledge their fears, their limitations and the possibility that they might be wrong on subjects they were once sure about."

If you enjoy the works of Wendy Wasserstein, you may also want to check out the following books:

Anton Chekov, *Three Sisters*, 1901.
Beth Henley, *Crimes of the Heart*, 1979.
Alan Ball, *Five Women Wearing the Same Dress*, 1993.

Summing up Wasserstein's oeuvre, the critic for *Contemporary Dramatists* felt the playwright's "strengths lie in her ability to create characters who laugh at themselves while questioning others. She serves as a role model for women who wish to be successful in the New York theater venue. All of her plays are quirky and interesting and offer strong roles for women." Similarly, Marks, writing in the *Washington Post* at the time of Wasserstein's death, declared that "her comedies will justly be remembered as vibrant documents of an urbane baby-boom generation and the more progressive view of women it embraced." James offered similar praise for Wasserstein's achievement in the *New York Times Book Review*: "Having charted her generation through nearly three decades of change, Wasserstein eventually found herself depicting aging baby boomers in a world collapsing around them. Her plays, which always seemed so much of their moment, have aged remarkably well. They're still affecting, still funny and even more resonant as time capsules." And Wolff also commended the life and work: "We are not past the need for what [Wasserstein's] work has to offer. Her abundant interest in ideas about gender and how patterns of behavior are inherited or changed is matched by her enthusiasm for the extended workings of Judaism, family, money, and art. What is more, at its best, Wasserstein's work manages to present a nearly anachronistic example of how to reject cynicism, remain hopeful, and yet retain a witty ironic edge."

■ Biographical and Critical Sources

BOOKS

Barnett, Claudia, editor, *Wendy Wasserstein: A Casebook*, Garland (New York, NY), 1990.

Ciociola, Gail, *Wendy Wasserstein: Dramatizing Women, Their Choices and Their Boundaries*, McFarland (Jefferson, NC), 1998.

Contemporary Dramatists, 6th ed., St. James Press (Detroit, MI), 1999.

Contemporary Literary Criticism, Volume 32, Gale (Detroit, MI), 1985.

Dictionary of Literary Biography, Volume 228: *Twentieth-Century American Dramatists*, Gale (Detroit, MI), 2000.

Feminist Writers, St. James Press (Detroit, MI), 1996.

Herrington, Joan, *The Playwright's Muse*, Routledge (New York, NY), 2002.

Newsmakers 1991, Gale (Detroit, MI), 1991.

PERIODICALS

Advocate, May 27, 1997, James Oseland, review of *An American Daughter*, p. 90.

American Theatre, April, 2006, Marsha Norman, "Wendy Wasserstein: 1950-2006," p. 20.

America's Intelligence Wire, May 5, 2003, Rick Weiss, "Wendy Wasserstein's Moldy Chronicles."

Architectural Digest, February, 1998, "Wendy Wasserstein: A Second Act for the Playwright's Central Park West Apartment," p. 30.

Atlanta Journal-Constitution (Atlanta, GA), May 23, 1993, Linda Simon, review of *The Sisters Rosensweig*, p. N10.

Back Stage, April 18, 1997, David Sheward, review of *An American Daughter*, p. 60; March 26, 1999, Roger Armbrust, "Wasserstein: Arts Not Elitist, but Democratic," p. 3; December 15, 2000, Julius Novick, review of *Old Money*, p. 48; February 16, 2001, Simi Horwitz, "Direct from Chekhov to Wasserstein," p. 19.

Back Stage West, September 10, 1998, Judy Richter, review of *An American Daughter*, p. 17; September 24, 1998, J. Brenna Guthrie, review of *The Sisters Rosensweig*, p. 13; October 8, 1998, Terri Roberts, review of *The Sisters Rosensweig*, p. 16.

Booklist, March 15, 1990, Ilene Cooper, review of *Bachelor Girls*, p. 1413; June 1, 1998, Jack Helbig, review of *An American Daughter*, p. 1709; May 1, 2001, Jack Helbig, review of *Shiksa Goddess; or, How I Spent My Forties,*, p. 1647.

Book Magazine, May, 2001, Penelope Mesic, review of *Shiksa Goddess*, p. 73.

Chicago, August, 1998, Penelope Mesic, review of *An American Daughter,* p. 27.

Entertainment Weekly, June 20, 1997, Mark Harris, review of *An American Daughter,* p. 28; May 1, 1998, review of *The Object of My Affection,* p. 42.

Library Journal, March 15, 2002, Thomas E. Luddy, review of *Old Money,* p. 82; December 1, 2004, Lynne F. Maxwell, review of *Sloth: The Seven Deadly Sins,* p. 118; March 1, 2006, Joy Humphrey, review of *Elements of Style,* p. 80.

Los Angeles Times, November 16, 2001, J. Wynn Rousuck, "At 51 and a Mom, Writer Wasserstein Scales Back a Bit," p. F28; January 7, 2005, Naomi Glauberman, review of *Sloth: Seven Deadly Sins,* p. E18.

Los Angeles Times Book Review, August 25, 1991, Charles Solomon, review of *Bachelor Girls,* p. 10; May 30, 1993, p. 6.

Nation, December 17, 1977, Harold Clurman, review of *Uncommon Women and Others;* February 18, 1984, Elliott Sirkin, review of *Isn't It Romantic.*

New Leader, December 7, 1994, Stefan Kanfer, review of *The Sisters Rosensweig,* p. 22; April 7, 1997, Stefan Kanfer, review of *An American Daughter,* p. 22.

New Statesman, June 26, 1998, Gerald Kaufman, review of *The Object of My Affection,* p. 51.

New York, June 29, 1981, John Simon, review of *Isn't It Romantic;* January 2, 1989, John Simon, review of *The Heidi Chronicles,* pp. 48-49; April 28, 1997, John Simon, review of *An American Daughter,* p. 105; December 18, 2000, John Simon, review of *Old Money,* p. 178.

New Yorker, December 5, 1977, Edith Oliver, review of *Uncommon Women and Others;;* June 13, 1983, Edith Oliver, review of *Isn't It Romantic;* December 26, 1988, Mimi Kramer, review of *The Heidi Chronicles,* pp. 81-82; April 14, 1997, Nancy Franklin, "The Time of Her Life," p. 62; December 25, 2000, John Lahr, review of *Old Money,* p. 166.

New York Times, November 22, 1977 Richard Eder, review of *Uncommon Women and Others;* December 12, 1988, Mel Gussow, review of *The Heidi Chronicles,* p. C13; October 23, 1992, Mel Gussow, review of *The Sisters Rosensweig,* p. C3; December 8, 2000, Ben Brantley, review of *Old Money;* October 25, 2005, Ben Brantley, review of *Third,* p. E1; April 20, 2006, Janet Maslin, review of *Elements of Style,* p. E1.

New York Times Book Review, April 23, 2006, Caryn James, "East Side Story," review of *Elements of Style,* p. 18.

Parade, September 5, 1993, Claire Carter, interview with Wendy Wasserstein, p. 24.

Publishers Weekly, March 2, 1990, review of *Bachelor Girls,* p. 68; April 23, 2001, review of *Shiksa Goddess,* p. 60.

Rolling Stone, April 30, 1998, Peter Travers, review of *The Object of My Affection,* p. 73.

Seattle Times, May 1, 1997; June 20, 2001, Misha Berson, "Wasserstein: Motherhood at Sixty Brings New Outlook."

Shofar, winter, 2003, Thomas P. Adler, review of *Shiksa Goddess,* p. 189.

Time, December 5, 1977, T.E. Kalem, review of *Uncommon Women and Others;* April 16, 1990, Margaret Carlson, review of *Bachelor Girls,* p. 83; April 20, 1998, Richard Schickel, review of *The Object of My Affection,* p. 81.

Variety, April 14, 1997, Greg Evans, review of *An American Daughter,* p. 100.

Village Voice, December 20, 1988, Alisa Solomon, review of *The Heidi Chronicles,*

Vogue, May, 1998, John Powers, review of *The Object of My Affection,* p. 154.

Washington Post, March 13, 1994, Judith Weinraub, "The Singular Romance of Wendy Wasserstein," p. G1; July 19, 2001, Michael Toscano, review of *An American Daughter,* p. T6; May 5, 2003, Peter Marks, review of *An American Daughter,* p. C1; January 19, 2004, Peter Marks, review of *Welcome to My Rash* and *Third,* p. C1; January 31, 2006, Peter Marks, "Women's Rib," p. C1.

Washington Post Book World, April 30, 2006, Elinor Lipman, review of *Elements of Style,* p. 5.

Washington Times, May 10, 2003, Jayne M. Blanchard, review of *An American Daughter,* p. D3.

Wine Spectator, April 30, 1998, Mervyn Rothstein, interview with Wendy Wasserstein, p. 361.

ONLINE

Doollee.com, http://www.dollee.com/ (June 28, 2006), "Wendy Wasserstein."

Internet Broadway Database, http://www.ibdb.co/ (June 28, 2006), "Wendy Wasserstein."

Internet Movie Database, http://www.imdb.com/ (June 28, 2006), "Wendy Wasserstein."

OBITUARIES

PERIODICALS

Chronicle of Higher Education, February 17, 2006, Tamsen Wolf, "Wendy Wasserstein (1950-2006)."

Los Angeles Times, January 31, 2006, Mike Boehm, "Wendy Wasserstein: 1950-2006," p. A1.

New York Times, January 31, 2006, Charles Isherwood, "Wendy Wasserstein Dies at 55," p. A1.

Washington Post, January 31, 2006, Joe Holley, "Heidi Chronicles Playwright Wendy Wasserstein," p. B6.

ONLINE

Village Voice Online, http://www.villagevoice.com/ (January 31, 2006), Michael Feingold, "Wendy Wasserstein, 1950-2006."*

Wally Wood

■ Personal

Born June 17, 1927, in Menahga, MN; died of self-inflicted gunshot wound, November 2, 1981, in CA; son of Max (a lumberjack) and Alma (a teacher) Wood; married Tatjana Weintraub, 1950 (divorced, 1968); married second wife, c. 1970. Married third wife, c. 1977 (separated). (divorced). *Education:* Attended Minneapolis School of Art, MN, and Burner Hogarth's Cartoonists and Illustrators School, New York, NY.

■ Career

Comic book and comic strip illustrator and writer, commercial artist. "Spirit" comic strip by Will Eisner, letterer, inker, and backgrounder, 1949; Fox Company, illustrator of romance stories, 1949; Avon, illustrator of romance, science fiction, horror, and crime stories, including *Space Detective,* beginning 1950; Youthful Magazines, *Captain Science* comics, illustrator, 1950; contributor of illustrations and stories to Ziff-Davis, 1950; EC Publications, *Weird Science, Weird Fantasy, Tales from the Crypt,* and *Shock SuspenStories,* interior and cover illustrator, beginning 1950, *Mad* comic book, illustrator, 1952-55, *Mad* magazine, illustrator, 1955-64; *Galaxy Science Fiction Stories,* cover and interior artist, 1957-67; "Sky Masters" comic strip, with Jack Kirby, 1958; Marvel Comics, *Daredevil,* illustrator, 1964-66; DC Comics, *Challengers of the Unknown,* illustrator; Dell, *M.A.R.S. Patrol,* writer and illustrator; Tower Comics, artistic director, creator, *T.H.U.N.D.E.R. Agents* comics, 1965-68; *Witzend,* independent underground comics magazine, founder and editor, 1966-69; *Creepy* magazine, illustrator; *Overseas Weekly,* creator of "Cannon," "Shattuck," and "Sally Forth." *Gang Bang* erotic comics, illustrator, 1979-81. *Military service:* U.S. Army 11th Airborne Paratroopers, 1946-48.

■ Awards, Honors

Best Comic Book Artist, National Cartoonist Society, 1957, 1959.

■ Writings

GRAPHIC NOVELS/COLLECTIONS

King of the World (first volume of "The Wizard King" trilogy), Sea Gate (New York, NY), 1978, Vanguard Productions (Somerset, NJ), 2004.
Odkin Son of Odkin (second volume of "The Wizard King" trilogy), privately printed, 1981, Vanguard Productions (Somerset, NJ), 2006.

Naughty "Knotty" Wood, Fantagraphics (Seattle, WA), 1998.

The Compleat Sally Forth, Fantagraphics (Seattle, WA), 1998.

The Compleat Cannon, Fantagraphics (Seattle, WA), 2001.

Alter Ego (first five issues), TwoMorrows (Raleigh, NC), 2001.

Spurlock, David J., editor, *Wally Wood Sketchbook,* Vanguard Productions (Somerset, NJ), 2001.

T.H.U.N.D.E.R. Agents Archives: Volume 1, DC Comics (New York, NY), 2002.

(With others) *T.H.U.N.D.E.R. Agents Archives: Volume 2,* DC Comics (New York, NY), 2003.

(With others) *T.H.U.N.D.E.R. Agents Archives: Volume 3,* DC Comics (New York, NY), 2004.

M.A.R.S. Patrol Total War, Dark Horse Comics (Milwaukie, OR), 2004.

Lunar Tunes, Vanguard Productions (Somerset, NJ), 2005.

T.H.U.N.D.E.R. Agents Archives: Volume 5, DC Comics (New York, NY), 2005.

T.H.U.N.D.E.R. Agents Archives: Volume 6, DC Comics (New York, NY), 2006.

ILLUSTRATOR

(With others) Harvey Kurtzman, *Mad Reader,* Ballantine (New York, NY), 1954.

(With others) Harvey Kurtzman, *Inside Mad,* Ballantine (New York, NY), 1955.

(With others) Harvey Kurtzman, *Mad Strikes Back,* Ballantine (New York, NY), 1955.

Augusta Stevenson, *George Carver, Boy Scientist,* Bobbs-Merrill (Indianapolis, IN), 1959.

Sue Guthridge, *Tom Edison, Boy Inventor,* Bobbs-Merrill (Indianapolis, IN), 1959.

Hazel B. Aird, *Henry Ford, Boy with Ideas,* Bobbs-Merrill (Indianapolis, IN), 1960.

(With Will Eisner) Julius Feiffer, *Outer Space Spirit, 1952,* Kitchen Sink Press (Princeton, NJ), 1983.

Stan Lee, *Marvel Masterworks Presents Daredevil,* Marvel Comics (New York, NY), 1991.

(With Jack Kirby) *Challengers of the Unknown Archives Volume 2,* DC Comics (New York, NY), 2004.

(With others) Harvey Kurtzman, *The EC Archives: Two-Fisted Tales Volume 1,* Gemstone Publishing 2007.

(With others) Harvey Kurtzman, *The EC Archives: Vault Of Horror Volume 1,* Gemstone Publishing 2007.

(With others) Al Feldstein, *The EC Archives: Tales from the Crypt Volume 1,* Gemstone Publishing 2007.

(With others) Al Feldstein, *The EC Archives: Shock Suspenstories Volume 1,* Gemstone Publishing 2007.

(With others) Al Feldstein, *The EC Archives: Weird Science Volume 1,* Gemstone Publishing 2007.

■ Sidelights

Wally Wood was "considered by many to be the most influential American comic book artist of the twentieth century," according to *ArtBomb.net* contributor Peter Aaron Rose. Best known for his work on the science fiction magazines of EC Comics during the 1950s, he also became a mainstay illustrator for *Mad,* beginning with its inception as a four-color comic book in 1952. He illustrated for numerous publishers, including Marvel Comics and DC Comics, and in 1978 also published a graphic novel, the Tolkien-inspired *The King of the World.* His later career was marred by the effects of alcoholism and depression, and much of his final artwork was geared for the erotic market, but his early illustrations for publications such as *Weird Science* helped, as *Entertainment Weekly* writer David Hochman noted, "form the images we all share of what spaceships, aliens, and the terrain of other planets look like." Such illustrations, often providing the artwork for tales by writers like Ray Bradbury, were detail-laden and pioneering in their use of new techniques to draw the viewer's eye to each panel. Writing in the introduction to *Against the Grain: Mad Artist Wallace Wood,* Maria Reidelback noted: "Wallace Wood's work for EC Comics' *Weird Science* and *Weird Fantasy* earned him the title of Dean of Comic Book Science Fiction, but EC publisher Bill Gaines put it simply: 'He was just the greatest science-fiction artist there ever was.'" Rose also commented that Wood "helped revolutionize a young comics industry accustomed to less complicated draftsmanship."

Struggling for Control

As Michael T. Gilbert noted in *Alter Ego,* "Wally Wood's entire life was an endless struggle for control." Born in 1927, in Menahga, Minnesota, the young Wood formed an early passion for drawing. Though this was discouraged by his farmer and lumberjack father, who wanted a more outgoing son, Wood's mother, Alma, a schoolteacher, encouraged such endeavors, even sewing his early cartoons into comic books. The family led a peripatetic life after leaving the farm in 1937, following the father from town to town with each successive job. Art and the comics formed a center of stability for Wood, and he began to copy the work of his favorite cartoonists, such as Will Eisner, Roy Crane, Hal Foster, and Milton Caniff. Wood graduated from

Wally Wood working at his drafting table, circa 1948.

high school in 1944, and a year later his parents finally divorced. He subsequently joined the Merchant Marines, serving for just over one year, and then enlisted in the 11th Airborne Paratroopers, and was part of the American occupation of Japan until mid-1947.

Again a civilian, he returned to Minneapolis with his mother and studied cartooning for about a year at the Minneapolis School of Art. Finally, in the summer of 1948, he decided to go to New York and attempt to break into the world of cartooning and comics. Wood also studied art in New York for a time, and soon found work with the "Terry and the Pirates" comic strip as a letterer, a function he also later played on Will Eisner's "The Spirit." Additionally, he began doing backgrounds and inking for Fox romance comics in 1948; his first signed work appeared a year later in *My Confession, #8.* He also began working for Avon publishers on titles such as *The Mask of Fu Manchu* and *Space Detectives,* teaming up with Joe Orlando on those titles and many others.

"Wood and his partners did fine work for Fox and Avon," Gilbert noted, "but it was at EC—Entertaining Comics—that he finally found a company worthy of his talents. . . . Surrounded and challenged by the greatest writers and cartoonists in the comics industry, Wood thrived." Joining EC in 1950, Wood was no longer paired with others as inker or doing the line drawings; now he was creating the entire artwork for covers and stories. Illustrating magazines and comics from *Mad* to *Weird Fantasy,* Wood "fearlessly tackled every genre in comics—whether science-fiction, war, or historical—and mastered them all," according to Gilbert. At EC, Wood became, by the young age of twenty-five, "the acknowledged master of futuristic sf ships and monsters," according to a contributor for *Bud Plant Illustrated Books.* Similarly, Gilbert noted: "Almost from the start, Wood's science-fiction art was in a class by itself. His gleaming rockets, intricate machinery, heroic men, lush women, and gooey monsters redefined the genre. . . . His pen and brush lines were always crisp, clean, and perfect."

Gilbert further commented: "Many still consider his EC work—drawn while he was still in his twenties—to be the best of his amazing career." At the same time that he was illustrating so many different titles for EC, he was also producing numerous illustrations for Avon and illustrated eight episodes of Eisner's "Spirit" comic strip. At about this time, Wood began using alcohol to help inspire and drive him to meet deadlines, a practice that later had heavy consequences.

The *Mad* Years

As the public demand for science fiction comics and magazines began to slow in the early 1950s, and as congressional oversight focused on the supposed violent content of comics, EC turned in a different direction with one of the their publications. In 1952, the editor and cartoonist Harvey Kurtzman began a satirical comic called *Mad*. Working together, Wood and Kurtzman produced various parodies of comic books, from *Superman* (dubbed Superduperman in *Mad*) to *Batman* (or Batboy in *Mad* parlance). These proved popular, and in 1955 *Mad* was reborn as a magazine with a wide assortment of zany humor. Wood's art appeared in almost every issue of the comic book version, and he continued to supply art for *Mad* into the early 1960s.

At the same time, the ever-busy Wood was turning out artwork for children's books such as *Tom Edison, Boy Inventor* and *George Carver, Boy Scientist,* for commercial advertising, for book covers, and also for men's magazines. Wood's erotic art would take on increasing prominence later in his career.

However, with the re-emergence of comic books in the mid-1960s, in part spurred by the popularity of Marvel Comics titles, Wood returned to the world of comic books. From 1964 to 1966 he drew Marvel's *Daredevil* comic book. By this time, however, Wood's personal life was beginning to unravel. His drinking was becoming a problem, and his marriage was also falling apart. He quit illustrating for *Mad* in 1964 when one of his stories was rejected.

In 1965, Wood was invited by Tower Publishing to create new super-hero comics. Thus was born his *T.H.U.N.D.E.R. Agents* team, featuring Dynamo, Noman, Lighting, and Raven. Writing on *Don Markstein's Toonopedia*, Donald D. Markstein noted that this comic "got rave reviews in fanzines of the time, and was quickly spun off into new titles." Such popularity was short-lived, however, and within a few years the comic ended. Wood created another heroic team with his *M.A.R.S. Patrol*, an acronym

standing for Marine Attack Rescue Service. This secret group of military specialists battled enemy agents wherever they could find them. Reviewing a 2004 collection of these comics, *M.A.R.S. Patrol Total War*, in *Library Media Collection*, Michelle Glatt felt that "what makes these comics interesting today is that [the patrol] is made up of culturally diverse members." Glatt concluded, "those who enjoy an old war comic or war movie will be greatly pleased." Reviewing the same title in *School Library Journal*, Erin Dennington found that the "stories remain a top-notch testament to Wood's genius."

The Final Years

In 1966, Wood started his own underground fanzine, *Witzend*, which featured not only fan mail, but also work by some of the most popular comics artists of the day. Wood contributed his own work to the magazine, publishing a comic strip called "The Wizard King" in the last several issues. These were later adapted into the 1978 graphic novel *The King of the World*, the first chapter in his "The Wizard King" trilogy. He self-published a second installment, *Odkin Son of Odkin*, in 1981, but the planned third part was never published. The books feature a medieval society of elves, the Immi, who live deep in the forest removed from the rest of the world. Their idyllic life is spoiled when a shadow falls over their village. A young Immi named Odkin, inspired

A hand-drawn Christmas card by Wood, circa 1950s.

BUCKY'S CHRISTMAS CAPER

Panels from "Bucky's Christmas Caper," a limited syndicated newspaper strip by Wally Wood from 1967.

and also tricked by the wizard Alcazar, decides to investigate and is then thrown into an adventure that finds him defending his world from the villainous Anark.

If you enjoy the works of Wally Wood, you may also want to check out the following:

The art of cartoonists and illustrators such as Will Eisner, Roy Crane, Hal Foster, Harvey Kurtzman, and Milton Caniff.

During the 1960s and 1970s, Wood took on a number of assistants, helping to train them in the cartooning art, but also using them as studio il-lustrators, helping to continue to churn out a wide assortment of projects under Wood's name. However, as Gilbert noted, Wood encouraged his assistants to draw like him. Added to the fact that his creativity was diminishing as a result of over-drinking, his artwork began to appear "increasingly stiff and homogenized," as Gilbert noted. "His heroes were often interchangeable." In the early 1970s, Wood turned to comic strips aimed at servicemen, producing sexy adventure tales involving spies and femmes fatales. "Cannon," for example, was a spy adventure yarn featuring John Cannon who battled everybody from neo-Nazis to Islamic terrorists. For Rose, reviewing a 2001 compilation, *The Compleat Cannon*, the tales were "simple, politically incorrect and woefully misogynistic." Another comic strip, "Sally Forth," featured a "sweet innocent in the classic Little Annie Fanny mold," according to Gilbert. In these tales, Sally attempts to "protect her long-lost 'virtue' from legions of horny admirers." For Gilbert, the strip was "silly stuff, but essentially good-natured fun." Similarly, Markstein felt the stories "are not very moving or insightful, . . . but there's something about them that has a timeless appeal."

Wood continued comic book work into the 1970s, illustrating for Marvel, DC, and Charlton, but also turning to erotica for men's magazines. Wood's final years were marked with ill health, resulting from years of alcohol abuse and overwork. His eyesight began to fail, and a minor stroke hampered his drawing ability. Then, when he was diagnosed in 1981 with kidney failure, which would necessitate dialysis, Wood decided to take matters in his own had. He shot himself with a pistol. As the contributor for *Bud Plant Illustrated Books* concluded: "If the first five years of [Wood's] career were meteoric in relation to his artistic development, the last five went down nearly as fast." A writer for *Comic Art & Graffix Gallery* summed up Wood's career and contribution to the world of comics and cartooning: "Wally Wood is most likely the best artist to ever illustrate science fiction comics, . . . but he was also one of the fifties top humorists. His use of ink to thrill fans of comic art will always be legendary."

■ **Biographical and Critical Sources**

BOOKS

Spurlock, David J., editor, *Wally Wood Sketchbook,* Vanguard Productions (Somerset, NJ), 2001.

Starger, Steve, and David J. Spurlock, *Wally's World: The Brilliant Life and Tragic Death of Wally Wood, the World's 2nd-Best Comic Book Artist,* Vanguard Productions, 2006.

Stewart, Bhob, editor, *Against the Grain: Mad Artist Wallace Wood,* introduction by Maria Reidelback, TwoMorrows Publishing (Raleigh, NC), 2003

Wood, Wally, *The Marvel Comics Art of Wally Wood,* Thumbtack Books (New York, NY), 1982.

PERIODICALS

Alter Ego, spring, 2001, Michael T. Gilbert, "Total Control: A Brief Biography of Wally Wood."

Comic Book Artist, July, 2001, Larry Ivie, "Ivie League Heroes," pp. 64-68.

Comics Journal, July, 1997, "Wallace Wood Issue."

Entertainment Weekly, October 16, 1998, David Hochman, "The Sci-Fi 100."

Library Media Connection, April-May, 2005, Michelle Glatt, review of *M.A.R.S. Patrol Total War,* pp. 83-84.

School Library Journal, May, 2005, Erin Dennington, review of *M.A.R.S. Patrol Total War,* p. 167.

ONLINE

ArtBomb.net, http://www.artbomb.net (January 18, 2007). Peter Aaron Rose, review of *The Compleat Cannon.*

Bud Planet Illustrated Books, http://www.bpib.com/ (June 30. 2006), "Wallace Wood Biography."

Comic Art & Graffix Gallery, http://www.comic-art. com/ (July 3, 2006), "Artists Biographies: Wallace Wood."

Comic World News, http://www.comicworldnews. com/ (July 1, 2006), "Wally Wood's 'Wizard.'"

Don Markstein's Toonopedia, http://www.toonopedia. com/ (July 1, 2006), Donald D. Markstein, review of "Sally Forth" and *T.H.U.N.D.E.R. Agents.*

Lambiek.net, http://www.lambiek.net/ (June 30, 2006), "Wallace Wood."

TwoMorrows Publishing, (June 30, 2006), Michael T. Gilbert, "A Brief Biography of Wally Wood."

Wallace Wood Foundation, http://www.comicartville. com (June 30, 2006).

Author/Artist Index

The following index gives the number of the volume in whichan author/artist's biographical sketch appears: